COMMUNALISM: A SOCIO-POLITICAL STUDY

Dedicated to the memory of
Mohan Das Karamchand Gandhi and
Sir Syed Ahmad Khan, two patriotic
Indian visionaries, who stood for
and made every conceivable sacrifice
for communal harmony in India.

COMMUNALISM:
A SOCIO-POLITICAL STUDY (—1947)

SATISH C. SETH

GYAN

GYAN PUBLISHING HOUSE

New Delhi-110002

COMMUNALISM: A SOCIO-POLITICAL STUDY (—1947)
[*Humanity, History, Sociology*]

ISBN: 81-212-0693-6

Published in 2000 in India by
Gyan Publishing House
5, Ansari Road
New Delhi 110 002

Laser Typeset at Alphabet, Delhi
Printed at Cahwla Offset Press, New Delhi

Contents

Preface

This study embodies a period Research on Communalism in India a facet of the Indian sub-continent. It's virulent form still affects one personally and in its geo-political context.

This historical study is based on an investigation of the secondary sources, which are available in the form of published official and non-official reports, periodicals, research journals, Presidential addresses of various political parties and other published material that had a direct bearing on the problem during the British Raj.

I am grateful to the National Archives of India for permitting me to consult the original records and documents of the Home and Legislative Departments of the Government of India for the years 1800 to 1947.

It is, however, worth mentioning that even though, I was given permission for going through the confidential records of both the Legislative Department and the Reforms Office down to 1947. The permission to consult the archives of the Home Department was however, restricted only to the year before 1901. My only regret in this respect is that, without knowing full details, it often becomes rather difficult for a scholar to make a correct analysis of the problem in hand. Such a handicap is likely to do some injury to truth. There is even a possibility that one may inadvertantly draw an incomplete or tendentious picture.

I feel it my duty to pen my thanks to various eminent Indian Leaders some of whom are unfortunately no more with us, such as Shri M. Ananthasayanam Ayyangar, Speaker, Lok Sabha, Dr. B.R. Ambedkar, the main architect of the Indian Constitution, Shri Purushottam Dass Tandon, and many others who had candidly discussed various aspects of the problem with me. I would also like to record my gratitude for the help and cooperation given to me by Late Shri V.D. Tripathi, Shri Ashok Mika, Dr. S. Gopal, Historian, Dr. B.A. Saletore, Shri N.V. Rajan, ICS, and Dr. K.M. Ashraf, Dr. C.J. Chacko and Dr. P. Saran of the Delhi University and Late Shri P.D. Gupta, Vice-chancellor, University of Agra.

The problem of social disharmony is not unknown to any multi-ethnic or multi-cultural society whether oriental or occidental. As we tend toward the new millennium, it is the duty and prime obligation of good governance to keep cummunal conflicts under control, no matter in what overt or covert form they may raise their naked head.

To influence future political dispensation and policies that uphold the tenets of secularism for inter-community harmony, a study of our recent past is not only essential but imperative, to provide some guidelines to all those who shall from time to time will be entrusted to run the Government of the Republic of India.

This socio-political study, makes no claim to be a comprehensive story of the configuration, and nuances that communalism took, even leading to an unfortunate partition of India. It is my fervent hope that many more erudite scholars shall study this problem *de novo* to guide the policy makers and help usher a harmonious co-existence of many communities and ethnic groups, almost of billion, Indians, to live in harmony while all of them would also enjoy a certain quality of life in future.

Satish C. Seth

Part I

The Prologue

The Prologue

When exactly was it that the term communalism was first used to signify a peculiarly Indian problem? It is a question to which there can be no definite answer — a question which is likely to remain one of the blanks of History. The most, one might venture to say is, that it was sometimes during the course of the nineteenth century that the term came to acquire its modern connotation.

According to the then Imperialist rulers of India, who actually coined this term, "Religious groups in India were usually referred to as, 'Communities', and inter-religious problems as 'Communal' problems. Since, the Hindus and the Muslims constituted the two largest and the most important sections of the indigenous population, and, since each had its own distinct religion, communalism was primarily taken to connote the communal antagonism and tension thereto, between Hindus and Muslims, as it manifested itself in various walks of life.

The validity of such a view, though not completely unjustified, is certainly open to question for more than one reasons whether their approach was correct or incorrect, and whether such an attitude was avoidable or inevitable, shall be judged later. Here, it is enough to state that the British over-emphasised religion. None of the sociological norms would ever admit religion as the only distinguishing criterion of communal classification. Even in a very narrow sense, communalism could not satisfactorily be equated to the problem of Hindu-Muslim relations in India. As we shall see later, a community is much more than a religious group, and, Communalism is certainly a social phenomenon of greater depths and variations than what it ordinarily happened to denote.

It may be well stated here that, as was natural, no one definition of communalism could remain valid for long. This peculiar term, that was used loosely to describe inter-communal relations of the natives during the gradual development of the British rule in India, changed its meaning according to the emphasis laid while using it on any one, or more than one aspect of ordinary social living, viz: religious, political, cultural or economic, etc. Thus, communalism, as also the problem of Hindu-Muslim relations, was to most purely a religious, to some just a cultural and to many others an exclusively economic and political question that faced Indians under the British rule.

Not only was this difference in meaning caused because of these basic factors but, as would be clear on examining the opinions of various eminent scholars, politicians, and historians, the change came because of the changed historical conditions and the ultimate objective which the users of the term had in their minds.

For instance, Mr. Rezaul Karim thinks that:

> "In order to gain certain ulterior motives which are generally hidden from public eye when any person exploits the religious passion of man he is truly a communal person and that method of subserving one thing in the name of religion is called communalism".[1]

Thompson and Garret, while historically analysing the problem, give more importance to the Indian social-organization. They do not lay so much emphasis on the religious or ethical as on the economic and political factors. They write:

> "Communalism is an old Indian problem which time does little to solve. Only to a small extent is this enmity based on race or religion. It may be better regarded as the revolt of the emancipated lower caste Indians against the social and financial domination of the higher castes".

They further add:

> "Almost invariably there is some economic basis to Hindu and Muslim rivalry — or later years all religions and castes have found it expedient to organise politically and they have discovered that disturbances are an easy way of attracting the attention of government to any grievance".[2]

Agreeing with the later remark of the above writers, K.M. Pannikar says:

> "The Hindu-Muslim problem in India, it must be repeated is not entirely a religious one. It is fundamentally a question of political power with an economic background".

In the light of the above observations, one is likely to conclude that Communalism connotes some sort of social unrest and communal agitation, as caused by the material needs and political aspirations of the natives, specially amongst the Hindus and Muslims. A.N. Sinha in his book, *A Guide to the Communal Problem in India* takes a somewhat different attitude.

To him Communalism appears, to be just an unhealthy manifestation of social disequilibrium and he is convinced that dubbing the problem of 'communalism' as a Hindu-Muslim question is more a matter of chance than of fact. He writes:

> "The real problem is exclusively the Muslim problem. It is not in fact a problem of Muslims versus Hindus, but of Muslims of India. In practice, however, as the Hindus form the largest community, the communal problem has come to be viewed as Hindu-Muslim problem".[3]

He further says:

> "The religious issues are only incidental and subservient to other issues; such other issues, I suggest are political desires to share in the 'loaves and fishes' of office is, thus, the basis of the communal question. This is a political problem of a handful of the educated classes who have drawn upon religion to lend weight to their demands."[4]

Summarizing his analysis he says:

> "Communal problem in India, is, therefore, a froth on the surface of the turbid social current. The superficial eddies may appear to move in all directions but the mighty sweep of social energy is moving with all the eddies in one direction only the winning a decent and satisfactorily material life by abolishing privilege, profit and prosperity. We must keep our perspective. The communal problem is not fundamental. It is a superficial symptom of a corrosive social disease."[5]

Viewed in this light communalism becomes that ideological exclusivism of which Muslims are in undaunted seeker, for it shall land them to a more secure, prosperous and powerful social life. This analysis obviously appears to be a bit out of focus, as the responsibility for any maladjustment cannot be imposed on any one group or any one cause alone. When in a given society, the communal role of its various constituents changes, the progress is seldom even.

> "Some parts change faster than others. When the different parts are inter-related, the varying rates of change produce a strain between the unequally moving parts".[6]
>
> Naturally the tension comes but it cannot be unilateral".

In any case, we leave the decision of the question as to "where does the blame lie", to a later period and turn to other views on communalism in the different aspects.

Considering that the urge for political domination and the ensuing greater economic stability were the two fundamental aspects of the communal problems in India, we are tempted to study a few more opinions in this connection.

According to F.K. Durrani:

> "Paradoxical as it may seem the communal question is itself the offspring of the growth of nationalism, and not something that was pre-existing and has become a hindrance to the growth of nationalism".[7]

He further adds:

> "Communalism and Nationalism are antagonistic forces, but they are also necessary accompaniments of each other, because of the peculiar constitution of the two communities concerned".[8]

Mr Durrani in suggesting that, "Communalism is a necessary accompaniment of Nationalism" in India, has forwarded a very interesting thesis. We cannot wholly dispute the validity of this statement in its particular reference to Indian conditions; still one is apt to raise the following pertinent doubts. Could this thesis stand good as a general rule or not? That is to say, if in any society in the world, the force of nationalism be present, would it not give birth to communalism and vice versa? Further, in India as such, was not the tide of nationalism a joint-revolt of the various communities in common? Are we to believe that since communalism implies a split in communal relationship, nationalism too was a split movement.

Perhaps Mr Durrani is driving hard towards the two nation-theory on the bold assumption that each community constitutes a nationality.

In this case, however, illogical, irrational and unhistorical, this theory might havę been, it succeeded in the creation of two nations in India. How far the credit for such an outcome should go to some other agency is a matter to be discussed elsewhere. It is indeed true that communalism had a definite relationship to the split tendencies' is the national struggle of India.

Judging communalism in its constitutional aspect, B. R. Ambedkar says:

> "Communalism as a peculiar Indian question has two different aspects. In its lesser intent, the communal question relates to the representation of Hindus and Muslims in the legislatures and in its greater extent the communal question relates to the deliberate creation of Muslim state".[9]

Examined in this sense, we face communalism as a well-known problem of majority vs. minority or as the problem of national self-determination, which cannot possibly be an Indian problem alone. As Dr Radha Kumud Mukherji writes:

> "The communal problem is a universal problem as it has been a physical impossibility that political and national frontiers should also coincide with racial, religious and social frontiers".

He adds:

> "Every State has to accommodate different elements and communities in its composition and there is no State which has been able to eliminate a minority".[10]

However, there is another school of thought that has never equated communalism to the question of a competing nationality that could legitimately claim for the right of separate nationhood. To this school of thought things appeared simpler and fundamentally different. As Jawaharlal Nehru in his autobiography remarks:

> "Hindu and Muslim communalism is in neither case, even bonafide communalism; but political and social reaction hiding behind the communal mask".[11]

Explaining this "social reaction" in much more lucid terms, an eminent scholar said:

> "When one speaks of the communal question ordinarily one has in mind the Hindu-Muslim question. There is, however, another communal question not less important.

> It is the question of the Hindu untouchables in relation to caste Hindus, of the Muslim depressed classes in relation to the Muslim community; of both as a part of the country's communal and political problem".[12]

Rajni Palme Dutt agrees to a considerable degree with these two opinions. Still he cannot conceive of any communal question without an economic base. As he writes:

> "The social and cultural backwardness is the expression and consequence of the low economic level and political subjection and not vice versa. The root problem is economical-political".[13]

He not only finds Hindus and Muslims as the only two parties committed to the communal ideology, but he finds some one else too far more responsible for forcing any such commitments of the indigenous communities.

Rajni Palme Dutt looks at the entire problem from an altogether different angle. To him it is neither the Hindu nor the Muslim who is at fault, but he tries to discover the evil in the very system under which they had to live. For he says:

> "Communal strife is, thus, a special product of British rule, and, in particular, of the latest period of British rule, or of the declining imperialism ascendancy".[14]

He further adds:

> "The Hindu and Muslim masses in India have not and cannot have different objectives. There is no such thing as a separate Muslim poverty and servitude and a Hindu poverty and servitude. In the hundreds of thousands of Indian villages, the overwhelming majority of Hindus and Muslims live under the same burden of landlordism, the same exactness of money lenders, under the same grinding imperialism and the attempt to promote divisions between them is only the attempt to protect this system of exploitation".

Obviously, therefore, according to Mr Dutt's views, communalism is nothing but a pure and simple gift of the British, as their rule promoted and multiplied communal divisions, which resulted in the"socio-economic rivalry not of the Hindu-Muslim masses, but the rising middle-classes", in India: He says:

"Hence, with the rise of the Indian bourgeoisie conditions of sectional rivalry existed which could easily assume a communal guise".[15]

Obviously enough, thus viewed, communalism seems to be a very comprehensive term that embraces many problems of Indian social, economic, religious and political conditions. The seemingly comprehensiveness, however, expresses more of the loose and vague use of the term, for it tends to extol and explain conflicting and contradictory ideals and aspirations of the natives.

While sometimes communalism appears to be a powerful force for "cultural and communal" progress; for 'social and economic' security, for registering ultimate triumph of the principle of self-determination, at other times it seems to be a force for communal separation, social disruption and mass exploitation.

Though the diverse and at times conflicting opinions make us feel bewildered, though they might be to some extent subjective, unscientific and irrational, they clearly point out the following three important facts:

Firstly, that in India communalism in general has signified inter-communal rivalries, and social tension caused thereby, due to the religious, economic, political or cultural differences of the rulers and the ruled.

Secondly, that communalism in particular has been that ideology which determined the gradual evolution of Hindu-Muslim relations both within and without their respective folds.

Lastly, that whatever might have been the factors responsible for the growth or communalism it was a triangular tussle of which:

"Hindus, the Muslims and the British constituted the three arms".

Obviously, therefore, any study of "The growth of communalism in India and the problem of Hindu-Muslim relations", shall have to take three important things into account:

(i) A study of the Hindu-social system as conceived by the early social scientists and as it finally emerged in the nineteenth century in India.

(ii) A study of the advent and rule of Islam and its influences on the Hindu-Muslim relations in India.

(iii) Lastly, a study of the nature, practice and consequences of the British imperialism in India.

It is obvious, therefore, that no study of the growth and development of communalism in India can be complete without an examination of the nature and consequences, of the action and inter-action of Hindu caste, Muslim religion and British Politics. It is in the light of the historical forces unleashed as also the conditions created by these three elements, that this dissertation attempts to delineate a socio-political history of communalism.

NOTES AND REFERENCES

1. *Muslims and the Congress* by Rezaul Karim, Calcutta (1941), p. VI.
2. *Rise and fulfillment of British Rule in India* by Garratt, G.T. and Thompson, Edward, pp. 623-25.
3. *To Philip Sober: A Guide to the Communal Problem in India* by A.N. Sinha. Himalaya Publications, Patna (1945), p. 15.
4. *Ibid.*, pp. 21-23.
5. *Ibid.*, p. 36.
6. *A Hand Book of Sociology* by William F. Ogburn and Meyer F. Nimhoff, Routledge Kegan Paul Ltd. Broadway House, London 1. p. 612.
7. *The Meaning of Pakistan* by F.N. Durrani: Sh. Mohammad Ashraf, Kashmiri Bazar, Lahore (1944), p. 86.
8. *Ibid.*, p. 87.
9. *Pakistan or Partition of India* by Dr B.R. Ambedkar; Thacker and Company Ltd. Bombay (1945) See chapter VI, pp. 89-95.
10. Quoted by Dr Rajendra Prasad in *India-Dividend*, p. 364.
11. *The Autobiography* by J.L. Nehru.
12. See *India Charter* by Jahangir Kotwal.
13. *India to-day* by Rajni Palme Dutt, p. 60.
14. *Ibid.*
15. *Ibid.*

Section One

The Analysis of Communalism

I. COMMUNALISM - ITS MEANING

The word, 'communalism' is conspicuous by its absence from the most standard and authoritative lexicons of the English language as well as from the *Encyclopaedia Britannica*.

It is in fact, a derivative of the word, 'communal' which in itself is a derivative of the words, 'commune' and 'community'.[1]

Firstly the word, communal on the authority of the *New English Dictionary on Historical Principles*, (Oxford), means something, "of or belonging to a commune".

Literally speaking, communalism, therefore, is the principle of the communal organization of society. It is a theory of government which advocates the widest extension of local autonomy for each locally definable community.

In this sense, a communalist is a supporter of this system.

Secondly the word, 'Communal' on the authority of the same dictionary means something "of or pertaining to a (or the) community".

In this sense, therefore, communalism means all that pertains to community and the communalist is the supporter of the community.

Thus, apparently, it seems that communalism stands for two different concepts, it is an attribute of commune on the one hand, and that of the community on the other.

But can this distinction go very far? Perhaps not.

Because, although politically or historically 'commune' may mean anything, yet it is but the body of commons, the commonalty. It is in fact, "a community".

Obviously, therefore, communalism is an attribute of community, or we may say that empirically speaking, "Communalism is the community in action".

II. COMMUNALISM - ITS NATURE

Empirically, we have defined communalism as 'community in action'.

In order to comprehend its nature, we must first examine the nature of the community and its components and the way they act.

Firstly, in principle, the community is like an organism since it is formed by a number of individuals for a specific end and each part has no meaning outside that composite whole. Infact "all the parts are essential to the whole and a disturbance arising at one point in the structure, is quickly felt in all other sectors"[2].

Secondly, it is truly a dynamic concept and like every life organism it is capable of growth. As a sociologist remarks "change and development of the community tend to occur in an orderly process termed succession. That is, the community grows through a series of stages that culminate in a climax stage at which relations are stabilized. A catastrophe, however, may destroy the rather delicate equilibrium and thus initiate a new succession of changes".[3]

Thirdly, like every life organism, a community displays a tendency to expand. Regarding this attribute of community Dr. Prasad writes:

> "The expansion of community beyond it is a function of thinking and ideas, tradition and loyalties and stops short or proceeds for, in accordance with their force and adequacy. Hence arise groups whose varying degrees of co-operation and conflict, amalgamation and separation, subjection and overlordship constitute the warp and woof of history".[4]

History is verily an account of the variability of human motivation and ideas. Every idea or human motive, first springs from one individual, which soon becomes a centre, a nucleus round which, in due course adheres a number of beings, with the result that after sometime the idea becomes, the 'be all and end all' of such an organic growth. The individual reels into the background, becomes a subservient to this "common consciousness of the common end", or the '*volanta generale*' or the 'super ideology' of the community.

Fourthly, therefore a community is absolute in nature. It is absolute and all correct, because it possesses an ideology which is the life sustainer of the adherents of that particular community, class or group, and if it is not so, the organization, is bound to disintegrate and will lose its compactness and wholesomeness.

Fifthly, a community is proselytizing in nature, for the community, group or class keeps on expanding, (however not always, although the tendency to expand is always there), and more and more individuals come to adhere to its tenets for, "social endorsement is a universal necessity, it springs from the innate sociality of men. Every one likes of fall in line with one's group".[5]

Summarizing its various characteristics, we can say that a community is like an organism. It is a dynamic concept. It is capable of growth it is absolute in nature. Being expandable it is proselytizing in its attitude.

Community Action

Having known the distinct features of a community, let us proceed to examine, "how a community acts?".

A community, since it always exhibits a tendency to expand, acts sometimes as a comprehensive whole i.e., just as a single group.

Secondly, as described above, just as 'thinking and ideas' 'traditions and loyalties' vary from one individual to the other, a community also expands, acts and reacts, not only as one single group, but through various groups or classes within its fold, that emerge and expire with the march of time.

Lastly, a community can also act through its smallest component, i.e., an individual commonly known as the leader.

Thus examined, the social structure of humanity at large would appear as a chequered pattern of divisions, small or big (that have been carved out by the millions of boundary lines crossing each other) forming a strange network of communities groups and classes of different castes, creed and colour, engrossed in a dynamic and unceasing process of action and reaction. However, this net-work has no static pattern, it keeps on changing, the change being in direct proportion to the variability of human motivation, social evolution and communal interaction.

Every society consists of several communities. Now as explained above, a community can act in three ways. It can act as a comprehensive unit. It can act through the various groups and classes, that form its inner structure. Lastly, it can also act through its smallest unit the individual i.e. the leader. Whenever it acts for its one single motive of 'progress or the all round development of the personality of the organization and thence that of the components', the action can adopt two different patterns viz. the non-aggressive pattern, and the aggressive pattern.

Communalism: Virtue or vice?

Examined in this way, therefore communalism, which empirically speaking is a 'community in action', becomes both a virtue and a vice.

It is a virtue when the community or its component groups act in a non-aggressive way. It is a vice when they act in an aggressive way.

The above will become more clear by the following statement of Muhommad Iqbal wherein he says:

> "The principle that each group is entitled to free development on its own lines is not inspired by any feeling of narrow communalism. There are communalisms and communalisms. A community which is inspired by feeling of ill-will towards other communities is low and ignoble. I entertain the highest respect for the customs, laws, religions and social institutions of the other communities; nay it is my duty according to the teaching of the Quran, even to defend their place of worship if need be.
>
> "Yet I love the communal group which is the source of my life and behaviour and which has formed me what I am by giving me its religion, its literature, its thoughts, its culture and thereby recreating its whole past as a living operative factor in my present consciousness".[6]

Even the authors of the Nehru Report, while discussing the separation of Sindh, echo the higher aspect of communalism. The report says:

> "To say from the larger viewpoint of nationalism, that no communal provinces should be created, is in a way

> equivalent to saying from the still wider international viewpoint that there should be no separate nation. Both those statements have a measure of truth in them. But the staunchest internationalist recognizes that without the fullest national autonomy, it is extraordinarily difficult to create the international state. So also, without the fullest cultural autonomy, and communalism in its better aspect is culture, it will be difficult to create the harmonious nation".[7]

The view that communalism is a virtue and a blessing has been accepted by people of various shades of opinion. A man is best known by the community to which he belongs. His personality and its all-round development proceeds step by step towards an apparent completion, through his association and identification with various social institutions and groups such as family, school and church.

Since the community happens to be

> "that process of social interaction, which gives rise to a more intensive or more extensive attitude and practice, interdependence and co-operation, collaboration and unification".[8]

It is in a position to influence him the most. Further, a community being a group of groups', is entitled to receive both voluntary and involuntary allegiance from its individual adherent. The individual and the community are interdependent; they are infact complementary in nature. They both give and take from each other.

The truth is that in any organic structure, both the parts and the whole are indispensable for each other. In fact, they are interdependent and complementary in nature. They both give and take from each other. It is needless to mention that it is always the 'whole' that dominates and the 'part' just acts according to the wishes of and in sympathy with the whole.

As the community grows, with the march of time, it develops an atmosphere of its own and gives to every individual a communal heritage, that is handed on from one generation to the other, becoming more varied, more rich and more intense in the process.

To an individual, this heritage is the most sacred and precious possession. He feels more proud and enamoured of it, than an individual of a community other than his own can feel of his individual possession. It is there in human nature that one loves and likes the objects of one's most intimate association, and in turn gets prejudiced towards others.

The communal heritage in culture consists of a complex body of several beliefs, customs, prejudices, developed and cherished by the members of any one community. Since every society consists of several communities, it presents a chequered pattern of such developments and diverse ways of living.

Communalism may, therefore, be regarded as a tradition that impresses itself on the attitude of all members of a society and that imposes itself on the behaviour of most members of the society.

Since it is the most powerful social and cultural cause of prejudice, communalism has a curious way of developing into a unifying and at the same time a disputing influence. As this attribute of community grows and gathers vigour, it begins frequently to travel beyond its proper domain and to aspire to concentrate power within itself even at the cost of others. Clifford Manshardt in his book entitled, *The Hindu Muslim Problem in India* correctly writes:

> "A man should be proud of his social heritage. But when pride of one's own community leads one to a hatred of other communities, communalism changes from a blessing into a curse".[9]

Thus, communalism is both a virtue and a vice, it is a blessing as well as a curse. In fact, it represents two different trends in social living.

In its higher aspects communalism would mean a 'Community in action' to promote social heritage. In its narrow sense it would mean a 'community in action' to promote social tension.

Communalism is thus a double-edged concept. In a given society it at once stands for culture and for tension.

Aspect of Communal Tension

Unfortunately, the term communalism has always been used to signify communal-tension.

The reason for such an association is obvious. It lies in the simple fact that "social existence is a competitive-struggle"

To live, each individual has to struggle. He has to do so in a competitive spirit in order to lead a better life than the one lived hitherto, a tendency to improve and out-do being inherent in human nature. Since the individual alone is too weak, he compensates for his weakness by leading a 'group-life' based on a principle of mutual cooperation and interdependence.

Such a change, however, does not alter, the operation of natural law of 'the survival of the fittest', which is a principle of universal validity. The competitive-struggle, that hitherto existed on an individual plane, now operates on the group-basis.

Tension:Inevitability?

Thus, in any human society, a "competitive struggle" amongst the various communities that constitute its largest groups, is inevitable. It is in the nature of the things that a 'growing, expansible and dynamic' group should somewhere and sometimes come in conflict with like, 'growing, expansible and dynamic' groups in any society or circumstances; more so, because each community has a will of its own which is by nature, absolute and proselytizing. Thus, in any given society, if several such 'absolute and proselytizing' wills are to exist, a state of tension is simply unavoidable until and unless any of the following three things be made possible.

Firstly, all of them, may arrive at a 'modus operandi' to co-operate amongst themselves.

Secondly, all of them may subordinate themselves to some still greater will.

Thirdly, they may cease to exist at all.

It is suggested that perhaps none of these conditions can ever be achieved. Hence, there cannot be a total cessation of conflict among the various communities.

Further, howsoever non-aggressive may be the action of a community to develop its culture, it is bound to be misunderstood and mistaken in a society of relative and interdependent existence. Since each community is like a life organism, it is bound to be dynamic; without being in action, it ceases to be a community at all and so long it is in action, in any society where other communities too are 'in action', the conflict and tension in various spheres of their contact are inevitable.

Hence, the term communalism fails to denote its higher aspect and has ordinarily come to signify communal conflict and tension.

When further examined from a larger point of view, it was found that as it is difficult to avoid social groupings, so is it difficult to have a society without some sort of tension; because the fact of classification proceeds from the fundamental fact of difference and the two together are concomitant to the fact of prejudice, which is the source of all tensions. Since, a community, (being a class of classes and a group of groups) combines in itself the largest elements of difference, it is a natural repository of prejudices and an obvious vehicle of tensions.

Tension is tension, call it by any name we like. The change is more extraneous, depending on the distinctive traits of the community in question.

It can be the fact of race, religion, language, colour or creed, acting alone or in combination, all being positive sources of prejudice, and hence powerful promoters of communalism, in any society or any age.

Thus, communalism is neither the privilege of any one age nor of any one society. It is an unavoidable phenomenon which not only that manifests itself in curious ways, in different forms but is in consequences the same.

Thus, analyzing the various forms of the communal question in general Rajni Palme Dutt says:

> "It is by no means a type of question peculiar to India. Under certain conditions, the mingling of diverse races or religions in a single country can give rise to acute difficulties, sometimes even riots and bloodsheds. Orangeman and Catholics in Northern Ireland, Arabs and Jews in Palestine under the Mandate; Slaves and Jews in Tsarist Russia; so called, 'Aryans and Jews' in Nazi Germany; These are familiar issues of the 20th century world without treading to go back to earlier examples. Anti-Semitism in Europe, 'Apartheid' in South Africa, 'Jim Crow' in the United States, or the colour bar in the British Empire illustrate varying types of these racial-religious divisions and antagonisms".[10]

III. COMMUNALISM - ITS CAUSES

It is evident that in any given society, cultural advancement and communal rivalry proceed hand in hand, and that communalism as an attribute of community has come to denote intercommunal rivalry and the consequent social tension instead of signifying cultural amelioration.

We now turn to investigate those causal factors that promote communalism, these are the factors that underlie the deterioration in human relationship, which is primarily a communal rather than an individual relationship evidenced by the following remarks of a psychiatrist of eminence like Alfred Adler.

He writes, "If the conditions of our life are determined in the first place by cosmic influences, they are also further conditioned by the social and communal life of human beings and by the laws and regulations which arise spontaneously from the communal life. The communal need regulates all relationships between the individual life of man".[11]

From whatever angle one might examine the causes of any type of tension, hostility and communal cleavage. The free and smooth existence of individual and social life can be attributed to three fundamental factors, viz. material, mental and moral.

The Material Factor

The material, or the economic factor, is the prime mover of communal relationship in any given society. This is a plain truth that if man wants to live he must have something to eat, meaning thereby that he should work, putting his labour into 'the production of immediate material means of substance'. As Marx said: Mankind must first of all eat, drink, have shelter and clothing, before it can pursue, polities, science, art, religion, etc."[12]

But man, as Darwin said, is essentially a weak animal and the "whole animal kingdom demonstrates the fundamental law that species whose members are incapable of facing the battle for self-preservation gather new strength through herd life. The herd instinct has served humanity to this end".[13]

Therefore we understand firstly that "Social life became a necessity, because through the community and the division of labour in which every individual subordinated himself to the group, the species was enabled to continue its existence".[14]

Secondly, we find history amply bearing it out that the conflict among individuals can be analysed in terms of their, 'economic needs', since the law of the jungle, viz. 'the survival of the fittest' operates with equal force and magnitude, in the human societies as well. Security, 'physical and economic', and more and more of it, has been the basic essential need of human existence throughout all ages, and all lands. It is the logic of group life that raises this fundamental necessity to a communal plane, since communities not only form a surer and potential stronghold of individual interests, but are capable of providing a better safeguard in a world of all-round competition. They cannot only serve their gregarious needs, but can also protect their members from external threats, provide greater social recognition and prestige, capture more political power, delivering thus, in every way, the largest possible material prosperity to their adherents.

Any such efforts to serve the basic economic needs of the members of the community, leads to a communal outlook and entails an unceasing struggle for greater economic security. When in a society in which many communities live, the competition for greater material gains becomes keener and varied, and opposed means are used to achieve this end; the communal spirit also becomes more intense and widespread, giving stimulus to rivalries, hostilities and tension between the various competing communities, and perpetuating communalism as an evil in the normal flow of human social-living.

Discussing the economic cause of the 'Communal-conflict', Jessie Bernard writes:

> "The basic economic conflict in modern communities involves buyers, and sellers .... In complex economic structures....... buyer-seller relationship may take a wide variety of forms, such as employer-employee, tenant-landlord, borrower-lender, consumer-producer, city-agricultural worker, patient-doctor, client-lawyer, one industry-another industry, or one region-another region".

She further adds,

> "But whether the conflict takes place in the labour market,

> the housing market, or the international market, the same fundamental pattern prevails".[15]

Conflicts of those types usually take a communal garb and different economic interests precipitate social-tension. Thus, a German would prefer to buy from a German and a Jewish patient would like to go to a doctor of his own community. Even if there be no such preconceived notions present, competing communities take no time to give a communal colour to any clash of economic interests. For example, in India any trouble between the tenant and landlord, borrower and lender or peasant and zamindar, mill owner and factory workers, led many a time to the spread of communalism in its worst forms.

Referring to the economic dissatisfaction of the peasants with their conditions, an American scholar of the Indian communal problem writes:

> "The situation has its bearing upon the communal problem where the landlord who is looked upon as the oppressor, happens to be a Hindu, while his tenant Muslim or vice-versa. There is scarcely a grave communal disturbance in the rural areas in which the thread of economic oppression cannot be distinguished in the tangled skein of causes".[16]

Illustrating the same point, A.R. Desai in his book, *Social Background of Indian Nationalism* writes:

> "The Moplah rebellion of 1922 had both communal and economic roots. The economic discontent of the Moplahs, who were mainly Muslim-agriculturists intensely exploited by the Nambudaris, who were Brahmin landlords in Malabar, canalized by the Muslim communalists into communal channels with the result that a revolt, predominantly economic in content but religious in form, broke out leading to tragic loss of life and property".

He concludes,

> "It frequently happened in India that where the Hindus were landlords and the Muslims were peasants, often due to instigation of communalists economic class conflict between them assumed communal forms".[17]

An important question can be raised here as to why such class-conflicts usually take a communal-garb? The answer is very simple and lies in the fact that in a competitive society, the community acts more or less like a trade union on the one hand, and an aggressive force on the other. In order to ring greater economic security, and to protect its individual adherents, it has to be both defensive and aggressive.

This economic conflict is not only, between the classes of buyers and sellers as enumerated by Jessie Bernard. There is another field of greater economic conflict. It is the competition for jobs and status. Since every community has desire to gain greater economic security for its adherents, the competitive struggle aggravates communalism, for example, in India during the British rule, the desire to share in 'loaves and fishes' of office was one of the basis of the communal problem. Every community wanted more seats than could be warranted by their numerical proportion either in the governmental office or in other public bodies such as the municipality, legislature, etc. Pandit Nehru in his autobiography thus sums up his impression.

> "It was all jobbery-big jobs, little jobs, jobs and seats for the Hindus, for the Muslims, for the Sikhs for the Anglo-Indians, for the Europeans: But in all jobs for the upper classes the masses had no look-in".[18]

In the words of Sinha, communalism is "Politics of the crawling belly; of the handful of communal intelligentsia".[19] Explaining as to why the communities fought for percentages he wrote:

> "The reason is that Indian economy is not spacious enough to give a free field to every one. We are confined to a narrow space and as we try to expand individually, as we inevitably must, we encroach on the opportunities of others. These latter must resist such encroachment and in resisting it draw upon all the weapons in their armoury including the weapon of communal distinction. In an uncertain world whatever certainty can be achieved by fixing communal percentages is a gain in itself".[20]

In conclusion he writes:

> "This economic want is the abiding source of communalism and no reform can uproot it unless we cure the evil of want".

The Mental Factor

The mental or the psychological factor is another important factor of primary importance that goes to make or unmake a normal communal existence in a society. The foremost fact to be noted is that it is in the minds of men that the seeds of every conflict or tension in the world, first germinate. G. Murphy, in his study of "Human Behaviour and Social Tensions in India" observes:

"When UNESCO has agreed that 'war begins in the minds of men' it has not by way of any reduction of emphasis upon factors other than the psychological which bring them in conflict, rather, it is an attempt to make clear that all the forces from which war springs are ultimately passed through the filter of human thought, feeling, and impulse before they lead to the decisions from which war follows".[21]

The behaviour of an individual and his relationship to others with whom he happens to live, depend not only on his individual thinking, feeling and imagination, but also on what others think, feel and imagine. However, a community furnishes a larger base for one's thought and action. Every community, during a course of time, fabricates some sort of organization, to which each individual adheres, both voluntarily and some times involuntarily. This organization springs from the minds of men. In the words of Arthur Hillman:

> "Communities have organisation quite apart from and more fundamental than the structures that find expression in their formal institutions. The characteristics, the habits, attitudes and interests of the people who make up the community, the situations in which they interact, and the 'rule of the game' in accordance with which their behaviour is regulated, the conceptions which people have of themselves and their fellows and of the community in which they live, are vital factors in community life".

He further adds,

> "These variables, the precise nature of which must be ascertained for each community, underlie the formal structure that may eventually crystalise and condition the success or failure of whatever preconceived scheme community organizer may seek to impose upon the community".[22]

Thus, we can safely come to three definite conclusions.

Firstly, that the seeds of all tension lie in the minds of men from where they grow in the form of individual attitude, belief and prejudice.

Secondly, that these individual attitudes, beliefs and prejudices eventually take a communal colour, because the communities themselves behave as a living individuality which is a true reflection of its adherents.

Thirdly, that howsoever an organized pattern the habits, attitudes and interests of the people who make up a community may assume, yet they are variable determinants and thus amenable to all correction.

These mental attitudes and psychological prejudices can be caused by more than one factor. Thus, "A certain amount of human prejudice may be due to single dramatic experiences or to recurrent experiences of a very simple sort, involving either gratification or frustration. In these cases we become prejudiced for or against an individual".[23]

Thus one unclean habit of one Muslim neighbour may develop a deep stereotype in the mind of a Hindu that all Muslims are unclean and hence untouchables, or one mischief by one Hindu seller can develop a prejudice in the mind of a Muslim that all Hindus are dishonest. In both these cases one can trace the psychological germs of communal tension.

Secondly, in many cases one may not have any parent belief but one can take over the outlook of those near him, since each community forms a little world of its own, that appears a different world to others. How this psychological aberration caused by one's sharing the group outlook, actually acts on a communal plane, is well stated by one of the world's foremost psychologists, Murphy Gardner. He writes:

> Now inevitably, since one must maintain ones stance in a complicated and difficult world, our people are good people; they tend to be near us, they satisfy our needs, they are on the whole warm and protective, and it is with them that we must stand if we are to make our way. Those who are outside of this little orbit of the personal world are viewed first with considerable caution and sometimes, if life treats

> us badly, with actual hostility. We early find, then the formation of a "we" group and a "they" group, a right group and a wrong group, from the point of view of our outlook and our hopes for making out of life what we want it to be".

He further adds,

> "The point is quite fundamental. It is not from the fact of diversity as such that hostility arises. Hostility appears when once the groups have been differentiated, so that one can see where the line of cleavage lies as regards skin, colour or religious practice or anything else, and then learns that the people who in the out-group do not share those values which are especially precious to us: if for example, we are Baptists they happen to be Catholics, their value system contains much that is not immediately real in them. If we care very much about our values, we may be exclusive toward people who do not fully share these".[24]

Clearly communalism thrives liberally on the right or wrong assumptions of certain communal values, which germinate, grow and flourish, in the minds of men.

These valuations have explosive possibilities. Given a slight spark of any psychological, imaginary or real interference or set-back, they lead to violent manifestions, in the form of communal riots and mob agitation. We may have both subjective or objective factors that provide this igniting spark. For instance, the sound of music from a Hindu procession passing through the street while the service in a mosque is in progress, or, the slaughter of a cow, in the open, may lead to violent repercussions. It happens when the minds of people are shut by the doors of mental prejudices.

There are times, when even an objective situation by giving rise to a sense of aggrievement, may be fraught with grave apprehension and fears for the community, ultimately leading to tension in society. As for instance,

> "We may have the scene in which only the members of one religious, racial or ethnic group can obtain special favours or privileges, particularly such as admission to educational institutions or admission to apprenticeships which give them in course of time desirable skilled trades to practice at the cost of other communities".

This kind of exclusivism would lead to a revaluation of communal relationship existing hitherto, and may raise issues seething with discontent. The Hindu-Muslim tension during the British rule amply bears it out.

Thus, any psychological valuation acts both ways however superficial or genuine it may be. It positively breeds communalism leading thereby to social tension. As G. Murphy remarks, "social tension is obviously present on both sides of the coin,on the side of those who try to break in and on the side of those who try to keep them out".[25]

We cannot ignore the fact of misunderstanding and illwill that the mental maladjustment of correct evaluation and consideration of others' point of view leads to. For instance, in a given society, even the status of being a minority community is sometimes enough stimulus to promote wrong psychological calculations. By its very act, the majority party is liable to being taken for a dishonest and harmful move. As Gardner Murphy writes:

> "Not only do we sense another group as interfering with our own progress; not only do we sense the situation is unjust; we develop from our own sense of immediate and obvious rightness and conviction that members of these other groups chronically and permanently take advantage of us. We thus raise what is a local and temporary hostility into a general and permanent one".[26]

There is no end to such psychological aberrations that turn into permanent prejudices and precipitate communal tension. Thus to a Brahmin, a Sudra is permanently impure; the Baptist may hate the Jew; the French Canadian thinks English Canadians aggressive;American may insist on fighting the Russians; and to Muslims, the Hindus may always appear unjust, irreligious and wrong; all this on the basis of any one single action of one individual or of a number of individuals done recently or in the remote past.

The truth however is that, in any small struggle in society, to which a number of communities are a party, be that struggle social, political or economic, be it real or imaginary, there is a fundamental tendency of communities to fight things on the basis of psychological foundations, having certain standardized pictures, stereotyped ideas, or preconceived notions, all being to a great extent pure and simple mental complexes. Thus, in some specific issue to quote Murphy again,

> "Usually a picture of the interfering group becomes standardized during this period of tension. 'They are the kind of people who take such advantage', 'They are always doing this' 'Never trust a Jew', 'Hit him again he is Irish'. 'The Americans are like that', and so on' with phrases which could be run to the hundreds, indicating the sense of chronic unfairness, unscruplousness and even moral depravity of those whose ways differ from our own".[27]

Elaborating the "formation of communal stereotypes", that are caused because of one's ignorance, irritation or frustration both at the individual and group level, Mr Murphy adds that these prejudices grow so hard that it becomes rather difficult to overcome them. He writes:

> But there is still one higher phase in the elaboration of prejudices. Just as we weave together spider-like a beautiful structure of our own essential rightness, decency, and adequacy for living, the capacity of our own people for high ideals, for hard work, for progress, initiative self-reliance and nobility, so we can expect any human group to develop its own sense of basic rightness. It may have to kow-tow; it may have to apologise for living with reference to others around it who may have some sort of superior status; but it has ways of getting even. It has ways of saying to itself in its own heart. We know our own ways are good.

Now, let us imagine this sense of rightness of our own group, encountering what we would call boorishness or crudeness in the behaviour of others. We come to a line when other people are simply chronically bad. They are chronically lazy, shiftless, dishonest, crooked, dirty, mean, violent or savage. Compare the words, 'cruel', 'dirty' and 'fanatical', applied by Hindus in Ahmedabad and Lucknow to Muslims.

One speaks of the prevalence in these connections of stereotypes, that is, fixed cliches or standardized epithets which are applied by members of one group to members of another group. The fact then that stereotypes are essentially moral and that we end up our sorry story of prejudice by assigning moral inferiority to our competitors, should be sufficient to suggest that explanations in terms of single shock experience, or those conditioned responses, are not likely to be altogether adequate as explanations.

In particular, the complex structure of the way in which we perceive our scheme in our own rightness, and the complex structure of perception of other groups in competition with ourselves and professing ways different from our own should carry us to recognition of the fact that we find prejudice existing difficult to overcome".[28] Summarising the causes of social tension, he concludes:

> "Thus we have so far two basis for hostility. First the direct and obvious interference with our goals which we might perhaps summarise under the word competitiveness, and second the matter of aesthetic annoyance or non-participation in our own form of correct conduct".[29]

We agree with Mr Murphy's views and venture to add that it is both the ignorance and indoctrination of communal values that precipitate social tension. In fact, it is the ignorance of fundamental truths that permits the prejudices to persist as 'pernicious venom'.

Secondly as Dr. Engene L. Caler writes:

> "The other side of coin is pictured in terms of cultural learning through indoctrination and habituation. Prejudice develops out of adult values and the status quo to which the individual is exposed, as well as out of social situation, generating insecurities".[30]

Explaining the helplessness of the individual and how in the majority of cases he has to succumb to communal-demand, Roback writes:

> "In order to play his role as a member of a particular group, the individual must accept the values of the group as his own. As a consequence of these pressures, he may find himself on the group for the determination of what is right and what is wrong. From this approach prejudice may also be an outgrowth of a competitive struggle between certain material and psychological returns."[31]

Thus, we find that during the course of ordinary social living, individuals have to accept the wrongs of their community as right. Communal loyalty, like every other loyalty, demands unquestioned obedience and implicit faith in its actions; It leads to an ever strained situation in the daily life. For example, during the courses of communal rivalry, it is not the dictates of individual thinking of right and wrong that prevail; it is the will of the community that matters.

One wrong follows another and is accepted as right by the sanction of the group that perpetrates it. It leads to individual indoctrination, the formation of stereotypes of honoured prejudices with high communal value.

Thus, these prejudices which are the product of multiple causation and which Allport defines as the "Negative Attitudes towards human beings that are held because of their membership in a certain group"[32], are a positive psychological source that spread communalism.

However, these group prejudices or the "Negative attitudes" may not act by themselves. As stated earlier, these psychological attitudes may be linked with any social issue, whether it is cultural, as between Sinhalese and Tamilians, or racial as between the Whites and Negroes in America, or, economic, say as between Arabs and Jews in Palestine; or political as between a Muslim minority or a Hindu majority in India; or, religious as between Catholics and Protestants in Ireland.

The result in all these cases is the same; viz. the loss of material understanding between different communities, birth of distrust and hostility and consequent release of forces of destruction of social harmony and promotion of tension. This tension may be designated variously as racial, cultural or communal.

The Moral Factor

The third important factor that promotes communalism is the moral factor, for in each society we find that every community presents its own code of morals which often clash with that of other communities, and hence the competing morals usually precipitate social tension.

According to the *Encyclopedia of Social Sciences,*

"Until rather recent times morals were not distinguished

> from manners. Together with ceremonials, they were techniques of behaviour believed to be efficacious in securing goods and averting evils; They were judged by identical standards as right and wrong. In the course of time, manners came to be identified with techniques recognized to be manifold, changeful and contingent morals, with a system presumed to be single, unchanging and necessary. They were called and they still are in certain quarters, not morals but morality and were ascribed to universal principles of right conduct endemic to mankind".

It adds,

> "The pluralization of morality into morals follows upon the recognition that morality also consists of manifold changeful and contingent techniques of conduct. Considered thus, morals so largely overlap manners, folkway, mores, law ethics and public opinion that only convention of fiat decides where these others leave off and morals begin".[33]

We however equate the moral factor with the socio-religious factor for two very clear reasons. Firstly, the morals envisage not only a definite code of conduct for the members of the community, they also expect a specified observance of some such code, thus, desiring a set behaviour both in the inter-and intra-communal dealings, whether done singly or through groups.

We can put it in another way and say that in every society the individuals whether they act through the community or by themselves usually evolve a code of conduct, according to their own genius which they call moral. This code not only forms the norm of judging individual and communal behaviour in the given society, but actual morality lies in a strict adherence to it without questioning the rightness of morals themselves. In short, morals deal with both individual and communal social-conduct.

Secondly, if there are two things most inseparably linked, they are morality and religion. As every religion expresses the moral spirit understood to be sanctioned and ordained by some spiritual and divine agency, morality, in itself can never be considered as separate from religion. It is needless to mention that these two elements sustain each other. As Horace M. Kallen observes:

> "But, the most pervasive sanction for any complex of morals, whether or not codified is religion. Religion is nearer the primary pattern of social complex than any other institution. Its sanctions involving supernatural rewards and punishments enter early into the consciousness of the young".

He further adds,

> "Orthodox cults thus continue to invest with moral sanction much that the secular world has reduced to manners".[34]

That any such code of morals is both ethical and religious has been accepted by all. In this connection, Alfred Bertholet says:

> "One of the most powerful and enduring aspect of the influence of religion upon human society lies in the sphere of ethics. The process is one of interaction rather than of unilateral causation".

He adds,

> "Cultural progress by stimulating the introduction of ethical standards in society contributes to the development of an ethical conception of god and the more exalted idea of god in turn, intensifies the social concern for morality".[35]

Examined in this light, it becomes clear that we may very well equate the moral factor to the socio-religious factor since it is a set of certain social practices with a religious sanction that go to form the moral code. But in a society in which there are different sects and communities professing different religions, one is likely to find a conflicting and varying pattern of communal ethics, demanding conflicting allegiance to certain social practices.

Thus, for instance, while the Muslim code of morality not only tolerates the slaughter of kine as a very ordinary necessity of daily life, but also presumes this social practice to be a religious act and a moral obligation of the community, the Hindu code of morality not only takes cow slaughter as a sin of the basest kind but also abjures any cruelty to living beings as an immoral and irreligious act, deserving even legal punishment in certain cases.

Many more instances can be cited to show that, "one group's virtue, to sum up, can be another group's sin. Obeying the Ten commandments, or following the gospel of Christ or of Marx may be beatitude or turpitude".

Obviously, the moral factor operates as a source of permanent discord in the harmonious existence of any communal relationship in a given society. But here a few pertinent questions can be raised. Firstly, how do certain practices acquire moral stature and religious sanction? And if they are moral and religious, how can the same thing be moral for a few and immoral for others? How at all can a human principle have conflicting allegiance?

Secondly, even if the sectional and divided values of morality be granted, are not such valuations liable to change within their own fold? If they do why can they not be forsaken for ever? If not, why?

Lastly, will their non-observance really make an individual immoral and a community irreligious? If not, why raise certain communal practices to such heights only to make social living complex, individual life more chained, and, communal relations permanently strained. And why go on ventilating off and on individual and communal grievances in the name of religion and morality, only to keep communalism permanently alive as an evil?

The answer to the first question is very simple, for we know that the fact of necessity is the first step that motivates human action. In order to provide a sense of stability to the fact of necessity, morality is associated with the mode of such social practices that deliver the goods in consonance to the communal conscience. Whatever is thus considered right becomes moral and even transcends to the divine plane.

As Kallen writes:

> "A necessity enters morals when it is consciously desired or rejected, pursued or avoided by a group. Food-stuffs, sex-objects, clothing, shelter, defence against diseases and enemies are such necessities. Consider primitive customs and codes; Australian traditions, Aryan Sutras, Israelitish commandments, are alike, meticulous, concerning what to eat and what not to eat, how to secure and prepare it, in what company to eat and so on. Cannibalism, which is a horror to us, has been a felt necessity to more than one ancient people, since it is based on the belief that men are what they eat and that to eat the strong, the great, the wise, is to become great, strong and wise".

He further adds,

> "The prescriptive dietary system of Todas, Jews, Brahmans, Moḥammadans, with their clean and unclean foods, exemplify the more positive elaboration of the same process in selecting and defining right.... codes deal similarly with the biological crises and conditions of the personal life,.. birth, puberty, menstruation, cohabitation, marriage and divorce, association with others. They regulate contact and communication between the sexes, between the generations between the castes, between the outsiders and insiders. Dress and decoration, themselves derivatives of the nutrition and sex complexes, also fall under rule codes prescribe how hair shall be worn; how a person shall be marked and dressed for hunting, fighting, courting, marrying, burying, and for contact with Ghosts and Gods".....[36]

Concluding the explanation of the formation of and continuation of habits, customs beliefs and social practices of different people, he says:

> "The generations transmit it, older infecting the younger with the feeling which the formula sustains. Since the originative force is forgotten another origin is automatically attributed. And all attribution seems to be summed up in the formula. It was Father's way-mos majorum".

Where societies are complexes of lesser groups, the importance of the father seems neutralized. Mos majorum ceases to be their way; it becomes a way which an original father of fathers, a king, a god reveals as his will for man. Mos majorum bifurcate into custom and code. The moral code is the will of God. It embodies sanctions, promises of reward and threats of punishments since its ordinances prescribe behaviour forms constantly subject to variation and lapse".

Where the code first imposed and then accepted is acknowledge by the general sentiment, it becomes a community ideal and expectation the "spirit" of the people of the times-glorified as the 'moral laws'.[37]

Each community thus develops many a "community-ideal" which are at the same time moral and religious. Thus, they have different appeal to different people, thus people have different necessities and a different communal outlook of life. This difference of communal growth is well nourished and maintained by the "community ideal", by a strict observance of certain socio-religious practices that uphold these moral ideals for the community.

Since any such communal observance is continued both by individual habit and communal coercion, communalism also continues to thrive. These beliefs of the community are seldom relinquished for they act as a source of power to the community. As Bertrand Russel writes:

> "The power of community depends not only upon its number and its economic resources and its technical capacity, but also upon its beliefs. A fanatical creed held by all the members of community often greatly increases its power. Some times it however diminishes it".[38]

Considering the way in which certain socio-religious practices of different communities, born out of conscious necessity, evolve themselves into a part of communal ethics and ideals, it is not difficult to answer the second question raised earlier, the question whether a change in the concept of morality entertained by a certain community is possible or not?

The fact is that every socio-religious practice is composed of two unequal components. The first part in it is the element of 'necessity', which is liable to change with the change of time and the needs of community. There is every possibility of the element of necessity, being not the necessity of the entire community but a clique thereof. Obviously, when the entire community gets conscious of this fact it can adopt the socio-religious practice attached to that necessity or reject it altogether as a slur on any decent existence. The practice of cannibalism or that of sati and untouchability in India can be cited as an illustration.

The second part that composes the socio-religious practice, is however, more rigid in its nature because it alone forms that element which is the source of strength and not often of immense power to a community. For instance, any custom or peculiar tradition of a community , once it has found a place in the moral code, assumes strength not by its nature but by the fact that it has a number of followers. The obedience that it extracts is what makes it a source of strength. Can that following be changed? Is it always rational? Clearly an individual obeys the communal commands not because he feels that a particular action demanded by society is good or bad in itself, but because it at once safeguards his place in society. It is not the question of rational discrimination, but of finding a support amidst social insecurities, of having an existence distinct and strong that a community alone provides. Such an adherence to the communal tenets can be altered with difficulty and that too through the course of a very long period.

In short, although it will not be very correct to say that the so-called moral attributes that are supposed to be absorbed in certain socio-religious practices of the community are unalterable in their import and sanctity, yet it would not be incorrect to say that whatever change comes, would be the result of a slow and difficult process. A systematic planning can even lead to their complete effacement.

This effacement can be achieved not by the effort of one individual but only if the entire community is animated with a revolutionary favour to cast off old marks and adopt less rigid, less narrow and more liberal human ways of communal living for its members. But seldom do communities assume such a bold outlook.

Communalism, thus continues to promote tension. It does so in direct proportion to the variability in the communal code of morality, as associated with the various socio-religious practices of different communities, as also to the rigidity with which these customs, traditions and beliefs are observed.

As to our last doubt, whether' their non observance will really make an individual immoral and a community irreligious' no categorical answer can be given. For instance, if today a Hindu goes and attends a feast given by Muslims or enters into an inter caste marriage, he remains as much Hindu after the act as before. Once again, if a Muslim does not sacrifice a cow or restrains his fanaticism and refrains from breaking to pieces an idol in a Hindu temple, he will continue to be as religious afterwards as he was before.

But can the community afford to witness any such action on the art of its adherent? Will the individual, who does so, be able to stand the fire of taboos and prohibitions envisaged by communal Pundits and Maulvis? The fact is that, once the community relaxes its control on the observance of the social practices evolved by it through its life time, it loses its strength and power, a contingency for which it is not prepared. The uniformity which is needed to give power to a community, is a 'uniformity in practice, depending upon sentiment and habit and it has to exist at the cast of individual's sense of discrimination and that of any intellectual conviction'.

It is here, that we can also find an answer as to why in spite of a number of points of agreement, different communities still retain a distinctive and often an exclusive bent of mind. They do not either let the fact or difference be forgotten, or tolerate any deflection from their tenets, for communal cohesion demands a "creed, or a code of behaviour, or a prevailing sentiment, or, at best, some combination of all three, without which a community disintegrates' and is likely to become subject to foreign infiltration.[39]

The fact is that, in a world where the 'fact of difference' be in itself a source of strength and a repository of power, communalism will but be a natural accompaniment. It is bound to increase as an evil, as long as there are number of such scapegoats as are a source of strength to one community irrespective of its consequences to others. The moral and religious factors have often been made such scape-goats, particularly so, because they have always appealed in different ways to different people, in spite of their uniform intrinsic import.

The fault lies not with morality but in the meaning that is given to this relative concept. It does not lie either inter-religion but with the rituals and the dogmatic rigidity with which God is worshipped. Ultimately, it is not the individual but his community that is to be blamed.

The cause of communalism in augmenting social tension lies deep in the socio-religious practices and the manner of their observance. It is they and other symbols associated with them that have promoted communalism, more so, because they had both moral and religious appeal combined in one place, and more so, because they prescribe to people a way of behaviour, that produces a most discordant and disturbing note to the neighbour community.

In every age, in every society, there have been numerous such socio-religious practices of neighbour communities that aroused heat and embittered inter-communal relations. In fact, these practices in the course being handed down from one generation to the other, also simultaneously carried along the source of irritation and conflict. Thus, communalism and tension have passed from one age to another and from one generation to the other.

In India, among the various socio-religious practices observed by the followers of different communities, the practice of untouchability amongst the Hindus (against which even the Muslims are not immune), is the most vicious dogma responsible for promoting a chronic and perpetual state of communalism.

The very element of discrimination exercised in any field gives birth to discontent and tension. And when discrimination is launched on such an unprecedented vast scale, as manifested by the practical application of this touch-me-not-ism, in almost every walk of life, the consequences are seldom anything but disruptive of every harmonious move of communal coexistence.

The curse of untouchability has very cruel and inhuman after effects. Still it has ever been observed with a systematic and religious fervour; any violation of the code thereof being considered as an immoral act. To dub certain communities as unclean, impure and low and to deprive their members of an equal and free association and movement in society, is likely to spread communal antagonism and social tension which is bound to increase when such a discrimination be hereditary. Writing about this phenomenon of hereditary untouchability of so many people in India, Dr. B.R. Ambedkar writes:

"This type of untouchability among Hindus stands in a class by itself... There are some striking features of the Hindus system of untouchability affecting the 429 untouchable communities.... the impurities of the 50-60 millions of the untouchables of India, quite unlike the impurity arising from birth, death, etc., is permanent. The Hindus who touch them become polluted thereby can become pure by undergoing purificatory ceremonies. But there is nothing which can make the untouchables pure. They are born impure, they are impure while they live, they die the death of impure and they give of untouchability affixed to them. It is a case of permanent hereditary stain which nothing can cleanse".[40]

Such a socio-religious practice that, not only keeps a certain section of society in a state of inescapable servility, accompanied by inferior status and undignified and low occupations, but also gags its intelligence, cripples its action, forbids its entry into public place and place of worship, prohibits going over to bathing ghats, and even to burning ghats, justifying all this on moral grounds, invariably gives rise to numerous grounds for frustration and a sense of ineffaceble humiliation deep into the hearts of the community, bringing disastrous results in any society persecuted whatever. The question whether such a practice can possibly promote happy inter-communal relations can be answered only with difficulty.

In India untouchability has been a natural corollary to the degenerated system of caste, that broke society into thousands of separate units, frequently hostile to one another and always jealous. The element of exclusiveness is a common feature of both the caste system and untouchability. Obviously understanding could possibly be created between communities if people were always to be kept at a distance from one generation to the other. Vincent Smith rightly observes:

> "the institution fosters intense class pride, fatal to a feeling of brotherhood between man and man. The Malabar Brahman who considers himself defiled if an outcaste stands within twenty paces of him cannot possibly be interested in a creature so despised. The sentiment pervades all classes of Hindu society in varying degrees of intensity".[41]

Communalism is bound to thrive in a society where communities live with social traditions, running counter to the human aspect of civilized existence. It matters little whether the venue of such a discrimination be America, South Africa or India. However, in India the socio-religous practice of untouchability was a serious blight on Hinduism. As a historian writes:

> "The more characteristic problems of the country centre round the institution of caste. Originally concerned with the preservation of ceremonial purity in social relations, the caste system has in the course of ages developed into an institution which rigidly assigns to each individual his

> position and his duties in the structure of orthodox Hinduism.......... Among the unfortunate results to which Hinduism has given rise must be counted the existence of the depressed classes who number about 60 millions. They are 'untouchables', that is to say, contact with them entails ceremonial purification on the part of the higher castes. In some parts of the country, they may be fairly termed 'unapproachables': since even their proximity implies pollution........ social ostracism so degrading, persisting through many centuries, has resulted in the erection of serious obstacles to manliness, independence and self help ... the main obstacles to their elevation lies in the social traditions observed by the great majority of the caste community:..[42]

But as stated earlier, what goes as a curse with Hindus goes well with Muslims too. It is a common feeling that whenever we hear any mention of depressed and suppressed classes and untouchability, we usually associate these epithets with the Hindu community. The classes in the Muslim community constituted by those whose ancestors came from outside India — the Sayyeds, Shaikhs, Pathans and Moghuls — have conceits of superiority that are in no way less proud than those found in the heart of Hindu society".[43]

Fazli Rubee, Dewan to the Nawab Bhadur of Murshidabad, in his book *The Origin of the Mussalmans of Bengal*, gives an idea of this equality and inequality, as it has to evolve through socio-religious usages. He writes:

> "From a religious point of view, of-course all Mussalmans stand on a footing of equality. But according to usage and custom the social position and a change of religion ... a low caste person on his embracing Islam is not allowed to hold familiar intercourse with high born Mussalmans.... Rigid and scrupulous regard has ever been paid by the Mussalmans to social and family dignity".[44]

That Hindus and Muslims alike, observe socio-religious practices, caste exclusiveness and untouchability with equal force and rigidity, has also been explained in detail by J.F. Kotewal an eminent authority on communalism in India. He writes:

> "The social democracy plea of Islam is not true to the facts of life as it is lived in Muslim society ... It would appear that just as the Hindus have their Avarna and Varna classes their low and high castes, so have Muslims their Momin and Shareif classes, their low and high classes".

He further adds:

> "The same untouchability is also observed here for instance, marriage with people of other communities is one of the offences and the prohibition on inter marriage extends to higher as well as low castes. The members of one group cannot gain admission to the other, etc.
>
> The above shows that the Mohammedans observe not only caste but also untouchability. There can thus be no manner of doubt that Muslim society in India is afflicted by the same social evils which afflict the Hindu society. Indeed the Muslims have all the social evils of the Hindus......"[45]

This is indeed one aspect of the communal problem, when it is created within the fold of a community due to the rigid observance of certain socio-religious practices as envisaged by the exponents of communal morality. There is however another aspect of the untouchability question when the inter-communal contact assumes a serious breach of religion and moral tenets. This aspect of communalism arises when Hindus call Muslims and Christians as *Mlechhas* and Muslims call the members of every other community as infidels and *Kafirs*. Such an attitude of indifference and mutual repulsion breeds communal hatred of the worst type in ordinary day to day intercourse and the social living, one comes across a Muslim treating a Hindu as a *kafir* and a Hindu giving a Muslim a treatment worse than meted out to untouchables for to the Hindu he is a Mlechha. As an analysts observes:

> "Since the invasion of India by the Musalmans the term has been applied by the Hindus to the Muslim invaders whom they classed along with Shudras, the untouchables. The Hindus feel polluted by the touch of the Muslims: to the Muslim the Hindu is a pagan, therefore polluted, whose touch would pollute a Muslim who is pure in body and soul".[46]

This attitude of mutual repulsion has persisted through the centuries, and is today one of the main obstacles in the path of fostering communal and political unity between the Hindus and the Muslims. It is evident thus, that in India, question of untouchability has been a chronic source of communalism in all its three phases. The truth however is, that no concept of morality or sacredness of any religious tenet is worth the name, until its observance, even if it does not promote healthy communal relations atleast does not disturb them either.

Any search of elements that make communalism an evil at the moral plane, therefore involves not only the investigation of the undesirable socio-religious practices, customs and traditions but also of the religions that give their tacit support and sanction? The fault lies therefore, not with the individuals, but with the communities and their concept of morality and religion. To sum up one could do no better than agree with Gandhi when in his reference to the communal problem amongst the Hindus and Muslims on a socio-religious plane he says:

> "The posterity will judge both the faiths by the manner in which the followers of each acquit themselves in the matter. However good Hinduism or Islam may be in the abstract, the only way each can be judged is by the effect produced by each on its votaries considered as a whole".[47]

IV. COMMUNALISM - ITS STAGES

Since the hoary past, India has been a land peopled by different races, speaking different languages and worshipping different Gods. The 'fact of difference' has been quite vividly and prominently stamped on the life and people of this land. However, amidst this chequered pattern of difference and diversity, group life continued to be the corner-stone of the Indian social life. The community[48] remained the main unit of this group-existence. It alone provided a cohesive framework within which people organized their activities and daily life. Thus, India has always been a land of many communities, each having its own distinct characteristics. The communal relationship of this conglomeration of communities in one land, forms the warp and woof of its history.

The growth of communalism was a two-fold process. In its higher aspect communalism led towards the growth of a culture that was rich, varied and colourful, as it had been evoloved through the genius of various communities acting in mutual cooperation and harmony.

However social life is not a very smooth passage. Every society has its own points of conflicts. The 'fact of difference' unprinted boldly, on every sphere of the life of Indians did lead towards the state of conflicts, hostility and tension, that manifested itself in occasional outbreaks and even in full pitched battles. Obviously the onward march of the life of the Indian communities also registers the growth and development of communalism in its lower aspect. It is in fact a record of "Social tension" as it came to pass due to the mutual discord and disharmony and concomitant antagonism and rivalries amongst the same set of communities.

We cannot say with any certainty as to when the cultural aspect of the Inter-communal life ends, and from where its lower aspect begins. Nor can there be drawn a dividing line between these two aspects, over a vast panorama of communal existence of the people in this land spread over many countries. One cannot indeed say as to when in the life of a community the elements of conflict cease to operate and that of cooperation start functioning. This much, however, can be said with certainty that history is a queer admixture of black and white. Every society in this world in its inter-communal life, two continual threads running parallel, one that of a higher and much more sublime nature, called culture and the other that of a lower and a rather unpleasant nature called conflicts.

The history of communalism, which in modern terminology exclusively denotes the lower aspect of the inter-communal relationship viz. that of communal conflict and social tension, records three distinct phases in its development from the earliest to the present times. It passes from the social to the religious and culminates in the political phase.

We now proceed to investigate the nature of each of these distinct phases of communalism in India in the ongoing chapters.

NOTES AND REFERENCES

1. 'Commune' : In its most general sense, commune is a group of persons acting together for purposes of self-government; specially in towns. Commune is now a term, generally applied to the smallest administrative division in Switzerland and France.
   All citizens in the middle ages were in the juridical sense of the word commune.
   'Community': a body of persons living together (though not necessarily at one place), and practising more or less community of goods or having a common objective and interest.
2. *Human Ecology - A Theory of Community Structure* by Amos H. Hawley, The Ronald Press, p. 64-65.
3. *Ibid.*, p. 65.
4. *The Hindu Muslim Question*. Dr. Beni Prasad. Kitabisthan, Allahabad, 1941, p. 1.
5. *Ibid.*, p. 3.
6. Mohd. Iqbal's Presidential address in the Allahabad Session of All India Muslim League. December, 1930 (Quoted from F.K. Khan Durrani's *The Meaning of Pakistan*, p. 207.
7. The All India Parties Conference Report (1928), p. 30.
8. Encyclopedia of Social Sciences, Vol. III (1951).
9. *The Hindu Muslim Problem in India* by Clifford Manshardt, George Allen & Unwin Ltd., Museum Street, (1936), p. 51.
10. *India To-day and Tomorrow* Rajni Palme Dutt: People's Publishing House, Delhi. (1955), p. 223.
11. *Understanding Human Nature* by Alfred Adler, Perma Books, New York.
12. *Marx Engels* Selected Works Vol. II. Foreign Languages Publishing House, Moscow, 1949.
13. *Understanding Human Nature* by Alfred Adler, p. 27.
14. *Ibid.*, p. 27.
15. *The American Community Behaviour* by Jessie Bernard.
16. *The Hindu-Muslim Problem in India*, Clifford Manshardt. George Allen & Unwin Ltd., Museum Street (1936), p. 54.
17. *The Social Background of Indian Nationalism*, by Dr. A.R. Desai, p. 166.
18. *Autobiography* by Jawaharlal Nehru, p. 293.
19. *To Philipsober. A Guide to the Communal Problem of India* by A.N. Sinha, p. 22.
20. *Ibid.*, p. 215.
21. *In the minds of men*, Murphy Gardner: B/B Basic Books, Inc. Publishers. Noy. (1953), p. 8.
22. *Community Organization and Planning* by Arthur Hillman. The Macmillan Col. N.Y. (Ind. Ed. 1951), p. xvi.

23. Murphy, *op. cit.*, p. 219.
24. *Ibid.*, p. 221.
25. *Ibid.*, p. 223.
26. *Ibid.*, p. 223.
27. *Ibid.*, p. 225.
28. *Ibid.*, p. 225.
29. *Ibid.*, p. 225.
30. In *Present Day Psychology* by A.A. Roback. Philosophical Library, New York (1955). Chxi 'social psychology' by Dr. Engene L. Gaier. p. 387.
31. *Ibid.*, p. 387 (1) *Prejudices - A Problem in Psychological and Social Causation*, by Allport G.W.: I. Soc. Issues 1950, 4, 1-26.
32. *Prejudices - A Problem in Psychological and Social Causation*, by Allport G.W. I.Soc. Issues 1950, 4, 1-26 (Supplement).
33. *Encyclopaedia of Social Sciences.* Vol. IX-X (Horace M. Kallen) The MacMillan Co., New York, Sept. (1951), p. 643.
34. *Ibid.*, p. 648.
35. *Ibid.*
36. *Encyclopaedia of Social Sciences* note by Horace M. Kallen. The MacMillan Co., N.Y. (1951) Vol. (IX-X), p. 644.
37. *Ibid.*, p. 646.
38. *Power: The New Social Analysis* by Betrand Russel. George Allen and Unwin Limited, London (Sixth Ed. 1948), p. 149.
39. See chapters X & XV entitled 'creeds as sources of power' and power and moral code's (Russel, *op. cit.*, pp. 149, 237.)
40. *The Untouchables* by Dr. B.R. Ambedkar; Amrit Book Co., New Delhi (1948), pp. 20-21.
41. *The Oxford History of India from the Earliest Times to the End of 1911* by Vincent Smith, p. 41.
42. *India in 1924-25* by L.F. Rushbrook, Williams, p. 262-65.
43. *The Indian Annual Register* ed. by N.N. Mitra Calcutta. 1938, Vol. 1, pp. 72-73.
44. Quoted in *The India Charter - a Study of Hindu-Muslim Communal Problem* by Jehangir Framjee Kotewal, Karachi (1944), p. 119.
45. *Ibid.*, pp. 119-21.
46. *Pakistan and Untouchability* by Ch. Afzal Haq, pp. 55-56.
47. "To the Hindus and Muslims by Mahatma Gandhi (Gandhi Series Vol. III) edited and published by Anand T. Hingorani, Karachi, Aug. 15, 1942. p. 126.
48. (Where-ever the members of any group, small or large, live together in such a way that they share not this or that particular interest but the basic conditions of a common life we call that group a community. See *Society: An Introductory Analysis* by R.M. MacIver and Charles H. Page London MacMillan & Co. Ltd. (1950), pp. 8-9).

Section Two

The Social Phase of Communalism

With the division of the ancient Hindu society into four distinct communities, communalism enters its social phase.

Chronologically speaking, the history of ancient India can be divided into four different ages, viz. (i) the Vedic Age, ending in the 7th century BC, (ii) the Buddhist Age, ending in the 2nd century BC, (iii) the early Hindu Age, ending in the middle of the 3rd century AD; and (iv) the later Hindu Age, ending in the 8th century AD.

Throughout these different periods, Hindu society reflects a gradual hardening of the social grouping that commenced with the scheme of Varna-organization (which subsequently evolved itself into the so-called caste system). It is seen that a gradual deterioration in moral values assigned to each community in the society sets in and (as we shall see) the development of caste system in India is but a sad commentary on the scientific Hindu outlook in regard to the problem of social existence.

For the ancient Hindu, the entire life of an individual was a kind of schooling and self-discipline. This life was supposed to be a transitory stage, a link in the long chain of births, past and future and it would cease when *moksha* or 'Final liberation' was obtained. The human existence provided but an opportunity to attain release from the cycle of deaths and births by living a life of Dharma, as laid down in the Sastras (i.e. scientific treatises expounding principles of Dharma). All the institutions, social or personal were supposed to be the means of 'Dharma Sanchaya' (accumulation of dharma). In other words, they were means to attain *moksha*, the ultimate goal of human existence. Two such means which the Hindu theory of social organization envisages, were the schemes of the Asrama and Varna. Both of them were institutional processes and, by following them an individual could live by Dharma, the mainstay of the entire moving world and also attain the coveted goal of *Moksha*.

The Asrama dharma was formulated primarily with reference to the conduct of the individual's life in the world. The Varna-dharma was formulated primarily with reference to the society in which the individual lived.

Though both these schemes concern themselves with the development of the individual and his association with society, yet the approach of the one was different from that of the other.

> "In the scheme of the asramas (*asrama-vyavastha*), the problem is approached from the point of view of the training or nurture (*srama*) of the individual through specifically provided environments at different stages of his life; in the varna-organization (*varna-vyavastha*) on the other hand, the problem is considered from the point of view of the larger group, and the individual's position is defined in this group with reference to his innate nature (*guna*), his tendencies and dispositions".[1]

It is primarily with the Varna-organization and its practical implications, that we are concerned here. According to Hindu philosophy in every thing that springs from nature, there are three *gunas* or fundamental qualities. These are firstly, *Satva* or light, which fully reveals Brahma or the divine element within and stands for purity. Secondly, *Rajas* or passion, which partially veils the Brahma within, and promotes activity. Thirdly, *Tamas* or darkness which obscures the Brahma within and produces stolidity.[2]

The temperament of an individual was formed according to the predominance in him of one or the other of these three constituents and under the Varna scheme it was planned that "for his own salvation as well as for social efficiency, an individual should be allowed to develop along the lines best suited to his natural endowments and that he on his part should perform the duties assigned to him in accordance with the predominant quality of the strand in his nature."

So viewed, the society gets divided into three major groups having individual adherents who represent either of the three fundamental *gunas* described above, and who follow some fixed callings in order to be true to Dharma and attain *moksha*.

This philosophy, however sublime and scientific, failed to maintain its purity for a long time. For since the Vedic Age "India is discovered as an agitated scene of conflicting tribes and races in which one group attempts to impose its civilization on the other. The Aryans and the non-Aryans meet in struggle and the war is waged not merely on the plane of politics and economics but also on that of cult and culture"[3] and by the time the early conflicts and convulsions could settle down to normal, we are confronted with a society divided into four communities represented by the Brahmins, Kshatriyas, Vaisyas and Shudras, the main pillars of the Indian social order which later on degenerated into caste system.

"Whether the system had 'already been formed', or whether it was merely in the process of formation in the Rigvedic Age, we have no authentic evidence to prove or disprove, but it is beyond dispute that by the end of the Vedic period, each of the four original orders had evolved into castes and had come to constitute its own special and exclusive social world.

Each was distinguished by its origin and its sacraments".[4]

It is indeed nothing short of a tragedy of human perversion that Varna organization was, in course of time replaced by caste-system. It was a change from 'open classes' to watertight compartments, from a social grouping on the principle of natural endowment and virtue, cooperation and equality, to a communal classification on the principle of heredity and privilege, competition and inequality.

As could be expected, this change precipitated tension between the various communities of the society. According to D.N. Majumdar:

> "The history of caste system in India is a record of a perpetual social tension and of protests and revolts against the prevailing social code which succeeded at times but very often failed in their objectives and which might have released individuals from caste-tyranny but put a tighter shackle round the social group".[5]

Social Groupings

Social grouping, as it came to pass in India, invites certain pertinent questions.

Firstly, how did it happen that a people so learned and scientific in their approach could not keep upto their schemes of social organization and on the contrary become communal-minded, so much so, that the society lived in a state of tension, as vicious and virile, as we have witnessed in our own times?

Secondly, is it not possible to have a society without any classification, whatsoever?

The answer to the first question lies in what we call "Human-natures." Having been given to understand as early as in the Purusha-Sukta hymn of the Rigveda which says that "the Brahma Varna represented the mouth of the Purusha, which word may be translated as 'the universal men' referring perhaps to mankind as a whole, the Rajanya, i.e., Kshatriya his arms, the Vaisya his thighs, and the Sudra his feet."[6] It was difficult to avoid insurmountable barriers being raised in society. For how could the representatives of mouth, degrade themselves to be the representatives of thigh or feet. In the nature of things, it is of course inconceivable that what has once been dubbed as love, could even spire to rise. And as the author of *Hindu-Social Organization* remarks:

> "Gradually, however, the Varnas came to be distinguished from each other. Each Varna became more and more marked of and separated from the other. The four Varnas came to be addressed in four different ways, differing in degrees of politeness as indicated by the terms *ehi*, *agachchha*, *adrava* and *adhava* respectively to be used for welcoming persons of the four different Varnas. Different sizes of funeral cakes (*pinda*) were prescribed for different Varnas".[7]

This is but an ordinary illustration of the way in which an estrangement between the four Varnas continued. The fact is that it was the group and not the individual that was made the unit or corner stone of the Hindu social polity. And a group is a group irrespective of the fact when and where it is constituted and by whom. Then the group's constituted by the Brahmin, Kshatriya, Vaisya and Sudra communities in ancient India, were not mere aggregates of people representing different virtues. They were well organized groups. They were communities with a definite consciousness of their purity and impurity, greatness and lowness.

As human nature would have it, those communal groups grew more and more conscious of their interest and could invent reasons for maintaining a status-quo.

The factors that encouraged communalism in its social phase are the same that promote it in the later phases. They are primarily economic and psychological and secondarily socio-religious. It is because of these factors, that the sublime and scientific scheme of Hindu social organization on the basis of equality and cooperation failed.

The Economic Factor

The economic factor clearly works behind the Varna-scheme and the subsequent communal estrangement. We know that a human being is not all intellect or spirit or appetite. He is a queer admixture of Satva, Rajas and Tamas. The material interest of the people however, led them to misinterpret the free movement of individuals to any calling to which they were best suited by nurture and nature, as it was envisaged by the original doctrine of Varna-Dharma. On the contrary, what was supposed to be a scheme for the individual development, was made a plan for the communal propriety. Hindu idealism did not plan a regimentation of virtues and accomplishments, but as human nature would have it, the particular interest of the people registered a victory over the real will of the Dharma-Sutras. And since there is no greater insecurity than the economic insecurity, the principle of heredity came to replace the doctrine of *guna*, to ensure and maintain thereby the security of economic interests and safeguard the communal rights and privileges for ages to come.

It was a communal conflict between the different parts of an organic whole. Is it conceivable indeed that a foot could ever dictate the top?

Manu has written, "Among the several duties, the most commendable (Visisthani) are, teaching the Veda for the Brahmana, protecting the people (*rakshanam*) for a Kshatriya, and trading (Varts) for a Vaishya".[8] Perhaps Shudra was destined for no other calling except to serve the Varnas, placed above him in a social hierarchy. For him, there was no other destiny than being born and dying as a Shudra. Manu, in one of his most conservative and communal advice says:

> "It is better to discharge one's own dharma incompletely or imperfectly (*vigunah*), than to perform completely that of another (*na parakyah sivanushtnitah*)".[9]

The Doctrine of Karma

The Varna-organization as it came to pass in India, is a tragic story of staunch Brahmin communalism in India, simply because they formed the uppermost strata of the Hindu society and could survive as long as the lower layers of society were kept at a standstill. The Varna-scheme got mented by the Indo Aryan concept of Karma and 'a certain taboo holiness', that came to be attached to the Brahmin for his accredited possession of a special spiritual energy (Brahma-sakti) born of the predominance of the Satva Guna (fundamental quality of revealing light) sustained and stabilized through well disciplined continuance.[10]

It is in this doctrine of Karma and 'a certain taboo holiness' (which is but a corollary of `scruple for purity') that we find the psychological-weapon or colossal energy, that communal groups have always used with effect. Communalism in this phase thrived much on such psychological prejudices.

Accordingly the doctrine became a philosophy of uncompromising determination and fatalism for it meant that "each one of us is under the influence of Karma (the deeds of the past life) and each of us must always try to see in what way he can be atoned for his karma and extricate himself from an evil doom ahead".

It was a subtle philosophy of conservative spirit and communal manoeuvre, which could have no scientific foundation whatsoever. It clearly meant that one who is born in a lower Varna should die as such in eternal servility following the Dharma of his Varna, as envisaged by the reactionary social pandits and may be that if he lives as such, he may be born again in a higher Varna. On the other hand, one who is born in a higher varna must live up to the duties and obligations of his varna, if he does not want to be lowered in the next birth.

The doctrine of Karma which in its simplest meaning implies that only right Karmas (action) should be performed by one in one's life, for on them depends the attainment of Moksha, came to be interpreted in a way which could best serve the communal interests of the 'Hindu Bourgeoisie'.

The Myth of Colour and Purity

Even the myth of 'Colour difference' and 'Racial superiority' entertained by Aryan invaders and subsequently used by Brahmin priesthood and Princely clans was nothing but a psychological instrument of effective use in maintaining communal cohesion and social supremacy.

As some eminent social psychologists have remarked, "some of the most potent of all needs have to do with the defence of the self. Many of our perceptions, cognitions, beliefs, and attitudes are so organized as to enhance feelings of self esteem or to remove any threat to such feelings ...... the need for superiority feelings is a strong and driving need in many individuals".[11]

The Brahmins were already in a privileged position and in self defence they developed 'many a wrong attitude and belief' and in every possible way, "degraded all occupations except their own and that of their patrons of the ruling class".[12]

Communalism was tremendously encouraged by maintaining the psychological fallacy that a Brahmin is forever a Brahmin and a Shudra is forever a Shudra.

Coming to the socio-religious factor, as the promoter of communalism we refer to the 'touch-me-not-ism', viz. untouchability. Perhaps the most glaring evil of communal organization of Hindu society was this doctrine of the Impurity communicated by the touch or contact of lower castes. It was a social stigma and a religious blight of the meanest order. It is an explosive promoter of communal tension in any society.

Like most social institutions, the origin of untouchability is supposed to lie in Aryans' emphasis on personal cleanliness and hygiene.

But what would have been a code of personal purity evolved itself in course of time into a code of group prejudice, used for the caste and communal interests. Untouchability became a part of their religion. The code of cleanliness turned into 'pride lifted to the level of religious fanaticism', incapable of recognizing the 'dignity of humanity'. It was an insult inflicted on one section of society by the other. Unfortunately it could never be eradicated in the social phase of communalism and it continued to be a potent and perennial source of communal tension in the years to come.

We conclude this introduction with a reply to certain doubts raised earlier. If a *coup d' ceil* of the evolution of World History be made, we shall come across two very important processes operating in human societies.

Firstly, that growth and decay go together.

Secondly, that conflicts and cooperation follow each other.

Everything in this world is subject to the process of growth and decay. Be it with man or material, idea or organization, prejudice or production.

Similarly, the conflicts may be mental or material, imaginary or real, psychological or substantial, the cooperation amongst the warring elements soon follows, be it voluntary or forced, sudden or delayed, genuine or superficial.

The above two processes operate simultaneously and dynamically. They operate in the minds of men and they operate in the outer world as well.

The scheme of Varna organization was a growing idea, but as was inevitable, a decay set in and, as human nature would have it, the perversion of certain ideas was accepted since it catered to the material interests and communal prejudices of the holders of social, political and economical power.

The experiences and needs of each community soon creates a body of traditions and standards, bound up with emotional accompaniments, justifying the set decay and so opposed as to stand in the way of association with others. Such a conflict of interests gives birth to prejudices and hate which continues in spite of its decay, for it is kept alive from generation to generation, 'particularly in cases where one of the community has risen to a higher level of culture that contempt for the lower community is persistent.

Communalism in its social phase amply bears it out, rigidity of the communal attitude and relationship between the four Varna being a proof of the same. The above explanation clears our first doubt raised earlier regarding the perversion of a scientific and sublime principle of Hindu social organization.

Regarding the second doubt as to, "Can't we have a society without any classification whatsoever, we positively say no, for man is essentially tribal. We proceed further reiterating our stand that, "Communalism is neither the privilege of any one age nor of any one society. It is an unavoidable phenomenon that manifests itself in ways, curious in different forms, but is in consequence the same".

NOTES AND REFERENCES

1. *Hindu Social Organization*, P.N. Prabhu. Popular Book Depot, Bombay 1954, p. 290.
2. This tripartite division of human soul, was borrowed from India by the great Greek philosopher Plato who constructed his ideal Republic on an assumption that State is nothing but human mind objectified and that human mind reflects three tendencies of reason, spirit and appetite same that are termed as *Sattava, Rajasa* and *Tannasa.*
3. *Influence of Islam on Indian Culture*, T. Chand. Introduction (p. ii).
4. *Caste and Structure of Society* by R.P. Masani.
5. Race and Culture of India by D.N. Majumdar, p. 104.
6. Hindu Social Org., P.N. Prabhu. (p. 291) Rig. 90, 12 Brahmano'sya mukha asid bahu rajanyan Kritah Uru tad asya yad Vaisyat Padbhyam Sudra alavta.
7. Ibid., p. 295.
   Satspatha Br. i, 14,12 : (from Dutt: *op. cit.*, pp. 85 H)
   Sat Br. xiii 8, 3, 11 (from *ibid*)
8. Manu. X. 95-96: 'na tveve jyaya sim vritim abhimayeta karhichit (from Prabhu Hindu Social Organisation, p. 307).
9. Manu X. 97 (from ibid. p. 309).
10. 'Caste, Race and Religion', in *Man in India* by Sarat Chandra Roy (from *Caste in India* by J.H. Hutton, p. 181).
11. *Theory and Problem of Social Psychology* by Krech and Crutchfield McGrow-Hill Publication (4th Edition), New York.
12. See Ibbstson's, *Punjab Castes* part I. Dr. Ghurye's *Castes and Race in India*, Chapter VII.
    Sir Herbert Bisley, *The People of India*.
    J.H. Hutton. *Caste in India*.

Regarding the second doubt as to, "Can't we have a society without any classification whatsoever?", we positively say no, for man is essentially tribal. We proceed further reiterating our stand that, "Communalism is neither the privilege of any one age nor of any one society. It is an unavoidable phenomenon that manifests itself in ways, curious in different forms, but is in consequence the same."

NOTES AND REFERENCES

1. Hindu Social Organisation, P.N. Prabhu, Popular Book Depot, Bombay 1958, p. 293.
2. This tripartite division of human soul was borrowed from India by the great Greek philosopher Plato who constructed his ideal Republic on an assumption that State is nothing but human mind objectified and that human mind reflects three tendencies of reason, spirit and appetite same that are termed as Sattava, Rajas and Tamas.
3. *Hymns in Praise of Indian Culture*, T. Chand Introduction (p. iii).
4. Caste and Structure of Society by R.P. Masani.
5. Race and Culture of India by D.N. Majumdar, p. 104.
6. Hindu Social Org., P.N. Prabhu (p. 281) Rig. 90, 12 Brahmano sya mukham asid bahu rajanyah krtah Uru tad asya yad vaisyah Padbhyam Sudra ajayata.
7. Ibid., p. 295
   Satapatha Br. I, 14, 12 (from Dutt op. cit., pp. 85 ff.)
   Sat Br. xiii. 4. 3. 11 (from ibid.)
8. Manu X, 75 [illegible] (from Prabhu Hindu Social Organisation, p. 307)
9. Manu X, 92 (from ibid., p. 309)
10. Caste, Race and Religion, in *Modern India* by Sarat Chandra Roy (from *Caste in India* by J.H. Hutton, p. 161)
11. *Theory and Problem of Social Psychology* by Krech and Crutchfield McGraw-Hill Publication (4th Edition), New York.
12. See Johnson's, *Plural Castes* part I Dr. Ghurye's *Caste and Race in India*, Chapter VII
    Sir Herbert Risley, *The People of India*
    J.H. Hutton, *Caste in India*.

Section Three

The Religious Phase of Communalism

With the advent of Muslims and their permanent settlement within the borders of the Indian subcontinent, communalism entered its religious phase.

It was in the medieval period of Indian history that the Muslims came to India and settled down permanently to establish their rule over Indian territory. This period is divisible into two ages - the early medieval age from the eighth to the thirteenth century; and the later medieval age from the thirteenth to the end of the eighteenth century.

In the early medieval period, they made a peaceful entry in the south while the sword was used for making a penetration into Sindh and the North-West region of India. It was during the later medieval period that they became one of the most powerful forces throughout the entire length and breadth of the country.

The advent of Muslims in this country presents a very interesting subject for sociological and historical survey; for unlike other invaders, they were not merely birds of passage but entered this land to stay on and to make it their own home. Curiously enough, there was hardly anything common between these invaders and the indigenous communities except that both were creatures of same flesh and blood, possessed with identical human instincts. The growth and development of Hindu-Muslim relations in India begin with such a positive handicap on both the sides.

Muslims came to India with the creed of Islam. It was a religion that maintained philosophy of life of action that was quite different and opposed to that of the invaded communities. Obviously, this fact of 'Religious-differences', was the fundamental source of social-tension in the medieval period. It alone governed the inter-communal relations.

The bedrock of Islam has been the prime belief in the 'oneness of God. As the Quran says:

> "Surely Allah does not forgive that any one should be made partner with Him.... and whoever makes one partner with Allah, he indeed strays off into a remote error".[1]

Islam is a proselytizing religion, and Musalmans are enjoined to offer to idolators the choice between conversion and the sword. The Quran even lays down rules of conduct for preachers among the people of scripture and of disbelief as well as among the followers.

According to the Quran:

> "You Muslims are the best community, that has been raised up for the benefit of mankind. You enjoin what is right, and forbid what is wrong, and you believe in Allah. And if the people of the scripture had believed, it would have been better for them. Some of them are believers, but most of them are transgressors".[2]

> "And from among you (Muslims) there should be a party who invite (people) to good and enjoin what is right and forbid what is wrong and there it is, that shall be successful".[3]

Not only this, the Quran prescribes a code of military discipline for its followers. Thus, 'the Quran calls upon the Muslims to preach and propagate Islam, to defend themselves in case of attack or oppression manfully like soldiers but just to the necessary extent and to guard against excesses".[4]

The truth lies in the fact,that according to the tenets of Islam, "this world would ultimately be reserved for believers, as to unbelievers, 'their abode is hall and evil is the destination' ".[5]

At the same time, "Islam combined the dualism of a universal religion and a universal state. It resorted to a peaceful as well as violent means for achieving their ultimate objective. The universality of Islam provided a unifying element for all believers within the world of Islam and its defensive offensive character produced a state of warfare permanently declared against the outside world, the world of war (*Dar-al-harb*)".[6]

Lastly that, 'the ultimate aim of Islam was always, in theory to wage a war with the Dar-al-harb and 'the Jihad (commonly called the holy war), reflecting the normal war relations existing between Muslims and non-Muslims was the state's instrument for transforming the dar-al-harb into dar-al-Islam. It was the product of a war-like people who had embarked on a large social movement of expansion".[7]

Thus, there enters into India the vigorous force of a virile community, armed with a religion which could never be a counsel of peace and order for a people who had hardly known any kind of order in the history of their civilization, cradled in the deserts of Central Asia. As a historian remarks:

> "For them (the idol-worshipping Hindus), Mahmud and his followers felt a bitter hatred which may be compared to that of the Puritans under Cromwell for the Irish. To grind images to powder, to raze temples to the ground, and to send idolators, without distinction of age or sex, 'to that fire which God has lighted for infidels, and those who deny a resurrection, say no prayers, hold no fasts, and tell no?, was a religious duty. India was a dar-ul-harb, a land of warfare, handed over by God to true believers to plunder".
>
> "The whole country of India is full of gold and jewels, and of the plants which grow there are those fit for making wearing apparel, and aromatic plants and the sugar cane, and the whole aspect of the country is pleasant and delightful. Now since the inhabitants are chiefly infidels and idolators, by the order of God and his prophet, it is right for us to conquer them".[8]

What was true with Mahmud, continued to hold good with all who came after him, for the person might have changed, but the principles did not change at all. Timur the Lane, commonly known as Tamerlane, was a Barlas Turk whose hordes had swept across the vast tracts of Central Asia. When he marched into Punjab from Samarkand, he is reported to have written in his autobiography:

> "My principle object in coming to Hindustan was to accomplish two things. The first thing was to wage war with infidels, the enemies of the Muhammadan religion, and by this religious warfare, to acquire some claim to reward in the life to come. The other was a worldly object: that the army of Islam might gain something by plundering the wealth of infidels; plunder in war is as lawful as their

> mother's milk to Musalmans who fight for their faith, and the consuming of that which is lawful is a means of grace".[9]

It can be clearly seen now that both in theory and practice, the general attitude of Muslims towards the un-Islamic people, and, particularly towards the Hindus, was always one of unscrupulous fanaticism and fury. This attitude could not be otherwise, for they were a community with claims of primitive freedom and had a zealous faith in the superiority of their God and their religion. For them the world consisted of two types of people: the believers and non-believers; and their only duty lay either in converting the latter to the fold of the former or, if that were not possible in exterminating them at the point of sword.

It was this devotion to faith that made them so virile, persistent and aggressive. Moreover, death had no fears for them for it opened for them the gates of paradise, with all its splendour and glories. As a historian observes:

> "The hope of becoming a Ghazi led the commonest Muslim to brave risks and cheerfully make sacrifices. He was never dismayed or terrified by the weary odds arrayed against him, for he was sustained by the belief that, if he died in the holy war, he would be admitted to the paradise and obtain the honours of martyrdom".[10]

It would not be out of place to quote here one of the Muslim war songs, which throws a very interesting and revealing light on that form of Islamism which is strongly fanatic. The song narrates:

> "It is the angel Gabriel who tells the prophet that bliss awaits those who die fighting against the infidel. The prophet tells his followers they are to gain paradise and be met by the houries, whose eyes are like the waxing moon, whose cheeks are like the young plantain leaves, who are soft as the petals of the young shoe flower.... the necks of the houries when they walk wave to and fro like the neck of a rutting elephant. But there breast is like a lake where-on are lotus flowers and they are always sixteen years old and very beautiful.
>
> "They come like sporting elephants, elephants to bear away those who die in battle and strive with each other saying 'I will take him - I will take him'. The prophet

> swore to his army that such happiness would be theirs if they died fighting bravely".
>
> "Omar was eating dates; when he heard this he cast them away. The prophet asked, why? He replied that he wished to waste no time eating dates. I wish to use my time for fighting and so saying he rushed like a lion among a flock of sheep, killed many and fled fighting; he met with death that he wishes for".[11]

This song further tells how the father fights against his son, for the faith is stronger than the bond of blood. In another song we find an equally fascinating account of heavens, along with a mention of the punishment that the cowards are likely to receive.

It begins ofcourse extolling Mahomed and subsequently it says:

> "The soul in our body is in the hands of God. Can we live for ever in this world? Must we not die once? Everything will die but God alone will not. Such being the commandment of God we will have no excuse when we are brought before him after death: so determine earnestly to fight and die. If we die fighting with the wicked men who attempt forcibly to burn this holy mosque, which is thc house of God, we shall obtain complete salvation".

The occasion to fight and die for the faith is then likened unto a vessel which has come to bear the faithful to the shores of bliss. They are invited to embark. How well for them that such a vessel has come for them: It will bear them to the broad gates of heaven. "Is it not for the arrival of such a vessel (sic) that we should pray":......" The pleasures of wealth or family are not equal to an atone of celestial happiness." Ofcourse, those who embark in the vessel (seize an occasion to fight and die) will soon be in bliss for ever.

"Our most venerable Prophet has said that those who die in battle can see the houries who will come to witness the fight. There is nothing in this world to compare with the beauty of houries. The splendour of the sun, of the moon, and of the lightening is darkness. Compared with the beauty of their hair which hang over their shoulders. Their cheeks,eyes, face, eyebrows, forehead, head are incomparably lovely. Their mouths are like coqals of gold; their teeth like the seeds of thalimathalam, their breasts are like cups of gold, the pomegranate, or are like beautiful flowers. It is not possible for the mind to conceive the loveliness of their breast and shoulders.... If they spit in the sea, the salt water becomes like honey, and its fragrant as attar. If they were to come down to this earth and smile, the sun, moon and stars would be eclipsed. Mortals would die if they but heard the music of their voice (Lore-ldi), when they wear red silk bordered with green lace of seventy folds, their skin muscles and bones can be seen through. Such is the splendour of their body. If they clap their hands, the clash of their jewels will be heard at a distance of 500 years journey. They clap their hands and dance and sing as they come like swans to the battle field. If a human being were to see their beauty, their dance of smile, he would die on the spot. Gently they touch the wounds of those who die in battle, they rub away the blood and cure the pain, they kiss and embrace the martyrs: give them to drink of the sweet water of heaven and gratify their every wish. A horse caprisoned with carpet set with precious stones will be brought and a voice will say 'Let my men mount; let them dance with the celestial houries".

Then the celestial coverings will be placed on their heads, they mount the beautiful horses which will dance and leap and take them to heaven, where they live in unbonded joy".

"Such is the fate that awaits those who die fighting bravely. At the dissolution of the world they will be sped like lightening over the bridge across hell. In heaven they will attend the marriage of Mahomet. They will be decorated with bunches of pearls and crowns of gold: they will be seated on the tusk of Mahomets elephant and enjoy supreme happiness. It is impossible to describe the pleasures which await those who die fighting bravely without flinching. All their sins will be forgiven and God will listen to all their prayers".

For otherwise is it with the cowards. "All his virtuous actions are ignored. He incurs the wrath of God. He will be written down as a renegade in the book of God. His prayers are vain. He will die a sinner and be thrown into hell where fresh kinds of torture will be given him. In hell are countless myriads of scorpions, snakes, worms, rightful dragons. It is a pit of everlasting fire". The pleasures of heaven and the pains of hell have been revealed to Mahomet, "who in his turn taught his disciples. It is the learned Musaliars who now hold this knowledge".[12]

These traits in the character of a Muslim are not only important for understanding the nature of Hindu-Muslim relations during the medieval period of Indian history, but even in the later period when these characteristics, continue to give a peculiar turn to their communal relations.

The demands of self preservation and religious propagation found a unique blending of material and spiritual interests in Muslims invasion of the foreign lands. History can give no better evidence of the dynamic and volatile energy that such an identification of diverse interests can produce.

Islam has been a great force. Its strength lies in the fact that there exists no antithesis between the material and spiritual interests of its followers. The pursuit of the economic interests automatically promotes the fulfillment of the spiritual interests and vice-versa. (Could it not be true as well for other communities?)

In India, what happened to be the source of strength to the united zealous followers of Islam, was the source of weakness of the disunited and tolerant followers of Hinduism: wherein exists a strong antithesis between the material and the spiritual pursuits. Sir Jadu Nath Sircar beautifully summarizes the difference that exists between the two communities:

He writes:

> "The Hindu is solitary, passive, other-worldly, his highest aim is self-realisation, the attainment of personal salvation by individual effort, private devotions and lonely austerities. To him birth is a misfortune and his fellow beings so many sources of distraction from his one goal. Not by enjoyment of God's gifts but by renunciation, not by joyous expansion but by repression of emotion, is he to attain to bliss.
>
> The Muslim on the other hand, is taught to feel that he is nothing if not a soldier of the militant force of Islam: he must pray in congregation: he must give proof of the sincerity of his faith by undertaking Jehad or active exertion for the spread of his religion and the destruction of unbelief

> among other men. He is missionary and cannot be indifferent to the welfare of his neighbours' soul: nay he must be ever alive to his duty of promoting the salvation of others by all means at his command, physical as much as spiritual.
>
> Then again, Islam boldly avows that it is good for us to be here, that God has given the world to the faithful as an inheritance for their enjoyment.
>
> The ancient Socratic ideal that "he who has the fewest wants is most like the gods", is peculiarly the Hindu's. No doubt, Islam too has its ascetics: no doubt Muslim theology recognises abstinence (*Parhez*) as good for the soul even of the householder. But in practice the immense body of Islamites loved to enjoy and considered it as no wise wrong to enjoy the good things of the world".[13]

Some find that the struggle between the two communities was a struggle between two different concepts of human life; As an Indian historian has observed:

> "The struggle between the two races was in reality a duel between two conflicting social systems. The old Aryan civilization with its splendid ideals of life in all its varied aspects, enfeebling by its varied and too much emphasis on the spiritual than on the material sides, was overpowered by its belligerent rival which did not disdain the love of worldly pursuits and enjoyments.
>
> The heterogeneous population of India with well marked social, religious and ethnological differences was easily conquered by a religious brotherhood which was organised on a military basis".[14]

This conquest of India, which resulted in the establishment of Imperial dynasties under Muslim rulers, make three things very clear.

Firstly, that the Muslims, in spite of their unbridled ferocity and missionary zeal that they displayed in their ware of plunders, massacres and conquests, failed to exterminate or convert the conquered.

Secondly, it was an identical failure on the part of Hindus to swamp off or assimilate the Muslim invaders and settlers, as they had hitherto done with a succession of immigrants like the Scythians, the Sakas and the Huns.

Thirdly, in spite of their being foreigners, "they made India their home and completely identified themselves with her people and became Indian through and through", so much so that in certain directions, one finds some sort of social fusion as well.

Granted that the Muslim came and settled here as one of the important section of the Indian population. Granted that in certain directions there came to pass, what we may call as Hindu-Muslim synthesis. Granted all that and all that would come under the head of Historical adaptability, still the question arises as to why Muslims could not be absorbed in the Hindu-fold?

There can be many differing explanations of this phenomenon.

One school of thought whose views we have already examined above, maintains that there was no possibility of a complete fusion between Hindus and Muslims, because the two communities envisaged different systems of social-living and each cherished an outlook on life that was diametrically opposed to the other.

Another very plausible opinion worth referring to is the one put forth recently by B.K. Malik, a sociologist. He says: "In the make-up of the Mohemmadan who came over to India, there was an element which made the stability of the fusion almost incalculable. The fact is that they came from the corridor of Central Asia, and as the latest converts to the Moslem faith on whom civilization rested like a thin veneer.

They were by no means races of peoples of a long-standing civilized traditions or settled habits which made for civilized life. And if the Hindu community has failed so far to stabilize its relationship with them in the manner it did practically with all the races and cultures that preceded them, the failure may well be traced to this uncertain racial element."

The issue perhaps was not so much between the Hindu culture and the Mohemmadan faith as between the civilized order of existence and some fundamental claim to primitive freedom".[15]

The above argument is not the whole of truth, for it was neither 'Muslim primitivism' nor any lack of longstanding civilized existence that came in the way of their being absorbed in the Hindu fold. Even before the Muslims, races which were as primitive and as uncivilized had come to India. Not only that, long after the Aryans had settled down with an elaborate scheme of social organizations, there were present in India people more primitive than thc Muslims who had not the least tradition of any civilization whatsoever.

As a matter of fact, it was neither the Islamic concept of a social order nor its claim to primitivism that arrested the gradual fusion amongst Muslims and Hindus. From whatever angle this issue might be examined, the only conclusion to which one reaches is that it was the proselytizing faith that was mainly responsible for a setback in the evolution of a complete communal synthesis.

For a social, order Muslims had a militant brotherhood; and in place of civilization, the Muslims had Islam, a missionary religion - an uncompromising faith. Summarizing very aptly these attributes of their faith that were opposed to Hinduism, that withheld this fusion, Lane Poole also stresses the very same point that we have discussed above.

> "The Muhammadan religion was a fighting creed; the extermination of the infidel and the destruction of idols were sacred duties; he who died in performing them was a Ghazi and went straight to the joys of paradise. The essence of Islam is brotherhood. All Muslims, of whatever race or social position, are equal in the sight of God. Merit was the only test of ability and a slave could rise to the throne of Delhi. In this it contrasted strongly with the endless divisions of caste-ridden Hinduism; and, lastly, the invaders were desperate men. They were carried forward by the lure of booty, by their own sense of superiority, and by their knowledge that if they were beaten there was no retreat; their only salvation lay in swords".[16]

Is it conceivable by any plane of imagination, that people so possessed could be absorbed in any social order other than that of the believers? To them the first and last truth lies in the simple creed.

> "There is no God but Allah
> Muhammad is Allah's Apostle".

In the words of Rawlinson, if we go into details we shall find that "Muhamadanism is the very anti-thesis of Hinduism: the one has been called the religion of the desert and the other that of the jungle",[17] obviously no complete fusion could have been a possibility.

Lastly, even the Hindu fold itself had lost its early elasticity and power of assimilation. For had this quality still been there, Hindu India could not have been conquered by any foreigner. It was not a mere question of 'religious toleration', Hinduism had never any scruples in this direction. For the followers of Islam it was a question of finding a place of social equality if not superiority in a society which was already split into rigid, communal groups as they emerged out of the fourfold scriptural scheme.

What could at the most be possible under these circumstances was not a fusion but a state of *Suam Cuique*.

As such, "after the Muslim conquest, the Hindu social system put itself on the defensive and tightened itself more than ever before. Priestcraft appropriated the authority which the state had so far exercised in a more flexible manner in social affairs. The machinery of social readjustment fell out of gear; the tendency to inflexibility really reflected a maladjustment but it steadied the system for the time. So, the two religions and corresponding cultures stood facing each other in the thirteenth century in the North and in the Fourteenth century in the Deccan".[18]

As would have happened in any other society, the struggle for religious supremacy, though fought on an economic, political and social plane, precipitated communal tension.

If we are to analyse the facts, we shall see that fundamentally the factors that aggravate communalism in the religious phase were none other than those we have witnessed hitherto operating in its social phase. The only difference was that, whereas in the social phase it was the concept of a particular type of social order that led to tension, in the religious phase, all these factors, ultimately led to one single goal, which was the source of this inspiration as well. It was the goal of "Religious Supremacy". The factors that aggravated communalism were economic, psychological and socio-religious in nature.

Self-preservation is the first need of human life. Land and labour have ever been the two major sources of human sustenance.

In the middle ages land had a special significance throughout the world. The medieval period of Indian history is a period of oriental feudalism. It had a hierarchical social set-up of which the king formed the apex and the peasant or the serf formed the base, an eminent historian aptly remarks:

> "In the medieval world and nowhere more so than in India the king was held responsible for the happiness of his people and with good reason he was regarded as a superman, as an incarnation of the deity or atleast god's representative on earth: he was invested with unlimited, unquestioned authority and the entire property in the land, he was, except in Catholic Europe, the head of Church and State alike".[19]

It is clear thus that every inch of land in the empire belonged to the king. He could give and take it back whenever he liked. The will of the King was the only will. Vox Populi had no significance then. The divine right theory was in full vogue. In assessing the cultivators, the principle that was kept in view was:

> "Exact from the peasant the last dam that he can pay :
> Leave for him just enough to exist and not to live".[20]

Obviously, therefore, in the religious phase of communalism, when everything followed the king, who followed Islam, the only true religion of the world; we can very well imagine the plight of non-believers, and, specially the Hindus. So though self-preservation is self-preservation for every community irrespective of its being the community of believers or non-believers; unfortunately, what constituted self-preservation for the Muslims proved mass-annihilation for the Hindus, for, as Lane Poole has remarked, "The very bigotry of their creed was an instrument of self-preservation" we do understand what this bigotry amounted: The great historian Barani, giving an interesting account of the reign of Alauddin writes:

> "The Sultan next directed his attention to the means of preventing rebellion, and first he took steps for seizing upon property, Whenever a village was held by proprietary rights, in free gift or as a religious endowment, it was to be brought back into the exchequer by a stroke of the pen. The people were pressed and amerced and money was

> exacted from then on every kind of pretext. All pensions, grants of land, and endowments were appropriated. The people became so absorbed in trying to keep themselves alive that rebellion was never mentioned".

He further adds:

> "The Hindu was to be soon reduced as to be unable to keep a horse, wear fine clothes, or enjoy any of life's luxuries. No Hindu could hold up his head, and in their house no sign of gold or silver or any superfluity was to be seen. These things which nourish insubordination, were not to be found. Men looked upon revenue officers as worse than fever; to be a clerk was a crime; no man would give his daughter to such. Ala-ud-din was a king who had no acquaintance with learning and never associated with the learned. He considered that polity and Government were one thing, and law another, 'I am an unlettered man', he said, 'but I have seen a great deal. Be assured that the Hindus will never become submissive and obedient though they are reduced to poverty. I have therefore given orders that just enough shall be left them of corn, milk and curds, from year to year, but that they must not accumulate hoards and property!' Next day he said, 'Although I have not studied the science or the book, I am Muslim of the Muslims. To prevent rebellion, in which many perish, I issue such ordinances as I consider to be for the good of the State and benefit of the people...".[21]

From Aibak to Aurangzeb, with the solitary exception of Akbar, Muslim policy towards Hindus had always been dominated and motivated by this communal outlook. "Hindus were in a ratio of six to one. Six men must be squeezed so that one may have an easy life". The 'life of a true believer of a true faith', formed the guiding principle of the ruling caste. As a matter of fact, throughout the rule of Islam in India, the country had no sound economic system. The sinister features of the Mughal economic system during the major portion of the Seventeenth century have been well described by Moreland in the following words:

> Weavers, naked themselves, toiled to clothe others. Peasant's themselves hungry, toiled to feed the towns and

> cities. India, taken as a unit, parted with useful commodities in exchange for gold and silver, or in other words, gave bread for stones. Men and women living from season to season on the verge of hunger, could be contented so long as the supply of food held out. When it failed as it so often did, their hope of salvation was the slave-trader, and the alternatives were cannibalism suicide, or starvation. The only way of escape from that system lay through an increase in production coupled with a rising standard of life, but this road was barred effectively by the administrative methods in vogue, which penalised production and regarded every indications of increased consumption as a signal for fresh taxation".[22]

The economic policies of the Muslim rulers continued to be a major source of communal tension in India and the victim of the misery described above was in most cases the Hindu. He had not only to tolerate the fanaticism and bigotry of Muslim rulers, but he had also to undergo the humiliations inflicted and indiscreet discrimination meted out to him. Muslim policy of taxation is a glaring illustration of this fact. Since Islam prohibits taxation of the believers, the basic principle of taxation under the Mahommedan rulers was the course of severe economic starvation of Hindus. Even the most humane of the medieval kings of India failed to be human in this respect. As Rawlinson writes about Firoz Shah:

> "In one respect Firoz Shah fell short of the standard of humanity of the great Akbar. Religious tolerance was unknown to him, and he considered it to be a religious duty to employ every means in order to induce his Hindu subjects to embrace Islam. 'I forbade the subjects infliction of any severe punishment on the Hindus in general, but I destroyed their idol temples and instead thereof raised mosques ...I encouraged my infidel subjects to embrace the religion of the prophet, and I proclaimed that everyone who repeated the creed and became a Mussalman should be exempted from the poll tax. Information of this came to the ears of the people at large, and great numbers of Hindus presented themselves and were admitted to the honour of Islam. Thus they came forward day by day

> from every quarter and, adopting the faith, were exonerated from the Jisya (poll-tax) and favoured with presents and honours'. The Brahmins, who had hitherto been exempted, were now ordered to pay like the rest. Furious at what they considered to be an insult to their order, they assembled outside the royal palace and threatened as a protest to starve themselves to death. Ultimately this tragedy was averted by a compromise, under which Brahmins were to pay a commuted sum of ten rupees a head. Attempts to spread the Hindu religion were sternly repressed, and it is said that a Brahmin was burnt alive for this offence. Hearing that certain new Hindu temples had been erected in defiance of orders, 'under Divine guidance I destroyed those edifices, and killed those leaders of infidelity who reduced others into error: the lower orders I subjected to stripes and chastisement, until this abuse was entirely abolished' ".[23]

The above details amply bear it out that the taxation policy of Mahommedans had a very important bearing on the Hindu-Muslim relations. It led to mass starvation as also wars and conversion from the Hindu to the Muslim fold. Hindus in a very large number embraced Islam in order to escape from the heavy burden of the tax.

In connection with the recruitment to public-services also, we find that the communal bias was usually in favour of the co-religionists. However, in the times of Akbar, a liberal policy was pursued in this matter. Della Valle, a traveller was impressed by the fact that "Akbar made no distinction between the 'Gentiles' and the Muhammodans as regards the army and public services".[24] But after him, the state of affairs was completely reversed. Hawkins another traveller noticed that "Jahangir reduced the number of Hindu captains and gave preference to Muslims".[25] During the reign of Shah Jahan there seems to start a policy of communal discrimination and greater hardships to the Hindus and other non-Muslims. He got Hindu temples and Christian churches demolished. According to Peter Munday: "Shaha Jehan, had command that all Hindu churches (place of worship) made in his time should be demolished".[26]

Bernier writes:

> "When Hugli was taken, the captured Portugese and their families were forcibly converted...... Displeased with the Jesuits, he ordered the destruction of Christian churches at Lahore".[27]

Even the pilgrimage tax was reimposed on the Hindus. Marrique in December, 1640 reached Allahabad and got himself registered at the customs House. He records:

> "Seeing that I was not a Gangetic pilgrim, they only took half a rupee from me. From the rest they took much more..."[28]

It was during the reign of Aurangzeb that the economic hardships which the Hindus had to face reached the breaking point. Communal discrimination was strictly observed according to the wishes of the emperor who tried his level best to undo what his predecessors had done to establish communal harmony. The famous traveller Mannuci writes:

> "He issued a general order commanding that all the Hindu public servants at court should be replaced by Muslims".[29]

Ovington, another traveller found at Surat that "the Muslims got the highest military and civil appointments only because of their religion".[30]

Aurangzeb started with a campaign against everything that was un-Islamic. His hand fell heavily both against the Hindus and the Shia[31] Muslims. Describing his drastic steps, which caused untold miseries to Hindus, an eminent historian observes:

> "Shah Jahan had stopped the building of fresh temples, but in 1969 Aurangzeb issued an order 'to demolish all the Schools and temples of the infidels and to put down their religious teaching and practices'. The Vishvanath temple at Benares was destroyed, and a mosque erected in its place, in the very heart of the most sacred of all Hindu cities. In the following years, the great temple of Keshava Deva at Mathura, erected in the reign of Jahangir at the cost of $ 350,000 was razed to the ground, and the richly-jewelled idols taken to Agra, where they were placed on the threshold of a mosque, to be trodden under foot by true believers. The very name of the town associated for

> centuries with the worship of Krishna, was changed to Islamabad. Thousands of places of worship were thus destroyed, to the consternation of pious officers Hindus all over India, and special officers were appointed to see that the Emperor's orders were strictly carried out".[32]

In the wake of this communal fanaticism, unleashed by the bigoted Emperor, followed the days of an acute economic crisis to the Hindus. To quote Rawlinson again:

> "Aurangzeb now proceeded to further measures which inflicted great economic hardships upon his Hindu subjects. In 1671 he dismissed the Hindu clerks in his service, but this order had to be partially rescinded as it was found impossible to carry on the administration without them. An octroi duty of five per cent was levied on goods imported by Hindus, while Muhammadan traders were exempted. But the most impolitic act was the resumption in 1680 of the Poll-tax on unbelievers. This tax was regarded as a badge of servitude. It is true that certain exceptions were made in the case of government officials and the very poor, but the general results were disastrous and many a Hindu who were unable to pay were forced to turn Muhammadan in order to escape from the insults of the collectors".[33]

The best and perhaps the most vivid picture of the consternation caused among the Hindu population of the capital after this tax was renewed has been given by the Muhammadan historian Khafi Khan. He wrote:

> "The Hindus round Delhi assembled in multitudes under the *jharokha* of the Emperor on the river-front of the palace, declaring that they were unable to pay and praying for the revocation of the edict. But the Emperor would not listen to their complaints. One Sabhath, as he went to prayers at the great mosque, a vast crowd of Hindus thronged from palace to mosque. Every moment the crowd smelled and his equipage was brought to a standstill. Then the elephants were brought out and charged the mole, and many people were trodden to death. For days the Hindus went on assembling and complaining but in the end they had to pay the Jisya".[34]

All this was done in due obedience to what the Prophet of Islam is supposed to have said:

> "Fight those who do not profess the true faith, till they pay Jizya with the hand in humility".[35]

In short, it is sufficient to add here that the economic life of the masses, and, in particular that of the Hindus was extremely insecure and miserable during the religious phase of communalism. In the name of religion, the worst atrocities were perpetuated on the economic plane in one form or the other. The collection of revenue, the imposition of taxes, the discrimination made in appointments to public offices, were but a few well-known aspects of the economic persecution of the Hindus. In themselves, these things may not mean much for every state collects revenue, and levies taxes. What mattered most was the stigma of humiliation and inferiority attached to them, a humiliation with which a vast majority continued to seethe for centuries under the rule of a bigoted and fanatic minority. As Sri Ram Sharma a historian remarks:

> "The Jizya was a very heavy burden to the masses. But it was not its burden alone which was irksome. It was a badge of inferiority round the necks of the unfaithful reminding them constantly that they formed a subject people under an alien rule".[36]

Under such conditions, a deterioration in the state of Hindu Muslim relations during the medieval period was inevitable. However, the economic system of the Mughals which was source of Hindu impoverishment, also led to their own dissolution. One could not agree less with the opinion expressed by Edwardes and Garret, who write:

> "We may therefore say, in conclusion that the Mughal state owed its decline and ultimate downfall to a combination of causes, of which perhaps the two most important were the uncontrolled domination of a selfish and extravagant bureaucracy and an inequitable economic system, which steadily impoverished the revenue producing classes of the population".[37]

Not much elaboration is needed to prove as to how much impetus was given by the psychological factor in perpetuating communalism during its Religious phase. The very clash between the people possessed too much with the magic of their own way of life and faith, was a sufficient cause for unavoidable disruption in the realm of thought and action. When religion so deeply covers every aspect of human life and when it is obeyed with an attitude as dogged and intolerant as the Middle Ages have displayed, social tension of the worst type is an inevitable concomitant. Medieval India was no exception to it.

We do not know indeed as to what Islam taught in its purest form. The first taste as also the repeated experience of it in India was nothing but a dogma of ceaseless bigotry and fanaticism. Muslim action and organization was nothing but religion debased on wrong notion, and a communal psychology that led more to the parting then to the mingling of ways.

A part of what was true with Islam was true with Hinduism also. The two religions had evolved round themselves all those customs, beliefs, and attitudes that perpetuate communalism, in one form or the other. However, the very fundamentals of the Muslim psychology of war and peace, as we have already examined in detail, in no way led to any peaceful coexistence with people other than that of the true faith. The protagonists of Islam had created a 'psychological sheath' of self-defence and expansion. It was founded on certain myths. Such as the concept of endless state of war between Dar-al-harb and Dar-al-Islam, the ultimate triumph of the 'God's elect' and the place in paradise to all who die killing unbelievers. Further, this 'psychological-sheath' was permanently safeguarded by the creation of certain stereotypes, an adherence to which, led not only to an automatic negation of the elements of mutual understanding, love and forbearance, but also to a complete annihilation of every form of civilized order. An eminent historian aptly describes this trait in the Muslim character when he says:

> "The very bigotry of their creed was an instrument of self-preservation: in mere self-defence they must hold together as God's elect in the face of heathen, and they must win over proselytes from the Hindus, whether by persuasion or by the sword to smell their isolated minority".

This creed of 'self-preservation' and 'self-defence' evolved through the 'self-proclamation' of being the 'God's elect', had brought in that state of mental perversion in the followers of Islam, which would not let them nor others live in peace. Besides, it would not be much wrong to say that their bigotry was too deep seated, to allow any free, unconditioned and rational thinking. Obviously, it was impossible for them to reconcile with any other community, its people, its culture and its social order. To a Muslim therefore, any effort to strengthen their 'psychological sheath' of communal-protection, meant expansion into the fold of unbelievers to convert them to Islam, not by word but by sword, not through explanation and cordial understanding of each others point of view, but through destruction of each others symbols and of faith and worship. Curiously enough, any setback in their efforts caused a sense of frustration which only inspired another attempt of ruthless aggression, more violent, more virile and over-fanatic. The raids of Mahmud of Ghazni bear ample illustration to this psychology.

It is clear therefore, that the very mental make up of a Muslim was quite opposed to that of a Hindu. Nevertheless, both harboured prejudices and stereotypes, calling each other infidel and Maleccha. To match Muslim's fanaticism and bigotry, Hindus had their own code of taboos and contempt, including many a wrong identification and personification, on either side. Since no attempt was made to understand each other, tension prevailed in its worst degree. Besides, we cannot overlook the fact that Hindu masses were an extremely frustrated majority that lived at the mercy of a tyrant minority that practised discrimination and mass annihilation with a religious fervour. The result is obvious: with minds steeped in darkness, and with a world full of differences, Hindus and Muslims even at a psychological plane lived in a state of acute communalism.

Finally, we come to the Socio-religious factors that helped in fanning communalism. We have already examined the characteristics of Islam as they stood opposed to Hinduism. Since the followers of the two different faiths observed different codes of morality, they came into clash in every walk of life. Here we refer to the curse of untouchability, an accompaniment of the caste-system.

Untouchability was a practice and had a religious sanction

behind it. In one sense, it was observed on either side, for if to a Hindu, a Muslim was an outcaste and unworthy even of any physical touch, then to a Muslim, a Hindu was a heathen, whose life observed not a second's existence. It amounted to a sort of social exclusiveness and it tremendously governed Hindu-Muslim relations in two contradictory directions.

Firstly, it proved to be a great hindrance in the smooth evolution of a Hindu-Muslim synthesis. The existing social order of the Hindus by the time of the advent of the Muslims had become 'assigned with its rigid strata of castes'. So though Muslims might have gained an upper hand politically, they continued to be social outcastes, and they were given the same treatment as the untouchables and the members of the lowest sections of society amongst Hindus. It created deep-seated prejudices by reason of the social taboos observed by both communities in the form of exclusive communality and in the ordinary daily living, when Hindus and Muslims lived together. This socio-religious practice kept the two communities constantly reminded of their pious or unpious status. It is quite natural that such a conscious spirit of discrimination did not foster the seeds of healthy communal relations.

Secondly, it led to a swelling of the Muslim minority as it received a large number of converts to Islam. By the time of the advent of Muslims, Brahmanical supremacy had been re-established and thus the rigidity of the caste-system and the evil of untouchability had been strengthened. Many a people accepted the new faith, which did not hold such a rigidity of social order. Describing the characteristics of this change-over, Prof. Humayun Kabir writes:

> "One reason which made a fusion of Hindu and Muslim outlooks not only easy but in a sense inevitable, was the fact that large masses of the native people entered the fold of the new faith. History tells us that there was no large-scale colonisation by the Muslims. It was a case of infiltration of small groups who came in successive waves. In some cases, those who were conquered, had the faith and outlook of their conquerors imposed on them. In many cases, there was no question of any imposition.

> There was a willing acceptance of the new faith by large numbers on whom the existing social orders pressed heavily. It also attracted those who had developed a sense of dissatisfaction with the prevailing religion of the country. It was therefore not only the oppressed and unprivileged, but also a section of the intelligentsia who were drawn by the simplicity and vigour of the new faith. There were no doubt many who were influenced by the worldly advantages offered by the new faith. Equally strong must have been its appeal to those whose innate sense of justice and human dignity rebelled against the rigidities of caste. The Muslim saints and faqirs by their example and precept must also have attracted large numbers to the new religion".[38]

We agree to the first part of the views expressed above that the large-scale conversion from the Hindu fold in one way helped in the evolution of some sort of Hindu-Muslim synthesis. As a matter of fact, it was not a fusion of an orthodox Muslim and an orthodox Hindu, but that of a Hindu without Islam and a Muslim with a Hindu way of life. Rawlinson explains this point in much more clear terms. He writes:

> "One of the chief features of Hinduism has been its power of assimilation. Other invaders, Greek, Saka, Kushan and Huna, were gradually absorbed into Hindu society. But the Muhammadans with their strongly marked religious characteristics, remained apart. They lived as a ganison in a hostile country, holding little or no intercourse with their subjects".

He further adds:

> "But it was inevitable that as time went on, these barriers should be gradually released though they were never entirely broken down. Hindus were largely employed as officials for administrative purposes, and in many districts Hindu chiefs were left undisturbed on condition that they submitted to their conquerors. Marriages between Muhammadans and the women of the country became more and more frequent, and the children adopted many of the customs of their mothers. Conversion to Islam was

> common among the lower orders on account of the tyranny of the caste system, the prospects of escape from the poll-tax and other social advantages, but the converts retained their Hindus mode of life to a great extent. They avoided the eating of beef and widow marriage, and the Muhammadan villager today consults the Hindu astrologer and propitiates the local god in times of trouble. The veneration of the tombs of 'pir' or saints is very popular, and Hindu peasants join the Muslims in the rites performed at these shrines, whose occupants are believed to have the power of averting disease or other disasters".[39]

The second part of Professor Kabir's thesis wherein he attributes certain conversions to "the implicity and vigour of the new faith and to its appeal to a 'sense of justice and human dignity', needs a much more objective scrutiny. This point of view is very much akin to the one which accounts for the spread of Islam among Hindus by stressing what has been vaguely described a democratic appeal to masses.

This point is assailable for more than one reason. It is not to be denied that in its fundamentals, Islam did offer certain concepts which are an approach to democratic values. However, it is a fact of human history that there has always been a glaring dichotomy between what is preached and what is practised. Islam is no exception and it is highly doubtful whether its followers did really profess those values at all. The history of Islam in India does not speak much for these values. The Islam that came to India showed on the whole, clearly marked manifestations of bigotry, intolerance and undemocratic spirit. Its concept of non-co-existence between the believer and the non-believer, its narrowness and fanaticism; its iconoclasm and ferocity, its policy of economic discrimination and heavy taxation of non-Muslims; its legal jurisprudence with rigid social laws, its feudal set-up and autocratic political rule; its clear distinction between Shurfa and Razil[40]. The stratification of its fold into some seventy-seven sects; its attitude towards women and slaves[41]; its treatment of minorities and lower classes: all these are traits which cannot be called democratic by any stretch of imagination.

An eminent scholar of the Hindu-Muslim communal problem says:

> "The social democracy plea of Islam is not true to the facts of life as it is lived in Muslim society. Much is made of the equality that lines up the Nawab, the Muslim nobleman, with the Muslim porter in the Friday prayer in the mosque. The Hindus also, in Bengal atleast, can show a similar habit of equality on the occasions of kirtans, devotional songs, when the Brahmin and the Doma (an Aavama caste man) sit or stand side by side and sing songs to the glory and beneficence of the Lord, penetrated with the belief in His words uttered to Narada — 'where two or three men are gathered together in my name, there I am in the midst of them'. This equality on occasions is not potent enough to create that habit which is the bed-rock of the democracy which the modern times demand".[42]

It is not an unknown fact that the feudal set up of Islam in India came to evolve a social order which had its own caste system and which was not free from the taint of untouchability. Even the converts who are said to have embraced Islam due to a democratic appeal in it, were not accepted on the terms of equality. To quote Professor Kabir himself:

> "The Muslim variation of caste is soon most clearly in the institution of feudalism. Inconsistent with the spirit of Islam in India, it became associated especially with the Muslims. Military conquest always tends to produce a feudal society, and in India it became a necessary element in the Muslim system of land administration. Absence of modern means of communication made the control of so vast a country as India from one common centre impossible. It was inevitable that a good deal of authority should be delegated to local representatives of the king. In time, they grew into petty chieftains or kinglings rather than administrators serving a central authority. Social life was disfigured by the existence of a large number of slaves both male and female in the household of Kings and nobles. Indigenous converts often failed to attain the social status of those who had foreign blood in their veins

> and in a plutocratic regime, the poor tended to form a separate class. Converts tended to carry over their caste prejudices to their new faith. Difference in social esteem among converts from different castes could not thus altogether be avoided".[43]

It is clear therefore that it was with no such misgivings of Islam being a democratic faith, that the converts came forth to embrace it. On the contrary, it was its undemocratic outlook on life which by making the life of unbelievers miserable and insecure, compelled people to seek a shelter to ensure greater security to their life, liberty and property.

It may be possible that Islam like all other faiths possesses distinct virtues that have an enduring appeal of their own; but it is doubtful whether they helped it in gaining coverts. The overall historical evidence tells a different story. It was not so much its virtue of simplicity, as its sword hanging perpetually over the non-believers; it was not so much its sense of justice, as its atrocities[44] that struck terror; it was not so much its gospel of human dignity, as its denial of this very dignity to the infidel; it was not so much its economic justice, as its economic oppression and exploitation; it was not so much its code of a pristine ethics, as its lax morality; it was not so much its democratic nature, as its undemocratic nature that gained for it a rich harvest of proselytes.

Strange as it may seem, amidst such a scene of communal discord and disharmony between the Hindus and Muslims during the medieval period of the history of India, one does discover a definite undercurrent of rapprochement between the followers of Islam and Hinduism.

Dr. Beni Prasad in his book entitled, *The Hindu Muslim Questions* says:

> "But as soon as the first waves of conquest, plunder and desecration had spent themselves, there began the operation of the forces, inherent in human nature, which interknit in human contacts into continual wholes and transform plurality into community. Hindu chieftains and soldiers were soon fighting under Muslim rulers against Hindus and Muslims alike. Sometimes later, Muslim captains and soldiers were to be found with Hindu rajas.

> Trade and Industry wore new relationships. Preaching and political influence brought millions of Hindus into the Islamic fold, inevitably with their own habits of thought language and manners. Some of them intermarried with the Muslim immigrants who in their turn had already begun to feel the grip of the land of their adoption - its climate, its intellectual atmosphere and its economic framework".[45]

It is indeed in the nature of normal human living that when different people live together in spite of their opposed modes of living and differing outlooks on life, they do influence each other's life in many ways.

Commenting on this aspect of Hindu-Muslim relations, as they came to pass during the Medieval period, Professor Kabir says:

> "It is not necessary to describe in detail the consequences which followed from centuries of common life. Throughout India, an initial clash was followed by fusion and synthesis. These contacts had a profound influence on the way of life of the peoples inhabiting this land. There were far reaching changes in their dress, food, language, literature, art, painting, architecture, music and philosophy".

He further adds:

> "In a way, rapprochement was inevitable from the very nature of the case. Administration cannot be carried on for long by mere force or with the help of imported functionaries. The needs of administration led to innovations which were in almost every case compromises. As a result of living in the land, the Muslim invaders were gradually absorbed into its economy. They developed an attitude, at first of toleration and then of appreciation and love for the culture of the land".

In the face of the wholesale destruction of Hindu temples, imposition of the hated Jizya, exaction of heavier customs duties from Hindus, dismissal of Hindus from Imperial services, prohibitions against the free exercise of Hindu religious rites and festivals; and occasional proscription on Hindu learning carried out by Muslim rulers, it may be somewhat difficult to agree with

Professor Kabir's thesis that the early Muslim invaders and the successive rulers really developed an attitude of toleration towards Hindus. It is true however, in course of time, the 'processes of geography of economy proved stronger than such racial exclusiveness' or religious intolerance. The Muslims were in any case a minority and, as such, were inevitably influenced by their contact with the Hindu majority. It was a process of mutual collaboration and an interaction of reciprocal influences.

As O'Malley writes:

> "Both Muslims and Hindus gave to and received from each other intellectual impulses, and there was a certain synthesis of culture to which the Muslims made contributions of substantial value".[46]

The efforts made towards a communal synthesis made themselves manifest in the realm of art and architecture, music and painting, fairs and festivals, language and literature, and, to some extent, even in religion and ritualism.

Discussing the synthetical development of the Art during the middle ages, an eminent historian observes:

> "The conditions in which the Indo-Muslim art grew up made it necessary that there should be a fusion of the two ideals. Hinduism recommended idolatry, while Islam forbade it; Hinduism favoured decoration and gorgeousness, while Islam enjoyed puritanical simplicity. These different ideals so strangely in contrast with each other, produced by their junction a new kind of art which for the sake of convenience has been called the Indo-Muslim art. Gradually as the Hindu master builders and craftsmen began to express Islamic ideals in the shape of brick and stone, the process of amalgamation set in. Both learnt from each other, and though the Muslim's handling of ornament was not so exquisite, he derived the fullest advantage from the new ideas and materials supplied to him by the Indian conquest".[47]

In the realm of architecture, new types were created which embodied the excellence of the traditional modes of both Hindus and Muslims. Havell in his famous work *Indian Architecture* writes:

> "In all the Indian Muhammadan styles.... at Delhi, Ajmer,

Agra, Gaur, Malwa, Gujarat, Jaunpur and Bijapur... whether the local rulers were Arabs, Pathan, Turk, Persian, Mougal or Indian, the form and construction in the domes of mosques and tombs and palaces, as well as the Hindu symbols which crown them; the mihrales made to simulate Hindu shrines; the arches often Hinduized in construction, in form nearly always; the symbolism which underlies the decorative and structural designs.... all these tell us plainly that to the Indian builders, the sect of the prophet of Mecca was only one of the many which made up the synthesis of Hinduism; they could be good Muhammadans but yet remain Hindus".[48]

What was true in the realm of architecture could be seen even in the realm of music and painting. It is indeed an undisputable fact that Mughals were great patrons of these branches of art. Thus, in these two spheres there occurred a good deal of 'give and take'. As an eminent historian observes:

"The Hindus and Muslims borrowed ideas from each other, and by their joint efforts contributed much to the advancement of the Hindustani music. New varieties of Ragas were introduced by famous singers. Sanskrit works on music were translated into Persian, and a large number of songs were composed which are in use to this day".[49]

Though painting was not unknown to Hindus, yet it received great encouragement from the later Mughal rulers, many of whom were great connoisseurs of painting, and this led to a greater adaptation of each others methods and approach. Abul Fazal writing about Akbar says:

"He (Akbar) gives it every encouragement as he looks upon it as a means both of study and amusement. Hence the art flourishes, and many painters have obtained great reputation.... More than a hundred painters have become famous masters of the art, while the number of those who approach perfection, or of those who are middling, is very large. This is especially true of the Hindus; their pictures surpass our conception of things. Few indeed in the whole world are found equal to them".[50]

The Mughal patronage of the art of painting did save it from decay and this great mode of expression of a people's soul', developed from sixteenth century onwards in common schools in the hands of Hindu and Muslim masters and became truly Indian.

Coming to fairs and festivals, we find that in Medieval times a considerable portion of the year was set apart for public festivals. Leaving aside, the reign or Aurangzeb who 'banned most of the Hindu and Persian festivals in the court', the two communities continued to celebrate their festivals with equal enthusiasm. In this connection, Dr. Chopra observes:

> "The Mughals could not escape the reaction of Hindu culture under its dominating influence, coupled with a keen desire to bring the two communities nearer, they adopted some of the Hindu festivals and gave them a place in their court calendar. Decorations, illuminations, fire-works, splendid processions, abundant display of gold, silver, pearls, diamonds and jewels by Muhammadans in India unheard of in their native lands, were the natural consequences of their contact with Hindu culture".

He further adds:

> "With the advent of the Mughals, a new era dawned over the social and political horizon of India. They took keen interest in the feasts and festivals of the people. Humayun adopted the *tula-dan*, or the weighing ceremony of the Hindus. Akbar went further and associated Holi, Dasehra, and Vasant with court celebrations. Jahangir and to a certain extent, Shahjahan continued the noble tradition".[51]

As mentioned above, a few of the important Hindu festivals had the recognition of the Mughal court during the times of Humayun, Akbar and Jahangir. *Ab Pashan* was a festival very similar to the Holi festival amongst the Hindus. *Id-i-gulabi* was another festival, in which the princes and the prominent nobles would take part and were greatly delighted in sprinkling rose water over each other. Even Vasant Panchami, that marks the coming of spring season, was observed at the court.

Rakshabandhan, one of the great festivals of the Hindus, in which a sister ties a sacred thread called rakhi, was honoured by Humayun and Akbar made it a national festival and had a rakhi tied on his wrist[52]. Jahangir called Rakhi s 'Nighadasht' and like

Akbar he ordered that the "Hindu amirs and the head of the caste should fasten rakhris on my arm."[53]

Even Dussehra was celebrated at the Mughal court. In the case of Diwali, another Hindu festival, Akbar took interest in the festive aspect of the celebration while Jahangir preferred gambling and sometimes ordered his attendants to play the games in his presence for two or three nights.[54]

It has been recorded in *Ain-e-Akbari* that Akbar also took part in the celebrations of the Goverdhaṇ Puja, a Hindu festival that followed Diwali, and was associated with the worship of the cow. On this day, cattle are washed, ornamented and fed and worshipped. Several adorned cows were brought before him. It was in his times that Shivratri another Hindu festival was also celebrated at the court. Jahangir also took interest in it.[55]

Periodical fairs were also held both by Hindus and Muslims. In medieval times, these fairs served a religious as well as a social purpose. Mughals used to impose special pilgrimage tax on Hindus at such occasions.

Coming to the realm of language and literature, one is taken with wonder at the most powerful synthesis that took place between the two communities, irrespective of their vast differences. Regarding this aspect of Hindu-Muslim relations. Dr. Beni Prasad observes:

> "The Indian Mussalmans adopted or shick to the Indian languages, though they often employed Persian and Arabic for higher education and the former also for administration. They naturally affected the dialect spoken near the capital city of Delhi...... with a large admixture of Arabic and Persian words, it appeared as Urdu".[56]

The foreign language made a great impact on the native languages. The Bahamani kingdoms gave a great impetus to the Marathi language. It is the opinion of an eminent scholar that "the elevation of Bengali to literary status was brought about by several influences of which Muhammadan conquest was undoubtedly one of the foremost".[57]

The fact is that both Hindus and Muslims very often used languages other than their own. Hindus wrote in Persian and Urdu while Muslims used Braja Bhasha, Avadhi and other Indian languages like Gujarati, Marathi and Bengali. An eminent Historian observes:

> "Akbar's reign was the golden age of Indo-Muslim Art and Literature. The Hindu and Muslim genius scared to the highest, and produced work of which any country may feel proud. The Imperial patronage was freely extended to Persian and Hindi literatures; and the Emperor showed equal interest in both".[58]

He further adds:

> "The Emperor was keenly interested in Hindi poetry and song, and his tolerant spirit attracted to his court the most eminent poets and singers from all parts of the country. The association of the most talented Hindus of the age with the Emperor secured official support for a class of writers who had been so far neglected or treated with contempt".[59]

Writing of the above items, Rawlinson says:

> "Some of the most important undertakings of the men of letters of the Mogul court were the translation into Persian of standard Sanskrit works. A deep interest was taken in Hindi Philosophy and Faizi the poet saurcate, rendered the *Bhagwat Gita* into Persian verse. Dara Shikoh was a student of Vedanta and the Upanishads. Persian abridgement of the Hindu Epics, the Puranas and the *Lilavati* (a treatise on Mathematics) was made".[60]

We also observe a marked rapprochement between the two communities in matters of religions and ritual. The synthesis in the direction took place because of the following three reasons:

> "In the first place, Hindu converts retained some of their ancient practices; some were only half converts. Mussalmans as a whole could not escape the influence of Hindu metaphysics and religious practices.
>
> Secondly, Islamic monotheism, brought into more conspicuous relief the monotheism or the henotheism of the Hindu systems of theology and partly inspired the Bhakti movements.
>
> Thirdly, there arose whole sects like those of Kabir (1440-1516), presumably a Mussalman, and Nanak (1569-1538)

which combined elements both of Hinduism and Islam. The same breadth of vision marked the hymns and teachings of Dada, Chaitanya, Tukaram and many others. A common point of view is clearly in evidence in a great deal, though not in all, of the neo-spiritualistic literature of medieval India".[61]

Similarly, we find that in many a Socio-religious practice, Hindus and Muslims came to follow each other's ways of observance. Thus, the Hindu venerated the tombs of Pirs and the Muhammadan villagers propitiated the local Hindu gods in times of trouble. Professor Kabir rightly observes:

> "The process of integration which followed profoundly changed the character of primitive Islam. We have already referred to the growth of Feudalism and of a kind of modified caste. Islam has always condemned a separate priesthood but there are unmistakable signs of such a growth among Indian Muslims. They also show a marked fondness for ritual and elaborate ceremony. Islam was iconoclastic, but Indian Muslims often display a veneration of saints and their tombs that remind one of the worship of relics. Mohammed stressed the uniformity of natural law and laid hardly any stone by miracles, but the Indian Muslim felt unhappy till he had built up a halo of sanctity, if not divinity, round his religious heroes. Muslims practice in India thus tended to conform to Hindu religious customs".[62]

So, in the perspective of centuries we see that in the religious phase of communalism, Hindus and Muslims whether consciously or unconsciously, successfully tried to replace conflict by co-operation and communal disharmony by communal harmony at various planes of day to day sharing of the ordeals of the life. Although it is clear that much depended on the will of the monarch, still the common man did establish a communal equilibrium which now and then was disturbed by the mischievous moves of the petty political and religious trouble mangers. 'Clashes were there, but the waters of life were rounding them and the 'blooming buzzing confusion was getting a new integration'.

We now conclude a study of this phase by reiterating our

thesis that even in the heart of worst conflicts there always exists, a nucleus of some common agreement. Human nature is the same everywhere. The basic needs of man have ever been the same. It is only the outward mode of life that has varied from one people to another, one place to another, from one age to another. The medieval period is an illustration of the part religion can play in predominantly shaping the growth of communal relations. We have seen how in spite of vast differences, people do find a via media between the seemingly incompatible religions.

The inevitable law of a harmonious social living as also the motive force of the historic evolution lies in the process of mutual adjustment and adaptation to the conditions that prevail from time to time.

A study of Hindu-Muslim relations during the medieval period thus conclusively proves that, as long as there are communities with different ways of living, disharmony is bound to exist. But every conflict can be followed by an attempt to cooperate which does bring harmony and concord.

The effort of Kabir to reconcile Hinduism and Islam by selecting elements common to both religions, to found a religion in which both communities would find a common meeting ground, is a creditable example of the same. We conclude with him that, "God is one, whether we worship Him as Allah or as Rama".

NOTES AND REFERENCES

1. Quran (116.18/4) (Quoted from the translation by M.S. Burney, p. 79).
2. Quran (109. 12/3) (*ibid.*, p. 76).
3. Quran (103. 11/3) (*ibid.*, p. 76).
4. Ibid., p. 89.
5. *War and Peace in the Law of Islam* by Majid Khadduri. The Johns Hopkins Press, Baltimore (1955), p. 59. (Quoted from Quran IX 74).
6. *Ibid.*, p. 63-64.
7. *Ibid.*, p. 53.
8. *India - A Short Cultural History* by H.G. Rawlinson (London: The Gresset Press) IV Ed. 1952, pp. 223-24.
9. *The History of India as Told by its Own Historians* by Elliot and Dowson. Vol. III, p. 389.
10. Ishwari Prasad : *op. cit.*, p. 178.

11. This narration has been taken from the report of Mr. William on the Moplerbs. These are the parts of their folk-song's composed in a mixture of Arabic, Hindustani, Malayaly, Tamil and other Indian Languages. See Govt. of India Records: Home Deptt. Police: March 1897: Nos. xix 31-64.
12. See *ibid.*
13. *History of Aurangzeb* by Jadu Nath Sarcar. Vol. V, N. C. Sarkar and Sons, Calcutta (1924), p. 483.
14. *Medieval India* by Dr. Ishwari Prasad (Introduction), (1928), p. XVI.
15. Quoted in *The Individual and Group* by B.K. Malik.
16. *Medieval India under Muhammadan Rule* by Lane-Poole (1903), pp. 62-64.
17. Rawlinson, *op. cit.*, p. 222.
18. *The Hindu Muslim Question* Beni Prasad: Kitabistan (1941), p. 8.
19. Jadu Nath Sarkari, *op. cit.*, p. 473.
    e.g. Upon the King : Let our lives, our souls,Our debts our careful wives Our children and our sins lay on the King (Shakespeare).
20. *The Commercial Policy of the Moguls* by D. Pant. (1930), p. 59.
21. Elliot and Dowson II; 179.
22. *From Akbar to Aurangzeb* by W. Moreland, pp. 304-5.
23. Rawlinson: *op. cit.*, p. 236.
24. *The Travels of Pietro Della Valle* ed. by Grey Vol. 1, p. 30.
25. *European Travellers in Mughal India* - An Appreciation by Y. Krishna. (Islamic Culture Vol. XXI No.3. July 1947, Quotes Hawkins, pp. 106-107), p. 221.
26. *Travels of Peter Munday in Europe and Asia* Ed. by R.C. Temple: Vol. II, p. 178.
27. *Travels in the Mughal Empire* by Bernier. Ed. by Smith pp. 176-77, 287.
28. The travels of Schartran Manrriqud translated and edited by Luard and Hoster. Vol. II, p. 147.
29. Y. Krishna. *op. cit.*, p. 222 (Manucci Vol. II, p. 154).
30. *A Voyage to Surat by Ivington*, (Ed. Rawlinson), p. 140.
31. Tavernier notes that the Shias were not allowed to celebrate the Muharam festival. (Tavernier 'Travels in India, by V. Ball Vol. II, p. 177).
32. Rawlinson, *op. cit.*, pp. 343-44.
33. *Ibid.*, p. 341.
34. Elliot and Dowson VII, p. 296.
35. (Quran, ix, 29) See *Mughal Empire in India* by S.R. Sharma. Part II, Karnatak Pub. House Bombay (1947), p. 152.
36. *The Religious Policy of the Mughal Emperors* by Sri Ram Sharma (1940), Oxford University Press, p. 12.

37. Edwardes and Carret: *op. cit.*, p. 364.
38. "Indian Muslims" by Prof. Humayun Kabir (an article published in *The Indo Asian Culture*. Vol. IV No. 3 Jan 1956 Published by Indian Council for Cultural Relations; New Delhi, pp. 287-88.
39. Rawlinson H.G., *op. cit.*, pp. 243-44.
40. Shurfa: literally nobles; Razil; literally, the Low.
41. The Muslims frequently referred to woman as Nagis-ul-Aqal, i.e., devoid of wisdom. Compare it with the Greek who lumped together woman with the slave and Manu, the Hindu law gives, who said "where woman are honoured the gods dwell".
42. The India Charter: by Jehangir F. Kotewal, pp. 119-20.
43. Humayun Kabir, *op. cit.*, p. 284.

    Ratish Mohan Agarwala in his book entitled *Hindu-Muslim Riots: Their Causes and Cures* (The International Social Literature Pub. Co. Lucknow 1943) enumerates fourteen causes of conversions to Islam (See Page 68). They may be briefly summarised as follows:—

    1. Many Hindus were converted to Islam as point of sword, sometimes under the orders, permission or connivance of the Muslim Kings and Emperors but very often by irresponsed 'Muslim' Generals and minor Government officials who felt themselves free to do whatever they liked specially in distant parts of the country away from the Central seat of Government; such as in Bengal, Malwa, Gujrat and Sind.
    2. Quite a large number of 'Hindus' girls and women were kidnapped by the Muslims and forcibly married or thrown into their houses and sometimes even boys and grown up males were kidnapped with a view to procure ransom money in return for them and were forced to become 'Muslims' if that was not available.
    3. Some Muslim Kings and Emperors imposed the Jizya on the Hindus under the pressure of which some 'Hindus' had to leave their ancestral faith.
    4. Many Muslim Kings and Emperors subjected the Hindus to so many political and social disabilities that some Hindus had to accept 'Islam' in order to get rid of them.
    5. Due to the suicidal policy of the Hindus of 'outstanding' and boycotting their own people on every little pretext many of those Hindus who were so 'outcasted' or 'boycotted' got themselves converted into 'Muslims' either because they wanted some society at least to live in and associate with or in order to take revenge on those who had insulted or humiliated them in that way.

6. Some 'Hindus' of both sexes look to Islam in order to avoid suffering in some way on account of the customs of dowry, sati; marriage in one's own caste or outside one's gotra; prohibition of widow remarriages, lack of divorce facilities violent or insulting treatment of their family people or relations untouchability and others.
7. Many orphans and helpless adults of both sexes for sexes for whom the 'Hindus' failed to make any provision were taken control of by Muslim proslytizing organisations which looked after them and subsequently converted them to 'Islam'.
8. Some 'Hindus' look to Islam on account of the love of Government appointments which they could obviously secure much more easily by so doing than by sticking to their original faith.
9. Some 'Hindus' who happened to be the courtiers of the 'Muslim' Kings and Emperors dined, drank and associated with them so freely that they ceased to care what faith they professed and in order to please their masters formally declared themselves to be Muslims.
10. Some Hindus of both sexes look to Islam in order to marry a male or a female of their choice belonging to the 'Muslim' community.
11. Some 'Hindus' fell into the society of Muslim friends under whose influence they ultimately got themselves converted to Islam.
12. Some Hindus who followed certain professions such as those of public women, butchers and others, had to mix so freely with both the Hindus and the Muslims that they look to Islam as a matter of pure convenience.
13. Some 'Hindus" changed their faith in order to carry out some threat to that effect which they had advanced to their family people or relatives in order to compel them to pay them some money or do something else against their wishes.
14. And finally we agree some Hindus might have taken to Islam because they honestly believed it to be a batter Religion than the faith of their ancestors.

44. "Mahmud went as far in 1624 as the town of Somnath ..... in Kathiawar in Western India, where in the storming of the town he slew fifty thousand Hindus because they would not be converted". (J.C. Archer. Kabir, Sikhism and Hindu-Muslim relations, p. 37).
45. Dr. Beni Persad: *The Hindu Muslim Questions*, pp. 8-9.
46. *Modern India and the West* by O'Malley, p. 8.

47. *A Short History of Muslim Rule in India* by Ishwari Prasad. The Indian Press Ltd. Allahabad. 1939, p. 191.
48. *Indian Architecture* by R.B. Havell, p. 101.
49. *History of India* by Dr. Ishwari Prasad (1944), p. 587.
50. *Ain Akbari* by Abul Fazal, Vol. I, p. 107.
51. *Some Aspects of Society and Culture during the Mughal Age* (1526-1707) by Dr. Pran Nath Chopra (S.L. Agarwala, Agra 1956), pp. 78-79. For greater details see Narly Travels p.119; Roc's Embassay pp. 378-80 (1926, Edition); Delhi Valle, p. 459; Manrique II pp. 200-4; De Laet pp. 101-2. Mandelslo p. 42. Tavernier p. 122; Storia II, p. 348: Bernier p. 272; Thevenot, XXVI. p. 47 and Qanun-i-Humayun, p. 76; Ain, I (1873), pp. 266-67; R. and B.I., pp. 78, 115, 160; Padshahnawa. I. p. 243; p. 243; MA. (Urdu), p. 51.
52. Badoni, VII, 261-62 quoted by Chopra, *op. cit.*, 92.
53. *Ibid.*, p. 92.
54. *Ibid.*, p. 93.
55. *Ibid.*, p. 93.
56. Dr. Beni Prasad, *op. cit.*, p. 9.
57. *History of Bengali Language and Literature* by Dinesh Chandra Sen, p. 10.
58. *History of India* by Dr. Ishwari Prasad, p. 588.
59. *Ibid.*, p. 592.
60. Rawlinson: *op. cit.*, 371.
61. Dr. Beni Prasad: *op. cit.*, p. 12.
62. Kabir, *op. cit.*, p. 291.

59. Ibid., p. 392.
60. Rawlinson op. cit., 37[illegible]

Section Four

The Political Phase of Communalism

With the advent of British Imperialism, communalism in India entered its political phase.

The English entered India as a trading company to carry on commerce. It was in 1600 AD that Queen Elizabeth granted a Charter to the 'Society of Adventures', which later on was constituted into the East India Company, under the title of 'Governor and Company of Merchants of London Trading into the East-Indies'.

Though they had set their feet on the shores of India much earlier, 'the Commencement of the Political supremacy in India of the Christian merchants of England dates from their winning the Battle of Plassey in 1757'.[1]

In no time, they eliminated the challenge from their European rivals for supremacy, built several factories, established diplomatic relations with various native rulers, annexed territory after territory and emerged as an eloquent illustration of the principle of 'the survival of the fittest'. They not only survived the early setbacks, but, within a span of a few decades, became the real masters of the land.

The entire political life of the British in India that ended on 15th August, 1947, can be easily divided into two distinct rules, viz.

(i) The Rule of the 'East India Company'.
(ii) The Rule of the 'British Crown'.

The Rule of the East India Company, came to an end with the Proclamation of Queen Victoria[2], read by Lord Canning, the first Viceroy and Governor-General designate by the same Charter on the Ist of November, 1858, in Allahabad.

It was only after the dissolution of the "Honourable Company", that an apparently 'responsible administration' of the country starts. This change, however, was a change in form and not in substance. Lord Irwin in his essay entitled, "The Evolution of Political Life in India", writes:

> "For many years indeed after the Government of India passed from the Company to the Crown, it is not easy to detect my essential difference in the actual character of the Government of the country. It remained an autocracy, but an autocracy continually tampered by the introduction of institutions and principles of very different kind".[3]

Be it as it may, "Exploitation and Counterpoise", have been the key-note of British rule in India both before and after Queen Victoria's Proclamation.

Commenting on the rule of the East India Company, that paved the foundations of an Empire for the British, an English Historian writes:

> "The establishment of the English power in India is an ugly one. It begins in feebleness and cowardice; it is pervaded by rapacity, it closes with a course of fraud and falsehood, of forgery and treason, as stupendous as ever lay at the foundation of a Great Empire.... Is it not in human nature that we should be reminded of the crimes which Clive and Warren Hastings, and all that shameless generation which surrounded them committed for our benefit?"[4]

Can there be a better testimony of British exploitation than this? Their reputation among the natives was appalling. Rev. Philip Anderson, describing the reaction of the people of Surat where they had established, 'their first factory' in India, writes:

> "As the number of adventures increased, the reputation of English was not improved. Too many committed deeds of violence and dishonesty... ...Hindus and Mussalmans considered the English as a set of cow-eaters, fire drinkers vile brutes, fiercer than the mastiffs which they brought with them who would fight like Eblees. cheat their own fathers, and exchange with the same readiness, a broadside of shot and thrusts of boarding pikes, or a bale of goods and a bag of rupees".[5]

The old Viceroy Shayista Khan, called them, 'a company of

base, quarrelling people and foul dealers'. But however, debased night have been their character, however, dirty their motives and however dishonest their methods, it is a fact that the English lived and ruled India in a way they liked the best, and the ends they thought fit.

The secret of their ascendancy lies not only in their unscrupulous and subtle plunder and exploitation of the indigenous population. It also lies in their subtle application of the Imperialistic policy of, 'Counterpoise'.

Imperialism likes to "divide and rule".[6] Fortunately for the British in India there was a vast and fertile field of mutually adjusted divisions which needed but little effort to get disturbed. What the distributor needed to escape the consequences, was a firm hold to the, 'balance of power' between the disturbed elements. British diplomacy in India did not fail here. The shrewd policy of 'Counterpoise' brought them every success. The entire social, political and economic life of India, once the, "brightest jewel in Britain's imperial crown", was totally disintegrated, so much so, that each man was set as a 'counterpoise' against the other. In the words of Karl Marx, who wrote a series of articles on India in 1853.

> "How came it that English supremacy was established in India? The paramount power of the Great Mogul was broken by the Mogul Viceroys. The power of the Viceroys was broken by the Maharattas. The power of the Maharattas was broken by the Afghans, and while all were struggling against all; The Briton rushed in and was enabled to subdue them all. A country not only divided between Mohammedan and Hindu, but between tribe and tribe, between caste and caste; a society whose framework was based on a sort of equilibrium resulting from a general repulsion and constitutional exclusiveness between all its members. Such a country and such a society were they not the predestined prey of conquest".[7]

The maintenance of British paramountcy was the 'dominant urge' of British in India and a policy of counterpoise suited them the most. Describing its practical application to the Indian conditions K.B. Krishna writes:

> "The British created artificially several classes. The moment these classes came into existence the struggle between them began. The British gave an impetus to these struggles. Princes, territorial magnates, industrial classes and Moslems, were brought into play to counteract the claims of the lawyers, schoolmasters, students and other middle classes .... Lord Lytton and Curzon spoke of a council of notables as a suitable counterpoise to the claims of the Baboos, whose organisation was the Congress".[8]

'Counterpoise' can be seen in every move of the British. Giving of weightage to one party and diminishing the influences of another, has continued all through with a shameless dexterity and uncanny simplicity. In this respect, the policy of 'Divide and Rule' helped them much. The counterpoise policy, used towards the ruthless tampering of the native lives needs no reiteration. As Prof. Abdul Majid Khan in his book entitled, *The Communalism in India - Its Origin and Growth*, writes:

> "Even school children know that the beginnings of British rule in India can be traced to the interference of the East India Company in the succession-squabbles of the heirs of Nizam-ul-Mulk, the Nawab of Hyderabad who died in 1748, and in the dynastic disputes between Chanda Sahib and Mohammed Ali, the two rival claimants for the Nawabship of Carnatic. In Bengal the unending enimity between Ami Chand and Siraj-ul-Daulah was astutely exploited. By and by the British Indian Empire grew".[9]

Sometimes, it was one class, sometimes another interest, that received a favour from British to counteract the rise of some other force in the country. If sometimes it were Zamindars and Princes who received the patronage against the peasants and masses; then sometimes it was members of the liberal intelligentsia who were used as a counterpoise against the mass revolt, as in the viceroyalty of Lord Dufferin. If, for Lord Ellenborough, the true policy lay in conciliating the Hindus; for Curzon, Minto and Sir Bainfylde Fuller, it was the Muslims who alone needed all care and patronage to counteract the once favoured Hindus. Is it any wonder to feel that the English even kept India divided into two parts viz, Indian India and British India, as a 'counterpoise' to each other.

To conclude

> "The main theoretical idea of this policy is the 'principle of communities, classes and interests'... From the beginning the idea has nothing to do with formal democracy. It is society concerned with a balance of interests, classes and certain religious adherents (communities) as each interest and class clamoured for power".[10]

"Power" is to politics, what profit is to economics. Having lost power to the British, Indian politics now switched its energies to regain the same lost power. It was a queer struggle between the forces of Imperialist autocracy and a chained India struggling for people's democracy. The three parties to it were the Hindus, the Muslims and the British.

In this tug of war for the acquisition of political power, there were involved certain 'problematic questions', that invite an immediate clarification.

The first is, "From whom did the British snatch political power? From Muslims or from the Hindus?"

The second is, "Having snatched once, shall they give it back? If so to whom and in what way?"

The most common, but of course a wrong notion entertained by Muslims has been that it was from them that the political power passed on to the Firanghis (Franks i.e. Europeans), the English Christian rulers of India.

In one of the specialized studies of the communal problem in India, W.C. Smith in his work entitled *Modern Islam in India*, has made a very interesting scrutiny of this psychological excuse of the Muslims that the British snatched the reins of political ascendency from them instead of the Hindus. Smith calls it a 'fallacious resentment' of the Muslims which for quite a sufficient period kept them unreconciled to any intercourse whatever with the new order.

He says:

> "Now it is true that they resented this and bitterly. We do not deny either the existence or the profundity of the resentment when we point out that the argument based upon it is fallacious. For the British, conquests were made from Hindu ruling classes, such as the Marhattas. In the

> Punjab where the Muslim question is at its height, the rulers were Sikhs. This does not prevent modern middle class Muslims in the Punjab and Western India from thinking vaguely that they used to be the rulers and hence compensating their capitalist frustration with offended pride".[11]

The fact, however, is that it was not the Muslims but the Hindus who were robbed of their political ascendancy, as will also be evident from a confidential minute, of Sir J.B. Lyall, written in 1887.

Sir J.B. Layall wrote,

> "In India as a whole it is more important politically to keep straight with the Hindus than with the Mohammedans. In Punjab it is very necessary to hold, the balance perfectly even between the two and to remember that before we took the country, the Hindus had the upper hand".[12]

The above view makes three things very clear viz:

(1) That it was Hindus and not Muslims, from whom the political power passed on to the British.

(2) That in framing any Government policy, Hindus and Muslims alone mattered the most, being the only important sections of the indigenous population.

(3) That while dealing with natives, 'Balance' (i.e.) Counterpoise, should be the chief guiding principle.

The above analysis clears the first doubt raised earlier. Now we come to the second. The sanest answer to this, an answer which can be valid for all times, is that the British did not acquire India to give it back. India was the single important factor in Great Britain's rise to the position of a power of the first magnitude.

As Joan Beauchamp wrote,

> "The plunder and exploitation of sub-continent of nearly two million square miles gave Great Britain an unquestionable advantage in the race for supremacy among the European nations, and her position as the controller of the market of a foreign population of three hundred million people gave immense impetus to her industrial development and enabled her to outstrip all competitors in the early years of the Nineteenth Century".[13]

It becomes clear that in this triangular tussle for the acquisition of political power, the British had no love either for the Hindus, or for the Muslims. They loved their own empire. They loved their own strategy of exploitation and counterpoise. They blatantly refused to make India their home. As the authors of *The Communal Triangle in India* have observed,

> "The great refusal enabled the English in India to retain his separate identity. He became the member of a super-Brahmanical caste, conscious of its superiority over the "Native" population and keeping itself proudly aloof from any contaminating contact with them. For him India became synonymous with the *Khansama* who cooked his food, the 'bearer' who looked after his personal comforts and the *Syce* who looked after his horses. These were also the people from whom he learnt what little Hindustani, he knew. He used it sparingly and only when he talked to his servants. At the office thanks God, he had a 'Bamboo' who understood the civilised English language.
>
> As he refused to make India his home, the thoughts of all the Englishmen were always fixed on the little island across the seas and he longed for 'England's green and pleasant land' with a longing that was not without a touch of nostalgia. Obsessed with this home complex, the Englishman instinctively began to look upon India as a land of fortune, a great reservoir of wealth whose sluices ultimately emptied themselves on the lovely plains of Devon and East Anglia. Nothing Indian was good enough unless it supplied some British need".[14]

What was true in the social life was much more true in the administrative and the political life of the country.

Warren Hastings had recognized the need of associating Indians with the administration and put his principles into practice. His policy was reserved by Lord Cornwallis and for more than forty years, the system of Government was one (which of-course continued to be the same in its spirit, if not strictly in form) in which, as Lord William Bentinck pointed out, there was an iron hand of power on the one side and monopoly and exclusion on the other.

> "In many respects", he wrote, "the Mohammedans surpassed our rules; they settled in the countries which they conquered, they intermarried with the natives; they admitted them to all privileges; the interests and sympathies of the conquerors and conquered became identified. Our policy, on the contrary, has been the reverse of this, cold, selfish and unfeeling".[15]

Obviously, "After the establishment of British rule", says O'Mally, "there were naturally many who desired to restore Indian rule of the old type and to recover place and power for themselves".[16]

Thus, it was in such a complex setting after the advent of an alien master, that India saw an unceasing struggle for political power between three communities. They were the disunited Hindu who in an age of advancing democracy being a majority community and, thus, being a natural successor to the power that be, impatiently sought freedom and the right of self-determination. The united Muslim who, bereaved by the downfall of Moghul Empire, lived in frustration, terribly fretful about his place in any political set-up in the future; and, the dividing English, who, unwilling to make India their home, but anxious all the same to govern it, continued to guard jealously the British Raj, with faithful adherence to the diabolic diplomacy of "Exploitation and Counterpoise".[17]

This struggle for political supremacy made every community extremely conscious of its own existence and future. It also made them cautious and suspicious of every other community that happened to be equally cautious and suspicious a competitor. As a matter of fact, this struggle dragged the entire country into a mire and wiped off every hope for a happy and harmonious existence among people. It was so, because the tussle was not between the Hindus and the Muslims alone. It was a general conflict between various 'communities, classes and interests'; who all sought some sort of social safety, economic stability and political security.

Naturally, therefore, we observe that the indigenous population reacted against the British masters in two different ways. One was the national resentment towards the foreign rule. The second was the communal approach directed towards the greater consolidation by each 'community, class and interest'. This is what has been vaguely described as nationalism and communalism trying to fan each other. The truth lies in the fact that we usually forget to appreciate the triangular setting of the problem. Thus, although this struggle for political supremacy had a national complexion, yet, in this competitive struggle, the rewards were obtained on a communal basis. The British recognition of the indigenous claim had an exclusive and communal complexion. To put it more correctly, we can say that "the patronage of communal activities had grown side by side with the growth of national sentiment in India".

The exact nature of the Indian political scene, which had both a national and a communal aspect, has been vividly described in the following words:

> "In the baffling maze of Indian history under British Raj, we are able to discover two distinct threads by which the Indian community sought to re-establish a pattern for its daily life. The national awakening and unrest following the British conquest first dashed itself against the armed might of the British Raj. Defeated and repulsed and severely punished, it turned to caste and religion to satisfy its inner hunger. Here under Government patronage, it acquired strength and gave meaning and significance, to thousands of frustrated lives. Government policies, clearly understood and intelligently pursued at last bore fruit. Today, India is becoming a land of communal organisations and communal loyalties and rivalries in the midst of which the voice of nation is struggling to make itself heard and understood. With clever checkmate and counterpoise, the British Government has tried to side track the wrath of the people from itself to the communal plane".[18]

It is not difficult to explain as to how the native reaction to the British rule assumed two contradictory forms — one anti-Imperialist and the other inter-communal, the former being denoted as nationalism and the later as communalism.

The explanation of this dichotomy may be sought in the British policy of exploitation and counterpoise. It was the creation of the British who had tampered with the native way of life. The force of narrow communalism was put forth by the British as an effect against the rising tide of the nationalist forces.

No one can deny that there were no communal distinctions in India before the arrival of the British. No one can deny either that, the communal quarrels and that too, between the Hindus and the Muslims were not there before the British came. In fact, some sort of social tension and antagonism did exist in India much earlier. The fact is that there can exist no society without some sort of conflict or some sort of decay. Yet, nature has its curious way of healing all the conflicts. Human forces are stronger than the forces of destruction. Every conflict is followed by cooperation among the warring elements. If this were not true, humanity could not have survived to this day.

The simple truth is that in any society each, "Community grows through a series of stages that culminate in a climax stage at which relations are stabilized. A catastrophe, however, may destroy the rather delicate equilibrium and thus initiate a new succession of changes".[19]

The British advent proved more than a catastrophe in the development of communal relations of Indians, particularly that between the Hindus and the Muslims. The communal harmony that they had evolved by now received a rude shock from which they could never recover. As the authors of the Sapru committee report observe:

> "Two such great sections of civilised humanity, thrown together for over a thousand years into intimate contact by the necessities of commerce, industry, social adaptation and political give and take, could not afford to live in perpetual discord. They, therefore, consciously evolved political and social adjustments, almost a cultural synthesis, which, but for the advent of dominating alien rule, might in the natural course of evolution, have perfected itself by now."[20]

Thus, we find that the impact of British rule did not help in a normal evolution of the various sections of the indigenous population. On the contrary, it disturbed the state of communal equilibrium in the country by "initiating a new succession of changes". It was to ensure the safety of their Raj that they caused disintegration of the village community and poisoned the life of the city. "They snapped the ancient threads that wove the people together" and created one class as an offset to another, they made the people conscious on a sectarian plane and turned India into a boiling cauldron of seething discontent making the life of an average Indian 'poor, frustrated and dark'. The authors of *The Communal Triangle in India* observe:

> "In this surrounding darkness of blight and frustration, where avenues of politics, education, the services were closed to the common man, the only ray of light, the only point of contact, the only straw, to which the average Indian clung with the desperation of a drowning man, were caste and communal loyalty. Here was something that he knew and understood, something too which offered contact and cohesion in a disintegrating world. The caste, at least, was not suspect in the eyes of the Government. They on the contrary encouraged caste feeling. What wonder if the people, baffled and frightened, got enmeshed in the complex of caste and sub-caste?"[21]

It is here indeed that we can discover reasons for the problem as to why the popular ferment caused by the British rule found two contradictory expressions in the simultaneous rise of nationalism and communalism.

Examined from any angle whatsoever, it is not possible to absolve the Christian rulers of their share in the development and spread of communalism in India. It is in the following three respects that there responsibility largely rests.

1. The destruction of the native structure by the British and the consequent unleashing of the forces of dis-equilibrium and disparity.
2. The creation of a State of fear psychosis and communal phobia replete with distrust, suspicion and fear, that consequently led to the loss of mutual understanding and tolerance between different communities.
3. The undue emphasis on things hitherto overlooked, which brought to light, in a magnified form, the forces

of communal discord and differences instead of concord and common interest.

On an analysis of facts, we find that the fundamental factors that fanned communalism in the political phase were none else than those we have witnessed hitherto in its social and religious phase. The only difference was that ultimately they all led to one single goal, the goal of political ascendancy which was sought by various communities.

NOTES AND REFERENCES

1. This victory came out of Sirajuddaula, the Viceroy of Bengal's defeat by Clive, the founder of, in the words of K.M. Panikkar, 'a robber-state'; It commenced an era of puppet nawabs, with the East India Company as a future king maker. Mir Jafar was placed on the throne of Bengal: Two clauses of the Treaty of the 15th July, 1757, mark the establishment of British political and military ascendancy; they made Mir Jafar impotent. These were, firstly that, "The enemies of the English are my enemies, whether they are Indians or Europeans", secondly that "Whenever I demand the English assistance, I will be at the charge of the maintenance of them". (*History of India*. Sinha and Banerji. 3rd Edn. 1950, p. 479).
2. "Queen Victoria's Proclamation to the, 'Princes, Chiefs and Peoples of India', announcing the transfer of the power to the Crown, expressly took up the threads of the Company's consistent policy, promising complete religious toleration and the maintenance of the 'ancient rights, usages and customs of India', and in the Act that followed it was laid down that, 'all acts and provisions now in force under Charter or otherwise in India shall continue in force'. Virtually the only change was the substitution at home of Secretary of State with an Indian Council of Fifteen members in place of the President of the Board of Control and the Court of Directors' (*India* by C.H. Philips: 1948. (Ch. IV, p. 77).
3. *Political India* (1832-1932) Edited by Sir John Canning. 1932. Ch. I, p. 11.
4. *British India, Its Races and its History*, by John Malcolm Ludlow, Vol. I. pp. 198-199.
5. *The English in Western India*, by Rev. Philip Anderson (p. 22). Quoted by Major B.D. Basu; *Rise of the Christian Power in India*, pp. 40-41.
6. "Divide et Impera" was the old Roman motto, and "it should be ours" Mountstuart Elphinstone.

7. *The Future Results of British Rule in India,* by Karl Marx, New York, *Daily Tribune,* August 8th, 1853; quoted by Joan Beauchamp in *British Imperialism in India,* p. 16.
8. *Communal Representation* by K.B. Krishna. George Allen and Unwin Ltd. Museum Street. (1939).
9. *The Communalism in India - Its Origin and Growth* by Prof. Abdul Majid Khan, Lahore: Paramount Publications, 1944, p. 33.
10. Krishna, *op. cit.*
11. *Modern Islam in India* - W.C. Smith.
12. Government of India Records Home Department Pub. B., Jan 1894; F.No. p. 309-414.
13. *The British Imperialism in India* by Joan Beauchamp: 1934, p. 11.
14. *The Communal Triangle in India* by Ashok Mehta and Achyaput Patwardhan, p. 80.
15. O'Mally, *op. cit.*, p. 87.
16. *Ibid.*, p. 87.
17. The words of a previous British administrator may be recalled here, "the fundamental principle of the English has been to make the whole Indian nation subservient, in every possible way, to the interests and benefits of themselves. They have been taxed to the utmost limit: every successive province, as it has fallen into our possession has been made a field for higher exaction .." Quoted from *White Sahibs in India* by Reginald Raynolds, p. 57.
18. *The Communal Triangle in India* by Mehta and Patwardhan, p. 102.
19. *Human Ecology - A Theory of Community Structure* by Amos H. Hambly, pp. 64-65.
20. *The Constitutional Proposals of the Sapru Committee.* Padma Publications Ltd., Mumbai (1945), p. 98.
21. *The Communal Triangle in India* by Mehta and Patwardhan, p. 99. Kitabistan. Allahabad. (1942).

Part Two

The Historical Analysis Pertaining to the British Raj

Section One

The Economic Aspect of Communalism

The British were primarily responsible for disturbing the economic equilibrium that had been established through the course of a few centuries in India. The economic factor operates on two distinct levels viz. the village level and the town level.

India has throughout been a predominantly agricultural country. The social base of village life has been the village community which is the chief form of association among the people subsisting mainly by agriculture; it is a group not of individuals but of families. Its characteristic features were the collective ownership of land, acceptance of the authority of a headman, as also the regulation of the communal affairs by representative bodies called Panchayats. In all cases, villages had an organization designed to make themselves supporting and self governing.

After the advent of the Muslims, the village lands were surveyed as a preliminary to the assessment of land revenue, in order to ascertain the proportion of the produce (or its cash equivalent) which the state could claim as its share of revenue. Except for the collection of land revenue, there was little State control over the villages and this was the only sphere in which the administrative machinery might be said to have extended to the villages. Land was, ofcourse, always regarded as the property of the sovereign, who was from time immemorial entitled to a share of the gross produce. The village contribution to the state earned for it the privilege of protection by the state. Describing the entire process, a historian observes:

> "Actually, it meant in practice that they (the villagers) knew little of Government except its exactions. The State performed no function of immediate benefit to the rural masses. In their eyes it appeared only as the power that

> levied taxes from them. The share recognised by Hindu jurists as the sovereign's legitimate right was one-sixth, but it was fixed at one third by Akbar, and this was not beyond the economic capacity of the cultivating classes. Neither Jahangir nor Shah Jahan had any idea of making their yoke easy or their burden light. The proportion of the produce due to the State was raised to one-half with the result that the peasantry were reduced to a mere subsistence level, as the other half was only sufficient to meet the cost of cultivation and provide a family with the necessaries of life. There was no margin left to meet the stress of hard times or seasonal calamities, and when famine broke out, there was universal distress and wide-spread starvation".[1]

The life of a peasant and that too of a Hindu peasant was quite hard in the Medieval period; and this economic factor played a very vital role in precipitating communalism to its worst degree. Contemporary records are full of the horrors of famine, mass exploitation and persecution, yet all these vicissitudes in the life of peasantry did not tamper with one institution that continued to survive even amidst such a state of ceaseless chaos and confusion. It was the institution called the village community.

In spite of the breakdown of the Mughal administration and power, the structure of the village community which now rested on the shoulders of Hindus and Muslims, survived every onslaught. Referring to the conditions that had emerged by the first quarter of the nineteenth century, O'Malley observes:

> "It would be a mistake to assume that the forms of government disappeared. They still existed but were made the instruments of arbitrary power and oppression. Moreover the social system did not collapse and culture was not destroyed. The institutions that governed personal relations such as the joint family and the caste system, were not affected by wars and revolutions, and they continued to regulate the internal life of Hindu society in the midst of tumult and strife".

Referring to the village community, he further says:

> "Unless, as sometimes happened villages were

> exterminated or abandoned, the communal form of organization represented by the village community still functioned, though the solidarity was often impaired by its members taking advantage of the general disorder to fight each for his own land. Owing to the tenacity with which the peasantry cling to their land and landed rights, the agrarian system, though thrown out of gear, was not broken up: in India village rights remain when kingdoms passed away. Those who fled before the storm returned when there was a measure of peace and security, rebuilt their houses, reclaimed the village land and re-established the proprietary shares which had existed before their disposition".

In conclusion he writes,

> "There was undoubtedly economic deterioration, but despite the disorder caused by war and mis-government trade and industry continued on a scale sufficient to make India the objective of European commercial enterprise".[2]

As we have seen, of all the commercial enterprises, the British were the most successful. They settled and began administering the land in the way that would suit the interests of the British Empire.

(i) Broadly speaking there were two schools of administration. One was led by Warren Hastings, 'who was convinced that the British power must be an Indian power, interfering as little as possible with Indian customs'. He laid down the principle that its authority should be founded on the ancient laws of the country. This policy was later on taken up at the instance of Sir Thomas Munro in Madras, Mountstuart Elphinstone in Bombay, and Sir John Malcolm in Central India.

(ii) However, the second school of thought which began to operate effectively towards the close of the Eighteenth century made its aim to remodel the administration on English lines. Lord Cornwallis was its leader. Unlike Warren Hastings, he excluded Indians from responsible office; issued in 1793 judicial regulations which were complicated by formalities of English procedure which resulted in the disuse of the village Courts of Justice known as Panchayats; and to add to the misery of the people, he introduced an English form of landed property and created a class of landlords which was hitherto unknown in India. He was convinced that State ownership of land was against public interest. He genuinely believed in the development of the economic resources of the country on the individual enterprise of 'a class of proprietors resembling English landlords'. This led to the disintegration of the village communities.

As could be expected, the British tampering with the indigenous way of life, resulted in communal disequilibrium and discord which led to communalism and an acute state of social tension in the country.

Describing the deterioration of the relations between the Hindus and Muslims, as a consequence of the destruction of the native structure, a sociologist says:

> "The Hindu-Muslim problem like any other problem followed inevitably from the structural change which came to pass in the whole of Indian life; it resulted in the loss and breakdown of the common and joint life in the community.... it being the sole cause of distress".[3]

He is referring here to the whole issue through what is known as the "Permanent Settlement". This policy which was the result of 'pecuniary needs of the British, introduced landlordism, for which the capitalist valuation of money in European policy' could alone account.

The mischief lay in the fact that a Hindu instead of a Muslim was chosen for the job of a landlord for he could 'secure the revenue' or 'deliver the goods'. He was wealthy and held control over trade and finance in the country. Elucidating the consequences wrought by this structural change, the sociologist proceeds to say:

> "Its immediate result was a serious disturbance in the relationship that prevailed between the Hindus and the Muslims upto that time. The creation of landlordism and the selection of the Hindus as landlords in large number, seriously affected the status and position of the Mohammedans, who had been exercising political authority and power during the Mohammedan rule. No community of men in any part of the world could face this sudden reversal in status with equanimity."

He adds:

> "There are authorities who hold the British policy was meant not merely as a calculating offence to Muslim pride, but as a step to deprive the whole community of its middle class, its only source of advice and guidance in time of distress. The large masses who were on the land, where four-fifth of Mohammedan community belonged were deprived by his policy of the rights and privileges which occupancy in the Indian system implied. Consequently the bulk of the Mohammedan community was not only deprived of their middle and aristocratic classes, but put at the mercy of landlordism which by accident came to be vested in the Hindus".[4]

Referring to this fresh cause of disagreement that naturally arose between the Hindus and Mohammedans, the sociologist in conclusions says:

> "It is here... that the origin of the Mohammedan problem is to be sought. Whatever disagreement between them might have been in past and however, they might have assured the proportions of serious cultural and religious clashes, the feature and character of the British phase of the problem can be wholly accounted for by the British policy which Lord Cornwallis introduced into India, or by the variants of his policy which were practised in other parts. The problem is entirely political or economic in its character and has no real connection with the religion and culture of the two peoples, whatever illusion the technique of the Mohammedan fight might create for the moment".[5]
>
> "The truth is", as the sociologist correctly writes that "not only the Hindu-Muslim problem, but every other problem which has been associated with the British period took its rise from this policy and the change that it brought about".[6]

As could be expected, because of the destruction of the native structure, particularly the village community, the embers of communal tension continued to glow. Quite later their intensity tremendously affected the British system of law and order, sometimes even leading to its partial paralysis.

For instance, towards the close of the Nineteenth century, the

Hindu-Muslim disturbances in India had become quite widespread. They even defied every attempt of the ruler to quell them, so much so, that at many a place, they acquired a seditious colour. It is during such a tragic state of time that the then Chief Secretary of North Western Provinces and Oudh, in an explanatory note dated, the 18th September, 1893, from Nainital addressed to the Secretary of the Home Department of Government of India confirms the above thesis. He emphatically hinted at the policy of British rulers in destroying the native structure.

He writes:

> "Sir Charles Crosthwaite believes that the true way of administering India is by enforcing village responsibility and compelling people to control each other, or if they cannot, to inform the authorities and to enable them to do it".
>
> "In these provinces the tendency for years has been to break up and disintegrate the village communities. We have attempted to keep order and suppress crime by means of an outside police who seem yearly to become more feeble and corrupt and are hated by the people".[7]

Yet another aspect of communalism on the economic plane, with a special reference to the Hindu-Muslim problem as it came to pass in India emerged with the rise of the middle-class in India. It was the result of the new capitalist economic structure which developed in India as an outcome of the British conquest. It was another way in which the British had tampered with the equilibrium of the indigenous communal existence.

The process of the rise of this middle-class in different parts of the country was an uneven one. The reason in part lay in the fact of 'uneven spread of the new social economy, both in time and tempo since this spread depended on the growth of political power of the British in India'. Elucidating this point a sociologist aptly remarks:

"The conquest of India by Britain resulting in the economic transformation which it led to, was not a single simultaneous event. India was subdivided by Britain by instalments and through stages. Different parts of the country became more or less economically transformed on the new capitalist basis in sequence of their political subjugation. Hence, new social classes came into being earlier in those zones which came under British sway earlier. This is why it was in Bengal, which was among the first prizes which fell to Britain and where the British Government created for the first time in Indian history, private property in land in the shape of Zamindari, that two of the new social classes, the Zamindars and the tenants, came first into existence. It was also therefore, in Bengal and Bombay, that first industrial enterprises such as jute and cotton factories were started leading thereby to the emergence of such new classes as industrialists and proletariat. Further, it was for the same reason first in these provinces that Britain established a complex, well ramified, administrative system and introduced new educational institutions, imparting knowledge in modern sciences such as modern medicine, law, etc., thereby leading to the growth of the professional classes first here".[8]

The rise of the various social classes in main comprised of the following two sets. In the rural areas they were principally the Zamindars; the absentee landlords; peasant proprietors; tenants and agricultural labourers; modern class of merchants and money lenders. In the urban areas they were principally the capitalists, (industrial, commercial and financial); the working class (belonging to industrial, transport, mining, etc.); the class of petty traders and shopkeepers (bound up with modern capitalist economy; the professional classes (e.g. technicians, doctors, lawyers, professors, journalists, managers, clerks; mostly people belonging to the intelligentsia and the educated middle-class).

Another striking feature of the rise of these new social classes, as also of the typically modern class was their uneven growth amongst various communities in India.

As Dr. Desai comments:

> "The process of the rise of the new social classes, among different communities was also an uneven one. This was due to the fact that certain communities were engaged in the pre-British period, in definite-economic, social or educational vocations. For instance, in pre-British society, mainly the Banyas, more traders and Shroffs, and the Brahmins, the custodians of education among the Hindus.

> In the new social environment, the Banyas were among the first groups (another being the Parsis) to take to modern capitalist commerce and banking and develop into new social classes, namely the commercial and financial bourgeoisie. Similarly, the Brahmins were among the first to study and assimilate the modern education introduced by the British Government and project a modern intelligentsia and an educated middle class".

He further adds:

> "The upper strata of the Muslim community in the pre-British period were, on the whole, divorced from medieval trade or money lending and were mainly engaged in military and administrative careers. Further, they predominantly resided in Northern India which came under British rule much later. The vast population of Bengal mainly belonged to the poorer classes. Hence, a modern intelligentsia, a modern educated middle-class and a bourgeoisie, on a substantial scale, sprang from within the Muslim community later than from the Hindus community"[9].

A proper understanding of this phenomenon of the unequal rise of the middle-class of the various communities needs a deeper historical examination of the conditions prevailing in the Nineteenth century in India. Primarily it was the result of a "communal lag", which was caused because of a difference in the nature of the reaction of the indigenous communities to the Western domination. The reaction of the Muslim was negative in nature, whereas that of Hindus had a positive outlook. As a result thereof, a "communal-lag" became inevitable and it had a deep influence on the relations between the Hindus and the Muslims, both in the Nineteenth and the first half of the Twentieth century.

In the case of the Muslims, the establishment of the foreign rule was in the nature of a triple shock. Religiously, it has placed them in a land which was no more Dar-al-Islam, but which had now become Dar-al-harb (land of war). Culturally, the Christian rulers envisaged a system which was quite opposed to the traditional Islamic way of life. From the political point of view, the British had removed them from the pedestal of power reducing them to the status of an insignificant minority. The Muslims reacted in a negative manner and thus suffered immeasurable material loss.

On the Religious Plane, the Muslims reaction expressed itself in the form of four movements, which are commonly known as the Communal rising of the Wahabis. They had four different leaders, viz. Shah Abdul Aziz of Delhi, Saiyid Ahmad of Bareli, Sheikh Karamat Ali of Jaunpur and Haji Shariat Ullah of Faridpur. These movements were known as the Wahabi movements because they all aimed at the reformation of Islam in India, similar to the manner in which a movement was started in Arabia by Mohammad bin Abdul Wahhab (1707-87) to purify Islam.

The communal rising of the Wahabis was both anti-Hindu and anti-British in nature.

Shah Abdul Aziz taught the need for purging Islam of the practices borrowed from Hindus. Abdul Ahmed Brelvi who was a saint-freebooter, launched a holy war against the Sikhs and the British. Doctrinally, he advocated a Muhamdi Tariqa or the way of Mohammad the Prophet. Karamat Ali tried to stabilize Muslim opinion. His main effort was to reconcile the anti-British opinion of Muslims, on the conditions that India was not a Dar-Al-Harb. The Faraizi's under the leadership of Haji Shariat Ullah of Faridpur also preached the purity of faith and conduct and obtained a large following among the peasantry. Since the population of the Eastern Bengal was mostly Muslim and the landlords mostly Hindu, movement was as much agrarian as religious, and it many a time resulted in Hindu-Muslim riots.

These puritan movements tremendously affected the Hindu-Muslim relations in India. The lower class Muslims emerged more communal than ever before, and the economic bitterness continued to increase on both the sides. W.C. Smith treats this movement as a purely class struggle. He says,

> "In addition to expressing an uprising of the peasantry against the landlords, the 'Wahabi' movement was also, especially in mid century a sort of Indian laddite movement, a protest of the Indian craftsman against the introduction of machine goods".

He further adds:

> "In any case, the affair was a class struggle, and the

communalistic confusion of the issue is evaporated. The movement made use of a religious ideology as class struggles in pre-industrialist society have often done, but though religious, it was not simple communalist.... none the less it did religious thinking and left a considerable section of the Muslim masses more susceptible to later communalist propaganda than they might otherwise have been".[10]

It was while referring to this communal aspect of the Wahabi movement that Dr. Sachin Sen wrote that,

"Historically speaking the Indian Wahabi Movement is the precursor of the Aligarh movement, the Khilafat Movement, the Pan-Islamic Movement and the Pakistan Movement which rocked Indian Muslims".[11]

Whatever might have been the impact of the Wahabi movement on the growth of Hindu-Muslim relations, its most serious aspect lay in its attitude towards the British. From Sittana Camp, in the valley of Swat at the North West Frontier border, to the plains of Bengal and down to the Southern Peninsula, the movement had spread itself through the length and breadth of the country. The British Government of India who in due regard to their policy of 'Counterpoise' had earlier ignored this movement as a purely anti-Hindu rising, became alert and made extensive enquiries, which unearthed the presence of a highly treasonable conspiracy in the country. As a matter of fact, the Wahabis had launched a religious crusade against their infidel conqueror and they involved them in many a military campaign.

The embers of Wahabi unrest continued to glow as late as the year 1870. Shurfrool-Oomrah - Bahadoor who happened to be a member of the Legislative Council in a memoranda for private information, addressed to Rt. Hon'ble Sir J.L.M. Lawrence Viceroy and Governor-General, dated the Adyar, Madras 14th August, 1865 wrote:

"I am sorry to say of the Mohammedan religious community which requires carefully to be watched and looked after and if what I have stated induces to action, which will arrest the growth and progress of this sect, and thus to a considerable extent destroy one of the disturbing causes of the peace of India, I shall feel myself sufficiently rewarded".[12]

As from the South India so from the East, H.L. Dampier Esq., officiating Secretary to the Bengal, in a letter addressed to A.P. Howell, Secretary to the Government of India, Simla dated the 16th November, 1868, informed:

> "It having been brought to the Lt. Governor's notice that an active movement of some kind was taking place among the Mohammedans of the Wahabi sect in several districts of the lower provinces, the Head of the Detective Department of Bengal Police was deputed to make enquiries into its nature and extent. From Mr. Reilly's (the deputed D.I.G. of the Special Bengal Police), enquiry it appears to be certain that a Jihad or a religious war against the British power has for sometimes been preached and collections in aid of the Hindoostanee fanatics on the Frontier made as a regularly organized system".

J.M. Reilly in his report further adds:

> "The extra assistant found that contributions were openly made in several villages contiguous to Kallia Chuck (a place) for a Jihad or religious war against the English with the intention of restoring the Mohammedan rule and driving the Kafir, English, out of the country".[13]

As could be expected, the Muslims as a community thoroughly antagonized the British against themselves, whose fury fell on them in a systematic policy of discrimination and legal oppression. In an important minute John Strechy wrote:

> "It is really preposterous that while we are told that there is ample evidence to show that certain persons have taken an active part in preaching a Jihad, and in collecting money for the avowed purpose of upsetting our Government, there should be room for doubt whether these persons are punishable under the existing law".[14]

Consequently, since from the 'beginning of the Eighteenth to almost the end of the Nineteenth century, the British looked upon Indian Muslims as their chief enemies or potential sources of danger', therefore, their hand fell heavily against Muslims than on those belonging to other communities. As early as 1843, Lord

Ellenborough, the then Governor-General of India, sent a warning to London and suggested 'the use of communalism to preserve imperialist use'. He wrote.

> "I cannot close my eyes to the belief that (Mohammedan) race is fundamentally hostile to us and our true policy is to reconciliate the Hindus".[15]

The upper-Muslim classes were the worst sufferers in this respect because their active participation in the mutiny of 1857 led, not only to their severe oppression at the hands of the Government, but also led to their economic impoverishment. As Yusuf Ali observes:

> 'The tragedy of the great revolt in 1857-58 marks the death of the old order, and brought political, economic and cultural disaster to the Indian Muslims. It made their sullenness, their aloofness, their suppressed hatred for the new order, more marked than ever. For many years afterwards the Muslims steadily lost ground in education, in the public services, and in the general leadership in India".[16]

On the cultural plane too the Muslims reacted in an anti-British spirit. Consequently, as a community they not only underwent a period of intellectual sterility, but in the long run they also suffered heavy economic loss. The result of the attitude of the Mohammedans has been aptly summarized by E.F. Bayley in one of his important notes. He wrote: "The truth is that, before the advent of the English, the Mohammedans were not merely the main political power but the main intellectual power in the state; they possessed a system of education which having been inferior in every way to that which we have now established, was yet by no means to be despised; it was capable of affording a very high degree of intellectual training and polish; was founded on principles not wholly unsound, though presented in an antiquated form; and which was, at any rate, infinitely superior to all other systems of education then existing in India; its universal acceptance by Mohammedans secured to them intellectual as well as material supremacy; indeed it was only through the medium of this education that Hindus could hope to fit themselves for even the smallest share of authority in their native country.

In fact, when we assumed the Government, it was to this system that we were compelled to look for the training of the large Native agency which we were obliged to employ; indeed it may be said that we continued mainly to draw upon this source for nearly a hundred years.

Naturally they received our system which, it may be said, was: "at once antagonistic to theirs", with suspicion and dislike; they did not believe in its superiority; it gave them no advantages over the Hindus, whom they disliked and despised: it failed to supply them religious requirements; it ran counter to their feelings and to their prejudices. It was even for a long time a very hotly disputed point among them whether education in any but a old tongue was lawful or not. Now there is favour for English and a stronger distaste in respect to education through the language of idolatrous Hindus, above all in regard to receiving education from a man of that race.

It is no wonder that they held aloof. Their own system of education now is no longer remunerative and has become less common among the poorer classes, whose position in the social scale has also somewhat fallen until at last there is danger that the entire Mohammedan community will rapidly be transformed into a mass of disloyal ignorant fanatics on the one hand, with on the other a small class of men highly educated in a narrow fashion, highly fanatic and not unwarrantly discontented, exercising an enormous influence over their ignorant fellow Mohammedans.

Lastly, from the political point of view too, the Muslim community underwent loss of power and dignity, loss of honourable employment, and the comforts of material life'. Because of their injured pride, general mental attitude was one of opposition to the British. Secondly, since they kept themselves aloof from English education, they also failed to justify for even ordinary administrative posts in the Government offices, because official business was conducted in English. Finally, the British attitude had also become stiff. After having tested Muslim hostility in the form of Wahabi Movement and the mutiny of 1857, they did not entertain much lively feelings towards them. As a result not only were they deprived of any position of vantage but their came a time as late as the year 1913, when in spite of a shift in the British policy, Muslim community could not supply even clerks. This can be very clearly seen from the following extract from an official minute of R.M. Craddock. He wrote:

> "The question of Mohammedans clerks is of great interest and importance. When I was in the Central Provinces as Commissioner and Chief Commissioner, I was exceedingly anxious to get many more Mohammedans into our offices, but it was most difficult to get the men. Mohammedans who wanted clerkships had insufficient education, and Mohammedans with sufficient education would not look at Clerkships".

He further added:

> "The number of Mohammedans in posts where the standard of education required is small is very satisfactory (e.g.) in the police, the forests, in the subordinate executive service, but directly higher and more technical education was required there were no men available, on the judicial side there were next to none. In the Medical, Public Works Department, and other technical services, there were a few in the lower branches, but next to none in the higher. In conclusion he said, "In the Central Provinces we drew largely on the United Provinces for our Mohammedans, the purely local supply being hopelessly limited. I cordially support any measure which will bring more Mohammedans into the public services, but it is at present a question of Education".[17]

The truth is that as stated earlier, since the very beginning the Muslims kept themselves aloof and isolated from the changes that were overtaking the country. Hindus, however, were sagacious enough not to alienate themselves from the same and tried to regain their lost ground by taking full advantage of the changing time. They might have opposed British rule in more than one way, but they took to English education only too readily, they valued it for its own sake, as the education for progress, as also because it unlocked the door to power and position. 'The Muslims were not among those who craved for the English education. A large number preferred an education which would give their sons a place of honour among the learned men of their community to one which would equip them for official or professional life'. The memorandum of Henry Thoby Prinsep, submitted on February, the 15th 1835, amply bears it out:

> "Undoubtedly", ran the memorandum, "there is a very widely spread anxiety at this time for the attainment of a certain proficiency in English. The sentiment is to be encouraged by all means as the source and forerunner of great moral improvement to those who feel its influence; but there is no single member of the education committee who will venture to assert that this disposition has yet shown itself extensively among the Mussalmans. It is the Hindus of Calcutta, the Sirkars (Accountants and Commercial managers) and Kulin (Brahman) connections, and the descendants and relations of the Sirkars of former days, those who have risen through their connection with the English and with public offices, men who hold that a knowledge of English is a very necessary qualification. These are the classes of persons to whom the study of English is as yet confined; and certainly we have no reason yet to believe that the Mussalmans in any part of India can be reconciled to the cultivation of it, much less give it a preference to the polite literature of their race or to what they look upon as such".[18]

Prinsep who was a member of the Committee of Public Instruction, opposed Macaulay's insistence on introducing English 'The Natives', said Macaulay,' are desirous to be taught English and are not desirous to be taught Sanskrit or Arabic'. English learning was the learning for which they are craving. The feelings of the Muslims were correctly interpreted by Prinsep. Muslims could attach themselves only to the traditional Islamic learning which comprised of Arabic language of their Holy Book, and Persian, the language of culture. Macaulay probably, could never understand this fact. Muslims insisted as they have always done, on the teaching of Islam as the true curriculum of education of a Muslim boy. Obviously, neither the Government nor the Muslims could benefit from each other. It was the Hindu who gained the most. He stole a march over his Muslim brethren in the field of educational and administrative posts.

Even at the cost of some repetition of ideas, we feel tempted to quote at length from a Memorandum of J.O. Kinnely Esq. It throws vivid light on the attitude of the two communities towards English education, and the consequent 'Communal lag' that it caused.

He wrote "I think that we may assume it as generally admitted that our Mussalman subjects are neither educated nor friendly, and I conceive that both these evils may be to a great extent removed."

In speaking of Mohammedans, I confine myself to the Sunnis. The Shiahs are few in number and confined to the large cities, such as Lucknow, Patna, Moorshidabad and Dacca. They exercise little influence on the mass of people, who are all Sunnis."

During the Mohammedan rule, Muslims were chiefly employed in the service of the state as judicial and executive officers; the land was the property of the ruling power, consequently they would not acquire large real estates, and the little land they possessed was Lakhiraj — granted as gifts by the different subedars, etc. They did not covet direct contact with the ryots, but looked higher and were either the official superiors of the large rent collectors, or afterwards created proprietors under our rule, or hangers on about the native courts, such as persons who belonged to the learned classes and subsisted on pensions granted to them by the rulers.

After our accession to the Diwani, matters remained as they were before. We took it under a kind of promise to carry on the Muslim rule as it then existed and we did so. The Mohammedan law continued to be the law of the land and the judicial and executive appointments remained in the hands of Mussalmans.

The first blow the Mohammeddan community received was of the Permanent Settlement Law which elevated the Hindu collectors, who upto that time, had held but unimportant posts, to the position of landlords, gave them a proprietary right in the soil, and allowed them to accumulate wealth which would have gone to the Mussalmans under their own rule.

The resumption laws fell heavily on the Mussalmans, and deprived many of the learned classed in Bihar and Bengal of the means of living respectably. The annexation of India and mutiny did the same for the Mohammedans of Delhi and Lucknow. It is not, therefore, to be wondered at, that these persons, who were fostered by Native Governments and despite trade, are unfriendly to our rule.

The determination on the part of Government to carry out a system of English education was unfavourable to Mussalmans, and a great boon to Hindus. The latter for ages, subject to a foreign power, had no dislike to learn the language of their rulers. As they learned Persian and oordoo, etc., under the Mohammedans, so they learned English under us.

But it was different with the former. They objected; they said that they feared lest an English education might undermine their religion, but this objection was not the whole truth. In reality, it was far more serious. According to the Mohammedan Law, as responded by Sunnis of the old school, it is not lawful to learn English, or the language of any other non-Mussalman people except for the purpose of answering letters, or of combating the religious arguments of that people. Learning a foreign language for any other purpose is not allowed. This antagonistic feeling has, to a certain extent, passed away but not wholly.

This question, and how far service under a non-believing Government is allowable, have often been discussed and decided by the learned classes....... At first, the change in Education did not effect the Mohammedans directly. They still held the chief appointments, but as the administration of the country has more and more been carried on in the language of its rulers, the learned Mohammedans sacrificed their positions to their belief, and those who learned English and took their place, possessed neither the position nor authority of those who went before them and even in the present day, English speaking Mohammedans possess but little influence except what appertains to their position as Government officials.

The abolition of the Mohammedan Law Officers on the introduction of the Penal Code deprived Mussalmans of mostly all the remaining respectable appointments, not requiring a knowledge of English and greatly checked vernacular education.

A few *Qazees* received Judicial appointments, but as a Mussalman once said, "Chuprassees, duftries and some peons are the only Mussalman officers in Bengal", and there does not seem much chance of improvement, for the High Court, by a late rule, has excluded persons not members of the Calcutta University from the Higher Judicial appointments. The relative number of Hindus and Muslims at present in the service of the Bengal Government are as follows:[19]

	Hindus	*Muslims*
Deputy Collectors, Sub Registrars & Assessors	242	40
Judicial Officers.	180	38
	420	78

But it may be said that the present state of the Mohammedan is the fault within themselves, that they have not learned English. No doubt this is true, but it appears to me totally beside the question, which is not what is the fault of the Mohammedans from our point of view, but whether it is wise in Government to strive and push on the people what they do not appreciate and do not desire, especially as a sound vernacular education will have the effect of inducing the people to learn English. The best answer to such a line of argument is the foundation of the Lahore 'Varsity .... Formerly it was the custom for all respectable Mohammedans to keep a kind of school in which the sons of poor Mohammedans were taught. As long as they were rich enough to support this, a certain amount of education was diffused among them, but when they lost Government service their means became narrowed and they rapidly fell into a state of ignorance.

The Government schools have never been freely resorted to, for the simple reason that there is no religious teaching; no provision for the appointment of Maulvies to teach Order, Persian or Arabic, and that the masters are Hindus, instead of Mussalmans. And although it may be argued that Government was right and the Mohammedans wrong in not attending them, the fact still remains the same, that Mohammedans have not and will not freely attend the schools under such circumstances.

These things are matters of feelings and not of reason because of saying prayers in Arabic or Persian.

I attribute the great hold which Wahabi doctrines have on the mass of the Mohammedan Ryots, to our neglect of their education.

When Sayyud Ahmud preached in lower Bengal, he made arrangements to render the movement permanent ..... In Bengal then Mussalmans were half Hindus. They adopted many Hindu customs and assisted at some of the Hindu religious ceremonies. His teachings progressed simply because it was in the main correct. Almost all the Bengalis became his disciples. Since then, great changes have taken place.

Mussalmans have become more religious, more estranged from the Hindus and have changed the mode of wearing their garments in order that they may not be confounded with them......

It takes it to be admitted that Government is bound to meet the wishes of the Mohammedan people on the question of education provided that they do not demand more than a fair share of the Government revenue, and that the teaching is loyal.

The system of secular education in Ireland has been strongly commented upon lately by both Protestants and Roman Catholics and if any doubts as to its propriety exist in Ireland how careful ought we to be in adopting the same system among an illiterate, fanatical people like the Mussalmans of India".[20]

The Hindu Reaction: It is obvious, therefore, that the reaction of the Hindus to the Western impact was not one of unmixed opposition. In fact, at first, they were levelled in a state of dilemma. They had hardly achieved political ascendancy over the despotic tyrannies of the Mughal autocrats when their independence was again lost to the British. Their immediate quest was one of re-emancipation from the new clutches. It was not so easy a thing, nor did they have any immediate solution except to live another life of servitude, and, if possible to try to reunite their own disintegrated community. As such, quite contrary to the policy of the Muslims, their approach was more towards the positive side of life and a large element among the Hindus, unlike the Muslims accepted Western education without any qualms.

It was this practical attitude of the Hindus that brought about the "communal lag" referred above. Thus they gained whereas the Muslims lost; they went ahead while the Muslims were left behind, and in spite of all their shortcomings and an acute sense of hostility towards the British, they stole a march over their other communal competitors in every walk of life.

Strange though it may seem, yet an historical examination of the facts clearly reveals that the secret of Hindu success, and of

Muslim failure to keep pace with the exigencies of the time, lay in their respective religion. Unlike Islam, Hinduism does not harbour any creed of non-co-existence. It holds a firm belief in the co-existence of thought and life. As O'Malley writes:

> "The spread of Western Education and ideals stimulated movements within Hinduism designed to preserve its essential principles and at the same time to remove excrescences which were opposed not only to the spirit of Hinduism but also the ideals spread by Western culture. What is the spirit of Hinduism? What are the essential principles? The spirit of science is not dogmatic certainly but the disinterested pursuit of truth, and Hinduism is infused by the same spirit. As I have remarked in another work(*), Hinduism sets itself of no such limits. It is comprehensive and synthetic, seeking unity not in a common creed but in a common quest for truth. Hinduism is more a way of life than a form of thought. It insists not on religious conformity but on a spiritual and ethical outlook in life. It is a fellowship of all who accept the Law of right and earnestly seek for the truth".[21]

He further adds:

> "The contradictory criticism urged against Hindu religion that it is pantheism and illusionism point to an imperfect understanding of the riches of spiritual life. Hinduism is a comprehensive religion which has sounded the depths of man's search for reality and has brought its results together in a vast synthesis which is able to help persons in different stages of evolution.
>
> The reactions of Hinduism to Western influences have varied from blind initiation of the West, to an unthinking hostility and opposition to it, with at present, a more balanced attitude. Hinduism, however, has the tenacity characteristic of a living organism, and the movements started by the more thoughtful reformers, the Brahmo Samaj, the Arya Samaj and the Rama Krishna Mission, are expressions of its spirit. All reaffirm the adequacy of the Hindu religion in its essence but demand a reordering of Society to suit Modern needs".[22]

On the religious plane, therefore, the Hindu reaction was more in the nature of a synthetic effort to seek truth and to reorder society by ridding religion of its degenerate practices and other associated evils. The Hindu Religious Movements were revivalistic in character and each community kept its pristine glory and religious purity as the norm of its present day reform. Referring to the causes which led to these movements Farquhar says:

> "The causes which have combined to create the movements are many. The stimulating forces are almost exclusively Western, viz. the British Government, English education and literature, Christianity, oriental research, European science and philosophy, and the material elements of Western civilisation; but the beliefs and the organisation of the ancient faiths have been moulding forces of great potency"[23].

The Hindu and the Muslim revivalist movements had a most striking feature of difference. They had quite opposite effects on the life of the respective communities. Whereas, in the case of Muslims, it led to a decadence of standards and loss of leadership, in the case of Hindus, it threw up a galaxy of liberal reformers and enlightened scholars. It is these scholars and reformers, whose efforts led to a renaissance or reawakening in the Hindu world, which brought Hindus to the forefront in every avenue of national life, whether political, economic or educational.

In the light of the historical investigation made above, we can trace out the root cause of the growth of communalism in the Nineteenth century India. The crux of the problem lies in the impact of the British system of economy and education and the consequent varied and uneven reaction of the indigenous communities. As Dr. Beni Prasad put it:

> "Contact Cross-fertilises cultures; the impact of the West set in motion new currents in the domains of religion, philosophy, literature, institutions and economics. India had integrated the new elements into a consistent whole. The intellectual and moral effort evoked by the root problems has necessarily been very complicated but it is possible to distinguish two tendencies sometimes running parallel to each other, sometimes reinforcing and

> sometimes conflicting with each other. From their interaction and from the accompanying political reaction, arose the Hindu Muslim problem in its present phase. The two tendencies may be designated for the same of convenience, modernism and revivalism"[24].

We have seen how the indigenous reaction manifested itself in both these tendencies. A Hindu middle-class which is, economically more secure, intellectually more enlightened, and, socially far purer, emerges sooner than the Muslim middle-class; for the community as a whole continues till the last decade of the Nineteenth century to be a community of illiterate, fanatic and frustrated people. It is to this fact of "communal-lag", that we attribute the growth of communalism. It was this disparity of the rise of the middle-class that led to mutual estrangement between different communities. Ultimately it was purely an economic question, as the growth of the indigenous population was to be fitted in the capitalistic economic structure introduced by the British. As Joan Beauchamp observes:

> "The expansion of British capitalism, which pursued its expioitation farther and farther into the country in search of raw materials and a market for manufactured goods, created in the process a class of Indian middlemen. The need of the British Government and commercial firms for clerks and other employees, on a far larger scale than could be supplied from England, was the basis for the introduction in India of the Modern education in the second decade of the Nineteenth century. From then on the Indian bourgeoisie grew very rapidly, capturing entirely the professions of medicine, law and teaching, and gradually accumulating wealth"[25].

Now, who was there qualified enough to enter these professions and to secure a share in the only large industry created by the Government namely, the public service? Who was it who had the Western education to assist him to adjust to these modern developments? Who had made himself more amenable to new masters?

Clearly enough, it was not a Muslim but a Hindu, who was more competent and qualified than the other competitors in the field. It was a strange coincidence that he formed a majority community, and hence he could capture a far larger share in the administrative, economic and political life of the country. It is this fact of 'communal-lag' which lies behind communalism. As W.C. Smith observes:

> "The fact behind this that the share of Muslims in middle class development is relatively weak lies at the very heart of the present day communal discord, as well as having contributed much to the rise of Communalism in the Nineteenth Century"[26].

We now turn to examine in some detail the efforts that different communities made in order to bridge the economic gulf that was an inevitable consequence of this uneven speed of progress in the new setting. This communal race of "struggle for existence", took the form of a scramble for the leaves and fishes which came by way of Government jobs, seats in the Legislative Assemblies, and various other facilities. Naturally, each community had to look up to the British for patronage and favour for it is they who distributed offices of profit and of dignity. What was true of the public services, was also true of the political advancement of the natives, for it too depended on the attitude of the rulers.

This struggle on the part of the indigenous communities expressed itself, at first, in the form of "prayers, petitions and protests". Each community was conscious of the fact that its material prosperity and advancement depended on the discretion and sweet will of the new master, and that it would not come by itself, unless it was sought as a special favour. From the British point of view, the concessions and the favours were to be distributed to a community as an isolated communal unit rather than as a part of a larger nation. Those benefits were not to be bestowed on the nation but on castes, creeds, and communities with a view to keep them apart. Each group, each class and each interest was to be encouraged or discouraged in accordance with the needs of the hour. British interest, we may reiterate, was confined to the ever increasing consolidation of the empire. As such, the policy of `Exploitation and Counterpoise' was a perfect complement of the larger policy that they adopted in the greatest "association of Indians" with the ruling party.

These efforts of the various communities for conciliation with the British and for competition amongst themselves throw an interesting sidelight on the disparity of the means they adopted at different stages. For instance, towards the closing decades of the Nineteenth century, the Hindus discarded the old conciliatory attitude, and taking up an agitational approach, formed political organization to fulfil their aims and objects — though these aims and objects were as yet in an amorphous state and not clearly formulated. It was exactly at the same period, that the Muslims, realizing the consequences of their old isolationist trends, made a beginning with a reconciliation to Western ways and education, which the Hindus had taken up long ago. Under the force of circumstances, the Muslims had to adopt precisely those means which the Hindus took up more than a century back, viz., a re-orientation and reformation on the Western lines, within their own communal field.

The tendency to organize a communal unit in order to gain political ends was invariably the consequence of the educational advancement on the Western lines. Thus, we find that the fact of "Communal-Lag" does not get annulled as time rolls by. It increases year by year intensifying communalism on all fronts. Before we examine its nature in the new setting that was ushered in after the close of the Nineteenth century, it is worthwhile to observe the way in which the various communities proceed in a cut throat competition for greater prosperity of one's community.

In spite of the fact that an overwhelming majority of the Muslim community in the ranks of the nobility as also of the commoners, was against the British Government, we come across few exceptionally important attempts to re-improve the Anglo-Muslim relations through an expression of their loyalty to British Government. The Mohammedans of Bengal were pioneers in this respect. They had organized themselves into an association known as the "Mohammedan Association". Quite a few prominent Muslims used to be its members. The names of Messers Fuzular Rehman, Abdool Baru, Mohd. Wajoeb, Rohmat Ali, Abdool Laiteef, Gholam Esa, Mohd. Abdoor Rowoof, Syed Murhumut Hosain, Abbas Ali and Mohd. Muzhar, stand out amongst those who formed its leadership. The association emphatically pleaded for the "good Government which British rule had introduced into this country". The association was conscious of the consequences that were to follow after the mutiny. Obviously, in order to plead the innocence of the Muslims as a community, they preached the sermon of implicit faith in the rule of the Firanghis.

Soon after the administration of the Indian territory was taken over by the British Crown, the association submitted an address to Queen, on the subject of Her Majesty's proclamation, vouchsafing their sense of gratitude and allegiance to the Crown, and beseeching an adequate and due distribution of posts and places of honour in the country. It is a document of great importance and we therefore give its full text. It runs as follows:

"To

> The Queen's most Excellent Majesty, May it please your Majesty.
>
> We your Majesty's most loyal and humble subjects belonging to the Mohammedan Community of India, beseech your Majesty's permission to approach your Majesty's throne, with these our most loyal and respectful acknowledgements for your Majesty's most Gracious Proclamation read to us on the Ist of the present month of November, 1856, by one of the secretaries of your Majesty's Indian Government.
>
> And we humbly beg to lay at Your Majesty's feet this the expression of our most complete satisfaction at the announcement made in Your Majesty's most Gracious Proclamation aforesaid of having assumed in Your Majesty's Indian territories.
>
> And we humbly beg to lay before Your Majesty also this the expression of our heartfelt gratitude for the gracious interest in, and solicitude for, the good and prosperity of Your Majesty's Indian subjects, evinced in Your Majesty's Indian subjects evinced in Your Majesty's Gracious Proclamation aforesaid.
>
> And we beg leave to lay before Your Majesty also this the expression of our deep appreciation of the value of the promises made and intention set-forth in Your Majesty's Gracious Proclamation aforesaid, more particularly of Your

Majesty's gracious intention to protect all Your Majesty's Indian subjects in the free exercise of their respective religions to secure them in the enjoyment of their ancient rights in the land to advance them according to their desert to posts of honour and/ trust in Your Majesty's Royal Service and to cause to be regarded in with care their ancient rights, usages and customs.

And we further crave to hereby most respectfully represent unto Your Majesty, our admiration of the Royal clemency which extends to persons guilty of having thrown off their allegiance to Your Majesty, in the course of the recent unhappy disturbance, the fittest pardon and oblivion of their offences and also our admiration of the judgment and discrimination, which exclude from the benefit of such pardon and oblivion, persons guilty of offences which it were alike unjust and impolitic to let go unpunished.

And we most humbly beg Your Majesty's permission to represent unto Your Majesty our earnest and deep-rooted belief and conviction that in the promulgation of Your Majesty's rules and that of Your Majesty's Heirs, and Successors over these territories is to be found the best and truest security for that prosperity and social advancement which it is Your Majesty's gracious desire to promote in Your Majesty's Indian Dominions and we further most humbly be such that Your Majesty will be graciously pleased to place truest and reliance upon the earnestness and sincerity of this our representation.

And lastly, we most humbly beseech Your Majesty's permission to join Your Majesty in prayer to Almighty God that, by vouchsafing strength and knowledge to all, He may enable Your Majesty and Your Majesty's Heirs and Successors to fulfil and realize the gracious intentions of Your Majesty's as contained in Your Majesty's most Gracious proclamation aforesaid.

"And we humbly beg Your Majesty's permission to subscribe ourselves as Your Majesty's most dutiful subjects:

Calcutta

14th November, 1856"[27].

This memorial was in the nature of a request to the Government of India that in any future distribution of posts of 'honour and trust', the Muslims should not be neglected. In a similar manner, on the religious plane too, the Muslims took certain steps to remove anti-British feelings from the minds of the members of their community. In this respect, the educated Bengali Muslims indeed played a very prominent role in bringing about a rapproachment between the Muslims and the British Government. In the year 1863, Moulvie Abdool Lateef, Khan Bahadoor, Member of the Legislative Council of the Lt. Governor of Bengal, founded a Society known as the Mohammedan Literary Society of Calcutta. The object of the Society was to impart useful information to the higher and educated classes of the Mohammedan community by means of lectures, addresses and discourses on various subjects in literature, science, etc.

The Society had aroused considerable interest in the Mohammedan community and its meetings were well attended by all the respectable members of that community. It had also obtained the 'cordial approval' of the leading members of Government and of European Society at the metropolis.

It was during the month of November, 1870 when the Wahabi movement had inspired Hijrat and completely alienated Muslims from the British rule, that the meeting was addressed by Moulvie Karamat Ali of Jaunpore. He was a well-known Wahabi preacher. He belonged to the Hanafi sect of the Sunnee Mohammedans. He had already worked in Bengal for the last fifty years. The subject of his speech was "that, according to Mohammedan Law, British India is Darul-Islam, and that it is not lawful for the Mohammedans of British India to make Jihad (a holy war)".

The speaker said, "British India which is at present a Christian Government, is Darul-Islam (country of Islam or safety), according to the dogmas of the Hanafi sect.

Such is the Fatwah (opinion of the Doctors of Mohammedan laws). For such is the assertion of ten celebrated law givers Inam Aboo Haneefali and the same has been laid down, either expressly or by implication, in all treatises of Mohammedan law current in India such as the Hidayah 'Sharbi-Vikayah', Jami-ur-Rumoz, Durrul Mukhtar and its two commentaries, the Tahtavee and the

Radul Muhtar; Fatwah Alamgeeree, Fatwah Kazee Khan, Baharur Raik, Nahrul Faik, Fusool Imadee, Nihayatul Murad, Ibrahim Shahee, Ashbah-wan-Nazair, etc.

Important opinions are those of Fatwah[28] Alamgeeree. According to it, Darul-Islam cannot become Darul-Harb until and unless the following conditions are fulfilled.

1. That the Rule of infidels is openly exercised and the Ordinances of Islam are not observed.
2. That it is in such contiguity to a country which is Darul-Harb, that no city of Darul-Islam intervenes between that country and Darul-Harb.
3. That no Moslem is found in the enjoyment of religious liberty, nor a Zimmee (an Infidel who has accepted the terms of permanent subjection to Moslem rule), under the same terms as he enjoyed under the Government of Islam.

After reciting many passages, the learned Moulvie called upon the meeting to consider that not a single one of the three conditions mentioned is to be found in this country.

He said "The first does not exist here. For although the Government of Christian Rulers prevails, still most of the injunctions of Islam are in force among the Mohammedans. The injuctions of Islam that have reference to worship and prayer are in force here entirely. There is no hindrance whatever to their observance.

The injunctions of Islam, that have reference to secular duties are also mostly in full force, in question of marriage, divorce, dower, maintenance, inheritance, gift, endowment, pre-emption, will and the like, arising amongst Mohammedans.

The Mohammedan law is strictly acted upon. It is in exact accordance with the rules laid down in the Mohammedan law that these questions between parties professing the Mohammedan religion are decided by the judicial officers, be the Christians or Hindus. And, especially in questions relating to Pre-emption, the injunctions of Islam are in force even amongst the Hindus upto the present day. The second condition too does not exist in this country. For, not to speak of the countries beyond the frontiers of India, there are many principalities in the very heart of the countries which can be undoubtedly termed Darul-Islam. And, as for the countries beyond the Western and North-Western frontiers of the country, they are all nothing but Darul-Islam.

As to the non-existence of the third condition in this country, it is so clear that no argument whatsoever is necessary.

On the contrary, it is a Christian nation that has come to this country Darul-Herb; and God has given that nation supremacy in this country, and it has become the Ruling Power.

Now, the entire Mohammedan population of this country amounting to more than one third of the inhabitants, have continued just as they were before the advent of the British, and the remaining two-third are Hindus, who were Zimmees (or living under a contract of permanent subjection) during the Mohammedans sway, and are worse off. The population of this country consists almost entirely of these two nations. The Christians, though the Ruling nations, are very few in number, probably less numerous than co-religionists in other countries, ruled over by Mohammedan kings — such as Turkey and Persia.

In conclusion he advised Muslims in the following words:

> "There is no need of Hijrat, for flight is incumbent on a Mohammedan from 'Darul-Harb', and not from this country which is `Darul-Islam'. If it be incumbent to fly from this country, then it would be likewise be incumbent to fly from Turkey and Egypt". The second question is "whether it is lawful in this country to make Jihad or not". This has been solved together with the first. For Jihad can by no means be lawfully made in Darul-Islam. Besides, there exists a cordiality between Turkey and Great Britain, waging of war against the Ruling power of this country, would be rightly pronounced rebellion; and rebellion is strictly forbidden by the Mohammedan law. Therefore such war will likewise be unlawful: and in case any one would wage such war, the Mohammedan subjects would be bound to assist the Rulers: and in conjunction with their Rulers, to fight with such rebels. The above has been clearly laid down in the Fatwah Alamgeeree".[29]

Karamat Ali's opinions were given a wide publicity to which even the Government had lent a tacit support. It had the desired effect and the anti-British feelings atleast of the educated Muslims were gradually toned up to some extent.

Another important effort to cover up the 'Communal-Lag', was made in 1882, when the Central National Mohammedan Association submitted another memorial pointing out the depressed condition of Mohammedans in Bengal, its causes and the remedial measures which, in the opinion of the Association, were required. Apropos this memorial, the Government of India recorded a Resolution, dated July 15, 1885, in which it was observed that:

> "In every Province admission to the superior departments in the service of Government was as a rule, regulated either by public competition, or by the candidate, and that in the opinion of the Governor General in Council, it was neither desirable on general grounds, nor for the advantage of the Mohammedans themselves that they should be exempted from the tests established to secure the admission of duly qualified candidates into the public services,, or that any special favour be shown them in open competition, examination of any description".

It further added:

> It is only by their own educational qualifications to the level already attained by other races that the Mohammedan can hope to win appointments that are awarded as the result of examinations. But there are large number of appointments, the gift of which lie in the hands of the local Governments, the High Courts, or local officers.
>
> The Governor General in Council desires that in those Provinces where Mohammedans do not receive their full share of state employment, the local Governments and High Courts will endeavour to redress this inequality as opportunity offers, and will impress upon subordinate officers, the importance of attending to this in their selection of candidates for appointments of the class last referred to".[30]

It is in this way, therefore that a beginning was made on the part of the British rulers to favour Muslims for a greater share in the offices of the State. In due accordance with the policy of "Exploitation Counterpoise", the British continued to favour the rising Muslim middle-class against the Hindu bourgeoisie, who had towards the close of the Nineteenth century assumed the role of staunch nationalists — a role that the Government looked upon with very suspicious and distrustful eyes.

Hardly a few years passed, when the members of the Central National Mohammedan Association sent another memorial to the Government, regarding the claims of Mohammedans to a proper share of state patronage. It reads as follows:

"May it please your Excellency—

> Your memorialists beg humbly to draw Your Excellency's attention to the difficulties under which in spite of repeated expressions of goodwill on the part of the Mohammedan community generally labour in obtaining a just recognition of their claims to a proper share of the state patronage.
>
> In 1882, Your memorialists presented to the Government of India through the Bengal Government a comprehensive Memorial pointing out exactly the position into which the Mohammedans had been reduced, the difficulties under which they laboured and the remedies which appeared to the Association necessary for their improvement.
>
> And in 1885 by a Resolution dated the 15th of July, Your Excellency's Government recognised the claims of the Mohammedans to an equal share in the consideration of Government and gave certain instructions for placing the Mohammedans on a more satisfactory footing in relation to other communities. In accordance with the resolution of the 15th July, 1885, the Government of Bengal was pleased to pass certain resolutions with the object of improving the position of the Mohammedans in the Public service. But your Memorialists regret to find that in spite of these Resolutions and in spite also of the fact that English education has made a decided progress in their recent years among the Mohammedans, the condition of our co-religionists has in no degree improved. From Statistics furnished to your Memorialists from the different Districts in Bengal and other Provinces and enquiries made in several Departments, we find that instead of an improvement there has been an appreciable retrogression.

> Your memorialists have ventured to draw the attention of the Local Government to these deplorable circumstances and they are fully convinced that every effort will be made to afford redress to the grievances which Your memorialists have set forth above.
>
> But Your memorialists venture to hope that Your Excellency will also be graciously pleased to place on record before Your Excellency's departure from India such recommendations as may seem advisable to Your Excellency for the legitimate assistance of the Mohammedan community and which may prove likely to strengthen the hands of the local Government in its endeavour to improve the position of the Mussulman community. And Your Memorialists as in duty bound shall every pray". [31]

In response to the above memorial, the Government of India reiterated the policy laid down in the Resolution of 1885. The local Governments were once again directed to absorb more Muslims than taken hitherto. An important minute regarding appointment to Public Offices recorded by an Honourable Member of the Governor General's Council on 21st September, 1888, reveals that the Government was positively desirous to have as many qualified persons as possible, while keeping a balance between the various classes and interests. The minute said:

> "We have of necessity to look to fitness quite as much as to nationality, and any action as the part of Government which gave rise to the motion that we are to appoint Mohammedans, as such, and be tender on the question of qualifications would only do harm to the Mohammedans themselves.
>
> As a matter of fact, it is only in Bengal, among the Provinces of Upper India where the Mohammadens in offices are disproportionately few. When the time comes to pass orders on the rules for the Provincial Service, we must emphasise the principle on which the public service commission insisted viz. That the rules must provide the best means (1) of securing the best natives in the Province (2) giving fair representation to the claims of all classes". [32]

This special treatment of the Mohammedans in its natural course become a principle of expediency. In 1886, the education commission set up earlier by the Government of India proposed a "differential treatment of the Mohammedan community in respect to education."

In its report it referred to three principal causes of an educational character which retard the prosperity of Mussalmans. It made the following observations:

> "Apart from the social and historical conditions of the Mohammedan community of India there are causes of strictly educational character which heavily weight it in the race of life. The teaching of the mosque must precede the lessons of the School. The one object of a young Hindu is to obtain an education which will fit him for an official or a professional career. But before the young Mohammedan is allowed to turn his thoughts to secular instruction, he must commonly pass some years in going through a course of sacred learnings. The Mohammedan boy therefore enters school later than the Hindu. In the second place, he very often leaves school at an earlier age. The Mohammedan parent belonging to the better classes is usually poorer than the Hindu parent in a corresponding social position: he cannot afford to give his son so complete an education. In the third place, irrespective of his worldly means, the Mohammedan parents often chooses for his son while at school, an education which will secure for him an honoured place among the learned of his own community, rather than one which will command a success in the modern professions or in official life. The years which the young Hindu gives to English and Mathematics in a public school, the young Mohammedan devotes in a Madrassa to Arabic and the Law of theology of Islam. When such an education is so completed, it is to the vocation of a man of learning, rather than to the more profitable professions, that the thoughts of a promising Mohammedan youth naturally turns".

The Commission in its recommendations said that among other measures to be taken for the official encouragement

> of education among Mohammedans, scholarships should be established for their benefits, to be awarded on the results of the Matriculation and First Arts Examination, and made tenable at Colleges".[33]

These proposals, the Government accepted only partially. But the fact that the Government was quite desirous to bring Mohammedans on equal terms with other communities is evident from the following note of 8th August, 1886 written by P. Nolan the officiating Secretary to the Government of Bengal. Before referring to the steps taken by the Bengal Government, he referred to a part of resolution recorded by the Government of India on the matter. It said that

> "Very much has been done by the local Government to meet the requirements of the Mohammedans in Bengal and it may fairly be said that they have now every opportunity offered them of securing a good education. If it is found that anything further is required in any part of the Province, or at any particular stage of the educational course, to advance the progress of the Mohammedan community, the Governor General in Council feels sure that his Honour the Lt. Governor will not stint the necessary outlay. For the attraction of Mohammedans to higher education a liberal provision of scholarships is essential, their wants must not be overlooked in the framing of any general scheme of scholarships for any Province in pursuance of the orders of the Government of India on the report of the Education Commission.
>
> These scholarships are not to be regarded as permanent foundations, but as an assistance temporarily given to a class which at present requires special assistance. The Lt. Governor notices with satisfaction the advance which has been made in the high education of Mohammedans within the last few years, and the increasing numbers in which they resort to the University. It may be confidently anticipated that with the special aid now offered, they will be able before long to meet all other sections of the community on equal terms".[34]

Once the ball was set rolling, the rest would follow by itself.

The Muslims went on clamouring for state patronage and their voice did not always go unheard and very often got them more advantages than they had even gained in the past.

The Muslims made these efforts in through the various associations that had cropped up in the country. As amongst the pioneer Hindus, so amongst the newly enlightened Mohammedans, there dawned a spirit of organization for public work and greater communal solidarity. The lead given by Muslims of Bengal was followed up by certain constructive efforts of the Muslims at Aligarh and in the Punjab. The most prominent of these associations were the Central National Mohammedan Association of Bengal, the Mohammedan Literary Society of Calcutta, the Naderaut-ul-Ulama Lucknow, the Anjuman-i-Islamia of Madras, the British Indian Association, Aligarh, the School of Theology, the Dar-ul-Ulam, Deoband, the Din-di-gal Anjuman and 'Anjuman Alimayat-i-Islam, of Lahore and the Central National Mohammedan Association, Punjab.

The avowed aims of all these associations were (i) to protect the Muslim faith and to propagate it further; (ii) to impart necessary education to Muslim boys and girls; (iii) to improve the social moral and intellectual condition of the Muslims; (iv) to bring home, to the Mohammedans the advantage of loyalty to the British Government (v) they all continued to seek for their community special treatment in the general life of Country.

In the year 1888, under the guidance of Nawab Abdul Majid Khan C.S.I. Raja Jahaandal Khan and Faquir Syed Jamaluddin and a few other prominent Muslims of Punjab, a petition was submitted to the Government of Punjab, requesting for a greater share in State Patronage.

The petitioners stated:

> "It is a common custom among public officers to fill up the vacancies through Sirishtadars, Head Clerks or similar officers, who are generally Hindus. These Heads of Departments as a rule, are naturally inclined to have the vacancies filled up utterly by their own relatives or by men of their own creed or religion. It is a fact that in 99 instances out of 100, Mohammedan candidates only learn of a vacancy when it is filled up.

It will be ungrateful on our part not to mention the fact that most of the European officers are always anxious to do full justice to Mohammedan candidates, but their only source of information being their Hindu subordinates, they are left under the impression that no qualified Mohammedans can be found, and therefore they are obliged to confer the posts on our Hindu brethren.

We further beg to submit that the principles conferring posts by competitive examinations in no way suited to the peculiar circumstances of this country, and more especially to this Province, which is considerably backward in the matter of education.

According to the present condition of the Mohammedans of the Punjab, such a system will practically exclude them from the Government service.

It is therefore most earnestly prayed that the Government may be pleased to invite the attention of the Heads of Department the relative position of the candidates not so much as regards their competitive ability as the qualifications necessary to fill the vacant post.

If it may be deemed necessary to have the competitive system at all, a certain number of posts in every Department ought to be reserved for Hindus and Mohammedans of the locality: on the occurrence of vacancies: Hindus only competing for the posts reserved for them and Mohammedans likewise for the appointment set apart for them in accordance to the general standard prescribed.

Association... does not mean to recommend the employment of unfit Mohammedans simply because they are Mohammedans, not to solicit any kind of undue favouritism to be shown to them by Government. We only beg for Mohammedans their fair share and the preservation of their just rights.

His Honour, as an experienced ruler of the Punjab, is in a better position to know the necessity of having a fair proportion of Mohammedans in public offices. For when they predominate in the population and on account of

> their growing poverty can resort to no other means of livelihood (Commerce, trade, etc.) and are obliged a great deal on government service; they must suffer and deteriorate if they cannot obtain help from Govt. It is therefore that the Government of India and all the Local Governments have always given their favourable attention to this subject".[35]

In response to this petition the then Government of Punjab, agreed to the preparation of a list of suitable Muslim candidates by the Association, and granted permission for its circulation among the Heads of Departments, who might thus be in a position to select more Muslim candidates for future appointments. In this connection, a semi-official letter from the Secretary to the Government of Bengal was also issued to all Heads of Departments and the Commissioner of the Punjab. It clearly brings to light the early British policy of subtle discrimination between one Community and another — a fact which spread communalism as a creed of intense social tension. The circular letter said:

> "In January last a memorial was presented to the Lt. Governor, on behalf of the Members of the Anjuman-i-Islamya of Lahore, which was signed by Mohammedans of various districts in the Punjab, drawing attention among other matters to the paucity of appointments held by Mohammedans in Government offices. This memorial, which was fully considered by Sir Charles Aitehison, has also been laid before His Honour the Lt. Governor, and Mr. Lyall desires me to convey the following remarks regarding the particular point which has been mentioned above.
>
> As regards superior appointments, the Lt. Governor has no reason to suppose that the claims of Mohammedans to posts under Government are not sufficiently considered, although the number of Hindus who obtain such appointments has no doubt steadily increased of late. It is impossible for Government to ignore the fact that Hindus as a rule have more largely availed themselves of the advantages of the higher education, than their Mohammedan brethren, and the preponderance of Hindus

among the extra assistants and Munsifs, some of whom are now appointed on a competitive examination, is the natural result of such a state of things. On the other hand, the proportion of Mohammedans who are now employed as Tehsildars has scarcely decreased during the last 5 years, and Lt. Governor believes that in other Departments there has been no marked diminution in the number of Mohammedans holding higher appointments.

But as regards the subordinate ministerial appointments, Mr Lyall thinks the matter is one which deserves attention. The Head ministerial posts in Government offices are very generally held by Hindus, and it is probable that Mohammedan candidates, for subordinate posts are not readily brought to the notice of those who have to dispose of patronage owing to the existence in many offices of an official clique composed of the Hindu elements.

The Lt. Governor will therefore be glad if you bestow your attention upon this subject and endeavour, as far as may be compatible with the best interests of the service and the supply of really qualified men, to assign a due proportion of subordinate appointments to Mohammedan candidates. Mr Lyall does not desire to lay down any rule regarding the proportion of Hindus and Mohammedans among the upper and middle classes of the population of the district, counting all the land owners, merchants and shopkeepers as included in one or the other of those classes".

The Muslims did not contend themselves merely with carrying on their chain of petitions, but, also tried to set their houses in order by formulating a new and constructive approach to Western education. It was the Aligarh Muslims who made the most significant contribution in this field. The pioneer efforts in this direction were made by Sir Syed Ahmed Khan (1817-98). When he came to the scene, he found the Muslim community in a state of stupor and dessiccation which followed as an aftermath of the mutiny. The Muslims all over India were falling into a 'state of material indigence and intellectual decay', and were going through a religious and political crisis; whereas the Hindus had stolen a march over them leaving them far behind in all walks of life. It was in these circumstances that Sir Syed Ahmed Khan came to the rescue of his community. He could realize that the key to the whole problem lay in adaptation to the new environment and in accepting the new instruments of progress; that had been created through the English education. Sir Syed launched his campaign of regenerating and lifting the Muslims community from a 'mire of defeat and shame' by working on two fronts. Firstly, he tried to remove the misunderstanding that had created a rift between the British Government and the Mussalmans of India and secondly he gave to his community the idea of a reorientation which came through the establishment of the M.A.O. College which ultimately grew into a big University for Muslims. He told the British in very plain terms that the main cause of the mutiny was not the hostility of the Indian Mussalman but a sheer fact of 'ignorance'. It was, as he believed, a case of 'ignorance' at both ends — ignorance on the part of the people of the intentions of the Government and ignorance on the part of the Government of the conditions of the people, or their needs, of thought and of life. He emphatically declared, "Had there been a native of Hindustan in the Legislative Council, the people would never have fallen into such efforts".[36]

Whether the revolt was really an error and whether or not it could be averted in the way suggested above is quite a debatable question. The crux of Sir Syed Ahmed's argument was an appeal for an increasing contact between the rulers and the ruled. In his famous *Risala Asbab-i-Baghwat-i-Hind*, he wrote:

> "The maintenance of friendly relations between the governors and the governed is far more necessary than between individuals; Private friendship only affects a few; friendship and good feeling between a government and its subjects affect a nation. The people and the government, I may liken to a tree, the latter being the root and the former the growth of that root. As the root is, so will the tree be".[37]

It need not be emphasized that when Syed Ahmed spoke of Indians, he was exclusively exposing the cause of the Muslims. In order to make his efforts more concrete, he further wrote an 'account of the loyal Mohammedans of India' entitled, *Risala Khair Khwahan Mussalman*.

From 1858 right up to 1898, Syed Ahmed Khan was the pivot round whom the Muslim politics moved. In 1866 he established a British India Association whose sole aim, in his own words , was that "Indians should come into contact with the Parliament for the preservation of their interests". The object of this Association was to form a link between the Indian and the representatives of the Crown in India.

Sir Syed had also to direct his energies towards converting the minds of his co-religionists as to infuse in them a more enlightened view of Islam. He was the first and last religious reformer; who summoned his people to return to the sanity and simplicity of primitive Islam. He denounced the superstitious and bigotary with which their faith had become encrusted; and told his people that the only instrument which could accomplish this regeneration was an education.

In his work entitled *Tahsib-ul-Ikhlaq* he gave a new interpretation to the Quran for which he was attacked violently. He was dubbed traitor and had to face such social persecution. Yet he stuck to his guns and nothing could daunt his leonine courage. His greatest contribution to the Muslim community came in the form of the Mohammedan Anglo-Oriental College at Aligarh which remained for long the *bete noire* of the pious Muslims'.[38]

In order to consolidate further the educational efforts as also to keep the Muslims aloof from the Indian National Congress (founded in the year 1885), Sir Syed laid the foundation of the Annual Muslim Educational Conference. The conference served a dual purpose - educational as well as political.

It was expected by the Muslims that through the activities of this conference, they shall overspread 'the whole of upper India with a network of societies, committees and individuals, all working harmoniously in the great cause, so that a big evil may be dealt with by a strong remedy and by the vigorous work of one generation the tide of misfortune may be turned and the Mohammedan nation may be set moving on the tide of progress of all the other nations of India'."[39]

Addressing the second session of the Mohammedan education conference at Lucknow, Sir Syed did great harm to the National cause by advising the Muslims to stay out of Indian National

Congress. As Mohammad Noven says: No Mussalman of note since then joined the Congress except one or two. Even Sayed Ahmed Khan's co-religionists who differed from his views on religious, educational and social matters and opposed him violently, followed him in politics and preserved their isolation from the Congress.

During the course of the third session of the Mohammedan Education Congress, he was received with the following address in commemoration of his visit to Lahore:

> "O! the most exalated of our nation; awaker of us from the drowsiness of neglect; a sage worthy of respect, bearing the appearance and qualification synonymous of the nation: real reformer: honourable and dignified leader: true patriot; and decent benefactor, endowing us with prosperity and progress: We sincerely esteem your visit as the source of our honor and pride, and are ready to lay even our eyes under your blessed feet wherever they go; and respectfully welcome your visit, which will add a good deal to our self respectability.
>
> It is to our great luck alone that you have honoured us with your visit, with a view to utilize the much esteemed and most essential movement of the Mohammedan Educational Congress to be held under your most distinguished auspices. We pray that the showers of Your Clemency may be poured forth on our heads in eternity, establishing our welfare, prosperity and happiness".[40]

The loyalist trend received its reaffirmation at the conference. Sirdar Mohammed Hayat Khan, in his speech said:

> "In the name of God, the most merciful and gracious....
>
> After thanking God, the omnipotent and the father of his creatures, we have first to thank our Queen Empress (cheers) and the British Government, under the shadow of whose benign empire, on which the sun never sets, we enjoy peace and tranquillity, and under which so many learned men and other gentlemen have been enabled to come from distant parts of India to the capital of the Punjab to confer together on the education of their backward and helpless nation (cheers).... Like the Messiah

he (Sir Syed) has rescued the boat of his followers and his great ancestors from the storm of ignorance in which it was sinking.

I have also to thank Mr Joseph Bech and his worthy son, who take an interest in the pitiful condition of out nation, for coming to attend this Congress".[41]

Sirdar Hayat Khan had made reference to Mr Theodore Beck, who was the Principal of M.A.O. College. The role played by the English Principals of the College has been most significant in promoting the economic and political advancement of the Muslim community. In fact, it was they who encouraged Muslim exclusivism and helped Muslims in reducing the 'Communal-lag'.

The speech delivered by Mr Beck in the above Conference is an illustration to point. He declared that the key to communal success lay in competing with the Hindus on all fronts; and it could not be possible by following a sitting on the fence policy; on the contrary Muslims would have to rise in the true tradition of their ancestors. Emphasizing this point he said:

"Again in Government appointments competition is the mania of the day. It is not good for Mohammedans to sit down and bemoan their fate. They have to enter into the lists and compete (Hear, Hear).

I have said that in 1886, the proportion of Mohammedan students was 44. This means that out of 1000 students, 44 were Mohammedans and 956 non-Mohammedans. Hence the number 44 has to be raised to 956 — that is to say where we have one Mohammedan now reading in the college there ought to be 22. (Hear, Hear). To change 1 into 22 is no easy task. It gives you however, gentlemen, a notion of the magnitude of the work before you. The Indian Mohammedans of the present generation have this great work to perform. If the task seem to you, impossible to recall to your minds for a moment what a handful of men in Arabia did 1300 years ago. These were the glorious founders of your faith and your civilization (Cheers). With such an example before them, Mohammedans cannot claim a right to despondency. The sun sets, but after 12 hours it rises again. I see signs of a new dawn for Mohammedans,

> and I look on this Conference as one of the golden clouds that herald the approach of day (Loud cheers) That is to say out of 100 students in the Punjab, 18 were non-Mohammedans... 18 has to be changed into 82".[42]

In his concluding remarks he said:

> "I may truly say that some of my dearest friends in the world are Indian Mohammedans.
>
> As to my taking an interest in the Mohammedan cause, both education and political, I may say that I certainly do take a great interest in it, and I trust I always shall. But for this I must assure you that I do not deserve the least credit, because I find that I have in my exile from my native land, no source of enjoyment than that which I derive from taking a part in your work (Applause).
>
> I have not met with so great kindness, even in England, from my own fellow countrymen, for whom I naturally cherish a most lively affection, as I have from my Mohammedan fellows subjects of our Gracious Queen Empress (Loud cheers): and I shall be bare indeed if I do not feel some gratitude towards them for what they have done to make my life happy in the land of my adoption".

With cautious but concrete British support, Syed Ahmed gradually gained ground for Muslims both in and outside the Government.

His efforts were not merely confined to a series of outspoken articles and speeches. He laid the foundations of the "Indian Patriotic Association of Muslims". It was an association set up as a platform where Muslim opinion might be focussed in contra-distinction to the Indian National Congress which was established in 1885. The objects of the Muslim Patriotic Association were as follows:

(1) To publish and circulate pamphlets and other papers for information of Members of Parliament, English journals and the people of Great Britain in which those mis-statements will be pointed out by which the supporters of the Indian National Congress have wrongly attempted to convince the English people that all the Nations of India and the Indian chiefs and rulers agree with the aims and objects of the National Congress.

(2) To inform Members of Parliament and the newspapers of

Great Britain and its people by the same means of the opinion of Mohammedans in general, of the Islamia Anjumans, and those Hindus, and their societies which are opposed to the objects of the National Congress.

(3) To strive to preserve peace in India and to strengthen the British rule; and to remove those bad feelings from the hearts of the Indian people, which the supporters of the Congress are stirring up throughout the country and by which great dissatisfaction is being raised among the people against the British Government".[43]

The truth is that Sir Syed did not make any secret of his communal role. He was frank and emphatic in his opinions. He did not intend to strangle the throat of his community by permitting it to tread any other path except one of unswearing loyalty and trust in the rule of the British.

His attitude towards Hindus was naturally shaped on the lines laid above. As such, it varied from an appeal of communal harmony to that of communal exclusivism. He deplored communal bitterness and said:

> "There is no person, who desires more than I, that friendship and union should exist between the two peoples of India and that one should help the other. I have often said that India is like a bride whose two eyes are the Hindus and Muslims. Her beauty consists in this that her two eyes be of equal lustre".
>
> He went on to say: "I have often given my nation to understand that slaughtering cows for the purpose of annoying Hindus is the height of cantankerous folly; if friendship may exist between us and them, but friendship is far to be preferred to the sacrifice of cows".[44]

His last important work was the establishment of the Mohammedan Defence Association of Upper India in 1893. It was in the nature of a political organisation and it also owed its origin to the counsel of Theodore Beck. He is reported to have addressed the meeting of a few eminent Muslims, who met on the afternoon of December 30, 1893, at the house of Sayyid Ahmed Khan, to formulate plans to organize Muslims for political purpose. Beck wanted the Muslims to follow a middle course between political abeyance and political agitation.

He said:

> "With the press pouring out a stream of political articles, our young educated Mohammedans will be drawn into the current to support or oppose the measures proposed... I think it would be a mistake to leave them without guidance".[45]

The objects of the Association were (a) to place the opinions of Mussalmans before Englishmen and the Government of India, and to protest their political rights; (b) to prevent the spread of political discontent among the Mussalmans; (c) to adopt all such means as would be helpful in strengthening the British, rule, in maintaining law and order and in creating a sense of loyalty among the people.

Beck was determined to keep off other communities, particularly the Hindus, from joining this association, in the way they had done in the case of the United Patriotic Association. On the other hand, he was keen to keep Muslims aloof from the upsurge of democratic and nationalist feelings that were fast gaining ground.

It is interesting to note that when, in 1889, Mr Bradlaugh introduced a Bill in the Parliament with the object of establishing democratic institutions in India, Mr Beck prepared a memorandum against it, and obtained a large number of signatures on it through the help of the students of the M.A.O. College, Aligarh, whom he sent to different places for this purpose. Walait's Husain Sahib writes in the Conference Gazette of Aligarh that one such group went to Delhi under the leadership of Mr Beck himself.

> "He (Mr Beck) himself sat at the door of Jama-e-Masjid and the students under his instructions secured signatures from those going in for prayers by representing that the Hindus wanted to stop cow slaughter and this was the petition to be sent to the Government against this move"[46].

However,

> "Having secured 20,735 signatures in this way in Delhi alone this marvellous petition was sent to be presented to the Parliament in England in 1890".[47]

The same Mr Beck in his opening speech at the establishment of this Defence Association complained that although the Patriotic

Association had secured signatures against Bradlaugh's Bill, yet it was a joint organization of Hindus and Mussalmans and had many organizations affiliated to it. He proposed that the Defence Association should avoid any such affiliation. It is worthwhile quoting a significant passage from this opening speech which reveals how Mr Beck harboured strong prejudices against the Hindus.

> "For the last few years" he said, "there are two kinds of agitations which have been gaining strength in the country — one is the National Congress and the other is the movement against cow slaughter. Of these, the first is entirely opposed to Englishmen and the second movement is against the Mussalmans. The object of the National Congress is that the political power of the English Government should be transferred to some groups amongst the Hindus, the ruling race should be weakened, the people should be given arms, the army should be weakened and the cost on it be reduced. The Mussalmans can have no sympathy with these objects. The object of the movement of cow slaughter is to prevent Mussalmans from cow-sacrifice and to prevent both Englishmen and Mussalmans from slaughtering cows for food. To prevent cow-slaughter they boycott their opponents to starve them into submission. This has resulted in bloody riots in Bombay, Azamgarh, etc. The Mussalmans and Englishmen have become the targets of these two movements. It is therefore necessary that Mussalmans and Englishmen should unite in opposing and that the establishment of democratic political institutions should be opposed as they are not suited to this country. We must therefore carry on propaganda in favour of true loyalty and unity".[48]

Beck later on sent another representation appended with signatures of many Muslims to England in which he voiced opposition to simultaneous examination for civil services, as it gave Hindus an opportunity to outclass Muslims. He declared himself against appointments being made by competitive examination and suggested that the Mussalmans should bank on their loyalty to the British Government to secure appointments. The Defence Association carried on propaganda in England also where Mr Beck himself delivered a lecture in 1895. In the words of Dr Rajendra Prasad, former President of India:

> "The thesis of this lecture was that Anglo-Muslim Unity was possible but Hindu-Muslim Unity was not possible and that parliamentary institutions were certainly unsuited to India. If they were established the Mussalmans being the minority would be overpowered by the Hindus who are in a majority. In this lecture he sometimes patted the Muslims on the back and sometimes threatened them with dire consequences if they did not behave and followed the policy of the Hindus".[49]

Beck in collaboration with Sir Syed had in fact taken upon himself the burden of opposing all the measures proposed by the Indian National Congress. For instance in 1896, in the Annual Report of the Defence Association he emphasized the need of a strong army and navy and stated that the Association was opposed to any cut in the military expenditure. It was a measure that was opposed by the Indian National Congress when the British Government under the Viceroyalty of Lord Dufferin was thinking of pushing on its forward policy on the Frontier and wanted to increase the military expenditure.

From the above one can easily form an idea of the way the British Policy, of 'counterpoise' and 'divide and rule' was subtly put into practice by an ordinary principal of an ordinary college parading under the subterfuge of an educationist, Beck not only shaped the Muslim politics but did all which even the best of diplomats could not have achieved for the Government of India. He indoctrinated the Muslim youth with anti-national and narrow communal ideas. He sowed the seeds which brought forth bitter harvest some fifty years later. It is small wonder that a few years later the Aligarh college came under the domination of Muslim League and its educational atmosphere and 'its liberalism was replaced by an almost historical religious enthusiasm intolerant and anti-national. Aligarh was by 1941, the emotional centre of Pakistan".[50] The climate created by Beck must have proved extremely congenial for such a growth.

It was in this manner that Muslim politics advanced itself under the cloak of educational reforms. Whereas the Muslims were thus greatly benefited by the loyalty that Sir Syed Ahmed gave to the British Empire in India, the Hindus and the national cause certainly suffered most by the services that Mr Theodore Beck rendered towards the building up of a sane empire in India.

The help of the British in promoting education amongst Muslims came from two clear motives. The first motive was to win over the loyalty of a bigoted and fanatic subject who had been since long a chronic source of danger to the British Raj. The second one was to groom the Muslims as an offset against the progressive Hindus, by helping the former in filling up the 'Communal-lag' between the two communities.

The above becomes clear from the minute of E.C. Baylay who supported an educational institution which may combine both English and Oriental ways of teaching. He wrote:

> "Anyway, as I have said, the Mohammedans will have some of this peculiar learning; they cannot do without it altogether. Questions of their law, their literature, their political attitude are continually arising which required a knowledge not wholly of a sectarian, kind to solve. If not available here, the persons who possess it will be sought elsewhere, and the guidance of Mohammedans in India will fall into the hands of bigoted men from without, taught in a narrow and too often disloyal school.
>
> It was avowedly to prevent this and to retain in our own hands the teaching of the learned class of Mohammedans that the Madarsa was founded. But the object has hitherto not been attained mainly because we have not used properly the instrument we had, but gave in to a purely Mohammedan teaching. What we should now do is, I think, to provide a place where Arabic language, literature, its philosophy, logic, grammar and to some extent Mohammedan law and history, may be taught leaving off the purely Mohammedan character at this stage and insisting on this amount of knowledge being combined with a fair knowledge of English literature, and some

acquaintance, greater or less, with the European science or European Philosophy'.

Enumerating the advantages that will result out of such an approach he further said:

> "By doing this we shall provide for Mohammedans the easy means of acquiring their distinctive learning. We should not teach it with its doctrinal accompaniment; there they may, and to some extent will, get elsewhere, but if we require in addition some European teaching, they will not go far into sectarian teachings: they will have little time and little inclination, and we should turn out Mohammedans, to whom their co-religionists will look with respect, who yet would, for the most part be men not bigoted but with enlarged minds, and who, while they were able to comprehend and enter into the feelings and thoughts of the Mohammedan community, would be filled to stand as interpreters between it and the governing classes.
>
> Without some such instrumentality, I feel assured that isolation into which the Mohammedan community has fallen of late years will become more complete and more intense, and this will be a most serious political evil, nor do I see how such an instrumentality can be furnished save by an upper or College department of the Madrassa, teaching according to Mohammedan school of teaching, but combining that with some considerable degree of European teaching and training".[51]

It need not be pointed out that the Mohammedan Anglo Oriental College, founded by Sir Syed Ahmed gave a concrete shape to Bayley's plans. It is an indisputable fact that without the help of the Government and their agents, the Muslims could not have advanced, how strong might have been the claims of their loyalty and devotion to the British. In this connection on the subject of raising Aligarh College to the status of a Mohammedan University, a letter written by principal Theodore Beck to Mr A.H.L. Fraser the personal secretary to the Viceroy throws a revealing light on the way the British were trying to help the Muslim community. We give its full text here.

M.A.O. College,
Aligarh.
Dated, the 11th Feb. 1899.

"My dear Fraser,

I don't feel quite certain as to the exact character of the information which you want for His Excellency the Viceroy about the proposed Mahommedan University, but I hope that in answering your letter, I shall mention the main points. I feel that it is extremely kind of the Viceroy to take so much interest in our movement and I hope you will convey to him my warmest thanks for enquiring about it.

First as to the origin of the idea. The idea was present in the minds of the founders of the College twenty-five years ago, a fact which is proved by the circumstances that Mr Syed Mahmud, then an undergraduate at Cambridge, wrote out a long scheme for the University for the consideration of the College Fund Committee. Again when Mr Mahmud asked me in England in 1883 to become Principal of the College, the aspiration that the College might expand into University was one of the chief features on which he laid stress. From time to time the idea was mentioned in various addresses to Viceroys and Lieutenant Governors, but the first time when it was definitely recognized by Government as a legitimate and probable outcome of our work was in the speech of Sir Anthony Macdonnell in 1896.

So far however, the idea of a University was confined to a few people and there seemed something ridiculous in talking very much about it so long as the institution was struggling to establish itself as a college of the first grade. By the time, however, that Sir Anthony MacDonnell made the speech I have referred to, the reputation of the place as a College was firmly established, and the occasion of the death of Sir Syed Ahmed when there was naturally a desire to find for him a fitting memorial, seemed appropriate for definitely launching the idea of a University for the Mohammedan Public as a practical aim to be taken up in earnest.

First a resolution was passed by the College Board of Management, then a committee was formed, subscriptions were invited, articles (of which I send you copies - See Appendix A & B of the Report of the Sir Syed Ahmed Memorial Fund Committee) were written by Mr Morison and myself explaining what was meant by the proposed University, and public meetings were held in many parts of the country.

The educated section of the Mohammedans took up the idea and it was formally adopted by the Mohammedans Education Conference (a body containing 800 members, and the most representative institutions among the Indian Mohammedans) in Lahore in December last. Letters approving of the scheme were received by the Conference from Nawab Emad-ul-Mulk, Syed Hosain Bilgrami, of Hyderabad, Mr Justice Budruddin Tyabjee of Bombay and Mr Justice Amir Ali of Calcutta showing that the leading Mohammedans all over India were prepared to support it. It may, therefore, be said now that the idea of developing and expanding the Aligarh College so that it may ultimately become a University framed on the model of the Universities of Oxford and Cambridge with a large staff of English and Mohammedan Professors has been adopted by the educated classes of the Mohammedans as the great object towards which they should lend their efforts for national improvement".

Writing about the prospects of the movement, he wrote:

"As to the prospect of success, we have a lakh of rupees from private individuals etc..... We are holding a meeting at Allahabad over which Sir Arthur Strachey has kindly consented to ppreside.

The M.A.O. College, unlike the other Indian Colleges, has already all the essential elements of a University in the germ. The students reside in the quadrangles and the Professors live within the College compound. Professors and students are alike animated by a strong *espirit de corps* and the old students look on it as their Alma Mater.

Nothing has been more encouraging throughout the

difficulties that we have experienced since Sir Syed's death than the warm support that has been rendered to the institutions by its old students. They have subscribed themselves and worked hard in collecting subscriptions. Such a phenomenon is, I believe, unique in India.

If we got our ten lakhs we should not only place the College on an absolutely firm basis but should enormously increase our work in quantity and improve it in quality. The Mohammedans would acquire confidence that they only needed perseverance to attain their end. The stream of popular subscription would continue to flow, and it is not unreasonable to hope that some wealthy men might be bitten with the idea and leave the College considerable endowments in their wills."

He concluded his letter with the following remarks:

"I do not wish to give too roseate a view of our prospects. The ordinary wealthy Mohammedan in India is not only indifferent to education but devoid of public spirit. He may give money for a mosque with an eye to his prospects in the next world. So far he has scarcely been touched by Western ideas. Our main supporters are among the middle classes who have but moderate means. So it may take a long time before the big endowments drop in. But meanwhile the continual effort to raise money in small subscriptions extends the popularity and the national character of the institution.

This is a brief outline of our present hopes which are possibly too sanguine.

But we consider what Sir Syed did commencing his work nearly a generation ago, when the bulk of his Mohammedan country men were entirely opposed to English education by determination and steadiness of purpose, I see no reason to look on our present scheme as unrealisable.

In conclusion I would say that the University we want to found is a residential teaching University, containing a group of Professors, scholars and students in daily intercourse.

> An institution that will perform the double task of educating loyal and energetic citizens belonging to the Mussalman upper and middle classes, and furthering research and the advancement of learning.
>
> Expressing once more the warmest thanks of all concerned with this proposal to His Excellency the Viceroy for his kind enquiry".[52]

This letter confirms the views expressed above that the British had in their heart nothing but contempt for Muslim backwardness and that their sole intention in giving them Western education was to train the Muslim middle-class into a batch of loyal citizens. Above all, what was desired, was the creation of Anglicized Mohammedans who could act as good interpreters of the British rule — a rule which was once described by Justice Mahmud, the son of Sir Syed, as 'one of the most wonderful phenomenon the world has ever seen".[53]

The impress of the English Principal, Mr. Theodore Beck not only brought a change in the life of the Muslim students but also in the life of their accredited leader. Mr. Beck 'assiduously tried to wean Sir Syed away from nationalism'. Whatever softer feelings Sir Syed might have entertained earlier for the Bengalis in particular and Hindus in general gradually hardened into a separatist philosophy. It came to a point where he said that India is two nations not one, a doctrine which later found its echoes and reverberations in Mr Jinnah's 'Two Nations Theory'. Sir Syed declared

> "It is our nation which conquered with its sword the whole of India".[54]

The change that had come in Syed Ahmed becomes quite apparent when we compare his later declarations with the views he held earlier. Previously he had said Hindus and Mussalmans constituted one nation, as the following extract from his writings will show:

> "The word nation (Qaum) applies to people who inhabit a country... Remember that Hindu and Mussalman are religious words; otherwise, Hindus, Mussalmans and even Christians who inhabit this country all constitute, on this account, one nation. When all these groups are one nation;

> then whatever benefits the country, which is the country of all of them should benefit all .... Now the time is gone when only on account of difference in religion the inhabitants of a country should be regarded as of two different nations".[55]

The truth, however, is that the policy of isolation as advocated by Sir Syed was a policy which desired to achieve greater communal solidarity under the veil of political expediency. Sir Syed did not intend to lose whatever little he had gained for his community.

The cause most dear to him was the cause of material prosperity and intellectual reawakening of his co-religionists. He was therefore, not prepared to leave the loyalist camp and join the Nationalist.

Sir Syed was a queer mixture of a feudal, loyalist and religious reformer. As such, he could neither come forth as a champion of the national cause, nor that of the Hindu-Muslim concord.

His attitude towards the Hindus, yet his feudal make-up and the fear of Hindu domination would not let him be any thing but a conservative and a communalist.

As an eminent historian remarks:

> "The Congress movement he defined as `a civil war without arms', 'and if', he went on, 'India were to be given, as Congress desired, an elective system based on weather or education or numbers, the whole council will consist of Babu so and so; and yet all Muslims,' he said, 'despised these fish-eating Babus of Bengal'. Simultaneous competitive examinations for the civil service would not in any event benefit the backward Muslims but if they were to be determined, he prayed that `we be allowed to use the pen of our ancestors'. Their clear policy, he maintained, was to boycott the Congress and to support the British.

He further adds:

> "Sir Syed's policy was frankly based on fear of permanent domination - educationally, economically, politically - of Muslims by Hindus".[56]

Sir Syed was dogmatic in his views that Parliamentary Government was unsuited to such a country, as India.

In 1883, in the course of a discussion on the Central Provinces Local Self-Government Bill, Syed Ahmed Khan said:

> I am convinced that no part of India has yet arrived at the stage when the system of representation can be adopted, in its fullest scope, even in regard to local affairs. The principle of self-government by means of representative institutions is, perhaps, the greatest and noblest lesson which the beneficence of England will teach India. But, in borrowing from England the system of representative institutions, it is of the greatest importance to remember these socio-political matters in which India is distinguishable from England. The present socio-political conditions of India are the outcome of the history of centuries of despotism and misrule, of the dominancy of race over race, of religion over religion. Traditions and feelings of the people and their present economic and political conditions are in a vast measure influenced and regulated by the history of the past; the humanizing effects of the British rule have not yet demolished the remembrance of the days of strife and discord which preceded the peace brought to India by the British supremacy. India, a continent in itself, is inhabited by vast populations of different races and different creeds; the rigour of religious institutions has kept even neighbours apart, the system of caste is still dominant and powerful. In one and the same district the population may consist of various creeds and various nationalities; and whilst one section of the population commands wealth and commerce, the other may possess learning and influence. One section may be numerically larger than the other, and the standard of enlightenment which one section of the community may be fully alive to the importance to securing representation on the local boards and district councils, whilst the other may be wholly indifferent to such matters. Under these circumstances, it is hardly possible to deny that the introduction of representative institutions in India will be attended with considerable difficulty and socio-political risks... The system of representation by election

means the representation of the views and interests of the majority of the population and in countries where the population is composed of one race and one creed, it is no doubt the best system that can be adopted. But, my lord, in a country like India, where caste distinctions still flourish, where there is no fusion of the various races, where religious distinctions are still violent, where education in its modern sense has not made an equal or proportionate progress among all the sections of the population, I am convinced that the introduction of the principle of election, pure and simple, for representation of various interests on the local board and district councils, would be attended with evils of greater significance than purely economic considerations. So long as differences of race and creed, and the distinctions of caste form an important element in the socio-political life of India, and influence her inhabitants in matters connected with the administration and welfare of the country at large, the system of election pure and simple, cannot be safely adopted. The larger community would totally override the interests of the smaller community, and the ignorant public would hold Government responsible for introducing measures which might make the differences of race and creed more violent than ever."[57]

On this score, Sir Syed could never reconcile himself to Hindus. Like every Muslim leader who came after him, he too suffered from the thought that Hindus being in a majority 'would be absolute masters as no Mohammedan Emperor ever was".[58]

Curiously enough, this single thought not only kept communalism alive but also led to the making of a separate Muslim State 'Pakistan'.

Sir Syed died in the year 1898 but his policies were continued by Mr Beck who also died a year later in 1899. It was now the turn of Mr Theodore Morrison who became the Principal of the College after Mr Beck, to continue the anti-Hindu Policy. His identification with the Muslim cause was not only new; for, it was under him that a branch of the Patriotic Association was started in England. One of his important missions, after assuming the charge of the

College, was to prevent the Muslims from merging themselves in the Nationalist upsurge, that was gradually gaining much strength. Not only did he oppose the demands for any democratic institutions for Indians, but also exerted his influence in prevailing upon the Mussalmans not to have any political organisation. In one of his letters, published in the Institute Gazette, he warned the Muslims against asking for democracy for "democratic rule would reduce the minority to the position of trewers of wood and drawers of water".[59]

He further harangued to the Muslims:

> In any opinion a political organisation instead of being beneficial would be injurious to the interests of Mussalmans because during the last twenty or twenty five years, the Government has been showing concession to them. If like the Congress, they also started an organisation and demanded their right and the Parliament were to appoint a commission, the Mussalmans would not derive as much benefits from it as they would if they were to leave their fate in the hands of Sir Anthony Macdonell".[60]

Theodore Morrison held sway from 1900 to 1905. He was followed by Mr Archbold whose contribution to the cause of the Muslims was perhaps the most significant as compared to other English Principals of M.A.O. College, Aligarh. It was through his efforts, advice and mediation that a deputation was arranged to meet the then Viceroy, to put up every grievance of the Muslims before the Government. During the long vacations in the year 1906, when Mr Archbold had been to Simla, he contacted the Private Secretary to the Viceroy, and in one of the most famous letters of modern Indian history, he informed Nawab Mohsin-ul-Mulk who was the honorary Secretary of the Aligarh College and who succeeded Syed Ahmed as the Leader of the Muslim Community, that the Viceroy has agreed to receive a Muslim deputation.[61] The text of Mr Archbold's letter ran in the following words:

> "Colonel Dunlop Smith (Private Secretary to the Viceroy) now writes to me that the Viceroy is prepared to receive the deputation of Mussalmans and intimates me that a formal petition be submitted for it. In this connection, the following matters require consideration.

The first question is that of sending the petition. To my mind it would be enough that some leaders of Mussalmans even though they may not have been elected, should put their signatures to it. The second is the question as to who the members of the deputation should be. They should be representatives of all the Provinces. The third question is of the contents of the address. In this connection my opinion is that, in the address, loyalty should be expressed, that thanks should be offered that, in accordance with the settled policy, steps are going to be taken in the direction of self-government according to which the door will be opened for Indians to offices. But apprehensions should be expressed that by introducing election, injury will be done to Mussalman minority and hope should be expressed that in introducing the system of nomination or granting representation on religious basis the opinion of Mussalmans will be given due weight. Their opinion should also be given that in a country like India it is necessary that weight should be attached to the views of zamindars.

My personal opinion is that the wisest thing for Mohammedans to do would be that they support the system of nomination because the time for introducing election has not yet come. Besides, it will be very difficult for them if the system of election is introduced to secure their proper share.

But in all these matters, I want to remain behind the screen and this move should come from you. You are aware how anxious I am for the good of the Mussalmans and I would, therefore, render all help with the greatest pleasure. I can prepare and draft the address for you. If it be prepared in Bombay then I can revise it because I know the art of drawing up petitions in good language. But Nawabsaheb, please remember that if, within a short time, any great and effective action has to be taken then you should act quickly".[62]

In his memoirs His Highness Agha Khan, who led the proposed deputation observes:

"Since 1875, and the transference of authority in India

from the East India Company to the Crown, the Muslims had, in a political sense, been more or less ignored by the British. Perhaps not unnaturally the new rulers of India turned away from those who, by religion and by language, were connected with the rulers who had been ousted. Muslims were not brought into the administration or into politics; few studied or read English. If the end of the Moghul Emperors was pitiable its effects lingered on for two generations in the sense of isolation and powerlessness which enveloped the Muslims of India in their own land. The Hindu majority were in an advantageous position under their new rulers; and they made full use of it. The Muslims had been for long what the French call "Quantite" negligible", but at long last we were going to be heard. The Viceroy, Lord Minto, had agreed to receive a deputation from us and I was to lead that deputation".

He further says:

"We were actually aware that we had long been neglected, that to the Hindu majority - as represented by its leaders in the Congress Party - we seemed a tiresome splinter in the flesh of the body politic, and that though there was great talk of nationalism we were not even considered in the aspirations that were being fostered, the plans that were being laid. They continued to send to the Viceroy's Legislative Council, third-rate yes-men instead of truly representative Muslims, with the result that our separate identity as a community and the status that would have appertained to it had been forgotten by the British.

He adds:

"Now we decided that the time had come to make a stand for a change in attitude. If constitutional advancements were to be mooted, we must have our say in their disposition".[63]

Thus arranged, Maulvi Syed Mehdi Ali Khan (Mohsin-ul-Mulk), Honorary Secretary of the M.A.O. College, Aligarh, addressed a request through the Principal of the College, Aligarh, asking His Excellency the Viceroy to receive a Deputation and address on behalf of the Indian Mohammedans to draw the attention of the Government to their rights and the "Communal-Lag", with which the community was severely suffering.

The Deputation that met the Viceroy, after he had consented to the same, was selected from a typically Muslim middle-class and landed aristocracy, of the Country. The Simla correspondent of the *Indian Daily Telegraph*, in its issue of October 3rd 1906, says:

> "The representatives of the Mohammedan community who were to present the address to His Excellency the Viceroy this morning at Viceregal Lodge collected in the Ballroom at 11 am. They numbered thirty-five and were seated in a horse-shoe facing His Excellency's chair. Precisely at 11 am, Lord Minto, preceded by his staff, entered the room, all standing to receive him. His Excellency was taken round and personally introduced to each member by the Aga Khan. The Khalifa from Patiala then asked permission for the presentation of the address and the Aga Khan then advanced and facing His Excellency read the petition given below, all the representatives standing".

The relevant portion of the address ran as follows:

> "May it please your Excellency, - Availing ourselves of the permission accorded to us, we, the undersigned nobles, jagirdars, taluqdars, lawyers, zamindars, merchants and others representing a large body of the Mohammedan subjects of His Majesty the King Emperor in different parts of India, beg most respectfully to approach Your Excellency with the following address for your favourable consideration.
>
> We fully realize and appreciate the incalculable benefits conferred by British rule on the teeming millions belonging to diverse races and professing diverse religions who form the population of the vast continent of India, and have every reason to be grateful for the peace, security, personal freedom and liberty of worship that we now enjoy. Further from the wise and enlightened character of the Government, we have every reasonable ground for anticipating that these benefits will be progressive, and that India will in the future, occupy an increasingly important position in the comity of nations.

One of the most important characteristics of British policy in India is the increasing deference that has so far as possible been paid from the first to the views and wishes of the people of the country in matters affecting their interests, with due regard always to the diversity of race and religion which forms such an important feature of all Indian progress.

Claims of the Community

Beginning with the confidential and unobtrusive method of consulting influential members of important communities in different parts of the country, this principle was gradually extended by the recognition of the right of recognized political or commercial organization to communicate in the authorities their criticism and view on measures of Public importance, and finally by the nomination and election of direct representatives of the people in Municipalities, District Boards, and above all in the Legislative Chambers of the Country".

The address further made an emphasis on the historical and political importance of the Mohammedan community and it urged upon the Government for a special consideration of the Muslims, irrespective of their status of a Minority Community. It said:

"The Mohammedans of India number, according to the census taken in the year 1901, over sixty-two millions or between one fifth and one fourth of the total population of His Majesty's Indian dominions, and if a reduction be made for the uncivilised portions of the community enumerated under the head of animist and other minor religions, as well as for those classes who are ordinarily classified as Hindus but properly speaking are not Hindus at all, the proportion of Mohammedans to the Hindu majority becomes much larger. We therefore desire to submit that under any system of representation extended or limited, a community in itself more numerous than the entire population of any first class European power except Russia may justly lay claim to adequate recognition as an important factor in the State.

> We venture, indeed, with Your Excellency's permission to go a step further, and urge that the position accorded to the Mohammedan community is any kind of representation direct or indirect, and in all other ways affecting their status and influence, should be commensurate, not merely with their numerical strength, but also with their political importance and the value of the contribution which they make to the defence of the empire, and we also hope that your Excellency will, in this connection, be pleased to give due consideration to the position which they occupied in India, a little more than hundred years ago and of which the traditions have naturally not faded from their minds.

The most important point to be noted here is that in order to compensate for the initial loss that the Muslim middle-class had suffered in an open competition amongst the various communities, they now tried to alienate themselves from their other fellow nationals and made claims' for a special treatment, on the grounds that they hold a distinct place in the country. As the address further said:

> "Still, it cannot be denied that we Mohammedans are a distinct community with additional interests of our own which are not shared by other communities, and these have hitherto suffered from the fact that they have not been adequately represented. Even in the Provinces in which the Mohammedans constitute a distinct majority of the population, they have too often been treated as though they were inappreciably small political factors that might without unfairness be neglected. This has been the case to some extent, in the Punjab, but in a more marked degree in Sind and in Eastern Bengal.
>
> Before formulating our views with regard to the election of representatives, we beg to observe that the political importance of a community to a considerable extent gains strength or suffers detriment according to the position that the members of that community occupy in the service of the State. If, as is unfortunately the case with the Mohammedans, they are not adequately represented in

> this manner, they lose in the prestige and influence which are justly their due.

Further on the address, harped another disability with which the Muslims had suffered and which had given lead to other communities particularly, the Hindus. It requested not only for a favour of communal weightage in the general distribution of the public offices, but it also requested for a relaxation of qualifications demanded of the Muslims. The address said:

> "We venture to submit that the generality of Mohammedans in all parts of India feel aggrieved that Mohammedan Judges are not more frequently appointed to the High Courts and Chief Courts of Judicature. Since the creation of these Courts, only three Mohammedan lawyers have held these honourable appointments, all of whom have fully justified their elevation to the bench. At the present moment, there is not a single Mohammedan Judge sitting on the Bench of any of these Courts, while there are three Hindu Judges in the Calcutta High Court, where the proportion of Mohammedans in the population is very large, and two in the chief Court of the Punjab, where the Mohammedans form the majority of the population. It is not, therefore, an extravagant request on our part that a Mohammedan should be given a seat on the Bench of each of the High Courts and Chief Courts. Qualified Mohammedan lawyers eligible for these appointments can always be found, if not in one Province then in another. We beg permission further to submit that the presence on the Bench of these Courts of a Judge learned in the Mohammedan Law will be a source of considerable strength to the administration of justice".

The most important point of the address referred to the representation of the Muslims to the Imperial Legislative Council. It said:

> "With regard to the Imperial Legislative Council wherein the due representation of Mohammedan interests is a matter of vital importance, we crave leave to suggest (1) that in the cadre of the Council the proportion of Mohammedan representatives should not be determined

> on the basis of the numerical strength of the community, and that in any case the Mohammedan representatives should never be an ineffective minority; (2) that as far as possible, appointment by election should be given preference over nomination; (3) that for the purpose of choosing Mohammedan members, Mohammedan landowners, lawyers, merchants and representatives of other important interests of a status to be subsequently determined by Your Excellency's Government, Mohammedan members of the Provincial Councils and Mohammedan fellows of Universities should be invested with electoral powers to be exercised in accordance with such procedure as may be prescribed by Your Excellency's Government in that behalf".

After having made a request for the establishment of a Mohammedan University, which may provide the Centre for the religious and intellectual life of the Muslims, the address concluded with the familiar. note of unswerving loyalty to His Majesty's Government of India, It said:

> "In conclusion we beg to assure your Excellency that in assisting the Mohammedan subjects of His majesty at this state in the development of Indian affairs in the directions indicated in the present address, Your Excellency will be strengthening the basis of their unswerving loyalty to the throne and laying the foundation of their political advancement and national prosperity, and Your Excellency's name will be remembered with gratitude by their posterity for generations to come, and we feel confident that your Excellency will be gracious enough to give due consideration to our prayers. We have the honour to subscribe ourselves, Your Excellency's most obedient humble servants".[64]

His Excellency, Lord Minto, after the address had been read out to him, rose and in an extremely sympathetic reply declared that he was entirely in accord with the views of the deputation, that any electoral system must take cognizance of the various religious beliefs of this great empire, and that the British Government would always in the future as in the past safeguard the political rights of the different communities entrusted to their charge.

After having appreciated the representative character of the deputation, he tried to eulogize the early British attempts to help the Mohammedan community. Later on, he talked of the Aligarh College and was all praise for the services of Sir Syed Ahmed to the Crown and to the Muslim community. Giving an assurance to the Muslims about the safety of their political future he declared:

> "And now gentlemen I come to your own position in respect to the political future, the position of the Mohammedan community for whom you speak. You will, I feel sure, recognize that it is impossible for me to follow you through any detailed consideration of the conditions and the share that the community has a right to claim in the administration of public affairs. I can at present only deal with generalization. The points which you have raised are before the Committee, which, as you know, I have lately appointed to consider the question of presentation (representation), and I will take care that your address is submitted to them, but, at the same time I hope I may be able to reply to the general tenor of your remarks without in any way forestalling the Committee's report".[65]

Referring to the question of political representation he further said:

> "The pith of your address as I understand it, is a claim that in any system of representation whether it affects a Municipality, a District Board or a Legislative Council, in which it is proposed to introduce or increase an electoral organisation, the Mohammedan community should be represented as a community. You point out that in many cases electoral bodies, as now constituted, cannot be expected to return a Mohammedan candidate, and that if by chance they did so, it could only be at the sacrifice of such a candidate's view to those of a majority opposed to his own community, whom he would in no way represent, and you justly claim that your numerical strength and both in respect to the political importance of your community and the service it has rendered to the Empire entitle you to

> consideration. I am entirely in accord with you; Please do not misunderstand me. I make no attempt to indicate by what means the representation of communities can be obtained, but I am as firmly convinced as I believe you to be, that any electoral representation in India would be doomed to mischievous failure which aimed at granting a personal enfranchisement regardless of the beliefs and traditions of the communities composing the population of this continent. The great mass of the people of India have no knowledge of representative institutions. I agree with you, gentlemen, that the initial rungs in the ladder of self-government are to be found in the Municipal and District Boards and that it is in that direction that we must look for the gradual political education of the people."[66]

In conclusion he assured the Muslims to have no fears and exhorted them to rely as firmly as ever on British justice. He said:

> "In the meantime I can only say to you that the Mohammedan community may rest assured that their political rights and interests as a community will be safeguarded in any administrative reorganization with which I am concerned, and that you and the people of India may rely upon the British Raj to respect, as it has been its pride to do, the religious beliefs, and the national traditions of the myriads composing the population of His Majesty's Indian Empire.
>
> Your Highness and Gentlemen, I sincerely thank you for the unique opportunity your deputation has given me of meeting so many distinguished and representative Mohammedans. I deeply appreciate the energy and interest in public affairs which have brought you here from great distances, and I only regret that your visit to Simla is necessarily so short."[67]

The Simla deputation which was a 'command-performance' achieved one of the biggest success in a series of persistent Muslim efforts to abridge the initial 'Communal Lag'. The achievement was made in the form of separate communal electorates and 'weightage' to the Muslim minority in any scheme for future representation.

The Muslim League

In the wake of the Simla Deputation, the All India Muslim League was set up in the year 1906. It was meant to be a purely sectarian-cum-political organisation, and right upto the liquidation of British Raj, it grew from strength to strength, consolidating "the pulling back of 62 millions of people from joining the ranks of the seditious opposition", to the British rule. Its earliest aims were:

(1) "Infusing in the heart of Indian Musalmans, a sense of loyalty for the British Government and removing any misunderstanding regarding any measure of the Government that might creep into the mind of the community.

(2) Safeguarding the political rights and welfare of the Indian Musalmans and presenting their demands and requirements before the Government in a respectful manner.

(3) Presenting among Indian Mohammedans the growth of ideas prejudicial to the other communities of the country".[68]

Henceforth, it was this body that directed, supervised and controlled the Muslim Politics in India. Its activities encouraged Communalism. In fact, the Muslim League can never wash off its hands from the charge of destroying the very basis of any healthy growth of Hindu-Muslim relations in India. The creation of Pakistan is an ample evidence of the fact that the League's policy was too irrational, separatist, and narrowly communal in its outlook.

To sum up, we can say that during its political phase, Communalism developed as a creed of social tension, due to the uneven pace of the Economic, Social and Political progress of the Hindus and Muslim communities.

The fact of 'Communal-lag', coupled with the British policy of 'exploitation and counterpoise', led to unconscious parting of the ways between the Hindus and the followers of the Islam. The emergence of the Muslim League as a protector of the rights of the Muslim community, did not help in bettering the Hindu Muslim relations. On the contrary, these relations grew worse. The technique of seeking protection through external props in the form of separate communal electorate, and various safeguards and other communal devices, did not and could not abridge the fact of `Communal-lag', that widened with the growth and advance of the Capitalistic rule of the British. It was inevitable therefore that the Muslim League should follow a separatist policy in the national struggle against the British. Muslim separatism sought its justification in the fear of future dominance by Hindus and pleaded that the last refuge of the backward Muslim middle-class lay in having a separate homeland where the Muslims could live undisturbed by other competitors without smarting under the handicaps imposed by this `Communal-lag' between them and other communities, particularly the Hindus. The key to Muslim political and economic prosperity seemed to lie only in a scheme for the `vivisection of India'.

This solution could be successful only on the plea that Islam was in danger in India. Once again it was the Muslim League that was the vanguard of such propaganda. The real danger for Islam did not come from any outside agency. It came from within , in its inability to adapt to the changed conditions. As W.C. Smith in his work entitled *Modern Islam in India* wrote:

> "If Islam, or any other religion, hopes to survive, it must adapt itself to the new world, must answer new questions and meet new needs. But men find it much easier to protect iràtely, than to work out those answers and those ways of meeting needs. Islam is indeed in danger, but the more conservative and the worse Communalist Islam is, the greater the danger".[69]

Categorically denying any other factor, except the economic he said:

> "And it is easily to let oneself be confused into thinking that the danger to Islam comes from Hinduism and the Hindus.... Because, Hindu culture, in India is more industrialized than the less advanced `Muslim Culture', therefore even the infiltration of Western bourgeois materialism can be interpreted as coming from (or atleast by way of) the Hindus. Less subtly, Islam is in danger in that the Muslim middle class and the Muslim lower class are being oppressed and dominated by the more highly

> developed, expansive, `Hindu' middle class Capitalism. Islam is indeed in danger too in the sense that the Muslim middle class is in grave danger of extinction being a petty bourgeois class in a collapsing Capitalist World".[70]

As such, the twentieth century Muslim demand for separate statehood and its constitutional recognition by the British in the form of Pakistan was illogical and irrational, though a successful solution of this lag was brought about by the historical processes of the nineteenth century.

This political solution of the material maladjustment between Hindus and Muslims in India, leads us to the following sociological axioms.

Firstly, that in a given society, a change in its structure, inevitably brings a change in the indigenous relationship.

Secondly, that any such transformation either in the social status, or in the possession of the economic means of production and distribution or in the political importance of the different communities, is likely to lead to social disruption in the society, more particularly, if the major social constituents were to progress at varying rates that cause a 'lag' between them.

Thirdly, the group that lags behind not only becomes a perpetual source of social-tension, but given support from the state, can even lead to a political disintegration.

The British impact in India brought an important change in the indigenous, social, economic and political life of the country. Communalism was the consequence of the mutual action and interaction of this structural change and disparity of native response that it evoked from Hindu and Muslim communities.

NOTES AND REFERENCES

1. "Modern India and the West" - A study of the interaction of their civilization. Ed. by L.S.S. O'Malley C.I. E. (Oxford University Press London, 1941) See Chapter I by O'Malley, p. 13.
2. *Ibid.*, p. 42.
3. "The Individual and the Group" by Dr. B.K. Malik. p. 76.
4. *Ibid.*, p. 74.
5. *Ibid.*, p. 75.
6. *Ibid.*, p. 75.

7. Records of Government of India, Home Department, File No. B. Public Jan. 1894. Nos. 309/414.
8. *Social Background of Indian Nationalism* by Dr. A.H. Desai: Popular Book Depot, Lamington Road, Bombay (2nd Ed. 1954), pp. 151-52.
9. *Ibid.*, p. 152.
10. *Modern Islam in India* by W.C. Smith.
11. *The Birth of Pakistan* by Dr. Sachin Sen. General Printers & Pub. Ltd. 119, Dharamtala Street, Calcutta. B. First Edn. (1955) p. 32.
12. Original Consultation: Home Department. Judicial. 9th Oct. 1869. No. 10/11.
13. Original Consultations. Home Deptt. Judicial. 27th March. 1869. 30/33.
14. *Ibid.*
15. Smith, *op. cit.*
16. O'Malley *op. cit.*, p. 398.
17. Government of India Records (Sub. Employment of Mohammedans in the Government of India Offices. Home Departments, note to the Legislative Department B. Sept., 1913. No. 51.
18. The Cambridge History of India (Ed. H.H. Dodwell: (1858-1918) Vol. VI, The University Press Cambridge (1932), p. 112.
19. In the Highest Grade in which the appointments dated from a previous generation, the Mohammedans did not much to complain of, as

    In 1869 there was one M. to two H.

    Now there was 1 M to 2

    Now " 1 M to 3 H.

    II. In the Second Grade

    1869 there were 2 M : 9 H.

    Now 1 M : 10 H.

    III. In the Third Grade

    1809 4M. to a total of 27 Hindus and Englishmen.

    3M to a total of 24 Hindus and Englishmen.

    IV In the Lower Banks

    1809 4 M : 30 of all creeds.

    4 M : 30 of all creeds.

    V. Among Probationers from whom the service recruited:

    2 M : 28

    Now there is not a single Muslim.

    It is however in the less conspicuous departments, in which the distribution of patronage, is less keenly watched by the political parties in Bengal, that we may read the fate of the Musalmans:

    In 1869

    1. In the 3 grades of Assistants, Govt. Engineers 13H and 1 M.

2. Among the apprentices : 4 H and 2 E and Zero M.
3. Among the Sub-Engineers and Supervisors of the Public Works Deptt. 24 H and 1 M.
4. Among the Overseers: 63 H. and 2 M.
5. In the offices of Account: 50H. and No Muslim.
6. In Upper subordinate Departments: 22 H. and No M.

But it is unnecessary to multiply instances of a fact that is patent in every page of the civil list.

F. Judges of Her Majesty's Court of Judicature in Bengal: 2 H: No M.

1869 II. Law Officers of the Crown: 4 E : 2 H. : No M.

III. Officers of the High Court: 21.

7 H : No M.

Barrister at Law 3H. : No M.

IV. But the list of Pleaders of the High Court, a sort of subordinate Barristers, tells the most cruel story of all.

This was a branch of the Profession almost completely in the hands of the Mussalmans with the memory of men still living.

Uptil 1851, Mohammedans stoutly held their own and in fact equals the whole number of the English and Hindu pleaders put together.

From 1851 the scene changes. A new order of men began to come to the front.

Different tests of fitness were exacted and the list shows that out of two hundred and forty natives admitted from 1852 to 1868, two hundred and thirty-nine were Hindus and only one a Mussalman.

239 : 1

V. Passing to the next grade in the professional, the attorneys, Proctors, and Solicitors of the High Court, there were in 1869.

27 H : No M.

VI. Among rising generation of articled clerks there were

26 H : No M.

It matters not to what department of profession, I turn, the result is the same.

VII. In the office of the Registrar of the High Court.

In 1869, out of 17: 6E, + 11 H and Zero M.

VIII. In the Receivers Office:

Out of 4 : 2 E + 2 H + Zero M.

In all the nookes and crannies of the Law, in the Offices of Account, the Sheriff's Offices, Coroner's Office and Office of Interpreters, twenty names were given.

20 : 8 E + 11 H + 1 M.

One Mussalman, the sole representative of the Mohammedan population on the list, and he is a miserable Maulvi (Law Officer) on six shillings a week.

Profession of Medicine.

Unhappily, the Medicine, as practised by the native doctors, scarcely ranks as a Profession among the upper classes of Mohammedans.

A Mussalman gentleman has two medical attendants:

(1) Tabib - Physician, Hakim

(2) Jarrah - Barber - Surgeon.

In 1869, Statistics stood thus - Among the Graduates of Medicine in the Calcutta 'Varsity.

1. 4 Doctors : 3 H + 1 E + 0 M.
2. 11 Bachelor of Med: 10 H + 1 E + 0 M.
3. 104 Licentiates of Medicine : 98 H + 5 E + 1 M.

(The above datas have been taken from the book entitled, *The Indian Mussalmans*, by Sir W.W. Hunter. Sir Hunter was one of the senior most civil servants of his time. His contributions to the History of India which came in the form of remarkable and scholarly books shall be long remembered).

(*) *The Hindu way of Life* by L.S.S. O'Malley, C.I.E. (1927).

20. Home Dept. Edn. Aug. 19, 1871; No. 2-8.
21. 'Modern India and the West' - A study of the interaction of their Civilisations (Ed. by O'Malley), p. 339.
22. *Ibid.*, p. 344.
23. *Modern Religious Movements in India* by Dr. J.N. Farquhar, (1915), p. 433.
24. *The Hindu Muslim Questions* by Dr. Beni Prasad, p. 18-19.
25. British Imperialism in India by Joan Beauchamp. Martin Lawrence Ltd. London W.C. 1 (1934), p. 163.
26. *Modern Islam in India: A Social Analysis* by W.C. Smith. Victor Gollanex Ltd. London (1946).
27. Original consultations: Home Dept. Ist Apl. 1859. Pub. A.Nos. 35/37.
28. This elaborate work on Md. Law in six quarter volumes was compiled in India in the days and under the order of Emperor Aurangzeb (Alamgeer).
29. Home Dept. Ind. Sept. 1872. B. Nos. 130-131.
30. Home Dept. Oct. 1888. Edn. Nos. 1-11.
31. Home Department (1888) Edn. Oct. Nos. 1-11. (The above memorial was signed by Mohd. Imamulaha, President of the Association).
32. *Ibid.*

33. Education Commission Report (1886), p. 580.
34. Home Dept. Edn. August 1886. Nos. 57 and 58.
35. Home Dept. Edn. Feb. 1889, Nos. 47-52 (Mohammedan Community and State Patronage).
36. *The Life and Work of Syed Ahmed Khan* by H. Col. G.F. I Graham William Blackwood and Sons Edn. and London (1885), p. 39.
37. *Ibid.*, p. 50.
38. Maulana Mohammed Ali - Coconada Congress (1921).
39. 'Muslim India' (Rise and growth of the All India Muslim League) by Mohammed Nowan. Kitabghar Allahabad (1942).
40. Home Deptt. (Books and Pub.) B. March 1889 Nos. 214-15.
41. *Ibid.*, (The Pioneer of the 4th ...... made).
42. *Ibid.*
43. The Aligarh Institute Gazette dated August 28, 1888, pp. 970-71.
44. See Political India (1832-1932) (Ch. IV. 'Mohammedan Movements by Theodore Morison') P.89.
45. Sic.
46. *Divided India* by Dr. Rajendra Prasad, p. 104.
47. Tufail Ahmad, *op. cit.*, pp. 311-12 (Quoted by *Ibid.*, p. 104).
48. Tufail Ahmad, *op. cit.*, p. 315 (Quoted by *Ibid.*, p. 105).
49. Dr. Prasad, *op. cit.*, p. 106.
50. Smith W., *op. cit.*, p. 30.
51. Home Deptt. Ed. June 1873, No. 74-111.
52. Home Deptt. Edn. Deposit. Nov. 1901. No. 4.
53. A speech delivered by Lord Lytton's arrival to inaugurate the College Library at Aligarh. See Grahm, *op. cit.*, p. 274.
54. *India* by C.M. Philips. Hinson's University Library, Stratford Place, London, W.1. p. 106.
55. *India Divided* by Dr. Rajendra Prasad, p. 99. Quoted from 'Musalmanon Ka Roshan Mustaqbal, by Tufail Ahmed, p. 283.
56. *Ibid.*, p. 106.
57. Noman, *op. cit.*, p. 34-36.
58. *The Muslim League* by Lal Bahadur: Agra Book Store, p. 4. (Quoted from the Aligarh Institute Gazette dated July 21, 1888, pp. 806-13.
59. Tufail Ahmed, *op. cit.*, p. 347
60. *Ibid.*, p. 350.
61. Viqar-i-Hayat, Pub. by Muslim Univ. Aligarh, p. 670.
62. *Roshan Mustaqbal*, by M. Tufail Ahmed, pp. 360-61
63. *The Memoirs of Aga Khan* by Agha Khan. Cassel and Company, London K.C.4 (1954), p. 92.
64. Quoted from *Pakistan or Partition of India* by B.R. Ambedkar, p. 428.
65. *Ibid.*, pp. 441-42.

66. *Ibid.*, pp. 441-42.
67. *Ibid.*, pp. 441-42.
68. The Aligarh Institute Gazette dated January 9, 1907, p. 6.
69. Smith, *op. cit.*
70. *Ibid.*

Section Two

The Psychological Aspect of Communalism

It is essential for a clear understanding of communalism in its political phase, to examine it from the psychological point of view. It need not be emphasized that the presence of the British had created an atmosphere of communal distrust, communal phobia and intense communal rivalry. As such, the masses moved with the time, more conscious of differences and disparity among themselves, than ever before. The various communities could not live to evolve into a composite whole. They were often over cautious, too jealous and too isolated in their inter-communal relations. The individuals belonging to various communities even fought on the basis of certain false notions, stereotypes and a few mental complexes, they entertained of each other. Such a state of affairs, which lacked the spirit of understanding and tolerance, was a sure ground where communalism as a creed of social tension could thrive in its most acute form.

One can easily single out 'frustration', experienced by the Indians as the most dominant factor which determined the relations between the Hindus and the Muslims. The history of communalism in this phase is verily nothing but an account of the maladaptive and adaptive reactions to the frustration that various communities underwent in their struggle with the forces of Imperial domination. The maladaptive consequence led to narrow communalism; and the adaptive consequence gave birth to the forces of nationalism, directed against the oppressive rule of the alien power.

The native reaction was all the more accentuated by an unscrupulous application of the policy of "exploitation and counterpoise" in the administration of the country. While exploitation inspired nationalist sentiments, the policy of counterpoise promoted a communal outlook amongst the indigenous masses.

Paradoxical as it may seem, both nationalism and communalism proved to be an outlet for frustrated emotions of the various communities. However, in the former, the forces of reaction were launched against the foreign domination in India, whereas in the latter, the forces of reaction manifested themselves through unhealthy rivalry amongst the communities themselves, each envying with the other for an enhancement of its economic and political status in any future set-up. The one led to the emancipation of the country, and the other to its political bifurcation.

It can obviously be asked as to what led to this state of frustration.

The truth is that, there were countless reasons for the people to feel sore and frustrated, reasons that cannot be easily summarized.

The enslavement of their country by aliens, however, was the chief source of frustration to the Indian people. It was a shock that the nation as a whole experienced. The sense of 'frustration' was not confined to the 'loss of political power', alone.

The sufferings through which the Indians passed under the British brought them a deep sense of frustration in almost every walk of life, be it moral or religious, social or economic, administrative or political. Behind every action of the British, behind every law that they enacted, behind every gesture that they made, there was latent, and utter sense of contempt for the black Indians. The favours that the Indians extracted were more in the nature of grudging concessions. They came only when the British diplomacy thought it fit to give. It will not be an exaggeration to say that the life of an Indian in relation to his master was the life of an outcaste — a pariaha in one's own land. It was for many years that Indians were 'excluded from every honour dignity or office which the lowest English could be prevailed upon to accept'.[1] For years together the life of Indians remained but a miserable tale of indigenous helplessness and alien atrocities. British exploitation and plunder of the native masses knew no end and as an Englishman writes "poverty more shameless, more naked and more undisguised"[2] than anywhere in the world, was what the white Sahibs gave to India.

British India knew no such thing as the fundamental rights of humanity. Repressive laws, ordinances and acts, were the only articles of the *Indian Magna-Carta*. Holt Markenzie wrote:

> "There is probably no example of a government carrying the principles of absolutism so completely through the civil administration of the country if that can be called civil which is in spirit so military".[3]

In every walk of life, whether civil or military, government had spread a network of fetters and they had chained life alike in public, prison and palace and made it equally miserable in either case. British terrorism and bloodshed made no discrimination between Hindu and Muslim, men or women. Gordon Halstead an American Missionary writes that in United Provinces "women were raped stripped naked and made to 'frog parade', through the streets".[4]

It is common knowledge that the British Army organized prostitution for its own purposes. It was done so under the patronage of Lord Roberts. The following is an extract from the circular memorandum issued in the name of Roberts as Commander-in-chief by Quarter Master-General Chapman and sent to every Cantonment in India:

> "In the regimental bazars it is necessary to have a sufficient number of women, to take care that they are sufficiently attractive, to provide them with proper houses, and above all, to insist upon means of ablution being always available.[5]

A Swiss Professor and former substitute delegate at the League of Nation, is said to have remarked that, "the only place where women were not safe in India was under the walls of British barracks".[6] The opinion was confirmed by Dr Sunderland, an American Missionary. He wrote: "In my own travels in India, I found that all communities in or near which soldiers were stationed particularly foreign (British) soldiers, regarded their presence as a danger to their women".[7] Naturally the natives suffered severe frustration at their inability, helplessness to resist the Feranghi oppression and prostitution of native dignity and honour.

Indians felt most grievously frustrated on the political and religious fronts. Politically the ruling caste of Rajas, Maharajas and nobles bleeded at their incapacitated and helpless state. This political insecurity was augmented by a sense of religious insecurity which happened to be the worst fear of the masses. The mere fact of the new masters being devoted to Christianity, a religion alien to that of the natives, was a sufficient cause of well founded fears, regarding the safe and uncontaminated preservation of their own benefits. If, to a Hindu, it was the rule of malechhas, then to a Muslim, the very fact of the rulers being the followers of a religion other than Islam, had converted this country into a land of infidels and hence a land of war, the *dar-ul-harb*. Henceforth it was not a place worth a moment's stay for a true Mussalman.

In short, British advent in India proved to be a calamity that brought both material and psychological privation to countless millions irrespective of their caste, creed or community.

In India, the Evangelical Christian missionaries had started working actively by the year 1793 (and they continue as yet, even after the British have left India). The missionaries usually get a helping hand from the Government. In spite of the instructions of the court of directors, who were 'more concerned with trading profits', East India Company did not hesitate to interfere with the native customs, traditions and religious rites.

The untrammelled pursuit of evangelization, proved to be an exceedingly disturbing factor in the life of Indian communities. Their policy of conversion and their attacks on the religions of Hindus and Mussalmans deeply hurt the susceptibilities of the masses, who could not receive any redress from their rulers in this respect, as in most cases they leaned to the views expressed by the fellow missionaries. Herbert Edwards, who was commissioner at Peshawar during the mutiny declared that 'Providence has placed India in British hands in order that the people might be Christianized'.[8]

In India, although the primary activity of the government had been 'an activity of conquest and annexation', yet the British sentiment both at home and abroad leaned strongly in favour of Christianizing India. No less than a person like Lord Palmerston said:

"Till India is leavened with Christianity, She will be unfit for freedom. When India is learned with Christianity she will be unfit for anything less; and England may then... leave the stately daughter she has reared to walk the future with a free Imperial step. I firmly believe this is what God meant England to do with India".[9]

Not only in moral and religious spheres, but the British interfered in social, economic, administrative and political systems. The tampering with the Indian way of life by the British knew no scruples or limits. Imperialism has everywhere been an unmasked and relentless force of aggression. Imperialists have seldom left unscathed any aspect of their victims life. The destruction of the religious and cultural base of the masses usually went along with the liquidation of their political set-up. We have seen at length the consequences of the destruction of the native structure on the life of Indians. It aggravated communal tension and unleashed forces of disequilibrium and fear-psychosis. However, frustration remained the keynote of the whole situation. As Mehta and Patwardhan aptly wrote:

"Thus the social, economic and political forces working on Indian society have created a situation whose keynote in frustration British rule is largely responsible for the social stagnation, economic debility and cultural indifferences that constitute the framework of our lives".[10]

The reaction of the frustrated Indians was both adaptive and maladaptive in nature. It gave birth to the forces of national emancipation as also to the forces of communal-tension. "By an easy transition, the reaction to life's frustration expresses itself in antagonisms *inter se*: Hindu-Muslim, Brahmin-non-Brahmin, touchable-untouchable. Such side stepping of resistance to British rule gains in momentum as it does not usually remain unappreciated in Government quarters. The reaction to British rule has thus assumed two forms - anti imperialist and inter-communal".[11]

It was in this manner that Nationalism as also communalism proceeded hand in hand under the British,

We know that the maladaptive consequences of the frustration are usually expressed in either of the following ways:[12]

(1) Aggression,
(2) Regression,

(3) Withdrawal,
(4) Repression,
(5) Sublimation,
(6) Rationalization and projection,
(7) Autism, and
(8) Identification.

The adaptive consequence of frustration are in main three viz:

(1) The substitution of goal,
(2) The Re-organisation of Perception of the problem,
(3) The Intensification of effort.

An historical examination of Hindu Muslim relations in India clearly reveals that the two communities underwent most of these phenomenons, as a consequence of the frustrations that they suffered under the British.

In the Wahabi-rising of the Muslims, we witness the first traces of a maladaptive reaction to the frustration suffered by that community. It manifested both through 'aggression' and 'retreat'. The former was expressed through the cry of a holy war i.e. Jehad against the British. In the latter manifestation, it was a call for Hijrat, a movement in which thousands of Muslims left India to take shelter in a land of Islam (*Dar-al-Islam*), thus, resolving their frustration by a psychological withdrawal from the un-Islamic land of war (*Dar-al-Harb*) that India had become after the British advent.

Another aggressive reaction to the frustration suffered by Indians, in which Hindus and Muslims acted in cooperation with each other, came in the form of a series of outbreaks starting with the famous revolt of Vellore in 1807, and culminating in a concerted attempt of the natives in 1857, which was "much more than a mutiny of sepoys and much less than a national rebellion".

Both these maladaptive consequences though anti-British in nature, also produced a serious impact on the hitherto existing relations between the indigenous communities. In both the cases, Hindu-Muslim relations were seriously damaged due to the presence of a third factor in the British. In the case of the Wahabi movement, they encouraged its anti-Hindu character whereas after the mutiny they adopted a policy that accentuated the communal-lag, existing between the Hindus and Muslims. As such communalism as a creed of social tension and disharmony spread like a wild fire, which often manifested itself in the form of communal riots and disturbances. What is much more important is the fact that the mutiny itself like the political holy wars of the Wahabis laid emphasis on the Muslim community of India being a distinct religo-political unit. Thus, frustration also led to a separatist tendency in the inter-communal relations in India with the Muslim community assuming the initiatives.

Yet another reaction to the native frustration found its outlet in the revivalistic movements, that agree both against Muslims and Hindus. These movements came as a measure of self defence against the Christian rulers and the crusading attitude of the Christian missionaries. As an analyst of the Hindu-Muslim question writes:

> "Psychologically, it was a partial restoration of the self-respect which had been deeply injured by political subjection. It represented at once resistance to Western encroachments, a recompense for the present degradation, a hope for the reign of righteousness in future".[13]

As we have already seen, in the case of the Muslims, these rivivalistic movements assumed both anti-Christian and anti-Hindu tendencies. Their main standpoint however always revolved round religious purification of Islam.[14]

Hindu revivalist tendency found its main outlet in religious reform movements like the Brahmo-Samaj, the Prarthana Samaj, the Arya Samaj and a few others like the Rama Krishna Mission, etc.

The Brahmo Samaj was established in 1828 by Raja Ram Mohun Roy (1772-1833). He was a religious reformer and a nationalist. He received education, customary to a Brahmin and in addition learned Arabic and Persian. He travelled throughout India and was in the employ of the British East India Company from 1804 to 1814. About him Hanskohn writes:

> "Roy was the pioneer of the renaissance movement in India, the first Hindu to break through the barriers between the ancient east and the modern west. He advocated that India adopt European intellectual achievement in order to further its own development. His numerous activities had

but one objective, to arouse India's spirit to free it from the deadening a ship or of medievalism. Though Roy's influence on European thought and social standards began to penetrate to a limited extent the circles of the high caste Hindus. He created a vernacular press and together with John Hare established the Hindu College in Calcutta, the first educational institute in India on Western lines. He was active in social reform and was instrumental in the abolition of the Suttee, the sacred Hindu-rite of immolating the living widow on the funeral pyre of her husband.

At an early age, Roy had come into contact with Islam and Sufism and had become critical of the polytheism and idolatry of the Hindus. Later, when he had learned English, his religious convictions were further modified by British liberal and rational ideas.

He became profoundly interested in religious reform and in 1828 with Davaraka Nath Tagore, he organised the Brahmo Samaj".[15]

"The Brahmo Samaj primarily aimed at social reform by `preaching a return to a purified and primitive Brahmanism combined with theism and humanitarian rationalism".[16]

The real importance of Brahmo Samaj lay in, "inaugurating a new era for the Indian people by proclaiming the principle of individual freedom, national unity, solidarity and collaboration and the democratisation of all social institutions and social relations".[17]

However, in the course of time a number of defects came to light in the Brahmo Samaj and a schism occurred in its own fold. Mr Parekh who before his conversion was a Brahmo missionary goes so far in his summing up of the Samaj as to say:

"Starting as an imitation of unitarian Christianity, it is to-day still merely a poor reflection of European Rationalism. To this intellectual bias it has added another which may well be called pharisaic and communal. It has become a kind of backwater of religious and communal life, separated by its own sense of self-satisfied superiority from the main currents of national life, which flows past it

> with a power and rapidity, which it can neither appreciate nor even understand".[18]

This severe judgement was not without some element of truth. Explaining the same H.C.E. Zacharias wrote:

> "Taking first the taunt of communalism, it must never be forgotten that in a country like India, not atomized by Western individualism, there is simply no room for unattached individuals. Membership in a caste of their own for those who refuse to comply with the traditional rules and taboos of the caste, into which they are born, is in India an absolute necessity: small wonder therefore that, on the one hand the English for instance have straightaway constituted a caste of their own: and that on the other hand converts to Islam-aye to Christianity- have likewise inevitably formed castes and sub-castes. What else could have been done by Ram Mohan Roy and his followers, who, were rejected by orthodox Hindu-Society, but to form a society of their own? English society would not incorporate them to let themselves be assimilated by Native Christian or Anglo-Indian society was equally out of the question; so was there really any alternative for them, but to develop into a caste with a social and religious code, a Dharma of their own?"[19]

The truth is that, Ram Mohun Roy had to begin by forming an 'elite which would be a leaven, working away gradually from above downwards, leavening the whole mass of Indian society". We agree with the contemporary and modern critics that the movement was never anti-Muslim in its outlook. On the contrary, it marked the beginning of the first organised expression of the Indian national awakening. Zacharias rightly comments:

> "Ram Mohan Roy and his Brahmo Samaj form the starting point for all the various Reform Movements — whether in Hindu religion, society or politics — which have agitated India during the past hundred years and which have led to her wonderful renaissance in these our own days".[20]

It was in 1867, that M.G. Ranade founded the Prasthana Samaj. It was yet another link in the revivalist movement of Hindus, and it had a programme of religio-social reforms on the lines followed by the Brahmo Samaj. Its activities did not make any significant impact on the development of Hindu-Muslim Relations in India.

It was in the year 1875, that the Arya Samaj was founded by Swami Dayanand Saraswati in Bombay. Another reformist group came into being when the Rama Krishan Mission was started by Swami Vivekananda in 1879. The cry of those preachers exhorting the people to, 'once again be ourselves' made a very wide impact on the Hindu community. The ancient Hindu Vedas and Upanishadas, were made the norm of future religious and communal life and unlike the Brahmo Samaj, the two groups opposed any compromise with the British. The vision to recreate the past Indian glory and the rejection of the British way of life made a deep impact on the frustrated Hindus. As an eminent historian remarks:

> "To the young frustrated Hindus, this doctrine was both timely and exciting: on the one side it afforded the strongest possible religious sanction for their political and economic grievances, on the other it enabled them to abandon the customary appeal to the doctrines of Burke and Mill and instead to turn directly to Hinduism. It was accepted that in this cause, all methods were justifiable in achieving the desired end, namely, the expulsion of alien influence and the political and spiritual resurrection of Hinduism. As one of their leaders wrote, "If thieves enter our house and we have not sufficient strength to drive them out we should without hesitation shut them up and burn them alive — we may kill even our teachers and kinsmen and no blame attaches if we are not actuated by selfish desires".[21]

The role played by the Arya Samaj in the life of this country is extremely significant as its activities were anti-sanatanist, anti-Muslim and anti-British in nature. The Arya Samaj was anti-sanatanist in the sense, that it was opposed to the orthodox notions of the, 'Sanatan Dharma' which is the religion professed by an overwhelming majority of Hindus. Dayananda Saraswati the founder of the Arya Samaj held that 'the born Brahmin was nothing more than an ordinary man'. He struck hard at the monopoly of the Brahmin in administering religious sacraments and in performing religious ceremonies. He denounced the worship of idols of Gods and Goddesses, and preached that only the Supreme being, the Primal cause of the Universe, the Universal and all-pervading spirit, should be worshipped, and none else. The great bulk of Brahmins were as ignorant of the Vedas as were the other Hindus. Even ceremonies were not necessarily performed according to Vedic texts. As such, Dayananda made an appeal to discard all the 'secular abuses and legendary accretions of orthodox Hinduism' and go back to the pristine purity of the Vedas, that alone could reveal the true Dharma. Thus, we find that the Arya Samaj was a movement directed towards a 'protestant' reformation of Hinduism which had become corrupted under the patronage and care of Brahmins, who were the chief exponents of Sanatan-Dharma.

It was anti-Muslim because it entertained a communal outlook and held a hostile attitude to Islam in particular and non-Hindus in general. It did a yeomen service to Hindus by a vigorous drive of reclamation and conversion of those Hindus who had left Hindu society and were now unacceptable to caste-Hindus. It was in this work of the Mussalman Mullah and the Christian Missionary, the Arya Samaj met with considerable success in reclaiming Hindus converted to other faiths and in stemming the tide of conversion of Hindus to other faiths. It also helped in raising the social status of the depressed classes among the Hindus and prevented them from leaving Hinduism and joining other religious denominations. The Muslims naturally felt provoked and retaliated. Funds were collected and Maulvies and Mullahs, Theologians and laymen deputed to check the movement. They were afraid about the increasing reduction of their followers. Fretful about the growth of Islam in India in the future, 'they took a very serious view of the situation and threatened to avenge the great insult as they called it, by Sword and fire. They not only breathed fire and swore vengeance on the Arya Samaj and its leaders like Swami Dayanand Saraswati and Swami Shardhananda, but also issued numerous Fatwas against those who had deserted Islam. A new movement called 'Tabligh' was started under the patronage of educated Mussalmans, in order to counteract the evil effects of Shuddhi. A vast propaganda was started to push on Islam by all kinds of means, even by violence, coercion and fraud. As Lala Lajpat Rai writes:

"Shuddhi and Tabligh thus set up one against the other,

created a situation the like of which was not known to Indian history. Riots, disturbances, murders, abduction of women and minors and other kinds of violence created an atmosphere of a warring camp in India. The Muslims hated the Hindu and vice versa. As result of these strained feelings, each party blamed the other for the excesses committed in communal riots. Shuddhi was not the direct cause of these riots. But the wound inflicted on Muslim sentiment by the Shuddhi was undoubtedly one of the basic causes which produced the atmosphere which led to these riots and other exhibitions of violence. The motives were partly political, partly economic and partly religious. For several years, it seemed that a pandemonium had been let loose".[22]

The Arya Samaj is still alive after having survived all these vicissitudes and crises. Its early revivalistic tendencies and its policy of 'conversion and reconversion of non-Hindus to Hinduism, that became a normal phase of Hindu life' did embitter the relations of the two communities. Hindu-Muslim relations thus grew worse each day keeping communalism alive as a creed of social tension in India.

The activities of the Arya Samaj because of their nationalistic and seditious ferver, were looked upon by the British as a, 'serious menace to England and her sovereignty'.[23]

The British Government of India took a very serious note of the activities of the Arya Samaj; the government made special confidential enquiries against it. The central Special Intelligence Branch observed, "The Arya Samaj is one of the most important of the modern seats and was founded by Pandit D. Saraswati, a Brahmin of Kathiawar, who having convinced himself of the untrustworthiness of the sacred books of the Hindus subsequent to the Vedas, formulated his new system and attacked the existing orthodox Hinduism. He aroused considerable antagonism, and his death, which took place at Ajmer in October 1883, was not without suspicion of poisoning. The Arya (lit. true) or, 'Vedic' religion is primarily the outcome of the solvent action of natural science on modern Hinduism. In the eyes of the Arya Samaj, the four Vedas constitute the only infallible revelation and the bases of the Aryan Faith is the revelation of God in the Vedas and the revelation of God in Nature and the first practical element in this belief is the interpretation of the Vedas in conformity with the proved results of Natural science. In its interpretation of the Vedas, the Arya Samaj found itself at issue with other Sanskritists. The three entities of Dayanand's philosophy, are — God, the Soul and Matter. The Samaj finds an efficacy in prayer and worship but greatly limits the number of ceremonies to which it accedes any meritorious power. It discourages the practice of bathing in sacred streams, pilgrimages, the use of beads and sandalwood marks, gifts to mendicants and all the thousand rites of popular Hinduism. It holds the futility of rites on behalf of the dead. Idolatry and all its attendant ceremonies according to the Aryans, have no basis in the Vedas and no place in true religion. The Aryas defend their religion from the charges of novelty and regard it as a revival of an old forgotten faith, the decay of which was mainly due to the Brahmins. The Arya theory of today is that, the real Brahmin is one who is a Brahmin at heart, that the Vedas are not confined to one class, and that all castes are equal before God. Though this is the theory of Aryas, in practice they will not eat or intermarry with people of other castes. The movement is to a great extent confined to the educated classes and one of the most striking features of its readiness to readmit into caste, converts to Christianity or Mohammedanism, who are willing to re-embrace the old faith. The Arya Samaj disapproves of child marriages and encourages widow remarriage. It has within its realm, female education, orphanages and schools dispensaries and public libraries and philanthropic institutions of all sorts. The Aryan doctrines have been formulated into a series of ten propositions and any person professing belief in the fundamental principles of the Samaj is eligible for membership. Whether the members of the sect are increasing or not is a moot point, but its strength is not to be estimated by members. The Aryas have an influence quite out of proportion to their numerical strength, from the fact that they are recruited almost entirely from the English Educated classes, and that their tenets are most popular among pleaders, government servant and others who have the greatest pretensions to mental enlightenment. It has been alleged that in the morning hymns of the Samaj, they ask for the deliverances from the rule of aliens. This has not been substantiated; but the following prayer written by Dayananda Saraswati was reported by the Punjab Govt. in October, 1889, to be used regularly by the members of the Samaj:

> "We are the subjects of the Lord of creation, and the supreme spirit is our King. We are the humblest of His slaves. May He graciously grant us the privilege of ruling in the world created by Him and enable us to dispense His true justice."

Though bitterly at variance with the orthodox Hindus in other points, they are at one with them in the matter of cow-preservation. A split has commenced in the current year between the vegetarian and the meat-eating members of the Samaj. Formerly Aryas kept themselves aloof from politics, but they are now freely taking part in all political movements."[24]

The British were extremely fretful about the growing sense of unity that was being actively fostered amongst Hindus, through the activities of the Samajists, and more particularly through the agitation against cow-slaughter-In India, the cow was to all Hindus a symbol of reverence. It was a unifying force that brought all Hindus together irrespective of their mutual differences of caste and sect.

The cow protection movement was originally started by the Arya Samaj of Calcutta, in Punjab in 1882. The movement resulted in an attempt in Lahore to get up a monster petition against kine killing. A committee under Swami Dayanand Saraswati was formed to secure cooperation of Hindus throughout the country. The government apprehended that the movement had not only the support of the Rajahs of Bettiah, Durbangha and Halwa of Bengal, Benaras, Hodhpur and of Marahatta pleaders of the Central provinces, but that it also had the support of the Indian National Congress (1885) a body of which the above persons were active supporters. A District Magistrate in the N.W. Provinces, describing this movement said: "The whole of Hindu population is driven into its arms by the tyranny of the caste and when once the League is established in any place, its grasp is so powerful that every man, woman and child must openly or secretly contribute to its funds or cease to be a Hindu".

As such, the cow-protection movement was later on taken up enthusiastically by the Hindu religious bodies, the Dharma Sabhas, throughout the country. At various places, 'Gau Rakshni Sabhas' (cow-protection societies) were established, whose leadership was taken up by the Brahmin officials, pleaders and school masters. Hindu Rajas and nobles gave their tacit support to this movement; the main supporters of this movement however were the Hindu trading and banking classes.

The cow protection movement naturally unleashed a devastating force of communalism. For the cow, which was a divine object to Hindus, was an animal of daily food for the Mohammedans and the English masters of India. Thousands of cows were daily slaughtered to provide beef for the British army and for the Muslim faithfuls. As could be expected, the movement took no time in precipitating an inevitable crisis; communal riots and disturbances spread out in an unceasing chain throughout the length and breadth of the country. In a review of the report of the Vernacular Press of Punjab in 1886, Mr Trupper wrote:, "The feelings connected with the slaughter of kine are politically, the most dangerous element in the Punjab. To the Mohammedans it is a welcome means of gratifying religious spite and also a symbol of their freedom from Hindu supremacy and disloyal Mohammedans may insidiously perceive that, by flaunting this emblem of their political enfranchisement in the eyes of their adversaries, they may rouse the anger of Hindus against the British Government except for whose tolerance practice would be suppressed. Either party may submit to British rulers preferable to the supremacy of the others but from both, foreign rulers must expect a certain kind and amount of antipathy and it is unfortunate that in the case of Sikhs and Hindus, such antipathy as there inevitably is, should be embittered in connection with the cow-question by a dangerous fanaticism directed against Mohammedans or against ourselves, or against both. All this, of course does not appear in the vernacular newspapers, but these remarks have been made to explain their tone with reference to kine killing".[25]

The British government found an ample scope in this movement to apply their subtle policy of divide and rule. They encouraged Mohammedan resentment and the inefficiency of their officials and other arrangements of law and order aggravated the intensity and number of communal riots. They assess this movement as communal-cum-political agitation. Commenting on the dangers of the movement, an official report said:

> "The primary danger is that the cow-protection question furnishes a common platform on which all Hindus of what ever sect however much at variance on other questions can and do unite. As a native official has well put it:, "To the Hindus it is the question of all questions and it will always be the war-cry of the discontented". While professed to be based on economic grounds, the agitation undoubtedly owes its success mainly to the religious element contained in it and perhaps also to the possibility that it may cause some embarrassment to an alien government. It must be held to be part of the Hindu revival of which the National Congress is another manifestation, the aspiration at the root of both being directed to the formation of an Indian nation and the displacement from power, place and emolument of the ruling race, who may however be permitted to guard India for its new Governors. The inflammable and seditious character of the utterances indulged in at cow-protection meetings has repeatedly been brought to notice. Though the movement is ostensibly directed against the Mohammedans, it is, as Sir. C. Corsthwaite recently pointed out, a form of disloyalty towards the British government and in this connection the preaching against the number of animals slaughtered to supply beef to the British soldier and to Europeans and the attempt made to rescue cattle destined for the commissariat are very significant. Though the movement has a strong hold in the Bombay Presidency and C.P., there is not much likelihood of any serious danger arising out of the movement thereon in Bengal. The real danger lies in its spread in the N.W.P. and the Punjab where serious disturbances between the Hindus and Mohammedans and collisions with the authority of government have already occurred. The Kuka rising of 1872 had its origin in the

> abhorrence of the sect to cow-killing and the recent riots in the Eastern districts of the N.W.P. are due to the spread of the agitation to those parts from the neighbouring districts in Bengal. It has often pointed out that under Mohammedan rules, the Hindus have made no attempt to raise this question and that before the time when the Hindus were stirred up by the existing political propaganda, the Hindus and Mohammedans hardly ever fell out with each other over cow-slaughter or went to the lengths they do now. Mohammedan organs in the Native Press throw the blame upon the new education and sometimes on the Government which they declare does not maintain strict neutrality and lean towards the Hindus. Hindu organs on the other hand charge Government officials with deliberately sowing dissension between the two communities, favouring the Mohammedans at the expense of the Hindus in order to divide and rule."
>
> The allusion in the first section of this note to be a belief current among the Hindus, that the Russians would put a stop to kine-killing if ever they should conquer India and to the Kukas looking to the restoration of the Kuka Raj (Sikh Kingdom) to effect the same purpose should not be lost sight of".[26]

It is apparent that just as in the case of the Wahabi Movement, the British did not take drastic measures so long as the cow-protection movement remained a purely communal agitation. It was in their interest to see Hindus and Muslims always arrayed against each other. The only cautions they would take were in the nature of keeping a balance between the two communities. Sometimes it were the Hindus and sometimes it were the Mohammedans who were backed up by the British. Sir J.B. Lyall referring to the rise of Arya Samaj and the connected movements, advocated a policy of conciliation towards Hindus in the Punjab. The reasons, as one of his confidential minutes will reveal were purely political. He said:

> "I gather from many quarters that an idea has prevailed lately among the Hindus (Sikhs included) in the Punjab that we are turning from them and favouring the

> Mohammedans. Some say we are more afraid of the Mohammedans, others that we are influenced by dislike of the Arya Samaj and the educated Hindu.
>
> I think I can see some justification or at any rate explanation of this feeling which is in my opinion, one we should do all we can to remove.... Again in cow-killing dispute, the Mohammedan position is naturally apt to appear the more reasonable to our officers, and in other riots between the Hindus and Mohammedans, the Hindus say, perhaps with justice, that we judge any turbulence or fanaticism on their part more severely than on the part of Mohammedans.
>
> In India as a whole, it is more important politically to keep straight with the Hindus than with the Mohammedans. In Punjab, it is very necessary to hold the balance perfectly even between the two and to remember that before we took the country, the Hindus had the upper hand."

The movement assumed alarming proportions towards the close of the nineteenth century. The Intelligence Service of the Government observed that, there can be no doubt that the agitation is fostered from purely political motives by persons who are in no way actuated by genuine religious feeling. Such propagandists, as Sriman Swami (the ex-convict Desikachari) and Ala Ram are busy preachers of dissatisfaction with the British Government and all its works:

> "The attraction to them of the movement is not the discord which it need tends to set up between Hindu and Mussalman, but the difficulties which it imposes on the British Government and its commissariat in supplying the troops with beef. They recognize that Mussalmans and Europeans alike, beef-eaters, that the question of kine slaughter is the most delicate and difficult one in the face of a Hindu majority who venerate the cow, and that the more the agitation is fostered, the greater our difficulties will become".[27]

The Report concluded by blaming the Arya Samaj, "to whose exertions the propaganda in Punjab is chiefly due-a religious body professing to restore the ancient Vedic faith in India."

These movements put British law and order to severe test. It was not the strained Hindu-Muslim relations that moved the British machinery; rather it was the fear of a, 'recrudescence of excitement' to the level of an armed sedition that created a stir in their heart. It was now that they realized the inefficiency of their working of the British machinery. In a minute, an executive councillor remarked:

> "It is much important to interfere with propagandism and to arrest the agitation that proceeds these outbreaks... we have gradually surrounded ourselves with such a web of law, legality and we get entangled in it, as soon as we attempt to interfere even in proceedings which we know to be dangerous to the public peace—witness the decision that a Brahmin's bull cannot be an object of theft and any attempt to restrain liberty is either at once challenged, by people in England, whose only ideas of administration are based upon their knowledge of the quiet and peaceful squabbles of English Parishes".[28]

However, all this heart-searching did not bring on the part of the Government any positive step to introduce some measure that might bring greater understanding amongst the subjects themselves, as also amongst them and their masters. More stringent laws and greater and more ruthless oppression was the only instrument of social justice that the Imperialist masters could use for their subjects. There were different opinions expressed on the subject, 'as to what should be the correct way of meeting such agitation'. It is interesting to note that the agitation was likened by all to a mutiny in making, though there were some suggestions for, 'not going for very strong measures', an anti-Hindu policy was generally agreed upon by the members of the Governor General's Executive council. The following note of one of the councillor's throws an interesting light on the British attitude towards revivalist trends amongst the Hindus:

"If I have, from the first, been opposed to the adoption of violent or precipitate measures for controlling this agitation, it has certainly not been because I looked upon it with indifference, or underrated the risks to which it exposes us; on the contrary, I doubt whether, since the Mutiny, any movement containing in it a greater amount of potential mischief has engaged the attention of the Government of India. The magnitude of the danger arises from this, that the agitation has supplied the whole of the disloyal elements to be found in the Indian community with a popular backing which they could not have obtained from any other source. The case presents a close analogy to that which has arisen in Ireland. Just as the Home Rule movement was comparatively powerless while its supporters limited their demands to political and constitutional reforms; so, I believe would any purely political movement in India be innocuous while it represented nothing more than the vague political aspirations of the half-educated classes, and asked for nothing more embarrassing than such reforms as the reconstitution of the Legislative councils or the amends of the Arms Act, or the separation of the Judicial from the Executive. But, as in Ireland, the Home Rule movement became really formidable from the moment when Mr Parnell's sagacity connected it with the Agrarian question, and thereby gave a material interest in Home Rule to every Irish peasant, so in India the unrest and discontent which have found expression in the Congress movement and in other political combinations, will, I am afraid, become unfortunately more dangerous now that a common ground has been found upon which the educated Hindus and the ignorant masses can combine their forces.

I am therefore, by no means disposed to treat the danger which has arisen with contempt but I am strongly of opinion, that we shall render it more dangerous still, if by precipitate or ill-considered action we afford a new stimulus to the movement, or if we are frightened into departing by an inch from the attitude of strict neutrality which the Government of India has hitherto observed in dealing with all questions.

It should be remembered that as Sir Antony MacDonnell has pointed out, we have to deal not with a difficulty of recent origin, but with one of old standing which partly owing to the revival of orthodox Hinduism, partly owing to the political unrest prevalent amongst the educated Hindus, partly owing to the tendency of the people to organize and to communicate to an extent under or before the means of communication and locomotion had been rendered as easy as they are at the present time is for the moment passing through an exceptionally acute stage.

The position is more complicated, because the movement is prima-facie a legal and blameless one. We should therefore, find that we had embarked in a struggle with the whole organization of Hindu caste, throughout India - a struggle into which I for one, should not enter with a light heart and which I would strain every effort to avoid.

As Mr Lyall has shown, the case of the Punjab is entirely different from that of other provinces in which Hindus and Mohammedans have lived together for over a century under British protection. An extension of the Punjab Rules to other parts of India would certainly be regarded as an enormous concession to the Hindus and a serious affront to the Mussalmans.

My own idea is that any attempt to register a stereotype customary rights would not only be impossible in practice; but would probably lead to a revival of the excitement which is fortunately dying away, and would place both parties to the dispute once more upon the alert".[29]

It is apparent, therefore, that the Revivalistic movements in India were pregnant with nationalistic sentiments. They were a positive index of the native unrest as caused by their subjection to an alien power. However, since the native resentment against the British found a communal outlet, the growth of nationalist feeling was subtly camouflaged by the British under the cloak of Communalism.

The British forgot that the cause of the unrest was not to be sought in either the role of the Wahabees or that of the Arya Samajists. It was to be sought in the nature and practice of the tenets of their Imperialistic doctrine for India. Lala Lajpat Rai refuting the charge brought by the Lt. Governor of Punjab, that wherever there was an Arya Samaj, it was the centre of unrest, aptly said:

> "There can be no progress without unrest, But, to be quite just, the Arya Samaj is not the true source of unrest in India. The Government itself with its educational policy and its Western methods of administration, has contributed materially towards that same unrest. The Arya Samaj may quite logically be pronounced an outcome of the conditions imported into India from the West, and as such, it has

> absolutely, no reason to repent or be ashamed of the share it has had in adding to the volume or modifying the character of the unrest that was the inevitable consequence of modern conditions of life in India".[30]

He further added:

> "That the Arya Samaj is one of the most potent nationalising forces, no one should need deny. The Arya Samaj aims at radical changes in the thought and life of the people. It aims at the formation of a new national character, on the fundamental basis of Vedic thought and Vedic life. It was essential for it to create dissatisfaction with the existing conditions in Hindu society; to create an ambition for better thought and better life, an ambition that was bound to bring about unrest. The Arya Samaj began its work by recalling the greatness of ancient India, and impressed upon the Hindus that the land of Vedas and Shastras had no right, 'to sink into the role of more critic or imitation of European letters' or European life. Yet that was at best the condition of the Indian mind at the beginning of Dayanand's apostolic career. The Hindu mind which, till then, could not get out of the vicious circle of mere forms or mere habits — and to some extent is even now in bondage — had to be broadened. So it had to be told that habit was only a factor in the evolution of character and not character itself; that mere personal refinement could not take the place of active ends and ideals, which are the elixir of life of all social organisms as of individuals; that mere, 'quietness, docility, resignation, and obedience' could not form a national character; and that it was necessary to foster also, 'strength, initiative sense of responsibility, and power of rebellion'."[31]

It is very true that both the Muslim and the Hindu revivalistic movements did infuse amongst their followers a spirit of rebellion, against the dominance of the Christian power, yet their impact on the inter-communal relations was not very healthy. In fact, these movements made both the Hindu and Muslim masses of the lower strata more communal than they were before.[32]

Their outlook became narrowly religious and thus narrowly

communal. It is obvious, therefore, that in spite of a common element in the opposition to the British rule and rejection of Western way of life, the nineteenth century revivalism led to a bifurcation of the nationalist awakening in India. As a scholar of the Hindu-Muslim question remarks: "The most serious aspect of revivalism in India in the 19th century was its bifurcation. The intellectual and emotional reaction of India to a very acute and unprecedented crisis of transition was taking a complicated form; one of its aspects was a return to different sources of inspiration. There was a real difference between the India of the Vedic age and the Arabia of the early Khilafat. Hindus and Mussalmans were going beyond the last thousand years, back to distant and divergent traditions and heroes and, therefore, further away from one another in certain departments of life. In fact, the two revivalisms stimulated each other competed with each other and became more and more different in outlook. Religious neutrality and expediency alike forbade the British Government to attempt to guide or harmonize them. It accepted them both and adjusted itself to them both, after a preliminary effort to suppress the extreme manifestations of the Islamic revival. Leadership rested in the hands of fervid puritans who were content with nothing less than the pure word of the gospel as they interpreted it. Revivalism weaned away the half-converts from the lingering Hindu beliefs and practices. On the other hand, the Hindu sub-castes which had adopted Muslim ways of living gravitated towards Hindu revivalism or modernism. Hindus and Mussalmans alike began to give up many practices which they had imbibed from one another and which had formed bridges between the two communities. Many areas of common life and thought have thus been restricted and many meeting places obliterated. Revivalism leads to the withdrawal of one community from the other's festivals which the natural forces of sympathy and imitation tend to make common to both. It fosters a conscious retention and accentuation of existing divergences and the invention of new ones in regard to diet and dress, manners and etiquette and magnifies them all into profound, 'cultural' diversities. It tends to diminish the common elements in the literary productions of the Hindus and the Mussalmans and fosters itself by claiming control over the education of the young and founding separate schools, academics, colleges and universities. It imparts its tone of literature, favouring the elimination of Sanskrit terms from Urdu and that of Arabic terms from Hindi, Bengali and other languages. Revivalism prompts organisation on communal lines and often assumes an aggressive tone which brings different communities into acrimonious debate over theological and other matters".[33]

It was the development of this Communal-cum-aggressive outlook, which gave to the British politicians a broad base on which to erect a political structure in India. The result was a growth of the Indian struggle of national emancipation which resulted in the territorial partition in 1947. Before we turn to examine the same, there is yet another link in the long chain of Hindu revivalism in India which deserves a significant scrutiny. It was the birth of an organized communal and militant movement amongst the Hindus.

In the wake of this communal revivalism and renaissance, just as the Muslim had evolved the All India Muslim League, as an organ of exclusively Communal-cum-Political activities, similarly Hindus evolved the Hindu Mahasabha that henceforth hold aloft the banner of a Militant Hindu communalism.

A few scholars trace the genesis of Hindu Mahasabha as far back as the year 1881, when an association known as Hindu-Sabha was formed. The founder of this Communal Organisation was Shri A. Shankaria. The duties of the Sabha were enumerated as follows:

1. To cite from the teaching of Vyasa, authorities for any doctrine or practice which they may uphold or against which they may oppose.
2. To give certificates of qualification and character to learned priests.
3. To encourage the marriage of girls after puberty and the remarriage of child widow.
4. To promote unity and good-will amongst the sects and the castes of India."

In its bye-laws the Association desired an All India set-up for its working and envisaged that 'the members and the patrons will cooperate so as to eliminate dogmas, schisms and practices opposed to the consolidation of the Hindu nation and the Sanskrit authorities held sacred by the nation and the Rishis."

Later on, it is in the writings of Lala Lajpat Rai that one discovers an idea of organizing a far more comprehensive Hindu organization. In an article published by him in the year 1901, the 'Hindustan-Review' he pleaded "the necessity of a Hindu Political Conference being organized." He quoted the following words of his article in his speech in 1909, where he wrote:

> "It should be the business of a High Congress or Conference to support and take as far as possible such steps that might conduce to their unity and strength as a religious nationality".[34]

A positive effort towards founding a Hindu organization came as a reaction to the unbridled and ferocious upsurge of Muslim communalism in India to which the British Government also lent its tacit support. It is curious to note that Hindu Mahasabha gradually assumed a shape during the same years which also witnessed the formation of the All India Muslim League. In the case of the Hindus, the partition of Bengal (1905) provided the necessary stimulus. This administrative measure of Lord Curzon was full of serious import as it disturbed the communal equilibrium of Bengal and unleashed forces of serious communal disharmony and riots. The Muslim saw in this measure, a positive triumph of their loyalist trends. Their show of happiness did not stop with thanks giving ceremonies but it let loose a terror of rapine and plunder in East Bengal. It was to check the Muslim hooliganism that a United Bengal Hindu Conference was held in 1907. Although the name of Hindu Mahasabha was yet in oblivion, yet according to the official chronicler of Hindu Mahasabha, its seeds were sown there. "It was however, in Punjab that the movement was ushered in the country with the formation of a Punjab Hindu Sabha. Its aims and objects were explained as follows:

> "The Sabha is not a sectarian nor a denominational one, but an all embracing movement and while meaning no offence to any other movement, whether Hindu or non-Hindu, it aims to be ardent and watchful in safeguarding the interests of the entire Hindu Community in all respects".[35]

It was in the year 1909, that the Hindu sentiments received a crude shock by the introduction of the Morley-Minto reforms that made a concession to the Muslims, and to them alone, of, 'Separate Electorates' i.e. the elections to the seats reserved for Muslims were to be made by Muslim voters only, besides giving Muslims and Sikhs weightage, i.e. they obtained more seats than would have been allotted to them on a purely numerical basis.

Several Hindu leaders in India criticized the timid policy of the Hindu community for not coming up with their own demands, to seek gains, that the Muslims were grabbing at their cost. R.B. Lala Lal Chand of Punjab while criticizing the policy of the Indian National Congress said, that Congress, besides ignoring the Hindu aspect of political question is proceeding on a wrong assumption of the United Nation; He declared:

> "Not only this, but they, the Muslims were given a political importance which they never possessed before, while the Hindus were lowered in the scale from the position which they had already occupied. And with all these events passing before their eyes, the Congress through its mouth-piece, the Indian National Congress Committee, moved not a little finger to render support or help the Hindu cause. Nay it did not even condescend to give an encouragement to the community in the struggle. On the other hand its main exponents tried to gag the Hindu mouth against even raising a lament".

He further added:

> "A movement is judged by its results just as a tree is judged by its fruits. A tree, however, bright and beautiful it may be in form and figure, yet if it bears bitter or poisonous fruits, will be shunned and avoided. The Congress may possess very high idea of a United India, admirable to look at from a distance, but if the result be bitter, I cannot conceive how a Hindu, who has the last spark left in him of the warmth of a Hindu feeling and patriotism can help and join the movement".

Just like Sir Syed Ahmed, he advised Hindus to abstain from joining the Indian National Congress which he said is trying to annihilate the interests of a Hindu nation.

> "Even apart from the question of political loss or gain", he said: my objection against the Congress is that it makes the Hindu forget that he is a Hindu and tends to damp his communal individuality into an Indian ideal, thus making him break. With all his past traditions and past glory, I regard this as a very heavy price to pay. The conversion to the new ideal means worse than the effects of foreign invasions that have hitherto hammered the Hindu community... Moreover, the other community has steadfastly refused to join hands and under the circumstances it appears to me to be pure imbecility and cowardliness to appear under United flag".[36]

Rise of Hindu Communalism

Thus, as 'an irritant and a reaction' to the Muslim communalism, Hindu communalism also gained strength. Almost in the same year Lt. Col. U.N. Mukherjee in his book entitled, *A Dying Race* wrote:

> "We Hindus are most ridiculously, most contemptibly ignorant. We have no idea about what is going on around us.... How do the two communities stand today? The Mohammedans have a future and they believe in it. Time is with them, time is against us. At the end of the year, they count their gains whereas we calculate our losses. They are growing in number, growing in strength, growing in health, growing in solidarity, we are crumbling to pieces. They look forward to a united Mohammedan world; we are waiting for our extinction.
>
> The wages of sin is death. We, Hindus have sinned deeply and damnably against the laws of God and Nature and we are paying the penalty. In our treatment of our co-religionists, dies the germs of our self-destruction. This is the history of the Hindus. The same process is going on round us".[37]

It is apparent therefore, that from Punjab to Bengal, throughout the length and breadth of the Hindu community a feeling of jealousy had been roused against the British patronage of the Muslim community. It was inspired from some such reasons that in October, 1909, the first Punjab Hindu conference was held at

Lahore under the Presidentship of Sir Protul Chandra Chatterjee. Rai Bahadur Lala Lal Chand was the Chairman of the reception committee and among other notable Hindus of Punjab, it was also attended by Lala Lajpat Rai.

Slowly and steadily Punjab Hindu Sabha carried on its work, keeping the flames of Hindu nationalism burning and keeping a vigilant eye on the progress of the Muslim League. The Honourable R.B. Shadi Lal (afterwards Sir), inaugurating the 1912 Session of the Punjab Hindu Conference urged the necessity of an All India Hindu Sabha and declared:

> "Suffice it to say that the events of the past four or five years proved beyond the shadow of doubt that with a body which could speak with the authority of the entire Hindu community behind its back and resist the aggressive action of the Muslim League, the Hindus would not have been in the plight in which they find themselves at present.",
>
> "I appeal to the Hindus of Punjab, to the Hindus of Hindustan, to combine and consolidate the forces for the future good of the country".[38]

It is thus apparent that the Hindu and Muslim communalism fed and fattened, on each other. Each provided the *raison d'etre'* and the stimulus needed for the other. The most immediate as also the farreaching influence was the gradual widening of the gulf between the members of the two communities, which manifested itself in an ultimate split.

The first session of the All India Hindu Mahasabha under the Presidentship of Maharaja Bahadur of Kasim Bazar met at Hardwar on 9th April, 1915. It was attended by prominent Hindu leaders of the time. The most prominent amongst them were Pandit Madan Mohan Malaviya, Shri S.C. Mitter, Babu Moti Lal Ghosh, Babu S.N. Banerjee and many others including Mahatma Gandhi and Swami Shraddhananda, who were also members of the subjects committee. The All India committee of the Mahasabha consisted besides others, of Babu Bhagwandas, Pandit Bishan Narain Das, Pandit Gokul Nath Misra, Sir Tej Bahadur Sapru, Lala Hans Raj and Dr Asutosh Mukherjee. The Maharaja Bahadur of Kasim Bazar in the course of his Presidential address said:

> "If therefore, we make efforts to set our house in order or hold closer together the scattered units of our state, it cannot imply a menace to any other community or faith".[39]

The Hindu Sabha movement with various vicissitudes, with rise and fall, thus continued to be the sole spokesman of the exclusively Hindu interests.

In the due course of time it considerably antagonized the Muslims because of launching the two movements of Shuddhi (i.e. reconversion of converts into the Hindu fold) and Sanghathan (i.e. the organization and solidarity of the Hindus) and by maintaining an unmasked anti-Muslim attitude.

The Shuddhi movement as also the Hindu Sanghathanist movement were meant to regenerate the Hindu race, by moulding it into a free and mighty nation. In this respect the Hindu Mahasabha was one with the activities of the Arya Samaj, and, more often than not the same set of leaders and missionaries led, directed and worked the Hindu Sabha as well as the Arya Samaj at many a local and provincial centre in India.

All these movements increased the tension between the two communities, and the fact that the movement had a distinct political bias made the tension worse. As V.D. Savarkar declared:

> "In a country like India.... Shuddi movement ceases to be merely theological or dogmatic one, but assumes the wider significance of a political and national movement".[40]

A clear cut departure in Hindu Mahasabha policy, from 'the cultural regeneration of the Hindu society' to that of 'political establishment of a Hindu Rashtra' became visible towards the close of the third decade of the twentieth century. It was in 1933, that it came out in open opposition to Congress. Bhai Parmanand in his Presidential address to the Ajmer session said:

> "I feel an impulse in me that the Hindus will willingly co-operate with Great Britain if their status and responsible positions as the premier community in India is recognized in the political institutions of new India".

It was in the year 1937, that Hindu Mahasabha redefined its aims. Mr Savarkar declared that, "the maintenance, protection and promotion of the Hindu race, Hindu culture, and Hindu civilization and the advancement of the glory of Hindu Rashtra, and with a view to secure them, the attainment of Purna Swaraj; i.e. absolute political independence for Hindustan by legitimate means".

At the next session, in his elaboration of the theory of a Hindu Nation, he said:, "Our politics hereafter will be purely Hindu politics fashioned and tested in Hindu terms only, in such ways as will help the consolidation, freedom and life growth of our Hindu Nation".[41]

It is against such a complex background of Hindu and Muslim Communalism that the forces of Indian National movement operated in the first half of the twentieth century in India. They were steered by the Muslim League for the Muslim community, by the Hindu Mahasabha for the Hindu community, and by the Indian National Congress for the Indian community and the Indian nation as a whole.

In the process of summing up, we can say, that since its very inception, the establishment of the British rule remained a positive source of disturbance in India. It was never liked by the natives. It could never evoke a spontaneous allegiance; on the contrary, it created seething discontent amongst the people of different communities. This discontent expressed itself at first through communal risings, like the Wahabi revolt, and, later, through the efforts of these communities to "remove the obstacles that impeded their growth". As such, the first mass consciousness of the people of India was very much in the nature of 'communal resentment' and 'communal frustration'.[42]

It is also clear that from its very beginning, this mass awakening amongst the various sections was of a divided nature, in the sense that it was grafted on a narrow social base; particularly so, because during the revivalistic phase each community derived its main sustenance from its religion. Thus, the first mass consciousness of the people of India was not national but a consciousness on communal and religious lines manifestinf itself through militant communal organisations like the Muslim League and the Hindu Mahasabha.[43]

Obviously, the birth of communalism recedes the rise of nationalism. It was out of communal revivalisms and renaissance that the nationalist movement sprang in India.

The rise of the Indian National Movement, can be regarded as an adaptive consequence of the frustration that the Indians suffered at the hands of their oppressive English masters. It was essentially the 'xenophobic and self-protective' effort of an old society and way of life to save and perpetuate itself; but at the same, it also showed the "striving of a Society threatened by the instrusion of alien forces to reconstitute itself in order to achieve a new place of dignity and equality" in its own land.

The growth of nationalism had been, in fact, a common feature of all the Asiatic countries that came under the dominance of Western powers. The initial frustrations caused by subjugation to alien powers impelled the slave people very often to hit back desperately and blindly at the foreign master. This kind of negative reaction was witnessed in the form of a Boxer rebellion in China, a sepoy mutiny (1857) in India, or, the anti-foreign movement that followed in the wake of Commodore Perry's minatory opening up of Japan in 1853. Nationalism came to the fore as a constructive force when subject nations cast off this negative attitude, in order to struggle for their liberation in a balanced and positive way. As Rupert Emerson comments:

> "Nationalism, then, is a positive and creative response to the shattering impact upon Asia of the Modern West. In consequence it means the appearance of a new clan, a new dynamism in a society which has come to insist on taking the control of its destiny into its own hands".[44]

The leadership of this nationalist sentiment among Indians was taken up by the educated middle-class intellectuals, of which majority happened to be that of Hindus. They had imbibed the knowledge of the democratic thought of the modern Europe and also of the nationalist struggles of freedom which took place in different countries. As Dr Desai says:

> "The educated Indians read about the war of independence of the American people, of the Halian struggle for national liberation from the Austrian domination, of the Irish struggle for freedom. They also studied the works of Thomas Paine, Spencer, Burke, Mill, Voltaire, Mazzine, and other writers who preached the doctrines of individual and national liberty. These educated Indians became the ideological and political leaders of the nationalist movement in India".[45]

These enlightened Indians started many a political organization, notable among which were the Indian Association founded by S.N. Banerjee in Bengal, the Bombay Association started by Dadabhai Naoroji and Jagannath Sankerseth in Bombay and the Samajainik Sabha established by Chipdunkar in Poona and the Mahajan Sabha in Madras. These associations aimed at the protection of public work, spread of education and improvement of the relations between the rulers and the ruled. In the wake of these organized efforts, came the Indian National Congress, to continue the fight for emancipation of the Indian Nation from foreign rule. It was founded by Allan Octavian Hume.[46] Hume was a liberal Englishman. He realized the real need of the India of his time. After his retirement from the service of the Government he gave most of his time in articulating a political awakening amongst the educated Indians. His circular letter to the graduates of the Calcutta University was a clarion call to the Indians to stand under the banner of nationalism. He wrote:

> "Constituting, as you do, a large body of the most highly educated Indians, you should; in the natural order of things, constitute also the most important source of all mental, moral, social, and political progress in India. Whether in the individual or the nation, all vital progress must spring from within, and it is to you, her most cultured and enlightened minds, her most favoured sons that your Country must look for the initiative. In vain many aliens like myself, love India and her children, as well as the most loving of these; in vain may they, for her and their good; give time and trouble, money and thought; in vain may they struggle and sacrifice; they may assist with advice and suggestions; they may place their experience, abilities and knowledge at the disposal of the workers, but they lack the essential of nationality, and the real work must ever be done by the people of the country themselves".[47]

Hume was also convinced that it was, 'of paramount importance to find an overt and constitutional channel for the discharge of the increasing ferment which had resulted from Western ideas and education'.[48] Not only this, he bluntly told the educated Indians:

> "Every nation secures precisely as good a government as it merits. If you, the picked men, the most highly educated of the nation, cannot, scorning personal ease and selfish objects, make a resolute struggle to secure......a large share in the management of your own affairs, then we your friends are wrong and our adversaries right.....only, if this be so, let us hear no more factious, peevish complaints that you are kept in leading strings and treated like children, for you will have proved yourselves such. Men know how to act".[49]

He therefore suggested that a national organization be formed for which 'if only 50 men good and true can be found to join as, founders, the thing can be established and the further development would be comparatively easy'.[50] The appeal received a nation-wide response and the Indian National Congress held its first meeting in Bombay in 1885.

It is apparent that the founding of this organization was one of the adaptive consequences of the indigenous sense of frustration. Frustration often leads to insight and reorganization of paths to the goal. The elite of the country now felt that a national union alone can bring a national emancipation. Mr W.C. Banerjee the first President of the Congress declared the promotion of intimacy and friendship among all lovers of the nation as one of the aims of this organization. It is true at that time people had no clear conception either of the cause or of the ultimate goal for which they had organized themselves.

As such, in its early phase, the Congress began its functioning with the blessings of the then Governor-General, Lord Dufferin. Its early policy was one of "prayer, petition and protests". But as this national organization went on meeting yearly at different places in the country, it swelled its membership and also, `tended to conform to a clear pattern'.

A few years later, the National Congress renounced its early loyalist trend and the concept of Swaraj was evolved as the ultimate political goal of the country. Dada Bhai Nauroji, in his Presidential address to the National Congress in 1906, declared:

> "We do not ask any favours. We want only justice. Instead of going into any further divisions or details of our rights

> as British citizens, the whole matter can be compromised in one word, "Self-Government" or, "Swaraj"' like that of the United-Kingdom or the colonies".[51]

Once the goal was clear, the progress to achieve it continued on right lines in an undaunted and inspired spirit. National sentiment found both the moderates and extremists, as its supporters. In spite of their different outlooks, they were one in the sense that they were both fighting a war against British Imperialism in India.

The Indian National Congress, however, absorbed not only Moderates and Extremists, but many more in its fold. In a slightly exaggerated and somewhat inaccurate account, Sir George Schuster and Guy Wint aptly summed up the role of Congress; They wrote:

> "The politics of British India have for long been dominated by Congress, and in the whole world there is perhaps no political party which altogether resembles, it. It is a collection of almost every conceivable interest and type of personality. It includes millionaires, mill-workers, landlords, peasants, saints, gangsters, professors, experts in international affairs, parochialists, liberals, anarchists, communists, ascetics, fanatical Muslims, and fanatical Hindus; and its liability is a large supply of visionaries".[52]

The above description amply bears out how the Congress gave a representation to the various, 'interests, classes and communities'. It is a strange irony of fact that because of British machinations and Muslim fanaticism on one hand and the overwhelmingly large Hindu membership of the Congress on the other, it came to be treated in course of time as a purely Hindu organization; which it never was. Even the most bigoted among the British admitted that:

> "Congress is not a political party in the sense known in the Western democratic countries, but a political mass movement of the kind which from time to time surges through a nation causing people of the most divergent types and interests to band themselves together and follow a leader".[53]

It is true that the Indian National Congress was to some extent constituted by the Indian bourgeoise of the time. It is also correct that in its early days:

> "Essentially it was a middle class Hindu and Brahman gathering from the principal cities, the aristocratic land owning groups from the countryside being poorly represented, and the mass of the people quite unconcerned. It fairly represented the new middle classes, lawyers and journalists forming the most prominent group".[54]

When all is said, the fact remains that it would be incorrect to call it a communal organization, in the sense in which the 'Muslim League' or the 'Hindu Mahasabha' were communal. It could not be so when Muslims, Christians, and Parsis and members of several other communities were its active members. Unlike the Muslim League and the Hindu Mahasabha, the Congress President could belong to any caste, creed and community. In fact, quite a few of the most prominent Presidents of the Congress had been Muslims and Christians, whose addresses are monuments of national idealism where one finds an emphatic refutation of the charge of communalism brought against the Congress. Speaking about the representative character of the Congress, Badruddin Tyabji said:

> "It is a meeting composed not merely of the representations of any one city or even of one province—but of the whole of the vast continent of India—representing not any one class or interest but all classes, and all interests of the almost innumerable different communities that constitute the people of India. I think we are fairly entitled to say that this is a truly representative national gathering".

Then, after criticizing the nefarious propaganda of those Muslims who were against the National Congress, the esteemed President most emphatically declared:

> "I atleast not merely in my individual capacity, but as representing the Anjuman-i-Islam of Bombay, do not consider that there be anything whatever in position or the relation of the different communities of India—be they Hindu, Mussalmans, Parsis or Christians—which should induce the leaders of any one community to stand aloof from the others in their efforts to obtain those Great general reforms which are for the common benefit of us all and which I feel assured have only to be granted to us".[55]

Mr Rahmutullah Sayani was the second Muslim President of the Congress. He compelled seventeen possible objections that the Muslims might raise against the Congress and refuted all of them in his Presidential Address to the Twelfth session of the Congress. He said:

> "All the Mussalmans in India have always lived side by side with the Hindus and mixed with them and co-operated with them both during the period of the Mussalman rule as also since then. In fact both the Mussalmans and the Hindus as also other races residing in this country, are all equally the inhabitants of one and the same country; are thus bound to each other by ties of a common nativity. They are all sharers in the benefits and advantages as also in the ills, consequent in common residence, all are subject to common joys and common sorrows and must necessarily co-operate with each other as humanity is imperfect and dependent on co-operation. The object of the congress is to give expression to the political demands of the subjects and to pray that their political disabilities may be removed; that the political burdens of the country may be lightened and its political conditions(may be ameliorated that the political state of the millions) of human beings who are their fellow countrymen may be improved and their general conditions may be rendered more tolerable. It is a most meritorious work, a work of the highest charity. No nobler or more charitable work could possibly be conceived.
>
> The only question is whether there should be two separate organisations, Mussalmans and Non-Mussalmans both simultaneously doing the same work, separate in name only, but identical in nature and interest, or whether there should be a joint organisation.
>
> Obviously, the latter is preferable especially as the Congress has no concern whatever with the religion or the religious convictions of any of its members".

To the objection:

> "That in as much as the Congress is a representative body and in as much as the Hindus formed the majority of the

> populations, the Congress will necessarily be swamped by the Hindus and the resolutions of the Congress will, to all intents and purposes be the resolutions of the Hindus and the Mussalman's voice will be drowned", He said:
> "It does not follow that because the Hindus form the majority of the Congress that resolutions of the Congress will be the resolutions of the Hindus. It is a standing rule of the Congress solemnly passed and recorded that if any proposal is disapproved of by the bulk of either the Hindus or the Mussalman, the same shall not be carried.
> Again so long as the Congress leaders happen to be men of education and enlightenment, men of approved conduct and wide experience, men in fact who have a reputation to lose the Congress will never be allowed to run its course for the benefit of sectional, private or party purpose. The Mussalmans, however, instead of raising puerile and imaginary objections from a distance, should attend Congress meetings and see for themselves what is going on in such meetings. Indeed they will find that even when one member puts forward cogent reasons in position such proposal is eventually dropped".[56]

In fact that the Congress was not a communal organization has been unequivocally admitted by all. Regarding the same, the opinions of Rezaul Karim make an interesting study. He said:

> "In order to prove that the Congress is a Hindu organization, one must have to show that its aim, ideals and principles are all for the Hindus. It does not matter how many Muslims are within it and how many are outside of it. Nor does it matter by how many Muslims or Hindus the Congress work is being carried on. If its aims and ideals are national, it is certainly a national organization".

He further said:

> " 'League and Mahasabha' do not allow members of other communities to take part in their deliberations. That is, the Hindu Mahasabha is exclusively for the Hindus, however broad a term that might be, and Muslim League is for the Muslims. Neither of these two organisations does ever think of uniting Indians into a composite nation.

Setting the above rule as a test..... "Congress is an organization which is open to the members of all the communities of India. Not to speak of Hindu, Muslim, Sikh, Christian, Buddhist, Parsi, Jew, even an atheist and agnostic can be its active member, can take part in its deliberations and can be elected President of the Congress (such as Mrs Besant, Wedderborn, Nauroji, etc.) It has nothing to do with the religion of its members. It is a political organization and its avowed aim is to win freedom of the country.

> All its policy and programme is for the people of the country, it embraces all, it absorbs all, but it never exploits religion for the sake of its objects".[57]

In conclusion he said:

> "Thus it is proved beyond doubt that the Congress is a national institution. As the Hindus in India are a majority community, it is not unnatural that in any organisation which is formed on an All India basis, their number will be overwhelmingly great. But that does not destroy its national character.
>
> The attitude of the Congress towards the minority communities specially towards the Muslims has been all through its eventful career, marked by perfect justice and equity. It has laid great stress on the removal of their grievances as a national organisation should do. It has passed various resolutions giving guarantees of safeguards to the religion and culture of the Muslims. It took up the cause of the Khilafat in right earnest. Several Muslims of hallowed memory held the post of Presidentship of the Congress with honour and distinction. It gave active sympathy to all the Muslim countries fighting for their freedom such as Turkey, Palestine, Egypt, etc.
>
> In spite of all these glaring facts, if any one still calls it a Hindu-organization, then we must say that he is either a man of perverted brain or a man who is bent upon doing mischief.
>
> The very fact that in spite of the vice propaganda of the Muslim League, thousands of Muslims are within the Congress, they are proud of it, shows that the Congress is not a Hindu-organization. However maliciously they may

accuse it, it is still a national organisation of the people of India".[58]

The growth and progress of the Indian National Congress as the chief exponent of the Indian public opinion made an important impact on the development of the Hindu-Muslim relations in India. In spite of its representative and national character, from Sir Syed Ahmad to M.A. Jinnah, it was maligned by all leading Muslims as a body that conspired to establish Hindu Raj in India.

The truth is that the keynote of Muslim thinking Organization and action in the political phase of communalism has been nothing but a deeply felt sense of frustration. Time and again as a community they suffered shocks that upset their communal poise and national outlook. Their first and foremost grievance lay in the seeming loss of political power with the transfer of sovereignty from the Muslim Emperors to the British. Then came the Wahabi rising and the mutiny which were crushed with a heavy hand from the new masters leading thereby to the creation of a wide gulf between the progress of their community and other sections of the Indian society. This lagging behind of Muslims was a sore cause of frustration to their intelligentsia and the rising middle class.

Obviously, the foundations of the Muslim mass-awakening sprang out of a sense of intense dissatisfaction over their own fallen lot and of jealousy over the superior status that their Hindu countrymen had acquired. Thus, even in the adaptive consequence of the native frustration, which manifested itself in the form of the Indian National movement, a majority of Muslims as we shall see failed to imbibe a truly national outlook. To the Muslims, their community constituted a nation and as such their nationalism remained out and out communal.

In the Muslim adaptive consequence we have already seen how during the course of the last few decades of the Nineteenth century, the Muslim elite of Bengal and Aligarh realized the futility of their early negative attitude and began to make for their early mistakes in not coming up to the changed conditions of life. In their first adaptive consequence, they assayed an 'insight' on the causes of their downfall and directed their energies in "reorganizing paths" towards a communal uplift to overcome British indifference and Hindu ascendancy. Curiously enough, even in their most positive outlook, the Muslim Westernization and reorientation remained primarily a communal matter. We have seen how their leadership as also the British interests desired them to keep aloof from the rising tide of nationalism in the country. The result was obvious. It kept the Muslims shut in their shells, they not only once again kept away from the National struggle, but also made it weak by siding with the Imperialist forces in India. What came forth from the Muslim side was not nationalism but the Modern Indian Communalism. As referring to the Muslim awakening an English historian aptly remarks:

> "Indeed it was the march of events - the rise of the Indian middle classes, the falling behind of Muslims on the road to power, place and wealth and their consequent tendency to invoke the whole strength of their community, rich and poor, educated and ignorant, to redress the balance that produced this modern form of Communalism. Essentially, modern Indian Communalism emerges as a middle-class problem and its chief causes arise through political and economic as much as through religious rivalry".[59]

In their second adaptive consequence to frustration, the Muslims showed a greater 'intensification of efforts', towards their goal of greater communal solidarity and uplift. In this direction the Muslims displayed three distinct trends.

In the beginning there was the Loyalist trend which had manifested itself with the extension of sovereignty of the British Crown over India. It was faithfully kept up by the All India Muslim League. This trend, as also the 'too narrow and too nebulous' policy of the Muslims received a rude shock when towards the close of the first decade of the twentieth century settled fact of the partition of Bengal was proclaimed unsettled, by the King emperor at the historic Durbar at Delhi. This revision was interpreted by them as a victory for the Hindu dominated Congress and a humiliation for the Muslim League. This trend received a second and a greater shock when during the course of the first World War, British policy towards Turkey and the Muslim Holy places in Arabia and Mesopotamia, exacerbated Muslim feeling. The British falsified the promises held out to Indian

Mussalmans about the Khalifa and as a reaction to the same the Muslims launched the Khilafat Movement in India. It is apparent, therefore, that by the close of the first World War, the Loyalist tendency of the Muslims had gradually become weak and had lost its early warmth and overt frankness.

These rebuffs not only made Muslims more hostile towards the Hindus, but also stiffened their attitude towards the general progress of the National Movement. Muslims became more and more communal. Henceforth, in matters of constitutional reforms in the country, they began to assert their claims with all bitterness and spirit of vengeance. The future Muslim stand was declared in the following words:

> ".......the case for the Indian Moslems, in its main lines, may be given succinctly. The position they acquired, not without effort, under the Morley Minto Act must not be imperilled by any subsequent legislation. It represents the very minimum that will satisfy their desires and remove their apprehensions. Concessions to Hindus direct or indirect, must be accompanied and balanced by corresponding concessions in just proportion to Moslems, so that their relative position shall remain undisturbed and the same. This will be the foundation on which Muslim opinion in India will stand".[60]

It is clear that the National cause suffered much due to repeated shocks of frustration which the Muslim community suffered time and again. Secondly, in their "intensification of efforts", Muslims adopted a conciliatory trend time and again they showed willingness to agree with the Hindu public opinion in India. Even the Muslim League showed enough catholicity by entering into a few pacts in order to achieve a `more direct and definite rapprochment between the two great communities'. This policy could begin because most of the leading Muslim members of the Indian National Congress for a number of years were also the Members of the All India League. M.A. Jinnah was one such prominent member who had once been a pillar of Congress but parted company after the Nagpur Session of the Congress held in December, 1920. It was he, who was mainly instrumental in bringing about an agreement between the two parties as `to the method of election of councils and the distribution of the seats' amongst the Hindus and the Muslims, an arrangement which is known as the `Lucknow Pact'. The pact was a surrender to the Muslims since the Indian National Congress, which had vehemently opposed the separate Muslim electorate and `weightage' conceded these demands. It would be clear that even in this agreement, the Muslim approach was more communal than national. They made a bargain in the interest of the Muslim community and not of the Indian Nation. In fact, Muslim policy continued to be same throughout British rule. They were always asking for more whether it be a few safeguards or reservations from the British or an acquiescence to the same by the Indian National Congress.

Another instance of a large-scale mutual agreement between the Hindus and the Muslims came during the Khilafat days, when Mahatma Gandhi, making a full use of a psychological moment, gave his unconditional support to the cause of Indian Mohammedans in their agitation against the British Government. The basic core of Gandhi's stand was the need for Hindu-Muslim harmony and understanding. He wrote:

> "I have already stated that if I were not interested in the Indian Mohammedans, I would not interest myself in the welfare of Turks any more than I am in that of the Austrians or the Poles. But I am bound as an Indian to share the sufferings and trials of fellow Indians. If I deem the Mohammedan to be my brother it is my duty to help him in his hour of peril to the best of my ability, if his cause commands itself to me as just.... It is expedient to suffer for my Mohammedan brother to the utmost in a just cause, and I shall therefore travel with him along the whole road as long as the means employed by him are as honourable as his end. I cannot regulate the Mohammedan feeling. I must accept his statement that the Khilafat is with him a religious question in the sense that it binds to reach the goal even at the cost of his own life".[61]

It was primarily the desire to bridge up Hindu Muslim differences that Mahatma Gandhi launched the forces of Indian National Congress in the service of the Indian Muslims. At the

Calcutta session of the Congress, the non-co-operation resolution was passed. It stated that "it is the duty of every non-Muslim to assist his Muslim brother in his attempt to remove the religious calamity that has overtaken him". A policy of progressive non-violent non-co-operation with the British Government in India, "until the said wrongs are righted and swaraj is established", was also adopted in the above resolution. Gandhi dreamt that "the solution of the Khilafat question is the attempt of Swaraj and vice versa". His governing belief was this that "no Government can withstand the bloodless opposition of a whole nation".

But could the Muslims of India come upto Gandhi's expectations? Could these conciliatory steps forge communal-harmony in India? Did this friendship and cooperation prove to be another step towards an early attainment of Swaraj? Probably not. The Congress tried hard to satisfy the Khilafat leaders. But Maulana Mohammed Ali was cast in a mould which could not serve the force of nationalism. Dr. Sachin Sen aptly writes:

> "With Gandhiji, the association of the Congress with the Khilafat cause was an attempt to cure the political paralysis of India. A new dynamic movement was needed, and that could be built up only through communal cohesion, harmony and understanding. Hence the Khilafat cause was pushed up by Gandhiji to generate a new unifying force in the political field of India. But the Khilafat movement under the leadership of Mohammed Ali upset Gandhijis speculation. The Khilafat movement encouraged the flight of Moslems to Afghanistan. The propaganda was carried that no true Moslem could live in India under British domination, as India was a Dar-ul-herb....Muslims also refused to worship the principle of non-violence which was the fundamental creed of Gandhiji. The speeches of the Ali Brothers were definite incitements to violence (Lord Reading who became Viceroy in 1921 secured an apology from the Ali Brothers for violent speeches through the instrumentality of Gandhiji). Reports were circulated that the Amir of Afghanistan was invited to wage war against the British Government and to convert India into a Dar-ul-Islam".[62]

Strange as it may sound, yet the Khilafat question failed to serve the progressive forces in India. Mohammed Ali, who also happened to be one of the leading members of the Indian National Congress and who even presided at its Kakinada session in 1923 "could not offer flowers in the shrine of territorial nationalism and secular democracy". During the course of his persecution, while pleading his case of not guilty, he came out in his true colours, when he stated:

> "Speaking as a Mussalman, if I am supposed to err from the right path, the only way to convince me of my error is to refer me to the Holy Koran or to the authentic of the last Prophet—on whom be peace and God's benediction—or the religious pronouncements of recognised Muslim divines past and present, which purport to be based on these two original sources of Islamic authority that demands from me in the present circumstances the precise action for which a Government that does not like to be called satanic, is prosecuting me today......I must either be a sinner or a criminal. Islam recognises one sovereignty alone, the sovereignty of God, which is supremo and unconditional, indivisible and inalienable".[63]

The truth is that, howsoever one might have tried, no reconciliation of Communalism could be possible with Nationalism. As such the Khilafat movement did a great harm to the normal development of the Hindu-Muslim relations in India. Dr. Sachin Sen writes:

> "The Khilafat crusade injured India. The latent Moslem feeling of hatred against unbelievers sprang up; the old Moslem religion of the Sword was reasserted; the extra-territorial allegiance to Afghanistan which was shown by Moslem leaders nourished pan-Islamic tendencies, the primary allegiance of Moslems to Muslim countries was stressed, the dream of establishing Muslim Raj caught many Indian Moslems; the loyalty of Indian Muslims to India was found to be spurious. The Khilafat encouraged the politics of the sword and introduced factors which widened the gap between Hindus and Muslims".[64]

Curiously enough the Pan-Islamic instincts as also extra-territorial allegiance of the Mussalmans were brutally opposed when Mustafa Kamal not only refused to receive the Khilafat deputation from India but he also abolished the Khilafat institution. The new Turkey separated religion from politics and it decried the Khilafat agitation as a reactionary movement. It was one of the rudest shocks in the history of Islam and the sense of frustration of the Indian Muslims grew immensely acute. Their wrath fell on innocent Hindus of India. The communal-relations assumed an explosive nature. It led to a ceaseless run of communal disorders throughout the country. Every naive act of either community was given a communal colour. Malabar registered one of the worst riots of the century.

The Mopla Rebellion of 1920, was a communal agitation carried out by the Muslim Organisations, the Khuddam-i-Kaba (Servants of the Mecca Shrine) and the Central Khilafat Committee. It was both anti-British and anti-Hindu. It aimed to establish Dar-al-Islam by overthrowing the British. Moplaas paralysed the administration and declared that Swaraj has been established. Having done so, they proclaimed Ali Musaliar as their Raja; Khilafat flags were flown, and Ernad and Walurenad were declared Khilafat Kingdoms.

They now turned to the Hindus of Malabar. In this connection Dr Ambedkar writes:

"But what baffled most was the treatment accorded by the Moplas to the Hindus of Malabar. The Hindus were visited by a dire fate at the hands of Moplas. Massacres, forcible conversions, desecration of temples, foul outrages upon women, such as ripping open pregnant women, pillage, arson and destruction — in short, all the accompaniments of brutal and unrestrained barbarism, were perpetuated freely by the Moplas upon the Hindus until such time as troops could be hurried to the task of restoring order though a difficult and extensive tract of the country. This was not a Hindu-Moslem riot. This was just a Bartholomew".[65]

It was not all in the coming years. At any procession or festival or any petty ground, "there was carnage, pillage, sacrilege and outrage of every species, perpetrated by Hindus against Mussalmans and by Mussalmans against Hindus — more perhaps by Mussalman against Hindu than by Hindus against Musalmans".[66]

All this encouraged communalism. Not only that, the nature of Muslim agitation caused much anxiety in the hearts of the Hindus. They deeply felt that "in thinking of an independent India the menace of Mohammedan rule has to be considered". Analysing the whole situation Mrs Annie Besant wrote:

> "Another serious question arises with regard to the Mohammedans of India. If the relations between Muslims and Hindus were as it was in the Lucknow days, this question would not be so urgent, though it would even then have almost certainly arisen, sooner or later, in an independent India. But since the Khilafat agitation, things have changed and it has been one of the many injuries inflicted on India by the encouragement of the Khilafat crusade, that the inner Muslim feeling of hatred against "unbelievers" has sprung up, naked and unashamed, as in years gone by. We have seen revived, as guide in practical politics, the old Muslim religion of the Sword, we have seen the dragging out of centuries of forgetfulness, the old exclusiveness, claiming the Jazirut-Arab, the island of Arabia, as a holy land which may not be trodden by the polluting foot of a non-Muslim; we have heard Muslim leaders declare that if the Afghans invaded India, they would join their fellow believers, and would slay the Hindus who defended their motherland against the foe; we have been forced to see that the primary allegiance of Mussalmans is to Islamic countries not to our motherland".[67]

Elucidating her argument, she further said:

> "The claim now put forward by Mussalman leaders that they must obey the laws of their particular prophet above the Laws of the State in which they live, is subversive of civic order and the stability of the State; it makes them bad citizens for their centre of allegiance is outside the Nation and they cannot, while they hold the views proclaimed by Maulana Mohammed Ali and Shaukat Ali, to name the most prominent of these Muslim leaders, be trusted by their fellow citizens. If India were independent, the Muslim part of the population — for the ignorant masses would follow those who appealed to them in the name of their

> prophet — would become an immediate peril to India's freedom. Allying themselves with Afghanistan, Baluchistan, Persia, Iraq, Arabia, Turkey and Egypt and with such of the tribes of Central Asia who are Mussalmans, they would rise to place India under the Rule of Islam — those in "British India" being helped by the Muslims in Indian States — and would establish Mussalman rule. We had thought that Indian Mussalmans were loyal to their motherland, and indeed, we still hope that some of the educated class might strive to prevent such a Mussalman rising; but they are too few for effective resistance and would be murdered as apostates. Malabar has taught us what Islamic rule still means, and we do not want to see another specimen of the "Khilafat Raj" in India".[68]

Similar fear was expressed in a letter that was exchanged between Lala Lajpat Rai and Mr C.R. Das. An anxiety was shown about the success of any attempt of Hindu-Muslim unity. The letter ran as follows:

> "There is one point more which has been troubling me very much of late and one which I want you to think carefully and that is the question of Hindu-Mohammedan unity. I have devoted most of my time during the last six months to the study of Muslim history and Muslim Law and I am inclined to think, it is neither possible nor practicable. Assuming and admitting the sincerity of the Mohammedan leaders in the Non-Co-operation movement, I think their religion provides an effective bar to anything of the kind. You remember the conversation, I reported to you in Calcutta, which I had with Hakim Ajmalkhan and Dr Kitchlew. There is no finer Mohammedan in Hindustan than Hakimsahib but can any other Muslim leader override the Quran? I can only hope that my reading of Islamic Law is incorrect, and nothing would relieve me more than to be convinced that it is so. But if it is right then it comes to this that although we can unite against the British, we cannot do so to rule Hindustan on British lines, we cannot do so to rule on democratic lines. What is then the remedy? I am not afraid

of seven crores in Hindustan but I think the seven crores of Hindustan plus the armed hosts of Afghanistan, Central Asia, Arabia, Mesopotamia and Turkey will be irresistible. I do honestly and sincerely believe in the necessity of desirability of Hindu-Muslim Unity. I am also fully prepared to trust the Moslem leaders, but what about the injunctions of the Quran and Hadis? The leaders cannot override them. Are we then doomed. I hope not. I hope your learned mind and wise head will find some way out of this difficulty".[69]

It would thus become clear that even the conciliatory trend of the Muslims could not beget any success. Their allegiance could never be bought, firstly because of their theological division of the world into Dar-al-Harb and Darl-al-Islam, and, secondly, because their extra-territorial loyalties, that manifested themselves in the nature of a Pan-Islamic movement in India. Mr Iyer aptly sums the chief characteristic of the Muslims when he writes:

"The mentality of the Muslims — whether of the Mopla of Malabar in the far South West of India or the Pathan of the North West — is the same. They are spurred to action only by religion. No mass movement among the Muslims was so great a success as the Khilafat though in the home of the Caliph, the people cared not a straw for him. The Indian Muslim has frankly not half the enthusiasm for Swaraj that he has for the resurrection of Islam. Famine in Smyrna would make a Muslim villager in Bihar sell his property and subscribe for the welfare of his suffering brothers across the distance, but he will be unmoved by the worst of famine in his own neighbourhood of Orissa. A careful study of the statements of the thousands of accused in the non-co-operation movement of 1921 would reveal that the Muslim emphasized the Khilafat whereas the Hindu laid stress on Swaraj. "The Pathan belongs more to the hills than to India", and the Mohammedans of India belong more to Arabia, Mesopotamia, Persia and Afghanistan than to India".[70]

It is thus apparent, that the national cause, in spite of several unity conferences that took place at various important places in India, could not receive any benefit, whatsoever, from the Muslims. The Muslims remained communal first, communal second and communal last.

The third and the final trend of the Muslim intensification of effort, may be termed as the 'Separatist' trend. In this, they followed those methods that were contrary to the general policy adapted by the Hindus and the Indian National Congress. The difference of approach was not merely confined to the ultimate good but it ran deep even into ways and means adopted to achieve those goals.

It was in this connection that one of the major crisis overtook Mr M.A. Jinnah, when he felt it essential to leave the Indian National Congress. Jinnah's ideology clashed with Mr M.K. Gandhi's. Till Gandhi appeared on the national scene, Jinnah had quite an important say in all matters, more so, because he was a popular member both of the Congress and the League. But after Gandhi's entry into Indian politics which led to his captivating the imagination of the masses and the members of the Indian National Congress, Jinnah had to undergo time and again qualms of painful frustration, as his proposals before went unheeded in the face of Gandhi's proposals. The biggest crisis came with Gandhi's programme of non-cooperation. Jinnah vehemently opposed it. At the Muslim League session of Calcutta, he advised his listeners in the following words:

"It is now for you to consider whether or not you approve of its principle, and approving of its principle, whether or not you approve of its details. The operations of this scheme will strike at the individual in each of you, and therefore it rests with you alone to measure your strength and to weigh the pros and cons of the question before you arrive at a decision. But once you have decided to march, let there be no retreat in any circumstances".[71]

The advice seemed ambiguous, but it was clear that he approved of neither the principle nor the details of Gandhi's plan.

In the realm of politics, Gandhi had evolved his own line of thought, organization and action. He was convinced that "it is the inherent right of a subject to refuse to assist a Government that will not listen to him".[72] Unlike Jinnah, Mahatma Gandhi did not consider non-violent non-cooperation as an unconstitutional method. On the contrary, he thought any cooperation with an unjust government to be such a method. He said:

> "It will be highly unconstitutional for the people of India to pocket every insult that is offered to them; it is highly

> unconstitutional for the whole of India to sit still and co-operate with an unjust Government which has trodden under its feet the honour of the Punjab. I say to my countrymen, as long as you have a sense of honour and so long as you wish to remain the descendants and defenders of the noble traditions that have been handed to you for generations after generations, it is unconstitutional for you not to non-co-operate and unconstitutional for you to co-operate with a Government which has become so unjust as our government has become. I am not anti-English; I am not anti-British; I am not anti-humbug and anti-injustice. So long as the government spells injustice, it may regard me as its enemy, implacable enemy".[73]

As opposed to Gandhi's views, Jinnah vehemently disliked the creed of non-cooperation. At Nagpur Congress he very frankly, told his political rival, "Your way is the wrong way: mine is the right-way — the constitutional way is the right way".[74]

Gandhi's programme of non-cooperation under the existing circumstances in India was an alternative to (a) meek and unconditional acceptance of tyranny and injustice at the hands of the Government (b) the method of Constitutional agitation as practiced by the Liberals, pressing for piecemeal reform; (c) the method of secret assassinations and open armed rebellion.

Gandhi was neither in favour of a slow and unjust progress nor in favour of the use of too radical and violent a method of gaining political ends. His radicalism was of a different nature. Dr M.A. Buch wrote:

> "Gandhi's differences with the Liberals as regards methods of obtaining redress of wrongs as well as attaining Swaraj are radical. There is nothing in non-co-operation which is unconstitutional. Gandhi's constitutionalism is bolder than the Liberals' constitutionalism. He does not want reforms; he wants revolution. His spirit cannot be satisfied with the slow patient modifications of the existing machinery".[75]

In *Young India*, Gandhi wrote:

> "Reforms have already failed as they are bound to fail because they imply a compromise and co-operation with the principle of evil"

> "Further, the acceptance of partial reforms takes away the ground under the reformer's feet. Science teaches us that a lever cannot move a body unless it has got a resting point outside the body against which it is applied. Similarly, in order to overcome evil one must stand wholly outside it i.e. on the firm, solid ground of unadulterated good".[76]

Cooperation with the Government for any selfish purpose or out of fear was to Gandhi an absolutely unworthy attitude. But all this logic did not make an appeal to Jinnah and so he parted company with Congress.

Clearly though, both Gandhi and Jinnah had the same political guru in G.K. Gokhale, yet they stood poles apart in their political outlook. Gandhi believed in 'suffering' - a suffering in which the whole nation participated. Jinnah, believed in a 'normal evolutionary method'. The break was inevitable.

Gandhi was an ardent Indian Nationalist. His philosophy was activistic. He was no legalist like, Jinnah. When Gandhi thought of a National emancipation, he could not think of its attainment without the support of the masses. To Jinnah, the struggle with the British was the struggle of an enlightened lawyer. As such, when Gandhi embraced the masses, Jinnah tried to isolate them. Jinnah the lawyer, and the politician, who was also the most well dressed man in the British 'Empiro' because of his personal temperament and ambitions, could not possibly adjust himself to the changed conditions.

Jawahar Lal rightly observes in his autobiography that, "temperamentally he did not fit in at all with the now Congress. He felt completely out of his element in the Khadi clad crowd demanding speeches in Hindustani. The enthusiasm of the people outside struck him as mob hysteria.....He suggested once privately that only matriculates should be taken into the Congress".[77]

Quite different in his make up in his approach as also in his selection of the means, Jinnah thus stood poles apart from Gandhi. Gandhi was a leader of a different stuff. His devotion to politics was not without a religious as also a mystic touch. He not only believed in coveting for a righteous goal, he also emphasized on the righteousness of the means adopted for a cause. Dr M.A. Buch wrote:

> "Gandhi is a saint among politicians and a politician

> among saints. In him the highest religious idealism is combined with a strong practical sense, a genuine passion for social service, an undying devotion to his motherland, and above all, the will to translate the religious idealism into concrete deeds of daily life. It is this blending of romance and reality, this yearning to soar into the sky while keeping his feet firmly planted on the solid earth, that is the secret of the matchless leadership of Gandhi".[78]

We doubt indeed if politicians can be saints or the saints can be politicians. Nevertheless, it can be well said for Gandhi that in spite of a strong vein of religious mysticism in his nature, he alone could give that leadership, which could take the people towards the positive goal of Swaraj.

His patriotism as also his nationalism were deep rooted in humanitarianism and unlike Jinnah, as long as he lived, Gandhi failed to find any difference between a Hindu and a Muslim struggle for independence. Hindu-Muslim unity was always one of the major planks of his programme for the achievement of Swaraj. He declared:

> "The union that we want is not a patched-up thing, but a union of hearts, based upon a definite recognition of the indubitable proposition that Swaraj for India must be an impossible dream without an indissoluble union between the Hindus and the Muslims of India".[79]

Whatever might have been Gandhi's views, they did not make an appeal either to the entire Muslim community, or to the mind of their leadership. The doctrine of truth and non-violence was too difficult a lesson to a people who had lived through the ages on principles quite opposed and different. Obviously, Congress methodology instead of bringing the two communities together, made the Muslims more aloof. As E.W.R. Lumbay writes".[80]

> "Moreover Congress was now becoming increasingly identified with a body of ideas and a political technique which the Muslims felt to be characteristically Hindu - the ideas and technique of Gandhi. There were the cult of the spinning-wheel; the use of fasts for political ends; the legalistic methods of negotiation; the insistence on the uplift of the Untouchables - the outcastes of Hinduism; all

> these had their roots in an India which had existed for ages before the coming of the Muslim conquerors. Politics of the Gandhian school, dealing so largely in gestures and symbols, were too amorphous and subtle for Muslims with their creed of simple assertions. Above all, there was the emphasis on non-violence. When campaigns of non-cooperation were launched, Congressmen were exhorted to eschew rigorously all methods which involved, or might lead to, violence. Muslims, though they had participated in the first non-cooperation campaign in 1920, which was undertaken largely in support of the Caliphate movement, could hardly be expected to be content in the long run with a method so alien to the warlike traditions of Islam".

When the frustrated and disillusioned Jinnah, who was once the "Ambassador of Hindu-Muslim Unity", came back after an eclipse of a few years of loneliness and dismay, he turned into an advocate of communal disunity.

To him, Hindu-Muslim unity became a mirage. His demands, his methods and his leadership gradually became too narrow and too irrational; and embittered Hindu-Muslim relations while causing a drag on the forces of nationalism. As the President of the Muslim league, he preached the gospel of separatism to its members, for in it lay his solution for a better communal understanding. He said:

> "We must think of the interests of our community. Unless you make the best efforts, you will fail and will command no respect and nobody will bother to consult you. Organize yourselves and play your part.
>
> The Hindus and Muslims must be organised separately, and once they are organised they will understand each other better, and then we will not have to wait for years for an understanding......I am helping eighty million people, and if they are more organised they will be all the more useful for the national struggle".[81]

It is thus clear, that while Gandhi's technique put the 'National' interest as the sinequanon of any political action, to Jinnah it was the interest of the 'Muslims' that supplied the best norm for all political attainments. It was, in fact the hurt pride of a frustrated leader, of a frustrated community, that asserted itself in the most irrational manner. Leuis Fischer aptly writes:

> "Hurt pride is a ferocious beast. Jealousy aroused by the bottom view of a rival mounting the ladder can become a mighty urge to achieve power in order to hurt him and others. Such motivations have made history. But history must help by offering the jealous one an opportunity, it must cup its hands under his foot to give him a boost. Historic events did form a stirrup for Jinnah's climb into the saddle".[82]

The unexpected rise of Jinnah to power was used effectively by him in wreaking vengeance on the Hindu community and Gandhi and the Indian National Congress in particular. In fact till the partition of 1947, his sole passion was to oppose and discredit every action of theirs. He got terribly obsessed with the nightmare of a Hindu-Raj. He said:

> "When you talk of Democracy you mean Hindu Raj, to dominate over the Muslims, a totally different nation, different in culture, different in every thing. You yourself are working for Hindu Nationalism and Hindu Raj".[83]

He would thus pose a question to the country and ask "can we Musalmans of India accept Akhand Hindustan, Hindu Raj over the entire sub-continent".[84]

As such, he became 'deaf to logic and blind to arithmetic' in his demands for the uplift of his community. The truth is that, a series of frustrations in private and public life totally shattered his personality and, in the later years, his megaltomania made him cast away the moorings of a healthy communal policy. In his 'intensification of League's efforts' he made use of all kinds of tactics and duplicity. While Gandhi was frantically trying to achieve Hindu-Muslim unity, Jinnah was fanatically striving for a permanent cleavage.

While Gandhi tried to adopt only fair means for the desired end, Jinnah violated all canons of righteousness for the cause to which he was wedded; viz. the partition of the country.

Mr Jones who interviewed Jinnah several times, was not much wrong when in his book *Tumult in India,* he wrote about Jinnah:

> "A superb political craftsman, a Machiavelli in the amoral

> sense of that description.... His personal defects are a somewhat hostile reserve, conceit, and a narrow oulook....He is an extremely suspicious man, who feels that he has been wronged many times in life. His repressed intensity borders on the psychotic. Withdrawn, and isolated, Jinnah is arrogant to the point of discourtesy.....".[85]

In the Machiavellian way, Jinnah exploited every situation to attain his end, and in the end he became the virtual dictator of Muslim League Politics. He brooked no opposition in party ranks. Mr Fazul-Haq tried it once and 'was thrown into the scrap heap'.

As pointed out by Dr Lal Bahadur, all opportunities to surround him with the halo of a dictator were fully utilized and his command assumed the force of law. He was always entrusted with the sole authority to negotiate with the Congress and the British Government. He became a dictator for all intents and purposes and thereby fully answered fascist traditions".[86]

It is correct that in the true fascist way Jinnah glorified the Muslim community and launched a hate campaign against the Hindus. His methods became communal and disruptionist. He utilised league's organisation to ventilate the economic grievances of the frustrated Muslims for which he did not mind the use of 'intimidation, threat, coercion and violence".[87]

Jinnah alone could annul the communal-lag with which the Muslim community suffered. "No one motivated by sordid landlord gains, or the clerk's ambitions of the educated unemployed, or the obscurantism of the mullahs (preachers), could have fused all these urges into a national crusade. That required somebody who stood above them, as Hitler personally stood above the financial and business aims of the German upper bourgeoisie and East Prussian land barons, Jinnah was the man. Incorruptible, rich and disinterested in economic benefits for himself, his furious hatred of Gandhi and Nehru, who had "worked under" him and driven him out of politics, plus his conceit and "repressed intensity" bordering on the psychotic, brought him back to politics in his sixties with a zeal that knew no principle except success".[88]

It is clear that Jinnah's violent irrational and communal policy was bound to negate the efforts of Gandhi who was wedded to non-violence, truth and communal-concord. It was this policy that ultimately made the irreligious Jinnah demand two religious states while Gandhi wanted only a united secular state.

It is in the above difference of outlook and technique of the two leaders that we can find the reason why Gandhi failed and Jinnah won, 'Irrational resoluteness even when it conflicts with self-interest never the less after makes history".[89]

Jinnah's individualism triumphed over Gandhi's humanism, and however kept in check, communalism continued to embitter relations between the Hindus and the Muslims.

In the final adaptive consequence, a "substitution" of goal was made. The Muslims having realized that turning out of the British was difficult, took the alternative goal of extracting whatever gains they could, by being loyal to the British and by preventing others from opposing their rule or from trying to dominate over Muslims. They now tried to perceive a similarity between the original goal of being anti-British and the alternative goal of being anti-Hindu. Henceforth, it was the All India Muslim League that became the chief spokesman of the Muslim community. Here again, we find that in its activities there was a persistent effort to eschew National politics as taken up by the Indian National Congress. We have already seen how the Muslim League tried to malign the rise of Indian Nationalism as cloak for disguised Hindu imperialism. Having taken up the role of a political broker, it tried to consolidate the position of Muslim Community in two ways.

Firstly, it extracted whatever concessions it could in the form of special safeguards, communal electorates and weightage in return for Muslim loyalty to the British. In its demands, the Muslim League had developed a neuropathic sentiment fed largely on abstract fears and suspicions that were made to appear plausible by its own irrational logic. The irrational element and the undesirable consequences of the same have been fairly described in the following lines:

> "In the brief analysis of the safeguards we see the working of a very interesting psychological phenomenon. The acceptance of safeguards to protect the Muslim interests began to isolate the Muslim community from the rest of India. The sense of isolation only helped to increase the

> feeling of insecurity which again sought safety in further safeguards. But the feeling could not be dispelled. On the contrary, at every step it seems to have gripped the Muslim League more firmly then ever, and like the witches in Macbeth, is driving it on from one impossible position to another. Caught in the coils of its irrational logic the Muslim League is driven to seek an escape in the desperate measure of Pakistan. Will Pakistan finally lay the ghost of insecurity? One can not definitely say but if the history of the past thirty five years is an indication, then one can make a shrewd guess as to the future. Feelings and appetites grow by what they feed on and their satisfaction is often vainly sought and hardly ever found".[90]

It was this demand of Pakistan, which became the second shaft of League's political philosophy. It resulted as a consequence of a split in the National movement, which came to be known as the two nation theory.

The doctrine developed from the time old Muslim fear of Hindu majority, an aspect of communal-lag which could not be annulled in any way. Rt. Hon. Syed Ameer Ali declared:

> "Unfortunately, the larger community has by its numbers obtained the practical administration of the country; the other is apprehension of losing every political right in the growth of Nationalism among their rivals".[91]

The Muslim solution to this dilemma was discovered by the famous Muslim poet, Sir Mohammed Iqbal in a territorial consolidation. In his Presidential address to the League session of 1930, he said:

> "It is clear that, in view of India's infinite variety in climates, races, languages, creeds, and social systems, the creation of autonomous states based on unity of language, race, history, religion and identity of economic interests is the only possible way to secure a stable constitutional structure in India".[92]

This separatist trend in the Muslim attitude reached its climax when in the year 1937, Congress occupied the reins of the Provincial administration. It brought the total cessation of the unitarian evolution of the Indian Nationalism. The doctrinal genesis of the two Nation theory in India was gradually given a practical shape. As Professor Coupland remarks:

> "So far the league's policy was merely negative: but from the autumn of 1933 onwards a new and positive doctrine was taking shape in Moslem minds. It countered the Logic of democracy with the logic of nationalism. If Indian Moslems were no more than a community within one Indian Nation, then, since they numbered only about one-quarter of the total population, they could scarcely expect to obtain an equal status with the Hindu community which numbered about three fifths. But the Moslems, it was now asserted were not a community, they were a nation, and nations are entitled to stand on an equal footing with each other in international society whatever their respective size may be and to exercise an equal right of self-determination".[93]

The claims of Nationhood were not purely cultured. The Muslims claimed to possess their own National homeland in those areas of North-West and North-East India in which the Muslims were in a majority.

It was a stand which was long accepted by the British public opinion, since the day they had occupied this subcontinent. In a letter published in the *Morning Post*, Mr Theodore Morrison then Principal of the Armstrong College at New-Castle had written much earlier in the twenties that India was two Nations.

He wrote:

> "your unequivocal support of separate electorates in the same article will be read with deep satisfaction by the Mussalmans of India: they are very seriously apprehensive that the British Parliament may, by a change in the Constitution deny them the right of choosing their own Representatives and leave them to the mercy of a Hindu majority. All Englishmen who know India at first hand will share their apprehension. Within the frontiers of India live two Nations, the Moslem and the Hindus, which entertain for each other the same feeling as do, for instance, French and Germans, and who differ from one another more profoundly than any two Nations in Europe".[94]

These were the British sentiments long before the Pakistan resolution was passed by League in 1940. The demand of a separate State on the basis of the claims of a separate nation was but a logical conclusion of the illogical forces that the League had unleashed with a tacit consent of the English rulers of India.

This split in the Indian National movement came in sharp conflict with the Congress doctrine of National struggle. In one of his letter to M.A. Jinnah, who in the true tradition of Sir Syed Ahmed, Sir Syed Ameer Ali and Sir Mohammed Iqbal had now assumed the leadership of the Muslim League, wrote:

> "......In the course of our discussions you have passionately pleaded that India contains two nations, i.e., Hindus and Muslims, and that the latter have their homelands in India as the former have theirs. The more your argument progresses, the more alarming your picture appears to me. It would be alluring if it were true. But my fear is that it is wholly unreal. I find no parallel in history for a body of converts and their descendants claiming to be a Nation before the advent of Islam, it must remain one in spite of the change of faith of a very large body of their children. You do not claim to be a separate Nation by right of conquest, but by reason of acceptance of Islam. Will the two Nations become one if the whole of India accepted Islam".[95]

Two days later, Jinnah replied in the following words, that sealed for ever any harmonious development of Hindu-Muslim relations in India He wrote:

> "We maintain that Muslims and Hindus are two major nations by any definition or test as a Nation. We are a Nation of a Hundred million, and what is more, we are a Nation with our own distinctive culture and civilisation, language and literature, art and architecture, names and nomenclature, sense of values and proportion, legal laws and moral codes, customs calendar, history and traditions, aptitudes and ambitions in short we have our own distinctive outlook on life and of life. But all the Canons of international Law, we are a Nation".[96]

Mr. Jinnah's stand for a separate Muslim State, on the basis of

'Two Nations Theory' when tested on the various touchstones that attempt to define the concept of Nation fails in its theoretical import as also its practical applicability. Yet it achieved one of the greatest political successes for the Indian Muslims."[97]

The fact remains that in any human society, it is not the difference of race or religion, of culture or caste, or, of language and literature, that ultimately goes to determine the entity of a Nation. The *raison d'etre* of a Nation lies more in the common consciousness of the people who are animated by a desire to live together irrespective of their mutual differences.

Muslims were positively a separate nation; not because they constituted a community with a different language, religion and culture, but, because they all desired to live separately from the rest of the Indians. It cannot be denied that British politics, Muslim fanaticism and, to some extent, Hindu rigidity had created a situation where an amalgam of Economic grievances and religious passion could be well exploited by a body of leaders belonging to the frustrated middle-class of the Muslim community.

When Jinnah talked of a separate Muslim Nation, he voiced the feelings of those people to whom their community and its communal uplift accounted for the only Nation in India to which Muslims could give a conscious allegiance.

> "Hindus and Moslems Are Separate Nations; Gandhi wants Hindu-Raj; Pakistan must be. This single-minded fanaticism, unreasoning passion and unbounded hate, wrapped in a person, untouched by suspicions of selfish motives had an enormous appeal to people whose hard lives and frustrations made them an easy prey to simple goals charged with emotion; Moslems will have their own state; Moslems will rule Hindus and Sikhs instead of being ruled; the Hindu merchant, industrialist, landlord; and official will go. The victims of Jinnah were as oblivious as he to the mathematics of minorities and to practical considerations. He gave them an intoxicating banner; Pakistan. He thought only of achieving Pakistan, never of the problems of Pakistan. In fact, for the first few years after he broached the idea, he even refused to indicate the future borders of Pakistan. The less concrete the project,

the more fascinating and the less attainable by criticism. The situation was a fanatic's paradise".[98]

It will be thus clear how the basic fact of 'communal-lag' led to a schism in the National Movement. This schism unleashed unforeseen forces of communalism and assisted by British ultimately registered a triumph over the Nationalist forces in India.

The historical investigation of the way the two communities revived, organized and fought against the foreign domination evidently proves the sociological truism that when the constituent elements of a social order once begin to act and react in an abnormal and disturbed atmosphere, then every aspect of their future relationship also has an abnormal growth.

The British rule had placed the indigenous communities in a state of abnormal existence of which frustration happened to be the keynote. The abnormal and disturbed state went deep into the minds of men. Each community was now encouraged to live in a state of suspicion, hatred and tension. It was more so, with the Hindus and the Muslims. They became extremely competitive and jealous and based their communal relations on mutual distrust and unfounded fear, which all the more aggravated their sense of frustration. It was this communal frustration which easily led to communal separatism.

To sum up therefore, it was as much the fact of economic discontentment as that of psychological discord that disabled efforts for bringing a communal rapprochement at various fronts and led to the final parting of the ways.

NOTES AND REFERENCES

1. *Note on Indian Affairs* by Hon'ble F.J. Shore, London (1837).
2. *The White Sahibs in India* by Reginald Reynold: The Socialist Book Centre Ltd., London (1946) 3rd Edn.
3. *Ibid.*, p. 69.
4. *Ibid.*, p. 69.
5. *The Moral Damage of War* by Dr. Walker Walsh, Boston (1906).
6. *Ibid.*
7. *Ibid.*, p. (see *India in Bondage* by Dr. Sunderland).

   ** The memorandum referred above further said "if young soldiers are carefully advised in regard to the ablution, and recognize that convenient arrangements exist in the regimental bazar (i.e. the Chakla or brothel), they may be expected to avoid the risks involved in association with women who are not recognised (that is licensed) by the regimental authorities".

Dr. Walsh who quotes this interesting circular gives example of how it was implemented locally. In one case, an officer had sent a requisition to a Magistrate "for extra attractive women for regimental bazar, in accordance with circular Memorandum 21a". Another complained that "there are not enough women, they are not attractive enough. More and younger women are required".

8. *Ibid.*, p. 59.
9. Reynolds, op. cit., p. 59.
10. Mehta and Patwardhan, op. cit., p. 103.
11. Ibid., p. 103.
12. *Theory and Problems of Social Psychology* by David Krech and Richard S. Crutchfield, McGraw Hill Book Company, N.Y. (1948), p. 55.
13. Beni Prasad, *op. cit.*, p. 24.
14. A sound though incomplete exposition of the Muslim revivalistic movements could be seen from the following extract from a sanad of Syed Ahmed Brelvi, the famous Wahabi Muslim Saint-freebooter in which he appointed Muhamad Hussain of Patna, as a Caliph. He wrote: "In the name of the merciful God, Be it known to those who seek the way of God in general and to those in particular, present and absent, who are the friends of Syed Ahmed, that the object of those who become disciples of holy-men by the ceremony of joining hands, is to secure the way of pleasing God, and depends on the observance of the law of his Prophet. He who believes that the way of pleasing God can be found without observing the law of the Prophet, is a false and deluded man. His pretensions are false and untenable. The Law of the Prophet is founded on two things.

    First: The not attributing to any creature attribute of God (Shirk-Polytheism). .

    Second: Not intervening forms and practices, which were not observed in the days of the Prophet and his successors or Caliphs (Bidat means innovations).

    "The former consists in disbelieving that angels spirits, spiritual guides, disciples, teachers, students, prophets or saints remove one's difficulties; in abstaining from having recourse to any of the above creations for the attainment of any wish or desire; in denying that any of them has the power of granting favour or removing evils; in considering them as helpless and ignorant as one's self in respect to the power of God; in never making any offering to any

Prophet, saint, holy man or angel for the obtaining of any object, but merely to consider them as the friends of God; to believe that they have power to rule accidents in life, and that they are acquainted in the secret knowledge of God in downright infidelity (*kufr*). No true faithful follower ought to be any one of the above dogmas".

"With regard to the second point non-introduction of novelties in religion consists in strongly adhering to all the devotions and practices in the affairs of life, which were observed in the time of the Prophet; in avoiding all such innovations (*bidat*), as marriage ceremonies, mourning ceremonies, the adoring of tombs, the erection of large edifices over tombs, the lavish expenditure on the anniversaries of the dead, the construction of *ta'ziyas*, and the like, and in endeavouring as far as may be practicable to put a stop to these practices.

A man must first leave off such practices, and next invite the attention of all Mussalmans to the fact, that it is as much obligatory on them to follow the law of the Prophet as to obey the commandment of God, in doing what he commands to be done, and in refraining from what he forbids".

Since the above is well impressed on my mind it behoves all who seek god to place the matter before their eyes, and now by joining each others hand to abide by it; and do so particularly, with Shaikh Mohammad Hussain, who has pledged to do the same by joining his hands with mine, and to whom I have fully explained all the above matter, and authorized him to take such views from you and to teach you holy practices in the room of myself. So it behoves the said Shaikh Mohammad Hussain to adopt the law as above explained, to direct his body and soul to God to follow the law in spirit and act to shake off any dust of shirk and innovations (*bidat*) that may on him to strife and incite people to make their views by joining their hands in his".

[*Calcutta Review* No. 100. pp. 89-90 (Quoted from 'Section from the Records of the Government of Bengal, No. XIII)"].

15. *Geschichte de nationaleu Bewegurg in orient* (Berlin 1928) Tr. by M.M. Green (London, 1929), pp. 56-61.
16. *Ibid.*, p. 61.
17. Dr. Desai. *op. cit.*, p. 255.
18. *Renascent India* (from Ram Mohun Roy to M.K. Gandhi) by H.C.E. Zacharias Ph.D. George Allen & Unwin Ltd., London, 1933.
19. *Ibid.*, p. 22.
20. *Ibid.*, p. 23.
21. Philips, *op. cit.*, p. 104.

22. *The Arya Samaj* by Lala Lajpat Rai. (1932), pp. 255-56.
23. *A History of Nationalism in the East* by Hans Kohn (1929), pp. 67-68.
24. Home Department Pub. 'B'. Jan. 1894. No. 309-414 (A report from D.F. Mc Cracken. Offg. Genl. Suptd. Thaggi and Dacoity Dept. 9th August, 1893).
25. *Ibid.*
26. *Ibid.*
27. *Ibid.*
28. *Ibid.*
29. *Ibid.*
30. *The Arya Samaj* by Lajpat Rai. Uttar Chand Kapur & Sons. Lahore (1932), pp. 293-94.
31. *Ibid.*
32. It is interesting to note the impact of these revivalistic tendencies on the relationship between Hindu and Muslim Zamindars and their tenants.
    (a) Inspired from Wahabi teachings a few Muslim farmers grew long beard in order to distinguish themselves from the fellow Hindu-peasants. On it, a Hindu Zamindar of Bengal, Kishen Ray, imposed a punitive tax of Rs. 2/8 on each such Wahabi peasant under him. The result was communal bitterness and riots amongst Hindus and Muslims. (See. Calcutta Review. Vol: ....)
    (b) Similarly, Hindu Zamindars, during the anti-kine slaughter movements did not permit their tenants from 'sacrificing cows or killing kine for food, it occassionally resulted in local riots.
33. Dr. Beni Prasad, *op. cit.*, pp. 25-26. Kitabistan Publishers, Allahabad.
34. *Ibid.*
35. A Review of History and Work of the Hindu Mahasabha and the Hindu Sanghthan Movement" by Indra Prakash (Pub. by Akhil Bhartiya Hindu Mahasabha; Reading Road, New Delhi, 2nd Ed. 1952), p. 13.
36. *Ibid.*, pp. 7-8.
37. *Ibid.*, pp. 9-10.
38. *Ibid.*, p. 16.
39. *Ibid.*, p. 19.
40. See introduction to Ibid. by V.D. Savarkar (old Edn.).
41. *Ibid.*, p. 190.
42. The Hindu Mahasabha Record Office. Presidential Addresses, 1937
43. *Ibid.*, (1938).
44. *Nationalism in Free Asia*. (Ed.) by Philip W. Thayer. The Johns Hopkins Press, Baltimore (1956), pp. 72-73.
45. Desai, *op. cit.*, p. 280.

46. The Indian National Congress owes its birth to a Scotsman, Allan Octavian Hume, who was for many years a member of the Indian Civil Service. Born in 1829, he entered the ICS in 1849 and was posted to Bengal. After serving in various capacities, he was Secretary to the Government of India from 1870 to 1879. In 1879, he was sent back to the districts because it was said he was inconveniently outspoken and expressed his views with great freedom without regard to what might be the wishes and intentions of his superiors. Lord Lytton offered him the Lt. Governorship of the Punjab but he declined the appointment on the ground that a Lieutinant Governorship meant a great deal of entertainment and neither his wife nor himself cared for this. Lord Lytton then recommended for the post of the Home Member but the recommendation was turned down by Lord Salisbury on the ground that Hume had stiffened Lord Northbrook against the repeal of the cotton duties.
    During his whole official career, Hume had formed strong views in favour of an early attainment of self government by India. He retired from the Civil Service in 1882 and began evolving a definite scheme for creating united public opinion in India and giving it effective expression. Lord Dufferin, the Viceroy, encouraged Mr Hume by telling him that as head of the Government, he found the greatest difficulty in ascertaining the real wishes of the people of India and that for purposes of administration, it would be a public benefit if there existed some responsible organisation through which the Government might be kept informed regarding the best Indian public opinion.
47. *Recollections and Reflections* by Chimanlal H. Setalvad; Padma Publications Ltd., Bombay (1946), pp. 273-74.
48. Philips C. H. op. cit., p. 100.
49. *Ibid.*
50. Setalvad, *op. cit.*, p. 274.
51. Congress Presidential Addresses: G.A. Natesan and Co. Madras (1935), p. 724.
52. *India and Democracy* by Sir George Schuster and Guy Wint. Macmillan & Co. Ltd., London. (1941), pp. 167-68.
53. *Ibid.*, p. 169.
54. Philips, *op. cit.*, p. 101.
55. See *Ibid.* Presidential Addresses, 1887.
56. See *Ibid.*
57. *Muslims and the Congress* by Razaul Karim, Calcutta, (1941), p. (vi).
58. *Ibid.*, p. (vii and viii).
59. Philips, *op. cit.*, p. 109.

60. *The Indian Moslems by An Indian Mohammedan*, London (1928), p. 249.
61. *Young India*, 2nd June 1920.
62. *The Birth of Pakistan* by Dr. Sachin Sen, pp. 71-72.
63. *Ibid.*, pp. 73-74.
64. *Ibid.*, p. 72.
65. *Pakistan or Partition of India* by Dr B.B. Ambedkar. Thacker and Company Ltd., Second Ed. (1945), pp. 153-54.
66. *Ibid.*, p. 177 (The number of the riots that took place is so large that they cannot be briefly summarized. It is one of the most unfortunate aspect of communalism and it continued till the partition took place in 1947. For greater details of the Riots upto 1947 see *Ibid.*, Chapter VII. As for the horrible conditions that prevailed during the Partition time. See (a) Stern Reckoning by Justice C.D. Khosla (b) *Now it can be Told* by Prof. Bali).
67. *The Future of Indian Politics* by Mrs Annie Besant, pp. 301-5.
68. *Ibid.*
69. Ambedkar, *op. cit.*, p. 68. (Quoted in *Life of Savarkar* by Indra Prakash).
70. *India in Crucible* by C.S. Iyer, p. 298.
    Report of the N.W.F. Committee (1924) Govt. Central Press, Delhi.
71. *Jinnah - Creator of Pakistan* by Hector Bolitho. John Murray A Lbemarle street, W. London. (1954), pp. 82-83.
72. See *Young India*, Jan. 5, 1922.
73. *Speeches and Writings of Gandhi*, pp. 530-2.
74. Hector Bolitho, *op. cit.*, p. 85.
    Dewan Chaman Lall recalled the above scene to Mr Hector Bolitho the biographer of Jinnah. Bolitho writes that when Jinnah made the above remark, he was opposed from many quarters.
75. *The Development of Contemporary Indian Political Thought* by Dr M.A. Buch. Good Companies Baroda (1939) Vol. II, p. 141.
76. *Young India*, 23, February, 1921.
77. *An Autobiography* by J.L. Nehru, pp. 67-68.
78. *The Development of Contemporary Indian Political Thought* by Dr M.A. Buch, Vol. II, pp. 1-2.
79. *Young India*, 19th Feb. 1925.
80. The Transfer of Power in India (1945-47) by E.W. R. Lumbay. George Allen and Unwin Ltd. (1954), p. 16.
81. Hector Bolitho, *op. cit.*, p. 112.
82. *Gandhi - His Life and Message for the World* by Louis Fischer (A Signet Key Book Pub. By The New American Library) 1954, p. 151.
83. *The March of a Nation: A Collection of the Most Important Speeches of Qaid -i-Azam Mr A. Jinnah*, p. 143.

84. The Indian Annual Register July-Dec. 1943, p. 290.
85. Louis Fischer, *op. cit.*, p. 150.
86. *The Muslim League - its History, Activities and Achievements* by Dr. Lal Bahadur, p. 352.
87. *Ibid.*, p. 352.
88. Louis Fischer, *op. cit.*, p. 102.
89. Louis Fischer *op. cit.*, p. 152.
90. Mehta and Patwardhan, *op. cit.*, p. 110.
91. *The Times*, Nov. 3, 1927.
92. Indian Annual Register, 1930. Vol. II, p. 334.
93. *India a Re-Statement* by Sir Reginald Coupland, Oxford University Press (London) 1945, p. 92.
94. Quoted in *The Indian Moslems* by An Indian Mohammedan, Ardenna Publication. London. S.W. (1928), pp. 189-90.
95. *Ibid.* Jinnah Gandhi talks (Nov. 1944).
96. *Ibid.*
97. See *The Making of the Indian Constitution* by A.C. Banerjee, Vol. 1. (1948), pp. 22-23.

    The Resolution of the Muslim League Lahore Session. March 23, 1940.

    "Resolved that it is the considered view of this session of the All India Muslim League that no constitutional scheme would be workable in this country or acceptable to Muslims unless it is designed on the following basic principle, viz. that geographically continuous units are demarcated into regions which should be constituted with such territorial re-adjustments as may be necessary, that the areas in which the Muslims are numerically in majority, as in the North-Western and Eastern zones of India, should be grouped to constitute independent States in which the constituent unit shall be autonomous and sovereign.

    That adequate, effective and mandatory safeguards should be specifically proved in the constitution for minorities in these units and in these regions for the protection of their religious, cultural, economic, political, administrative and other rights and interests in consultation with them; and in other parts of India where the Mussalmans are in a minority, adequate, effective and mandatory safeguards shall be specifically provided in the constitution for them and other minorities for the protection of their religious, cultural, economic, political, administrative and other rights and interests in consultation with them."
98. Louis Fischer, *op. cit.*, p. 153.

85. [illegible] op. cit., p. 198.

87. Ibid., p. 293.
88. [illegible] op. cit., p. 148.

90. [illegible] op. cit., p. 186.
91. The Dawn, March 1, 1947.

94. [illegible]
95. [illegible]

Section Three

The Socio-Religious Aspect of Communalism

Finally, we come to the moral factor and the part it played in aggravating and accentuating communalism, in the political phase. As already discussed, the moral factor operates through the observance by various communities of certain socio-religious practices in their daily life. In this phase, the socio-religious factor operated exactly on the pattern of economic and psychological factors. It had a triangular setting formed by the interconflict of Hindus, Muslims and the British.

The course of Hindu caste rigidity and the concomitant stigma of untouchability, to which even the Muslims were not immune, continued to be a powerful source of social tension in India. Curiously enough, even the British cannot vindicate themselves from the odium of having encouraged and practised untouchability in their social life. For them, every Indian, irrespective of caste, creed and colour was no better than an untouchable rather he was also an unapproachable, like the *panchams* and *periahs* of South India. Racial discrimination and social discrimination, may connote two different things, but, when put in practice, by the members of a society, they do not differ in their form and content. They are invariably the creed of prejudice, hate and unceasing hostility amongst those who observe it and those who are its victims. It is a sheer outrage on human dignity to dub any one community as bad and immoral. The West has always blamed India and, particularly the Hindus in this respect. The charge is quite correct but is not the whole truth.

The curse of social and racial discrimination, which had its sanction both in the code of religion and in the code of morality of the contemporary exponents of society, was one of the main undercurrent of communalism, in India.

The second content in which the socio-religious factor operates, is the realm of religion itself. It is clear to us that all the three communities had different religions. As such, not only did their concepts of good and bad, of truth and untruth differ widely but the zeal and enthusiasm with which they were practised and propagated formed an important factor in keeping the different communities alert and suspicious of the members of any community taking inspiration from gods different from their own.

It is a well known fact that the community is a growing and a dynamic concept. Where a particular community holds a proselytizing creed, it is but natural that its zeal for conversion should give rise to tension in a society where so many communities exist in a state of mutual interaction. Obviously Christianity and Islam because of their proselytizing tendencies generated a deep undercurrent that engulfed people in a vicious circle of communal unrest and antagonism.

However, on taking a dispassionate and objective view of the matter, it would appear that it was not so much the Christian but the Muslims who confused a zeal for religion with ruthless bigotary. As such it was difficult to expect that the Islamic concept of morality and religion could be anything but a disquieting element in the complex texture of Indian social life.

The socio-religious practises of the Christian rulers of course were quite different from those professed by the Indians.

However, the British responsibility lay not so much in stressing the differences, as in laying overemphasis on the points of difference between the practice of the indigenous communities. They played a subtle imperialistic game, to which the magnifying of these facts of difference was suited par-excellence. The Hindus were made to appear as more rigid and fixed in their social outlook than they were in reality; on the contrary Mohammedans were passed off as much more intolerant and separatist in their religious outlook than was warranted by the actual life of the country.

The responsibility for this distortion and destruction of the native life was never accepted by the British. They have always denied having tampered unscrupulously with the indigenous institutions and way of life. Very clearly, they camoflauged their subtle destruction of the harmonious relations existing hitherto amongst different communities. Their stand was just in keeping with their fundamental policy of Divide *et impera*, a corollary to the theory of Balance of power. In the case of India, they could make good of 'differences of religion' that existed. Thus, Religious groups in India were referred to as 'communities' and inter-religious problems as 'communal problems'.[1] Accordingly communalism came to be defined as that 'Ideology which has emphasized as the social political and economic unit the group of adherents of each religion and has emphasized the distinction, even the antagonism between such groups; the words, "adherent and religion", being taken in the most nominal sense".[2]

The British stand on the Hindu-Muslim question can be aptly summarized in the words of Sir Hugh Mcpherson who served for a time as Secretary for the Home Department of the Government of India and also acted as a Governor of Bihar and Orissa in 1925. He writes:

> "The differences which separate Hindu and Muslim are essentially religious. They may be re-inforced by historical tradition, by political rivalries or by economical contrasts, but for the great masses of the population it is the religious issue alone that counts".[3]

It was the bogey of religion and religious differences on which the British Imperialists in India thrived for centuries.

It is in laying undue emphasis on the religious differences of the indigenous population that the real mischief of the Christian ruler lies. The importance attached to the religious cleavage was so acute that the fact of religion came to pass as the sole criterion of group distinction, social living and political achievements. Describing the legacy of British India, Dr Sitaramayya aptly writes:

> "At Railway stations, dining halls for Brahmins and non-Brahmins are separately arranged in the South India while Hindu Pani (water) and Muslim Pani are separately served and stocked in Central and Northern India. It is unfortunate that when you give evidence in law court or write out your description registering a document you have to mention your caste. Thus, what is required to be overlooked was emphasised according to British regulations. This only added fuel to the fire of

> communalism which had always been there for the very names of the Indians bear suffixes which indicate their caste and sub-caste".[4]

One has to admit that the Socio-religious problem as presented by the various communities before the British administrators of India was quite complex and intricate by itself. The differences of religion along with the difference in many other social observance of Hindus and Muslims certainly needed a very delicate handling on the part of the authorities. Often they did give this problem a serious think in an attempt to try their best to solve it as fairly as possible. The main guiding principles of the British administration in India were summed up by Sir Charles Crosthwaite in the following words:

> "They are, first on the part of Government itself, an imperial toleration of all creeds; secondly, a fixed determination to maintain the lawful liberation of all its subjects, and sternly to repress any person who infringes the lawful liberty of others; thirdly, when dispute arises as to what are the lawful liberties of any class, to decide according to established custom and usage by patient enquiry from those who know the usage".[5]

The soundness and wisdom of these principles cannot be questioned. Yet, if we examine them in the true historical perspection of their application in actual practice, we come across a shocking contrast between the theory and fact. To realize this we have only to take up each principle and put it to a thorough investigation. The principle of toleration of all creeds in its deeper reality was essentially diplomatic and vague. Apparently, toleration on the part of the British was not an unqualified or imperative principle that could have been put to some set norm. Since there was no constitutional guarantee or check on the administration, since the executive was neither responsible to the legislature nor to public opinion, it was extremely arbitrary in its decisions, and, quite often inconsistent and mischievous in its handling of the affairs of the natives. The question of the slaughter of kine is an illustration to point.[6]

It is well known that the Hindus hold the cow as very sacred and intensely dislike its slaughter. On the other hand, Muslims and the Christians, not only do not object to cow slaughter but also eat beef without any moral scruples. The 'Cow' and its slaughter has, therefore, always been the cause of violent controversy between these communities. It is more so because if Hindus celebrate the festival 'Gao-dhan', when the cow is worshipped with ceremonial-cum-religious reverence; the Muslims celebrate the Bakar-Id festival for which their socio-religious enjoin a meticulous observance of "sacrifice" and for sacrifice the Indian Muslims have in particular chosen the 'Cow' as the most propitiating.

Obviously, this difference between the socio-religious practices of the two communities continued throughout the British rule to be a chronic source of communal tension and disorders, between Hindus and Muslims.

There is enough contemporary evidence to establish clearly that British rulers cannot escape the charge of having deliberately encouraged communalism, for they tackled the question not on its merits but in accordance with the exigencies of the British Empire.

Looking back to the days of Ranjit Singh, when Punjab had yet not been annexed, we find that the British had prohibited kine-slaughter, but as soon as Punjab was annexed, all such prohibitions were removed. One would like to demand an explanation on why it was so? What type of a tolerance was this, which could change its nature with the change of territorial sovereignty? Was it not due to boost up the Mohammedans so that the indigenous communities might remain busy in fighting with each other and help the foundations of the British empire in continuing to go deeper and become stronger?

An answer to the above queries is indicated by the following secret letters which were exchanged between the British authorities. They clearly reveal that the real necessity of this new move arose to fulfil the demand for beef needed by British army though it was enforced under the cloak of permitting and tolerating socio-religious practices of the Muslims. The text of the letters run as follows:

Lt. E. Dursterville, Sub-Assistant Commissioner, General, in a letter dated the 4th April, 1849 addressed to the Officiating Assistant, resident of Mooltan as follows:

> "As the Punjab is now annexed, by orders of the Right Honourable the Governor General of India, I have the

honor to inform you that I propose entering into an agreement for the supply of beef for the European troops at the station as I conclude, you can have now no objection thereto".

In his reply Lt. Hugh James, the Acting Assistant Resident said, of the 4th instant, and in reply to state that the Right Honourable, the Governor-General has notified that he will allow no interference with the religious customs of the people; and the question therefore still remains open... So, postpone the measure, till I can receive the views of the President on the subject."

In a few days time the Assistant Commissioner of Mooltan received the following letter from the Lahore Residency.

No; 6, Dated 10th April, 1849.

From: Major E.B. Edwards C.B.
Officiating Secretary to the Board of Administration,
General Department, Lahore.

To

The Assistant Commissioner , Mooltan.

"Your letter on the subject of killing oxen for the consumption of the European troops.

You were quite right to act up to what you deemed the literal meaning of the Proclamation of 29th March, but the Board believes the spirit of the paragraph quoted in the margin to be opposed to your interpretation.

'The British Govt. will leave to all the people whether Mussalmans, Hindoo, or Sikh, the free exercise of their own religion; but it will not permit any man to interfere with other in the observances of such forms and customs as their respective religions may either enjoin or permit' Govt. Proclamation. 29th March, 1849.

The Governor General of India they conceived desired in that Proclamation to extend perfect religious freedom to all classes in the Punjab and your interpretation would obviously make every Mohammedan a slave to the religion of his Hindoo neighbour and this with out absolutely interfering with his own religion. The Mussalman, however would probably put the case to you much stronger even than the above. He would say, "It is true the Koran does not enjoin me to eat beef as an article, of faith, but my race has had this prohibition laid upon it for generations by prosecuting conquerors of another creed, and it has become throughout Asia the sign and symbol of Hindoo triumph and Mohammedan degradation. These persecuting Hindoo conquerors have in their turn been conquered by a tolerant Christian power and I claim the benefit as I have endured the hardships of subjection".

3. The Board therefore are distinctly of opinion that the Right Honourable the Governor General fully contemplated and intended the removal of that prohibition against the slaughter of kine, which we have hitherto maintained in the Punjab out of defence to a Sikh sovereign.

4. But the very same reasons which lead to this decision should make it a duty of all civil officers in the newly annexed countries so carefully and strictly to regulate the slaughter of kine in their districts as to render it as little offensive as possible to the prejudices of the Hindoo population. For instance, it should not be permitted within the bounds of cities, towns or villages where Hindoos and Mussalmans are mixed but under severe penalties should be removed to a distance of not less than 300 yards and even then should be away from any thoroughfare. Civil officers should themselves, in every large town, appoint a spot for the shambles and butcher's shops, if they value the peace of their districts and particularly take care that the Mohammedans do not select the neighbourhood of any Hindu Fakeer's hut or religious building.

On no account ought beef to be exposed for sale in shops within the towns, even though slaughtered outside, and Mussalmans should be severely punished for ostentatiously parading what they know will offend their Hindoo neighbours.

5. In short, the first tendency of the reaction will be to make Mussalmans abuse a privilege, from which they have been so long debarred, and it will become necessary to protect from insult, the Sikh and Hindoo so lately in the ascendant.

This correspondence will be forwarded to Government for information and final orders, but the Board request that you will meanwhile act upon these instructions."

The above interpretation of the Board was approved by the government of India and it is interesting to examine the orders passed by the Right Honourable the Governor-General of India (dated Shimla, the 21st April, 1849). The minute reveals in a glaring light the diplomacy of the British rulers, to distort the meaning of the Christian principles of Justice and tolerance, and have it whenever it suited the interests of the Empire.

Dalhousie wrote:

"Acquaint the Board that Mr James has not correctly constructed even the literal sense of the wording of the proclamation. It declares that no man will be allowed to interfere with the practice by his neighbour of customs which that neighbour's religion permits, and consequently that the Sikhs cannot be allowed on the ground of religious tenets of his own to prevent the Mussalman preparing the food which the Koran does not forbid.

Perfect toleration to the Sikh does no include recognition of and impunity for, intolerance on his part towards his Mohammedan neighbour.

The Governor General intimates that the Board has correctly interpreted both the spirit and letter of the Proclamation. He fully approves of the regulations they have issued on the subject. He requests that they will intimate this, his approval to all their offices and that they will at the same time inform them that the Governor-General regarding the question as one deeply affecting the peace of the country and the ready and satisfactory establishment of our rule will hold the civil officers severely responsible for measures being taken to ensure that the regulations shall be strictly attended to by all, whether Europeans or Natives.

The Governor-General will send a copy of this letter of his Board to the C-in-C, requesting him to enjoin on all Military authorities close attention to these regulations, and he desires that the civil officers will immediately report any disregard of them by those who may be beyond their immediate control'.

(Signed) (Dalhousie).

With such a sanction at its back, the machinery of the Government of India, was immediately put into action and cow-slaughter was permitted not so much for the sake of Mohammedans, of religious tolerance, or of the peace of the country, as for the permanent and solid establishment of the British rule.

H.M. Elliott, Secretary to the Government of India addressed the Board of Administrators for the Affairs of the Punjab in the following words:

> "I am directed to acquaint you that Mr James has not correctly constructed even the literal sense of the wording of the Proclamation. It declares that no man will be allowed to interfere with the practice by his neighbour of customs which that neighbour's religion permits and consequently that the Sikh cannot be allowed on the ground of religious tenets of his own, to prevent the Mussalman preparing the food which the Koran does not forbid. Perfect toleration to the Sikhs does not include recognition of and impunity for intolerance on his part towards his Mohammedans neighbour.
>
> The Governor-General desires me to intimate that you have correctly interpreted both the spirit and letter of the Proclamation and he fully approves of the regulations you have issued on this subject.
>
> You are requested to intimate this His Lordship's approval to all the officers subordinate to you will at the same time inform them that the Governor-General; regarding the question as one deeply affecting the peace of the country and the ready and satisfactory establishment of the British rule, will hold the civil officers severely responsible for measures being taken to ensure the strict observance of the regulations by all, whether Europeans or Natives."[7]

Such then was the application of the British principle of 'impartial toleration of all creeds'. As to the second, the very word 'Liberty' was a misnomer in the Imperialist Code and without entering into a dilatory exposition of this question we can say, that enough liberty was given to all subjects, to do things that could promote inter-communal rivalry and tension. As regards the repression of the persons who infringed the liberty of others, the rule was applicable to all except the British themselves who had enslaved millions under the Imperialist banner.

If the third rule were to be strictly followed, all communal disputes arising over the observance of the indigenous socio-religious practices, should have been decided by an appeal to, 'established custom and usage' of the realm. However, the rule was more often than not applied, and sometimes even perverted to the point of ludicrousness. Here are the orders given by Finley, a top British official, to regulate the trouble which are expected to arise because of the celebration of Muharram (a Muslim Festival) and JalJhulani (A Hindu Festival):[8]

> "All music shall cease on the processions approaching within 30 yards of a mosque, or 20 yards of a tazia or 10 yards of a Sabil, and shall not begin again until a distance of 30 yards from a mosque, 20 yards from a tazia and 10 yards from a Sabil has been reached .. no Sankhs or shells or horns will be allowed to be sounded on any pretext, except on the bank of the Jamuna."[9]

To sum up, we can safely reiterate our former stand that communal harmony was never the aim of the British masters in India. They had no love either for Hindus or Muslims, or any other sect. Their only love was the consolidation of the British Empire in India, which is made clear by G.M. Ogilvie, who was Financial Commissioner in Punjab. He declared:

> "The spirit of Mohammedans is far more aggressive than that of Hinduism and we must not overlook the fact although the Mohammedans may in some parts of the country appear to have ranged themselves. On the side of the Government, their attitude in this matter essentially just as much founded on religious fanaticism as is that of the Hindus.
>
> It should therefore be the policy of the Government while firmly suppressing the seditious conspiracy of the Hindus to show clearly that it will not tolerate any aggressive or provocative action on the part of the Muhammadan".[10]

We find an echo of the same views in one of the most unequivocal assertions of Sir Devis Fitz-Patrick, who was the Lt. Governor of Punjab.

"It should never be forgotten and there should never be any hesitation in laying down the principle that it is one of our first duties towards the people of India to guard the safety of our own dominion."[11]

The socio-religious factor aggravated communalism, partly

because of its inherent complexity and partly due to British diplomacy; it also led to Hindu-Muslim bitterness, by precipitating communal riots which became a permanent feature of Indian social life under British rule.

NOTES AND REFERENCES

1. *In the Minds of Men* by Gardner Murphy. B/B Basic Books Inc. Publishers, New York, 1953, p. 44.
2. *Modern Islam in India: A Social Analysis* by W.S. Smith Victor. Gollen Ltd., (London), 157.
3. Political India, *op. cit.*, p. 109.
4. Quoted from *Group Prejudices in India.*
5. Home Deptt. B. Pub. Jan. 1894. Nos. 309-414 (Subject Agitation against Cow Slaughter).
6. The practice of sacrificing kine at the annual festival of the Muslims which coincides with that day in ceremonies of the Meccan pilgrimage on which the victims are slaughtered at Mina is widely spread in India. The festival is popularly known as the Bakar-id, a name which is generally, though probably erroneously interpreted as rendering kine, particularly appropriate as victims. The great majority of Indian Muslims are Sunnies and followers of Abu Hanifah, whose tenets enjoin the punctual observance of the sacrifice, as an obligatory duty (though not expressly ordained in the Koran), by all who have means sufficient to perform it.

   The same rule, which is also recognized by all schools of Mohammedan Law declares that, while, the 'minimum' obligatory offering for each free adult Muslim is a sheep or goat, the offering of a camel, bullock, ox or cow or buffaloe is equivalent to seven sheep or goats and thus by such single offering seven persons can participate in the sacrifice. (Report from Lord Lansdowne G.G. and Viceroy of India to Lord Kimberly, the Secy. of States, on the subject of Hindu-Muslim Relations. 1893, Pub.: No. 210-13)
7. Home Department Publication, December, 1893, Nos. 210-213.
8. Shimla Records. Home Deptt. Pub.: Feb. 1891. Nos. 61-91.
9. a) Muharram: Is the name of the first month of the Mohammedan year, which like all other months of the Muslim calendar, being lunar, shifts its place backwards by about eleven days each year when compared with the solar months, new moon (or rather the first appearance of the crescent of the visible moon) to New moon. The Hindu months, which are also lunar, are counted in Upper India. (In Bengal the reckoning is from New moon (Amavasya) to

new moon. From full moon to full moon; but the Hindu lunar year differs for the year of Islam in that it is kept in approximate accord with the solar year by the intercalation of a thirteenth month every third year. The Muslim year, on the contrary, has rejected the intercalation which prevailed before the Prophet's time, and now hears no fixed relation to the solar seasons; The months progressing backwards year by year, may fall at any season while the Hindu months recur approximately at the same period of the solar year; The Muharram is the name generally given to the first ten days of the month called the Ashura, which is a sacred season of Prayer and meditation for all Muslims. It is, however, specially associated in India and Persia with the events which led to the death of Hussain, the Prophet's grandson, who was slain in battle at Kabala by Yazid in a forlorn attempt to oust the House of Umayyah from the Caliphate. The battle and its preliminaries lasted throughout the sacred days, and Hussain was killed on the tenth. The last four days, being the day of his death and those which immediately preceded it, included many harrowing scenes, and their commemoration is the occasion of much religious and enthusiastic excitement among Indian Mohammedans. Strict Sunnies who recognize no special title to the succession to the Caliphate in the family of Ali (as the Shias do) rather, hold aloof from the fanatic demonstrations of the populace. But everywhere in India the occasion is one of the great popular agitations among the lower classes of Mohammedans and processions with banners and wardrums, parade the streets. The *tazias* (called more properly *tabuts*) in Southern India are representations of Hussain's tomb, and are carried about like *bkrs* on the tenth day of commemoration of his burial".

b) The Jal Jhulni: Is a very minor festival, at which the image of Krishna is taken out from its temple, carried through the streets, and bathed in the Jamuna the image being swung in the water, hence the name.

10. Home Department Publication. B. January, 1894, 309-414.
11. *Ibid.*

Section Four

The Explosive Aspect of Communalism

No study of communalism in its political phase would be complete unless it takes up an investigation into the nature of communal riots and disturbances that took place under the British rule.

In India, as elsewhere, communal riots have always been an index of social unrest. Their history is not only a record of an acute disorganization and disruption of normal social existence, but also happens to be a sad commentary on the development of Hindu-Muslim relations in India.

A riot ordinarily speaking, is an outbreak of temporary but violent mass disorder. As, *Encyclopaedia Americana* observes:

> "Riot is, a disturbance of the public peace, attended with circumstances of tumult and commotion, as were an assembly destroys or in any manner damages, seizes or invades private or public property, or does any injury whatever by actual or threatened violence to the persons of individuals".[1]

The fact is that although, "the web of human relationships which constitutes community is a very strong and flexible one, yet it is not completely a proof against violent tearing. We can say that each society is always, "under the weather", from chronic tensions. Riots are but one manifestation of such disruptive stresses operating both within and without the communal fold. Broadly speaking, therefore, riots are not a disease in themselves, but the symptoms of some other diseases inherent in a given social system.

It is, therefore, the difference in the nature of the disease that brings a change in the character, scope and intensity of the riot, In any social set-up, individual or group dissatisfaction, followed by more violence and a general sense of consternation constitutes a riot.

Rioting bears testimony to the fact that there exists a strong sense of dislike, difference and dissatisfaction among certain groups of people, in a given society or social order. It also indicates that these groups tied to these differences whether differences of thought or action, custom or convention, race or religion, that, sometimes, they cannot but break into a fit of violent aggression against each other. In each case as K.Semillie observes,

> "Riots are an index of social unrest. Although civilisations and historical periods, those which have been truly symptomatic have directly reflected their chief force of conflict. The most significant types have been religious, political, economic and racial. Such riots are as much a symptom of social disease as pain is a symptom of biological disorder".[2]

Sorokin, however, does not regard the occurrence of these disturbances as something abnormal. To him any riot is a purely social and cultural phenomenon, in which the original system gets unsettled. As Cowell in his work on Sorokin observes:

> "The occurrence of important social disturbance in the life of social bodies is so frequent that the recurrent outbreaks, like tensions and sickness in individual human organisms or storms in nature must be regarded as a normal occurrence in the life of any society group on an average; for all the countries studied, there has been one significant disturbance for every five years of peace".[3]

As we have already noted, communalism in India happened to be a chronic ailment of the Indian social organism of which communal riots were a symptom. Every phase of communalism in India records an account of riots; although as K. Semillie observes, they do differ considerably in their character, scope and intensity, but unlike Sorokin's analysis their frequency is far greater, particularly during the course of British rule.

In the political phase of communalism three things make themselves quite obvious:

Background

(1) Firstly, that under the British rule the indigenous population lived a politically emasculated life. It was a life of economic privation, social degradation and cultural chaos. The misery inflated on society was so intense that individuals and groups lost

their moorings and communal equipoise. Obviously, the disturbed equilibrium manifested itself in all avenues of life, be it economic, political, social, religious or economic. Riots were but one manifestation of this wave of general inequanimity.

(2) Secondly, that it was a period of long and agonizing frustration, a frustration suffered at two levels. If, on the one hand, Indian communities got frustrated at the hands of British administration and diplomacy, then, on the other hand, their uneven pace of social, political and economic progress and the indiscriminate patronage received at the hands of Imperialist masters, made their relationships more strained. Thus, hit by an acute sense of frustration and lost in a mire of shame and defeat, the communities turned against each other, more cautious, more jealous and far more aggressive in their general outlook. Riots painfully record such an abysmal state of communal cleavage.

(3) Thirdly, therefore, as is evident from the first two points, Indian society gradually emerged into a society of cautious, jealous and competing communities. The Indian communities were harrowed all the time by a sense of ever increasing political insecurity. The emphasis henceforth lay more on mutual differences than on points of agreement, socially because, 'the fact of difference' alone regulated the distribution of the Ruler's frown and favours. It was alone a society where religion constituted a vital fact of difference, amongst various communities. Naturally, therefore, in many communities, particularly the Muslim community, and quite a section of Hindu community, the religious and political matters got intermixed, as earlier in the case of the Wahabees and the Arya Samajees, and, later on, with the followers of the Muslim League and the Hindu Mahasabha. It was not all, even the national struggle against the oppressive force of Imperialism, could not present a joint front for a common end. As time passed, it was not, 'swaraj' for which Indian communities fought with the alien rule. With many, the question of political emancipation became also a matter of safeguarding undefined religious insecurity.

For instance, "The religious ideal of Islam, Mohammad Iqbal declared is organically related to the social order which it has created. The rejection of the one will eventually involve the rejection of the other. Therefore, the construction of a polity on national lines, if it means a displacement of the Islamic principle of solidarity, is simply unthinkable to a Muslim".[4]

The most unfortunate development lay in the fact that the element of mutual distrust and suspicion was not only limited to the vague fear of future political set-up and religious security, but had its full play even in the ordinary course of daily life. The communal relations became so delicate and strained that any naive set of either community was enough to make the other community feel aggrieved. It was indeed difficult to decide the point wherefrom political motives and religious chauvinism starts.

The truth is that the amalgamation of religion with politics is a highly explosive mixture. It takes no time to get ignited in an atmosphere already charged with fear and distrust. Communal riots in India were a sign of such explosiveness.

Such were the conditions that formed the background of the sporadic and too frequent occurrence of communal disorders in the political phase of communalism. The fact is that the struggle between the forces of imperialist domination and of national emancipation could not bring about a smooth and healthy synthesis, where the country could move forward as an organic whole. Out of this political struggle, there arose, certain forces that disturbed the sense of equilibrium amongst the indigenous communities, that made them conscious of their communal-lag and other differences, and that led to an undesirable amalgamation of religion with politics. Communal riots were precipitated where those forces operated in the realm of day to day material, mental and moral life of the people.

It is one of the most unfortunate aspects of the Indian history that no attempt was ever made to analyse the causes and growth of the various violent disturbances that occurred during the British rule in this country. Time and again the British Government of India did collect statistics, regarding the place of riot, its apparent cause and also the number of casualties on either size; but they did not care to probe into greater details. As late as the year 193[illegible] in the Memoranda submitted to the Indian statutory commission by the Government of India, the chapter on the communal disorders clearly stated:

"In the attached statement statistics are given of communa[l]

> riots which have occurred between Hindus and Muslims.... No attempt is made to investigate historical origins, or to examine and assess the underlying motives which might be held to have influenced, or to be influencing, the ebb and flow of the rivalries and contentions of the two communities. In particular, no inferences are drawn from these statistics".[5]

Referring to the Government's silence in this matter, Mr K.B. Krishna writes:

> "In this the Government of India is guilty of a two fold deliberate evasion. It avoided formulation of the question. It thereby avoided solution.
>
> This further strengthens the conclusion that its only interest in the communal problem is to seek a source for a policy of counterpoise. It also gives the impression that communal disorders break out in India for no reason whatever".[6]

It is not difficult to explain the above attitude on the part of the Government of India. For the British rulers, the riots were a most common place occurrence, very often they did not take them with the seriousness they demanded and merely looked on as silent spectators. In some cases, we come across unofficial evidence of an implicating nature which involves the authorities responsible for law and order.[7]

Obviously, any honest investigation of these disorders, besides being a reflection on the poor state of administration and an inefficient state of law and order would have exposed the British in a manner disastrous to them.

Reporting about the Salem riots, a European correspondent in The Madras Times, dated August 23, 1882, commented:

> "The gubernatorial mind does not seem to be affected in the least by the condition of affairs in Salem: perhaps, it will remain so until a Collector or Judge is killed, and then it may awake to the necessity of doing something. For the past month matters have been at a most serious crisis; and the hatred of the rival factions does not diminish, but rather increases as time goes on.
>
> The Mohammedan, seem to have the sympathy of certain residents in Salem; and report affirms that this sympathy

is at the root of much of the mischief that has been done. However, this may be the whole affair is a specimen of gross maladministration and until prompt and active measures are taken, Salem will continue to be the scene of riot and tumult.

He further added,

"The existence of a mosque in Shivapett must be a continual taunt to Hindus for three Hindu temples are situated quite close to it, and had been there long before the Mohammedans erected their building. It is a prevalent notion that the Mosque was put there because the collector or under whose regime it was built, had a Mohammedan butler: and it adds fuel to the fire of Hindu hatred when this is remembered. The race of butlers is by no means an insignificant factor in the Government of India. This secret may be a gross exaggeration but if Hindus believe it, it is none the less mischievous.

Referring to the indulgence of the government, he writes:

"The curious circumstances of the collector's absence during both the riots requires explanation.

Each time when the tumult was at its height this gentleman was at Ovsoor, the most remote corner of his district. Of-course, he came into Headquarters when the rioting was over and showed great zeal: but the occasion was gone. The head assistant was in Salem; but I humbly submit that the responsibility of such a station, in a time like the present, is too much for a young civilian, however clever and gifted he may be. That the Hindus mean business is apparent from the way in which they demolished the offensive mosque: the bazar people refuse to sell anything to Mohammedans: and if the Hindus catch a stray follower of the prophet, the way they ill-treat him indicates "war to the knife and the knife to the hilt" policy that will give perpetual trouble to the Government.

Mohammedans are going into Salem, from various parts of the districts and there is danger that dis-affection will not be confined to Salem only.

The Mohammedan population by far exceeds that of the

> Hindus in the Northern part of the district: Krishnagiri, Variembady and Tripatore might easily take sides in a business like this, and furnish the Hindus living near them."

He concluded his report with the following remarks:

> "How wisely we govern may be inferred from the way things are managed and mismanaged. Given a Head Assistant Collector and his peons, a Superintendent of Police with his Inspectors and about thirty constables, a town containing 50,000 population one half having the other half with all the cruel bitterness of religious fanaticism.
>
> These two parties meet in deadly strife whilst the peace making officials must look on."[8]

There is no dearth of documentary evidence to show that the British, by ignoring the serious implication of the communal disturbances, helped in recurrence and intensity as also in the havoc that followed with each outbreak. The negligence of the British officials was deplored time and again, not only in the native press, but also in the Council of the Governor-General of India. On the occasion of the riots in the Bareilly District, one of the members of the Viceroy's Council observed:

> "I think that at any rate, until the trials are over, we had better give no opinions. The trials may throw new lights on the matter. Meanwhile I must say that I altogether disbelieve the conclusions of the Lt. Governor and the other high authorities that no blame attaches either to the police or to the magistrate for not taking special precautions. The object seems to be to show that nobody is to blame for anything. Having myself had a great deal of experience in former times of disturbances of this kind in Rohilkhand, I assert that it is absurd to say that "the authorities had no means of becoming cognizant" of what was threatening. I equally doubt whether the authorities deserve all the praise that has been given to them for vigour in putting down the riots after they had begun. What can be a more significant fact than this - that all the officers, while the Bareilly riots were going on "were seated in buggies and carriages".[9]

The characteristic British policy consisted in always emphasizing the religious differences of the indigenous population and just keeping quiet over misery, the panic, and the social unrest caused by these riots. They never tried to go deep into the question, as to what actually aggravates the degree and increases the frequency of these dub-breaks. In one of his reports to Lord Kimberly the Secretary of State, Lord Lansdowne the Governor General of India depricated any analysis or publication of the riots. He said:

> "These despatches may, if you consider it advisable, be published at home after careful revision: but I depricate the publication of confidential information relating to origin and progress of anti-kin and killing agitation.
>
> First — even if our confidential reports are excluded, a full report as to origin and causes could not fail to excite bitter controversy and rekindle the flame of fanaticism now happily subsiding.
>
> Secondly — it is most undesirable that we should show our hand and tell those concerned how much we know".[10]

A historical examination of the past records clearly reveals that it was the Economic factor that worked behind most of the riots. Since, the trouble used to be between the tenants and landlords, borrower and lender, peasant and zamindar or mill owner, and factory worker belonging to different communities, predominantly economic conflict usually assumed a religious and communal form. The Maplah or the Mapilla outbreaks are a classic example of the same. In most of the cases, these riots showed the cleavage between the landless and the landed, between the Muslim tenant and the Hindu landlord. The Muslims of Malabar are known as Moplahas or Mappillas. Mostly they live on land, which is in the hands of Hindu landlords. During the British rule they became notorious for their occasional risings directed both against their Hindu neighbours and the administration of the British.

The first serious outbreaks in modern times occurred on 8th September, 1873 at Walluvaned Taluk since the Government started keeping troops in the Malabar District. The Moplahs had forcibly captured lands belonging to Hindu proprietors to use them as sites for mosques or for the internment of their dead. This resulted in bloodshed and firing. The Government of Madras was also put to a difficult situation. They were faced with the equally important and to some extent conflicting problems - viz. to enable the Moplah community of Malabar to acquire in a lawful way, such lands as they reasonably needed for purposes of religious worship and of sepulchre.

Mr Cunningham, Advocate General for Madras, submitted a bill entitled "Malabar Religious Sites Act 1874". This bill proposed to enable Mohammedans to acquire by a compulsory process, in the District of Malabar, sites for mosques and burial grounds. The bill caste some interesting sidelights on the communal tension in Malabar.

Hon'ble Mr. W. Robinson in his minute[11] dated 20th August 1874 wrote:

> "It will be an easy matter both to frame and execute that part of the proposed law which deals with the compulsory transfer of Hindu property to the religious uses of the Moslem inhabitants, for the Hindu proprietors of Malabar are as a rule most reasonable, and are on the whole by no means so intolerant as they are represented to be, even under the sore provocation which they habitually suffer. They certainly arc law-respecting and loyal subjects of the State: so that distasteful as such measures may seem to them at first, I anticipate little difficulty in respect to an equitable and reasonable adjustment between the sectors in regard to the acquisition of land for mosque purposes, if the Magistrate only exercises tact and judgement as cases for administration arise ... But a very much more difficult task lies before us, viz. that of putting a reciprocal restraint on the lawlessness and provocation of the Moplah sect. Finally I advise with utmost deliberation in the matter, for I will not conceal that I believe we are entering on a very embarrassing and difficult arbitration between two religious sects, who are both actuated by the same peculiarity harsh disposition - an arbitration which it will be scarcely possible ever to make acceptable to both parties, and which will too often satisfy neither.
>
> Nor must we ignore the fact that when we had done all,

> we shall leave their mutual animosity much where we found it, with the addition that the interference of the state may turn both parties against the public officers. Still I believe that legislation is required both for the protection of the rights of the Hindus and relief of the Moplahs but I depricate precipitation of any kind".

Here can be seen the difficulty that the variety of conflicting communal interests in India, presented before the British. But the fact is that they had no love for either community. Their first and last and only love was the safety of the Imperialist Raj of the Christians. They were not prepared to do any thing which might in the least precipitate any trouble for them, or, commit them to anything in future.

Obviously therefore, British neutrality was a qualified neutrality and their justice was nothing more than a diplomatic dispensation made at the altar of expediency. With them it was never a question of punishing the wrong and rewarding the just. It was on the contrary always a problem of striking a balance of power. Their handling of the communal question in India amply bears it out.

Expressing his views on the proposed 'Malabar Sites Bill', Hon'ble J.D. Sim in his minute made an extremely lucid exposition of the communal problem in Malabar. He did not hesitate to confess that hitherto the British Government had failed to protect innocent Hindus from the Muslim raids but he cleverly concluded with the traditional appeal to hold a balance, He said:

> "It must not be supposed that the Moplahs of Malabar are the only class in Southern India who meet with difficulty in procuring sites for the purposes stated. It is well known that in Tanjore, Madura and Tinnevelly, native converts to Christianity still experience considerable difficulty in obtaining sites for Churches and even for schools and our records show that in several instances the aid of Government has been invoked. But these converts are a law abiding class.
>
> Most of the missionary alertly prefer trusting to the influence of time enlightenment and conciliation rather than to legislation or Government intervention; and the

Government has felt debarred by the positive injunctions of the late Honourable Court, from deviating from the strict line of religious neutrality.

The difficulty is, I understand, gradually diminishing - the natural result of respect for established rights and of submission to the law.

With the Moplahs of Malabar the case is otherwise. The difficulty is certainly not diminishing, it is perhaps increasing in intensity.

The reason is, I think, patent. The Mohammedan religion is essentially an aggressive one; and the great bulk of the Moplahs now are converts or descendents of converts from the lower castes of Hindus who add to the fervour characteristic of converts, feelings of bitter animosity engendered by previous degradation.

The higher castes of Hindus on the Western Coast are proverbially proud of their social status, and intolerant of the lower castes to a degree scarcely known elsewhere.

The Hindu of low caste when he embraces Mohammedanism at once rises in the social scale: he passes from the condition almost of the slave to that of an equal and the remembrance of past wrongs naturally render him devoted to the religion which has done so much for him. His want of education adds to his bigotry, and where his new faith seems to require it, neither rights nor laws are regarded.

The daring and defiant invasion of rights in building mosques without and against the consent of the Hindu landlord aggravates all the evils of religious antoganism and makes Nair and Moplah inveterately hostile.

The Hindu naturally resents unlawful encroachments by fraud and violence, on rights which are his by law and immemorial usage, and of which we, as the Government are bound to secure him the safe and full possession. Mr Cunningham, as I have already said, has overlooked the great importance of this feature of the case. His bill is really little more than a law to enable one set of men to obtain what belongs to another. The Hindu landlord has law and right on his side, and I believe, as a rule, would be tolerant enough if secured from lawless aggression by the Moplah.

I must confess to a deep regard for the rights of property: every principle of justice and policy seems to me to require that we should uphold them in their integrity. I cannot but think that in past we have not afforded the Hindu landlords of Malabar the protection they were entitled to expect, and that our failure to do so has added greatly to the difficulties we have now to face. Our policy now must be firm and decided. We must not let the Hindu imagine that his rights are insecure: we must not let the Moplah fancy that he will gain his end by lawless violence... In his covering letter, Mr Cunningham alludes to the possibility of the Government taking up sites under the existing land acquisition law, as for "Public purposes", and paying the price out of the treasury. The proposition seems to me preposterous. If the Government are to adopt such a course in Malabar for the benefit of the Moplah, they must do so everywhere else for all other denominations. But the more serious objection to the course lies in the fact that it does not provide for the second object in view. We should still require a law to prevent forcible usurpation of land by the Moplah".

He further said,

"I consider that liability to deportation under the Moplah Outrages Act should be expressly declared part of the penalty for infraction of the Act: and removal of mosque or burial ground should also be explicitly required. It must be remembered that the consequences are not more riots or affrays, but murderous outrages, such as have no parallel in any othere of Her Majesty's dominions.

The severest penalties are necessary to prevent their occurrence, and no reasonable objection can be raised to the enactment of such penalties, when as in this case, all plausible reason for such lawlessness is being removed by special legislation of a Charter not conceded to any other class of Her Majesty's Indian subjects.

There is another point which merits serious consideration

in connection with this subject. If we are not cautious how we encroach on the rights of the Hindu landlord of Malabar, it may happen that they may exercise their rights as landlords and refuse to have Moplah tenants. The Moplah grievance will then be that they cannot get land to cultivate, and the special interposition of the Government will be invoked, possibly by lawless turbulence to encroach still further on proprietary rights. Prudence, I think, requires that we should make it distinctly understood that the step we are taking is the last we can or will take in that direction and some shall dispel ambitious hopes on one side and allay natural apprehension on the other".[12]

Mr Sim's views are important in as much as they unequivocally acknowledge the following factors viz:

(1) Firstly that the Mohammedan religion is essentially aggressive in nature and that the Moplah outbreaks in most cases displayed a frustrated aggression pattern directed against innocent Hindus.

(2) Secondly, that most of the Moplahs lived at an exceedingly low economic level and being mostly Hindu converts showed a great intolerance to Hindus.

(3) Lastly, that British administration had so far failed to prevent the Moplah menace which was both anti-Hindu and anti-British in nature.

The President of the Madras Legislative Council also admitted the inefficiency of the administration and advised a balance between penal coercion and just concession. He said:

"There are two modes of preventing the recurrence of popular violence both of which are usually adopted by civilised Governments. One is, to punish such violence severely when it occurs: the other is; to remove any just ground of complaint by which it may have been incited. The Government of Madras had hitherto adopted only the first of these expedients and it must be confessed that they have done so with vigour. If the necessary slaughter of the actual offenders, - if the exile and imprisonment of all known or suspected accomplices or instigators, - if the exaction to the verge of ruin, of fines from the indigent inhabitants of the surrounding district most of whom are innocent, - are not the measures of sufficient severity, no measures could well be so.

What we are now proposing to do, is to rectify the error of former administrations by putting in motion that other expedient prescribed by the rules of good government, and unaccompanied by which no policy of repression has ever in similar cases been known to succeed, - the removal of the injustice which is admitted to have mainly led to these outrages:

Our present task, and our chances of radically curing the evil, is to redress the balance as between penal coercion and just concession: and this is what will be effected by the bill".[13]

The bill however was finally disallowed by the Governor General of India but as a precautionary measure more troops were stationed at various places in the district. But all these arrangements proved far from satisfactory and once again the outbreak flared up in the year 1885. The official report sent to the Secretary of State said:

"The intended victim of the fanatics was a Hindu named Kandassari Raman, a native of the village of Malapuram. About 10 years ago this man became a convert to Muhammodanism (the religion of the Moplahs) and married a Moplah girl but in the course of a few months he returned to his own religion and people.

His conversion had excited considerable attention and his sudden defection was deeply resented by Moplahs. Raman's house was thrice set to fire to, and in June last a savage attempt on his life was also made".[14]

In spite of the fact that the British Government in India understood well the real nature of communal tension in Malabar, they never tried to remove the root cause of disturbance. Once again, after the affray of 1885, same old steps were taken. A complete disarmament of the Moplahas in the Taluks of Ernad, Calicut and Walwanaad was ordered and more troops were stationed at important centres of the District.

The lawlessness and fanaticism of the Moplahas, however, could not be cured by mere stationing of troops. Moplahas were an extremely frustrated lot. "They were bitter, bitterly anti-Hindu bitterly anti-British, bitter against the world that gave them only misery". So as could be expected, the arrangement of the government ended only in a failure. The year of 1894 and 1896, witnessed some of the worst riots of the country.

The Moplahas have indeed been a strange section of Muslims in India. They would ruthlessly kill every Hindu who came in their way and would fearlessly embrace death by attacking the armed police, as also by "going out in open" to face the military firing directed against them.

Hon'ble Mr Winterbotham, was specially deputed to make extensive enquiries into these disturbances and he too arrived at the conclusion that 'poverty and ignorance of the world' were two significant reasons for the communal disturbances in Malabar. He was also emphatic on the fanaticism of the Moplahas on an additional factor of unrest. He said:

> "Every Hindu within possible reach of the gang (of Moplahas) remains in mortal terror of his life till the gang is destroyed and this pitiable condition of the law-abiding section of the inhabitants should not be forgotten when considering the propriety of the prompt and drastic measures taken to restore public security".[15]

The most interesting and highly satisfactory explanation of the causes and nature of the riots in Malabar is found in the reports of F. Facwett, Superintendent of Police, Malabar District. In his report addressed to the Inspector General of Police Madras, dated 5th June, 1896, he writes:

> "... the Mappila difficulty far from receding in the distance, like the suttee and thugee is really becoming more serious. We have here to do with people who are capable of assuming easily that condition of mind to which death is of all things most delightful - death under certain terms, that is....
>
> We must try otherwise to ascertain something like the rate of multiplication of the Mapillas as compared with Hindus in the dangerous quarter and what are the checks to

population, for these have serious bearing on property and the rate of wages, to say nothing of going out to be a Sahib. Indeed, the Mapillas in Ernad illustrate more painfully how that men multiply in geometrical progression, while provisions multiply in arithmetical progression. That which increases as 1, 2, 4, 8, 16, 32, 64, 128 is kept back by that which increases only as, 1, 2, 3, 4, 5, 6, 7, 8. Following the dictates of their creed as felt by them they endeavour to bring into the world as many children as ever they can. If a man is well to do, he has more than one wife at a time, but no matter how poor he is he always has a wife, - If one dies he has another at once - from the age of 18 to his death.

The Super abundant is pressed out of existence by some form or another of misery: The law is as certain as gravitation. The mode of destruction is of course uncertain: it is the thing itself which is certain and not to be avoided. It has been said, 'the question whether the condition of a people at any given time be improving or deteriorating ... depends on whether improvement be increasing faster than population, or population than improvement. We have seen how that, under the inexorable law of population, the Mapilla is born to more than the ordinary share of trouble. We will now see whether his improvement is *paripassu* with his increase - whether it is sufficient to meet it.

Among the Hindus of Malabar everything in the way of marital arrangement and inheritance makes for maintenance of the Tarawada (Joint family). It must be preserved at all costs. The Tarawada and not the individual, is the unit which must be preserved. That it suits Malabaris is obvious if for no other reason that it is a popular institution not framed by any cunning law giver, but grown naturally as the customs regulating life grow; and many of the Tarwads are very old indeed. How suited to the people, it is seen by the Mappillas of North Malabar retaining the Marumwakkatyam law of inheritance while otherwise remaining strict Mohammedans.

Now while among the Hindus everything goes towards retaining property in the family, among the Mappillas it is exactly the other way. Strong in their religion, the Mappilas of Ernad will not depart a hairs breadth from the Mohammedan law under which on one man's death, his property is divided. Sons get an equal share. Now the number of children has been usually too large. In four cases there were twelve children and in one case thirteen. This is tremendous... Given this enormous increase in population and the subdivision of property, the resultant misery is terrible to contemplate. Of course, it is only too often that the father having a large number of children with not a rupee to be divided among them, the children are thrown on the world in complete destitution to aggravate the misery which is the worst thing of all.

In one family, the father's hut was put up for sale in order to pay for the funeral. It was worth nothing and none would buy; and the only available way in which it was possible to raise Rs 3 was by evacuating the hut and getting the value for two Jacka trees in the compound. The material of the hut, worthless in an ordinary way, were carried a mile to erect a small hut in the forest.

Mapilla do their best to multiplty and spread their creed in population, and then they follow the law of sub-divisions. They are a mixed race and clearly it is a mixed race in which the rate of multiplication is exceptionally rapid.

With very rare exceptions, every individual Mapilla is married in his teens and by the time he arrives at the age when the Nayar (Hindu)) marries, he has several children......".[16]

It is obvious that Mr F. Facwett has made a great improvement on the investigations of his predecessors. Every one knew so far that poverty was one of the main causes of the Moplah trouble, yet no one tried to go deep and to find out as to what led to this poverty. Mr Facwett's was a remarkable thesis based on extensive research and collection of first hand statistics and data.

He observes that the Moplahas are an extremely poor lot and

that they owe their poverty to a high rate of increase in their population and a proportionately lower rise of income. Secondly, as compared to the increase of Muslim population of Malabar, there is a comparatively lower increase of Hindu population, as a consequence of which there is a decrease in Muslim's average financial status per family. It is this economic inequality between the two communities coupled with the abject poverty and the frustration caused thereby in Moplahas, that lies behind the communal riots in Malabar.

In the second part of his thesis Mr F. Facwett tried to explain the second root cause of the Moplaha outbreaks. Herein he analyzes the element of fanaticism amongst the Malabar Muslims. He wrote:

> "We are now prepared to understand how it is that the Mapilla community struggling hard in the sisyphean labour to live, for ever being thrown back like the ripples on the beach, may well become dangerous if animated by genuine fanaticism. Nearly all our criminals throughout Malabar are Mapillas. Exceptions are few. And I am afraid that some share of crime in other districts too is due to Mappilas of Malabar". [17]

Facwett adds: We must proceed etiologically:

> When a civilised community such as that in Liverpool adopts Islam as a creed there is no great change brought into the ordinary course of life. Whether the civilised entering Islam adopts the exalted interpretation and which is said to have been Mahomet's meaning or whether, as is usual, religion has really very little hold on life on the most civilised people in the towns, the fact remains that they do not feel bound to go out, become Shahids and kill all those whose persuasion is not theirs.
>
> If the town councillors of Liverpool decided tomorrow that such a thing as a mosque should not lift its minarets in their midst, and that it should be destroyed for a temple of Rimmon, there would be no bloodshed. There would be letters in the Mercury, some talk and violent language: but no one would go out and die for it. If their attitude is prosaic it is sensible.
>
> We have come to allowing without demur our oldest and

> most hallowed churches in the city being knocked down and graveyards of the honoured dead being turned into playgrounds for making healthier and already over-teeming population."[18]

After contrasting the attitude of the civilized followers of Islam with those who are more or less uncivilized, Mr Facwett went at length to describe the fanatic approach of Muslims, as contrasted with the milder attitude of Hindus, in religious matters. He said:

> "If the shrine at Mambram or the Malapuram mosque were to be destroyed by tomorrow by order of Government, there is hardly a Mapilla in Malabar who would not give his life to avenge the disgrace to his pearl like faith. There would be blood and blood and blood. The most insignificant shrine, a wayside mosque, even though no better or larger in structure than a hen house, cannot be moved without much blood being shed. Why is this?
>
> When a Hindu temple is desecrated and made abominable by a handful of Maplieas no one raises a hand to avenge the insult to the religion. Nor will those of that creed stand up to save their temple. The Gods or goddesses, Siva, or Bhagavati, must look after themselves in there ebullitions of excitement. If their shrine is made a place for filth or even for the slaughter of the sacred cow, they must look on with equanimity.
>
> All that is looked for is ceremonies which will make it just as sanctified as ever it was and the disgrace is swallowed. Why is this? The people are much the same in blood. Not in Ernad but in other parts of Malabar they are quite the same in the blood, it is to be found in the creed. During the Goudan war we had unmistakable evidence of the extraordinary influence which Islamism has on the lower and uncivilised races.
>
> What made the immortal "Fuzzy Wuzzy" of Kipling's ballad such a `first rate fighting man'? Really, nothing but the effect of Islam on his receptive nature. It is a creed which as if by magic turns the submissive into heroes. We have evidence of this here. The Cherumous and Kanakans,

> inferior races, serfs, in Malabar are submissive to the last degree; in their lives they are the most harmless of beings exemplifying many of the virtues which are supposed to be exclusively Christian and always in peace.
>
> But one of these adopt Islam and many do hereby and he is changed altogether. The Psychic effect is marvellous".[19]

The fundamental factors that led to Moplah disturbances were also the factors that worked behind most of the communal riots that occurred between Hindus and Muslims. It was usually "economic malaise", coupled with "psychological stereotypes" and "socio-religious differences" that brought about communal outbreaks, which disturbed the peace and tranquillity of the life of the Indian communities.

To sum up we can say that the communal disturbances in India were a positive indicator of the fact that communalism in India owed its growth largely to the religious fanaticism of the Mohammedans and their embitterment over the material ascendancy of the Hindus. The Muslim dissatisfaction over the backwardness of their community was well exploited by the Machiavellian diplomacy of the British and the result was discord and perpetual disharmony.

H.J.S. Cotton, who was the Chief Secretary to the Government of Bengal, attributed the frequent occurrence of communal riots to the following three reasons, viz.:

(i) Mohammedan aggressiveness,

(ii) Official bias in favour of Mohammedans,

(iii) Official mismanagement and incapacity.

In one of his official letters, addressed to the Government of India, he said:

> "Since his return to Bengal, the officiating Lt. Governor has had reason to think that in some of the riots which have occurred, the Mohammedans have been the immediate aggressor: he has also regretfully to admit that in some cases the riots might have been prevented had there been greater prudence, resolution and alertness on the part of the local authorities".[20]

This is how communalism assumed an explosive character during its political phase. If, on the one hand, these outbreaks indicated a state of social unrest in India, then on the other, their frequent occurrence spoke ill of the way British India was administered. C.S. Ranga Iyer in his analysis of this aspect of communalism, observed:

> "The frequent communal outbreaks must be attributed partly to the communal electorates and communal propaganda and partly to the alien control of the police. No Government has seriously attempted to put down the communal movement as compared with the steps that they have taken to suppress sedition. An indigenous administration will show as much alacrity in putting communal outbreaks as in suppressing political violence".

He further said:

> "The communal riots have thoroughly discredited the police and the present administration of law and order. If the government had taken half the precaution that they generally take to prevent political riot or to snuff out the revolutionary clubs, there would have been no communal riots".[21]

We entirely agree with the views expressed above. The British interest in suppressing riots was conditioned by their own motives of the safety of their empire in India. In their administration of this vast subcontinent, they forgot the simple political truth that, if the instrumentality of the state fails to bring the desired ends of peace and harmony in a given society, it needs a thorough change in its practice and personnel. It was an alternative for which they were not prepared, and, hence, the communal explosiveness continued to manifest itself in the form of bloody riots that kept communalism alive as a creed of social tension in India.

NOTES AND REFERENCES

1. *Encyclopaedia Americana* (1953), Vol. XXIII. Americana Corporation.
2. *Encyclopaedia Social Science*. Vol. 7, p. 386.
3. *History, Civilisation and Culture: The Historical and Social Philosophy of P.A. Sorokin*, by F.R. Cowell, Adam and Charles Black, London, 1952.
4. *Speeches and Statements of Iqbal*, Al Manar Academy, Lahore, 1944, p. 9. Muslim League Presidential Address, Allahabad Session, 1930.

5. Memoranda submitted to the Indian Statutory Commission by the Government of India, Vol. I, 1930, p. 96.
6. *The Problem of Minorities or Communal Representation* by K.B. Krishna, George Allen and Unwin Ltd. Museum Street, 1939.
7. (a) See *White Sahibs in India* by Reginal Reynold Ch. XII (He gives details of the Chittagong Riots of August, 1931, wherein a non-official enquiry committee, reported that the "disturbances were caused by British Officials and non-officials with Mohammedan police": The author also mentions the use of "Agent Provocateurs" by the Government to instigate communal riots.
(b) See *British Imperialism in India* by Joan Beauchamp, p. 147 (During the Bombay riots 1929 and the strike movement" Pathans and the other primitive tribesmen were imported by the Government as black-lags.
(c) See Cawnpore Riot Enquiry Committee Report, 1930.
8. Home Deptt. Judl. B. July 1882, No. 350-351.
9. Home Department. A. Pub. 5th Aug. 1871, Nos. 145-7 (Minute of 21. 7. 71 by J.S.).
10. Home Deptt. Pub. Dec. 1893, Nos. 210-213.
11. Government of India Records: Leg. Dept. 1874, Nos. 5-7 (Proceedings Madras Govt. Judl. Dept.).
12. *Ibid.*
13. Govt. of India Records: B. Home Deptt., Political, May 1885, Nos. 101-110.
14. Govt. of India Records: B. Home Deptt., Political, May 1885, Nos. 101-110.
15. Home Deptt. Police, March, 1897, Nos. 31-64.
16. Government of India Records: Home Dept. Police, March 1897. Nos. 31-64.
17. *Ibid.*
18. *Ibid.*
19. *Ibid.*
20. Government of India Records: Home Deptt. 4 Oct. 1893, No. 1462.
21. *India in Crucible* by C.S. Ranga Iyer. London Lelwyn and Blount, 1928, Lt. Paternonster House, Paternonster Row, R.C. 4, p. 292.

Section Five

The Constitutional Aspect of Communalism

Finally we turn to examine the constitutional aspect of the problem of communalism, of which, "Communal representation", formed the most important element. The history of communal representation in India, which ultimately led to the partition of the great subcontinent in the year 1947, is a record of three dominant aspects of Indian political life under British rule.

Firstly, it is the history of the growth and working of the 'democratic principle in India'.

Secondly, it is the history of the 'counterpoising policy of the British in India, a history of the offsetting of one section against another'.[1]

Thirdly, it is the history of the development of communal relationships, as they came to pass particularly between the Hindus and Muslims on the political and constitutional plane.

In one word, the history of communal representation in the record of the constitutional gains and losses through which each community underwent, in its struggle with the British, in order to make the country's alien political governance truly representative and akin to the governed. It was a struggle that commenced with India's first war of liberation and the consequent transfer of power from a Mercantile company to the British parliament.

We know well that the Indian Revolution of 1857, in which all communities joined hands to fight against the British, brought a great change both in the form and spirit of the British government in India. The Indian Revolt had completely taken the Imperialist masters by surprise and shock. It resulted in bringing about certain changes in the light of Queen's declaration. It brought forth:

(i) 'The final abolition of the dual system initiated in 1784, the dissolution of the company, the transference of all responsibility for Indian government directly to the crown'; and,

(ii) The realisation of the fact that any further continuance of British Raj would be impossible without having sufficiently intimate contact and understanding between Indian Public-opinion and the government. It seemed unwise to continue, to legislate for millions of people with few means of knowing except by a rebellion whether the laws suit them or not.'[2]

The need for an association of natives with the working of the machinery of government was fully realized, yet it was a matter of controversy as to what type of contact it should be: Was Britain expected to play a role of a benevolent despot - a role which seemed paradoxical, which prided itself on its old established parliamentary institutions and its great tradition of resistance to autocracy in Europe?

Or was it to be a representative government run on parliamentary lines? a form without many supporters and about which it is interesting to note that even so staunch a champion of parliamentary government as John Stuart Mill, felt that in India, representative government was, 'wholly out of the question'.

The truth is that on this point, British statesmanship always remained in a state of dilemma. Warning the commons against making innovations hastily, Macaulay said:

"The light of political science and of history is withdrawn- we are walking in darkness - we do not distinctly see whether we are going. It is the wisdom of a man so situated to feel his way, and not to plant his feet till he is well assured that the ground before him is firm".

It was however, not because of any such warnings or moral scruples, but because of other factors, that the British could not give any effective instrument of Indian administration, which might in time satisfy the indigenous demands. These factors may be summed up as:

(i) The conservative element deeply embedded in British character. Their concessions and constitutional acts were never inspired by any long range theories about the future; they were accustomed to make characteristic British response to an immediate practical need.

(ii) The unsatiated Imperialistic ambitions and the safety of British Raj in India. This end could best be achieved by keeping anti-imperialistic forces in check and by holding a balance between the various classes, communities and interests. The policy of counterpoise inevitably withheld the evolution of a simple polity that could be run on smooth democratic lines.

(iii) The indigenous conditions: even if the British had no sinister motives, the fact remains that the Indians were still politically uneducated and were an extremely disunited lot. Progress in India therefore could only be slow.

As such, the question of a future political set-up in India presented quite a problem to the British. As Gladstone said:

> "In an Asiatic country like India, with its ancient civilisation, with its institutions so peculiar, with such diversities of races, religions and pursuits, with such an enormous extent of country and such a multitude of human beings as probably, except in the case of China, never were before comprehended under a single government. I can well understand the difficulties that confront us in seeking to carry out our task. All other parts of the British Empire present us to a simple problem in comparison with the problem which India presents.[3]

It was amidst such circumstances, that the native demand for greater and active association with Indian administration was feebly met before Mutiny by the Charter of 1833 and after it by the Indian Councils Act of 1861.

The Act of 1861, authorised the Governor-General to enlarge his council for purposes of legislation, by addition of not less than six nor more than twelve members. They were to be nominated for two years, of whom not less than half were to be non-officials.

In moving (June 6, 1861) for leave to bring in the East India Councils Bill, Sir Charles Wood, the then Secretary of State said:

> "I rise to move for leave to bring in a Bill of the greatest possible importance to our Indian Empire. It modifies to a great extent that Executive government and what is of still greater importance....it alters the means and manner

> of legislation. I can assure the House that I never felt more responsibility than in venturing to submit to it a proposal of so important and grave character. It is hardly necessary for me to mention that the power of legislating for 150,000,000 whose welfare it indirectly affects is a matter of the greatest importance and I am quite sure that to those who have ever studied the inherent difficulties of the question will be no less apparent.
>
> We have to legislate for different races with different languages, religions, manners and customs, ranging from the bigoted Mohammedan, who considers that we have usurped his legitimate position as the ruler of India, to the timid Hindu, who though bowing to every conqueror is bigotedly attached to his caste, his religion, his laws, and his customs which have descended to him uninterruptedly for countless generations.
>
> But added to that we have English settlers in India differing in almost every respect from the native population-active, energetic, enterprising, with all the pride of race and conquest, presuming on their superior powers and looking down in may respects and I am afraid of violating in others, the feelings and prejudices of the Native population with whom nevertheless they must be subject to laws passed by the Legislative body in India. Such are the circumstances under which we are to legislate and I regret to say that the recent mutiny has aggravated these difficulties. The unlimited confidence which a few years ago was felt by the European-population in Natives of India has given way to feelings of distrust."

He adds:

> Many of the greatest mistakes into which we have been led have arisen from the circumstances that we have been, not unnaturally, perhaps, for arranging everything according to English ideas... The House can hardly be aware of the extraordinary and inherent difficulties in devising a system applicable to the whole of India. It behoves us to be most careful, as a rash step may lead to most dangerous consequences... To talk of a Native

> representation is therefore to talk of that which is simply and utterly impossible. Then comes the question as to what extent we can have a representation of the English Settlers in India. No doubt, it would not, be difficult to obtain a representation of their interests but I must say that of all governing or legislative bodies none is so dangerous or so mischievous as one which represents a dominant race ruling over an extended Native population".

In conclusion, he suggested the addition of a few natives and said,

> "Honourable Gentleman will have noticed the great success which has attended the association with us of the Talukadars of Oudh and of the Sirdars in the Punjab in the duties of administering the revenue, and Lord Canning has borne testimony to the admirable manner in which they have performed their duties. I believe greater advantages will result from admitting the Native chiefs to co-operate with us for legislative purposes; they will no longer feel, as they have hitherto done, that they are excluded from the management of affairs in their own Country, and nothing, I am persuaded, will tend more to conciliate to our rule, the minds of natives of high rank'.[4]

It is undoubtedly true that India lacked two of the main pre-requisites of the representative Government viz. a sufficiently educated electorate and a sufficiently homogenous society. Naturally any constituted progress in the realm of representative government was bound to be slow. In fact, any such future possibility too was seldom imagined. It was rather difficult for the British mind to think in these terms. There's is "a mind which habitually concerns itself with speculations about the future".[5]

Obviously in 1861 though the Indian Councils Act, introduced a small non-official element, yet no attempt was made to create representative chambers. These non-officials were supposed to co-operate and advise in the business making Laws.

It was in the time of Lord Dufferin that the question of communal representation was once again seriously taken. The Dufferin Reforms committee suggested that steps should be taken to secure the representation of various classes and interests. Lord Dufferin wrote:

> "By this means the field of Public discussion will be considerably enlarged and the various administrations concerned will be able to shape their course with the advantage of a more distinct knowledge of the wishes and feelings of the Communities with those interests they may be required to deal than has hitherto been the case, for those wishes and feelings will be expressed not, as at present through self constituted, self nominated, and therefore untrustworthy channels but by the mouths of those who will be the legally constituted representatives of various interests and classes".[6]

As yet there was not the slightest intention on any side to introduce representation on Western Lines. In a despatch addressed to the Secretary of State in 1892 at the time when the New India Council Bill was being brought before Parliament, the Government of India indicated 'Communal Representation at the future of action. It said:

> "Indian society from historical causes to which we need not now refer is essentially a congeries cf widely separated classes, races and communities, with divergences of interests and hereditary sentiment which for ages have precluded common action of local unanimity. Representation of such a community upon such a scale as the Act permits can only be secured by providing that each important class shall have at least the opportunity of making its views known in the council by the mouth of some members specially acquainted with them".[7]

It was emphatically observed by the Home Government that there was no intention of giving the enlarged councils the character of representative Chambers. Lord Curzon, then Under Secretary of State of India, while introducing the Bill in the House of Commons asserted that the Bill was intended to "provide the means by which, representatives of the most important sections of native society may be appointed to the Councils."[8]

It is here that we can see the beginning of an Anglo-Muslim alliance. It was bound to come in one way or the other for the

British had now started backing the Muslims as an offset to the rising, tide of the Indian National movement. Besides, even the Muslim community had changed its negative outlook. They were now trying their level best to embrace the Western education as to bridge up the communal-lag between them and the Hindus.

The Muslim demand for a 'separate consideration' of their claims was not confined to the field of education alone. It was extended to the realm of political reforms. We have seen how Sir Syed while pressing for greater association of the ruled with the working of the Government opposed the system of representation by election in connection with the Local Self-Government Bill in 1883.

It was in the same year that Mohammed Yusuf who was a Mohammedan of Behar made the first Muslim claim for a 'separate-representation' of his community in a speech delivered in the Bengal Legislative Council in reply to Mr G.C. Pauls opposition to the Local Self-Government Bill which men like Rai Bahadur Kristo Das Pal Maharaja Sir Jatindra Mohan Tagore and Raja Digambra Mitra had opposed the introduction of Local-Self-Government in the Calcutta Municipality, he spoke for the adoption of the Democratic principles. He said:

"If an opportunity is not afforded there never will be a beginning. There is no school for education in political matters where people should first go and qualify themselves in politics in the abstract before you could put them in charge of a District for the purpose of self-government but if the people are sufficiently advanced and educated in a general way you may safely entrust them with the duties of self-government although they may not have had a trial before. To entrust them with such duties is to begin with their political education which can only be acquired by practice, and not by going to any particular School."[9]

Mohammed Yusuf then claimed separate representation for the Mohammedans. He quoted in support of his argument the 47th paragraph of the Report of the Commissioner of the Presidency Division who had remarked "that the agitators in this matter are Hindus, and that Local Boards, constituted as proposed will be comprised almost entirely by Hindus to the exclusion of Mohammedans".

Mohammed Yusuf said:

> "The Council will be pleased to remember that though in most places the Mohammedan population forms a minority as compared with the larger bodies of the Hindus, still in many places they form a large population of the population. Or it may be that in some places, though fewer, the case is the reverse, and the Hindus form a minority. In such cases, when there is party spirit and angry feeling between the classes of the people, it is necessary to reserve power for the representation of the minority. The Bill proposes to provide for this by nominations but it would be an advantage and a more fit recognition of the claims of the Mohammedan population if provision could be made in the Bill for the election of Mohammedans by reserving a certain number of membership for that community".[10]

It is thus interesting to note that since the very beginning of the political awakening among the Muslims they were conscious of their status of a minority community and as such were keen to have a separate treatment in any scheme of representation in future. Mohammed Yusuf's demands were remarkable in two ways, firstly, that he anticipated the demands made by the Agha Khan deputation of the 1906, and secondly, that he was more liberal and less communal in his outlook. He did not claim 'separate-representation' for the Mohammedans only, but for any minority community, be it Hindu or Mohammedan by religion.

It was therefore with the above background and an eye on the permanent interest of the British Empire that a stress of favouring the important communities in India took its birth. Lord Kimberley, speaking on the Indian Councils Bill of 1892, in the House of Lords, made a demand for some provision to secure the representation of minorities. He said:

> "It has been found in this country not very easy to protect the interests of minorities by any contrivance that can be devised: but there must be found some mode in India of seeing the minorities such as the important body of Mohammedans who are frequently in a minority in parts of that country are fully represented".[11]

It was thus the beginning of a Constitutional bait to catch the loyalty of the major minority community in India. Thus when Lord Cross the then Secretary of State in India sent the copy of the Act of 1892 he suggested the following terms on the steps to be taken to obtain, "the representation of the views of different races, classes and localities". He wrote:

> "Where corporations have been established with definite powers, upon a recognised administrative basis, or where associations have been formed upon a substantial community of legitimate interests, professional, commercial or territorial, Your Excellency and the Local Governors may find convenience and advantage in consulting from time to time such bodies, and in entertaining at your discretion an expression of their views and recommendations with regard to the selection of members in whose qualifications they may be disposed to confide".[12]

The philosophy that lay behind the 'separate representation' was the giving of representation to types and classes rather than areas and numbers. As such after the receipt of the Secretary of State's instructions, the Government of India defined for each province the classes which were of sufficient importance to require representation. Thus, the classes considered to require representation in the province of Bengal were as follows:

> "(1) Hindus,
> (2) Mohammedans,
> (3) Non-official Europeans and Anglo-Indians,
> (4) Merchants, traders and manufacturers,
> (5) The planting community,
> (6) The population of the Presidency town,
> (7) The urban classes of the mufassil,
> (8) The rural classes,
> (9) The professional and literary classes.
>
> It was recognized at the time that this classification was a cross division: a person representing the professional or urban classes might also represent the Hindus; and a person representing the rural classes might also represent the Muslims.

> It will be noticed that the classes in Bengal to which the Government of India considered that representation must be secured comprised communities (for instance, Hindus, Muslims and Europeans), classes (for instance the urban, rural and professional) classes, and interests (for instance, commercial interests)".[13]

The Act of 1892 did not openly recognize either direct election or even communal and class representation. However, the two things appeared under the disguised principle of Nomination upon recommendation. It is clear that the Government wanted a few yes-men, whom it could easily get through nomination than election.

It was on such instructions that the method of nomination was adopted to give representation to various classes, interests and communities. The selection of all the non-officials who are associated with the Government went to the native chiefs, the business magnates and the members of the landed aristocracy. Invariably, every such nomination at the same time was also a representation of one community or other. The candidate, be he, a Raja, a zamindar or a merchant, would also be a Hindu, a Sikh, a Muslim or a person belonging to any other community. As such, if on the part of the natives, different communities used to vie with each other to seek a place for their own members, the Government also took special care to keep a communal balance in any such representation.

This is how quite unobtrusively communal representation came into being. It needs no reiteration that the principle of nomination led to a spirit of unhealthy rivalry and communal antagonism among the various sections of the country. Muslims should be appraised, not on grounds of numerical strength alone but also in respect to the political importance of the community and the service it has rendered to the Empire. As a consequence, the Act of 1909 gave a constitutional recognition to the principle of communal representation in India. It helped the Muslims by introducing the special Muslim electorate and by giving them "weightage", that is, by giving them more seats than could be allowed to them on a purely numerical basis.

In actual practice the creation of separate electorate meant:

(1) that the Muslims now possessed a double vote as the Muslim electorates were superimposed upon the general electorates, in which also qualified Muslims were competent to vote;
(2) that the British Parliament accepted the political importance of the Muslim community as distinct from its numerical strength;
(3) that the franchise in the Muslim constituencies, which elected direct to the councils was wholly different from the franchise qualifications in the general constituencies, in which the district boards and municipalities intervened between the primary voters and their representations in the councils.

The double vote possessed by Muslims was a source of grievance to other communities. They also resented the fact that in the special Muslim constituencies the franchise was based upon property, educational and service qualifications and had a more liberal basis than the franchise in the general constituencies. It is apparent that the concessions that were made to the Muslims were radically inconsistent with any comprehensive notion of democracy, but the British statesmanship looked at the entire question from an altogether different angle. Lord Minto clearly stated his position:

> "I am no advocate for representative government in India in the western sense of the term. It could never be akin to the instincts of the many races composing the population of the Indian Empire. It would be a western importation unnatural to eastern tastes."[14]

The other plank in the British stand was its over-emphasis on the differences between the Hindus and Muslims. Lord Morley was insistent on the point that, "the differences between Mohammedanism and Hinduism is not a mere difference of articles of religious faith: it is a difference in life, in tradition, in history, in all the social things as well as articles of belief that constitute a community".[15]

Finally, the Government of India was keen to set a counterpoise against the rise of nationalist elements. Nationalism in India could be easily offset by promoting communalism. It was Muslim India that could help in this respect and it could be possible only by driving a constitutional wedge in the growing national consciousness amongst the Indians. Such a policy of introducing communal principle in the constitutional machinery of the Indian State was in line with the view that the policy of counterpoise or balancing one class or one community against the other was absolutely vital for the preservation of the British paramountcy in India. Minto in his speech before the Legislative Council said, "An increased representation of Indian interests and communities would not weaken but strengthen British administration."[16]

The native reaction to the Act of 1909 was one of extreme dissatisfaction. The Hindu community resented this move strongly. Long before the Act came into force, the Government of India in one of their Despatch No. 21, dated the 1st October, 1908 addressed to the Secretary of State, wrote:

> "These proposals are as a rule, adversely criticised by the Hindus who regard them as an attempt to set one religion against the other, and thus create a counterpoise to the influence of the educated middle class."[17]

Unmindful of any such opposition, the Act of 1909 was passed and when the regulations were published, the Indian National Congress placed on record its strong disapproval. It is here indeed that we find the introduction of certain elements that led to the beginning of a political discord among the indigenous communities. E.W.R. Lumbe while analyzing the nature of the Hindu-Muslim conflict in India is right when he says that along with the economic and socio-religious factor that worked behind the communal tension, another factor, viz., the struggle for political power was now added in a more tangible form.

He writes,

> "This concession to the Muslims of separate electorates marks the beginning of the Hindu-Muslim conflicts in its twentieth century form of its struggle for power. Some foreigners, and even some Indians have taken it at its face value as a religious conflict such as the world has hardly seen for over two centuries. It is true that even in recent years religion has played an important part. The Hindu and Muslim faith stand in sharp contrast not merely in

doctrine and worship but in the elaborate social system of which each is a centre and which govern daily life in so many things from food and dress to marriage and inheritance; and all this has created a perennial cleavage in Indian society. Religious feeling was certainly an invariable auxiliary in the Muslim League's rapid rise from 1937 onwards; and in the last years before the transfer of power the cry 'Islam in danger' played a tremendous part in whipping up the mass support for the League which enabled it to capture the North West. With the religious element in the conflict is associated an historical element; the Hindus look back to the Maurya and Gupta empire, the Muslims look to the Mughal empire which was founded on invasion and conquest. Nor must the economic element be ignored. The Hindus, with their traditional aptitude for business, were better equipped than the Muslims to take advantage of the industrial and commercial revolutions when these reached India. Similarly, they were more ready to adapt themselves to the alien system of education, and were accordingly more successful in the competition for posts in the administration as these were thrown open to Indians by the British.

He further adds,

"But if religion, history and economic competition were the only ingredients in the Hindu-Muslim conflict of the twentieth century, it would be hard to explain why during the previous century, in spite of sporadic communal riots and certain amount of bickering, the two communities had on the whole lived fairly peacefully side by side. The reason is, of course, that the political element had not yet been injected into the conflict. The Government, neither Hindu nor Muslim, did not arbitrate in the religious quarrels of the two communities; but its neutrality was the result of its being both alien and autocratic, and there was no question of its ceasing to be either in the foreseeable future. Hence the communities had nothing political to quarrel about. India was in fact a country without politics, or at least without party politics.

> But this state of affairs could endure only so long as Indian nationalilsm has not become strong enough to win from the British at least the promise of self-government. As soon as there was any probability of limited transfer of power there rose the question of who would inherit the power the British would be relinquishing."[18]

It was this problem of inheritance that made the principle of communal representation a veritable cause of discord in the political phase of communalism in India. Muslims stuck to it as the only positive safeguard of the interests of their community. Jinnah said:

> "As far as I understand, the demand for separate electorates is not a matter of policy but a matter of necessity to the Muslims, who require to be roused from the coma and torpor into which they have fallen for so long. I would therefore appeal to my Hindu brethren that in the present state of position they should try to win the confidence and trust of the Muslims, who are, after all, in the minority in the country. If they are determined to have separate electorates no resistance should be shown to their demands."[19]

The demand was so pleasant that in spite of Congress' initial opposition to such a mode of representation, its leaders entered into an agreement with the Muslim League in 1916. This constitutional agreement is commonly known as the 'Lucknow Pact'. It was for the first and only time that Congress accepted the principle of separate electorate. With regard to Mohammedan representation, the Lucknow Pact stated as follows:

> "Adequate provision should be made for the representation of important minorities by election, and that the Mohammedans should be represented through special electorates in the Provisional Legislative Council in the following proportions:

Punjab	one half of elected Indian members
United Provinces	30% of elected Indian members
Bengal	40% of elected Indian members
Bihar	25% of elected Indian members
Central Provinces	15% of elected Indian members
Madras	15% of elected Indian members
Bombay	one third of elected Indian members.

Provided that Mohammedans shall not participate in any of the other elections to the Legislative Councils.

Provided further that no Bill, nor any clause thereof, nor a resolution introduced by a non-official member affecting one or the other community, which question is to be determined by the members of that community in the Legislative Council concerned, shall be proceeded with, if three-fourths of the members of that community in the particular Council, Imperial or Provincial, oppose the Bill or any clause thereof or the resolution."

With regard to the Imperial Legislative Council, the Lucknow Pact made the following proposal:

"The franchise for the Imperial Legislative Council should be widened as far as possible on the lines of the electorates for Mohammedans for the Provincial Legislative Councils, and the elected members of the Provincial Legislative Councils should also form an electorate for the return of members to the Imperial Legislative Council. One third of the Indian elected members should be Mohammedans elected by separate Mohammedan electorates in the several provinces, in proportion as nearly as may be, in which they are represented in the Provincial Legislative Councils by separate Mohammedan electorates.[20]

The Pact was a surrender to the Muslims. Naturally, it not only whetted their appetite but also made them confident in making a good bargain in any scheme of future reforms. It is needless to mention that the entire process was anti-national in its import, in the sense that communal electorates are opposed to the teaching of history, and that wheresoever introduced they have been instrumental in perpetuating class divisions and to stereotype existing relations.[21] The Congress in lending its consent to a wrong principle, acknowledged the triumph of communal policy over a democratic and national policy. Dr Sachin Sen aptly comments that if self-government was the ultimate goal, communal representation was not the road for the same. He says:

"The Lucknow Pact blessed communal representation and separate electorates. It was the Muslim case, pampered by the bureaucracy and British Politicians, that for a people

> divided by race, religion and caste, a system of communal and class representation was not merely inevitable, but actually the best.
>
> Communal representation, they say, is healthy for the development of a non-political people. But students of history must note that responsible government becomes meaningless, unless the territorial principle triumphs over the tribal principle. It must rest on a sense of the common interest, on a bond compounded of community of race, religion and language. The compounded of community of race, religion and language. The spirit of common citizenship cannot flourish on the soil, made muddy and murky by communal representation. Political camps on the basis of religious creeds teach men 'to think as partisans and not as citizens,' force representatives to behave as delegates of the community, and a national representation becomes impossible. If self-government is the goal, communal representation cannot be the road. It will divide people and half the self governing principle."[22]

Be it as it may, the Lucknow Pact proved to be an unfortunate child of expediency in more than one way, Firstly, it confirmed the Anglo-Muslim thesis that India was two nations, and secondly, it conclusively gave to Congress an unwarranted recognition of a Hindu communal organization, and finally, the acceptance of a split in the system of electorate gradually paved the way for an ultimate split of the country into two dominions in 1947.

It was in the year 1917 that the British Government made a historic announcement, which said:

> "The policy of His Majesty's Government, with which the Government of India are in complete accord, is that of the increasing association of Indians in every branch of the administration and the gradual development of self-governing institutions with a view to the progressive realisation of responsible Government in India as an integral part of the British Empire."[23]

The importance of the announcement lay in a positive implication that "some day responsible government in India was to be completely realised without breaking its association with the

British Empire - a concise description of the rise of the self-governing colonies' dominion status."[24]

A few months later, Lord Chelmsford, the Viceroy and Governor General of India, while elaborating the significance of the above announcement reminded the Indian Legislative Council of two pertinent questions that he had posed earlier, viz.,

1. What is the goal of British rule in India?
2. What are the steps on the road to that goal?

He said, "We came to the conclusion, which, I trust most Hon. Members will agree, was inevitable - that the endowment of British India as an integral part of the British Empire with self-government was the goal of British rule, and His Majesty's Government have now put forward in precise terms their policy in respect of this matter, a policy which I may say that we as the Government of India regard in substance as practically indistinguishable from that which we put forward."

With regard to the second question, he said, "after a careful and detailed examination of the ground, we arrived at the decision that there were three roads along which an advance should be made towards the goal. The first road was in the dominion of local self-government, the village , the rural board and the town or municipal council... The second road, in our opinion, lay in the domain of more responsible employment of Indians under Government. We felt that it was essential to progress towards the goal that Indians should be admitted in steadily increasing proportion to the higher grades of various services and departments and to more responsible posts generally."

He further said, "We come now to our third road which lay in the domain of legislative councils. As Hon. Members will readily appreciate, there is no subject on which so much difference of opinion exists and with regard to which greater note is required for careful investigation and sobre decision. I may say frankly that we as the Government of India recognise fully that an advance must be made on this road simultaneously with the advance on the other two, and His Majesty's Government in connection with the goal which they have outlined in their announcement have decided that substantial steps in the direction of the goal they define, should be taken as soon as possible... As I have told you,

Mr Montague is coming on my invitation to consult informally with myself, the Government of India and others... I am anxious that when Mr Montague arrives we - and in that pronoun I include all those representative bodies and others mentioned in the announcement - should have ready, to face before him, all the materials which will enable him to form a seasoned judgement."[25]

This statement made the various Indian communities alert and they all waited upon Mr Montague, the Secretary of State, when he came to India to discuss the future form of the Indian government in accordance with the spirit of the August announcement. As a consequence of all such consultations a report on the Indian constitutional reforms, which is commonly known as the Montague-Chelmsford Report was published as a recommendatory document.

The joint authors made a remarkable survey of the communal problem in India. They were unequivocal in their denunciation of the principle of communal representation. Yet, they concluded, that, "So far as the Muslims are concerned the present system must be maintained until conditions alter, even at the price of slower progress towards the realisation of a common citizenship."[26]

During the period when the new reforms were under discussion, three distinct trends emerged regarding the subjects of Muslim representation.

Firstly, there were the extreme separatists who insisted on absolute isolation.

Then there were the moderate separatists, who would give the Muslims full and adequate representation by means of special Muslim electorates and would also maintain their participation in the elections of the general electorate.

And lastly, there were the non-separatists who objected to any sort of class representation by separate electorates.

The proposals of the Government of India were in a line with the moderate separatist trend. His Excellency Lord Chelmsford in September 1918 made it absolutely clear that communal representation was the only feasible mode of representation in India.

He said, ".... Hon'ble Members will probably expect something from me on the vexed question of communal representation. I cannot help thinking that much more has been read into our proposals than they were intended to convey. We wished indeed to make it clear that in our opinion communal electorates were to be deprecated for the reasons set out in our report. But it was in the main to the method of securing communal representation, communal electorates that we took exception, and not to communal representation itself. The careful reader of the report will see that we regard this as inevitable in India and that we clearly contemplate the representation of those communities and classes and interests who prove their case before the Committee shortly to be appointed to examine the question. I am most anxious that the fullest representation should be secured to the various classes and the communities in India; but I am frankly doubtful myself whether the best method for securing that representation is through a system of separate electorates. However, I am content to leave the unravelling of this important question in the hands of the Committee, who will have the fullest evidence placed before them and will be free to make such recommendations as they think right unfettered by our Report."[27]

The views taken by the franchise committee were not only favourable to keeping communal electorates for Muslims everywhere, but also recommended the same for Sikhs in the Punjab, for Indian Christians in Madras, for Anglo-Indians in Madras and Bengal and for Europeans in the three Presidencies, United Provinces, Bihar and Orissa. The Government of India then observed:

> "We feel the objections of principle to the communal system as strongly as the authors of the reforms report, but see no advantage at this stage in reiterating them. India is not prepared to take the first steps forward towards responsible Government upon any other road. The road does not lead directly to that goal and we can only echo the hope expressed by the Committee that it will be possible at very distant date to merge all communities in one general electorate. Under existing conditions we see no ground on which the Committee's proposals can be questioned."[28]

The Government of India Act of 1919 which came as a result

of all these deliberations incorporated in the main recommendations of the Mont-Ford Report. It upheld the principle of communal representation in spite of the severe condemnation that the system received in the House of Commons and Lords. On December 3, 1919 when the Government of India Bill was under consideration, Colonel Wedgewood said:

> "The principle on which English representation has been based is that the members represent the whole of the community, and to adopt for India an entirely different system, whereby the representatives represent different sects and religions, is going back on all the principles which have made representation in the House of Commons a model for all other Parliaments in the world. It is most unfortunate that this Bill has been whittled down to establish this communal representation."[29]

He also criticized the Southborough Report as also the Joint Select Committee of the Parliament for having 'widened enormously the scope of special representation.' All such denunciations proved of no avail. Mr Montague explained that no one objected to communal representation more than he did. Yet he regretted that it was the only alternative.

The Reforms did not merely re-affirm the protection accorded to Muslims by separate communal electorates. They went further and extended that type of protection in particular provinces to the other minority communities: for instance, to Sikhs in the Punjab; to Europeans in Madras, Bombay, Bengal, the United Provinces, Bihar, Orissa and Burma; to Anglo-Indians in Madras, Bengal and Burma; to Indian Christians in Madras and to Indian and Karens (on a limited scale) of Burma. In a few cases protection was given by the reservation of seats, e.g. in Bombay seats were reserved for Marathis and in Madras for non-Brahmins.

In the Act of 1919 the representation to Muslims followed broadly the lines laid down in the Lucknow Pact. As such, although the Indian National Congress characterised the Reforms as "inadequate, unsatisfactory, and disappointing" it had to accept the provisions of communal representation.[30]

The Act was a real triumph for the Indian Muslim. His early misgivings losing the gains obtained through the Act of 1909 had proved false; for, in spite of the condemnation of communal electorates in paragraphs 226-30 of the Mont-Ford Report, the Act retained the separate electorate as well as the weightage to the Muslims.

Finally the provision of a limited provincial autonomy in the form of Dyarchy, as envisaged by the Act of 1919 was "launched through the propelling force of communal representation." As such it did not further the cause either of democracy or that of self-government. In a word, the Reforms registered another victory for the communal forces in India.

A word may be added here about the mode of representation that came to be adopted in the case of the local bodies.

We have already noticed that even before the arrival of Lord Minto a "class system of representation to select fit representatives" had found favour with the Government.[31] It was, however, Lord Minto who started the issue of communal representation, even for the local institutions. The official opinion in the matter came out in the following instruction issued in August 1907:

> "... As the constitution of the provincial legislative councils must largely depend upon the municipalities and district boards, it is suggested that Local Governments should introduce into their systems of election and nomination for these boards the principle of assigning a fixed proportion of seats to each of the leading classes into which the population is divided by race, caste or religion, and permitting the members of that class to select its own representative."[32]

Broadly speaking, the legal position, which continued to be the sole guide for many a year in future was that, "under the laws of most provinces local governments possessed powers to fix the amount of representation to be given to a particular class of the inhabitants in a municipality, but for district boards the power was merely to fix the total number of members of the board and the number of members of each tehsil in the district."[33]

Later on the Royal Commission on Decentralisation in India also echoed the feelings of Lord Minto. In its Report the Commission observed that, "Having regard to the very different circumstances of different areas, we think it essential that the system adopted in each should be such as to provide for the due representation of different communities, creeds and interests. It has always been recognised that it is the duty of the British administration to protect the interest of the various communities in India, and to secure impartial treatment to all. Moreover, in the cognate matter of the selection of members for legislative councils, the discussions which resulted in the passing of the Indian Councils Act of 1892 embodied the emphatic testimony, not merely of distinguished Anglo-Indian officials, but of British statesmen, as to the necessity for securing special representation of Muslim and other minorities, and as to the danger of allowing undue predominance to any one class."[34] As to the mode of election to municipalities it said, "As regards the methods of election we need only repeat what we have said in the case of sub-district boards, that members should be chosen in ways best suited to local conditions, as laid down in the Government of India Resolution of May 1882. The main object should be to secure an effective representation of the various classes in each town, and the selection of fit representatives... A class system of representation, which exists in Rangoon, and in some of the Punjab Municipalities, seems to have worked fairly satisfactorily."[35]

The Commission, it is apparent, harped the traditional British thesis that Indian population consists of different communal interests and that they need balanced representation to communal lines. It is implied that Muslims were supposed to be the most important of all the various communities, classes and interests the majority which could bring the desired state of balance particularly against the majority which invariably consisted of the Hindus.

The above recommendations were given powerful support in spite of a staff opposition from several quarters. Mr R.C. Dutt the only Indian member of the Commission, opposed this mode of election. In his note of dissent he said:

> " Separate election by caste not creeds is not known elsewhere in the British Empire, and would introduce a new element of discord and disunion in India. The British Government, while wisely exercising its power of nomination and appointment to help minorities and backward classes, has generally taught the people of India

> to ignore distinctions of caste and creed of civic life. A different policy, accentuating existing social and religious distinctions by attaching to them distinct political rights, is likely to breed dissensions and trouble in a country like India."[36]

The Government were not affected by the fears of the state of dissension and trouble that was likely to follow the adoption of communal representation in India. It welcomed such a scheme, probably because, in a troubled state, divisions and differences strengthen all the more the hands of the imperialistic rulers. However, opinion in this matter inclines sometimes in opposition and sometimes in favour of communal representation in local bodies.

In 1918 the Government of India initiated a proposal for the special representation of minorities on municipal boards and rural boards by retaining the practice of nominations.[37] With the passing of the Act of 1919 local government became a transformed subject entrusted to the administration of Ministers. It is interesting to note that although each province adopted its own pattern of representation of local bodies which varied from representation by nomination to representation by separate election, yet by the year 1923, the principle of communal representation by separate electorate, came to be adopted in the United Provinces, Bengal, Bombay and Assam.

The truth is that by now in no scheme of future representation was it possible to avoid the principle of communal representation. The Muslims would refuse to have anything less than they had obtained in the past. Besides, to the British mind the principle of communal representation was the only adequate instrument of political enfranchisement of the natives. Accordingly, by extending the principle of representation on strictly communal lines, to all public institutions, be they Central, Provincial or Local, the virus of communalism was permanently injected in the political system. A cleft growth of the movement for emancipation was thus inherent in the entire logic and the way Indians were made to acquire a semblance of self-government.

The post reform period in India witnessed a gradual deterioration of the relations between the Hindus and Muslims. It seriously affected the political progress of the country. Many a serious attempt was made to stem the tide. The most significant one was the Bengal Pact of 1923 of which Mr C.R.Das was the chief architect. It was designed to settle Hindu Muslim differences by providing for communal representation in the Bengal Council and in local bodies in the proportion of 60:40 in accordance with the population of each community. It further provided for the grant of 5 per cent of Government appointments to Muslims. This Pact was rejected by the Congress and the plans of evolving a national pact between the Hindus and the Muslims did not mature. As such the entire political atmosphere was left charged with greater communal distrust and suspicion.

The crux of the entire controversy now aggravated the question of separate versus joint electorates. Gandhi, who was in favour of some transitional expedients, observed:

> "Our goal must be removal, at the earliest possible moment, of communal or sectional representation. A common electorate must impartially elect its representatives on the sole ground of merit. Our services must be likewise impartially manned by the most qualified men and women. But till that time comes and communal jealousy or preferences becomes a thing of the past, minorities who suspect the motives of majorities must be allowed their way. The majorities must set the example of self-sacrifice."[38]

The minority community, however, was not prepared to make any sacrifice whatever. In its sessions held during 1924-26 the All India Muslim League continued its adherence to separate representation for Muslims. In the session held in December 1926, Mr Jinnah declared:

> "There is no escaping from the fact that communalism does exist in the country. By mere time and sentiment it could not be removed. Nationalism could not be created by having a mixed electorate."[39]

The British never took a constructive stand on the question. They criticized their own doings, yet they strengthened them in every possible way. The majority report of the Reforms Inquiry Committee (1924) observed:

> "It must be admitted that in principle these provisions are open to constitutional objection, and most of us look upon them as an obstacle to political advance, but we consider that the abolition of any special communal electorates - and in this we include reserved seats -is quite impracticable at the present time. The objections of the communities concerned are, in our opinion, far too deep rooted to enable us to justify any recommendation in this respect."[40]

The wishes of the Muslims were thus time and again upheld by the ruling party. In reply to an address presented by Muslims in Poona, the then Viceroy stated:

> "The question of communal representation about which you have expressed anxiety is of great complexity. I have said elsewhere its only justification is that it should be the means through which every community should feel free to give what it can to the common cause of the service of India. But if this ultimate purpose is obscured and if communal representation comes to be regarded as an end in itself, then it has the effect of narrowing the horizon of our loyalty. What was designed to promote the cause of unity may quickly become the seed-bed of division when different communities have to live together. It is incumbent upon each to recognise that the cause of peace demands a wide measure of mutual toleration and restraint. That which we claim for ourselves, we must be ready to accord to our neighbours. This spirit, if it may but grow, will be found to be a better and more lasting solvent for the present discords than any artificial methods of representation, but until we can reach this state, communal representation in some form is likely to be necessary and it is probable that a substantial modification of it must largely depend upon the general consent of all communities."[41]

It is thus apparent that political aspect of communalism instead of getting solved became more and more involved, due to the difference of opinion that existed on the problem of joint versus separate electorate. In May 1927, the All India Congress Committee, Bombay, emphatically declared that in any future scheme of representation so far as representation in the various legislatures is concerned, joint electorates in all the provinces and in the central legislature be constituted. The same stand was reported in the unity resolution adopted at its Madras session in December 1927.[42]

Meanwhile on this ticklish question, a schism arose in the Musiim public opinion. In the year 1927, the All India Muslim League met both at Calcutta and Lahore. These were rival meetings of the same body owing to differences of opinion between the leaders. In a resolution adopted at Calcutta session the surrender of the valuable right of separate electorate was accepted on condition of Sind being constituted into a separate autonomous province and of reform being introduced in the North-West Frontier and Baluchistan Provinces. At the Lahore session the idea of joint electorates whether with or without specified number of seats was declared as totally unacceptable to the Indian Muslims.[43]

Quite opposed to the Muslim opinion, the All India Liberal Federation placed on record its deep conviction that for the early attainment by India of responsible government, it is of paramount importance that the unfortunate communal differences should be composed. It confirmed that, "National patriotism can best be developed by a system of joint electorates, qualified by the reservation of seats for important minorities until it be possible with the goodwill of the communities concerned to dispense with reservation of seats."[44]

The All India Hindu Mahasabha met at Delhi and passed a resolution stating that, "communal representation is fundamentally opposed to nationalism and there should be uniformity of franchise for all communities in each province"[45]

It will be clear from the above that the Indian public opinion was terribly divided in itself, and that it always failed to formulate an agreed national demand. It was in order to arrive at some common conclusion that an All Parties Conference was held in Bombay in 1928.

The Conference appointed a committee under the chairmanship of Pundit Motilal Nehru with members belonging to different political parties, groups and schools of thought. It envisaged the constitution urging that dominion status for India should be the next immediate step: secondly, the new responsible

Government of India should take over British rights and obligations towards the Indian States, and thirdly, that the first stage in settling communal problem should be the abolition of the special electorates. Its views on the communal representation were as follows:

At the Centre:

(1) there shall be joint mixed electorates throughout India for the House of Representatives (the lower house in the centre) and the Provincial Legislature;

(2) there shall be no reservation if seats for the House of Representatives except for Muslims in Provinces where they are in minority and non-Muslims in the N.W.F. Province;

(3) such reservations will be in strict proportion to the size of the community. Muslims or non-Muslims where reservation is allowed to them shall have the right to contest additional seats, but no weightage is to be allowed.

In the Provinces:

(1) there shall be no reservation of seats for any community in the Punjab and Bengal.

(2) In Provinces other than the Punjab and Bengal there shall be reservation of seats for Muslim minorities on population basis with the right to contest additional seats.

(3) In the N.W.F. Province there shall be similar reservation of seats for non-Muslims with the right to contest other seats, and the reservation of seats where allowed, shall be for a fixed period of 10 years.[46]

The Nehru Report also envisaged a scheme for the fundamental rights. Therein it said, "There shall be no state religion for the commonwealth of India or for any province in the commonwealth, nor shall the State either directly or indirectly endow any religion or give any preference or impose any disability on account of religious belief or religious status.

The above provision was more in the nature of an affirmation of the secular concept of State. Clearly it remained more as a pious wish amidst the general state of deterioration of the inter-communal relations that lasted before and continued after the publication of the Report. Apart from the constitutional provisions of the Nehru Report, it made a very significant contribution by differentiating between the two aspects of communalism - one higher and the other narrow. In its higher aspect, communalism was described as culture. In fact, the separation of Sind from Bombay Presidency and the provision for a new Kanarese speaking Hindu province in southern India was conceded more on cultural than on communal grounds. The report deplored communalism in its narrow aspect and therefore the pith of the entire proposals centred on eschewing the principle of communalism from the Indian politics, which alone could ameliorate the Hindu-Muslim relations for greater national good.

The provisions of the Nehru Committee Report were given a national hearing. They were considered at a meeting of the All Parties Conference held at Lucknow in August 1928, and was also discussed at an All Parties National Convention held in Calcutta on the 22nd December, 1928. The result of all these deliberations proved in no way fruitful to the problems that faced the framers of the Indian Constitution. Mr Jinnah wanted four amendments to the Nehru Report:

(1) The fixation of one-third representation in the Central legislature and the distribution of Moslem seats according to Moslem adjustment.
(2) The statutory majority in Bengal and the Punjab.
(3) Residuary powers in provinces.
(4) The separation of Sind

It is apparent that Mr Jinnah was not prepared to skim out the virus of communalism from the Indian politics. As such the Report failed to bring the desired result.

The Nehru Report in spite of its giving favourable concessions to the Muslims was rejected by them as they insisted on the retention of separate Muslim electorates and even on the extension of communal representation into the central execution. In fact, the disagreement on the Report brought about unity amongst the divided leadership of the Muslim League. The frustrated Mr Jinnah came out with his fourteen points as the future minimum of the Muslim demand.[47]

The new demand of Jinnah reaffirmed faith in Communal representation by separate electorate and it asked for increased constitutional concessions and cultural autonomy to the Muslim community. It is needless to repeat that as time passed, the Muslim demand was gradually becoming more and more still, unreasonable and anti-national in its import. Such an attitude brought an inestimable loss to the cause of communal concord in India and the parting of ways became more wider than before.

Meanwhile after a labour of two and half a years from the British side the Simon Commission in spite of a concerted opposition from various sections of the Indians came out with its review of the working of the Montague-Chelmsford reforms.

The Commission while deploring the failure of the Act of 1919 recommended an immediate extension of the parliamentary practise in its fullness at the Provinces. In its opinion "each province should as far as possible be mistress in her own house",[48] under the control of a popular ministry.

Unlike the Montague-Chelmsford Report that had simply hinted about the possibility of a Federation, as also exceeding the suggestions of the Nehru Report, the Simon Commission report envisaged that Federation was the only practicable form of Government for the whole of India. However, it was against the reproduction of the British Parliamentary system at the Federal centre.

While dealing with the communal problem in India, the report felt that "the coming of the reforms and the anticipation of what may follow them have given a new point to Hindu-Muslim competition". The report behind that communal disturbances were "a manifestation of the anxieties and ambitions aroused in both the communities by the prospect of India's political future".[49]

The view of the Commission though not unfounded were to a great extent a partisan opinion. It failed to expose the British responsibility in aggravating Communalism in India. Not only that, it miserably failed in prescribing a healthy solution for the growth of a sound democratic principle in India. It recommended the retention of the system of communal representation through separate electorate, which, it said, was too firmly rooted to be abolished by the British even though it marked a complete departure from British parliamentary practice.

The Commission did not agree with all the demands incorporated in Mr Jinnah's fourteen points, yet it recognized for the first time that a communally formed legislature also envisaged an executive constituted on communal lines. In other words, every Ministry formed, should be a coalition in which at least the major communities would always be represented. The Commission observed that, "In some Provinces we conceive that a reasonably stable Ministry is hardly possible without the inclusion of Ministers from the main minority groups. In others prudence would dictate the adoption of a similar course".[50]

It becomes quite clear that the Commission instead of making any useful suggestion, in the true Imperialist tradition made more way for a smooth infiltration of communalism in politics. An English scholar aptly says:

> "Yet while acquiescing in the continuance of the Parliamentary system, modified by Communalism, the commission clearly betrayed their conviction that it was not the best possible system for India. In the same sort of language which British statesmen had so often used before 1917, they pointed out that the British parliamentary system had been slowly moulded by British character and history; it was like a garment they said, which fits the wearer because it has been long worn, but will not necessarily fit any else".[51]

Obviously, the Simon Commission report also failed to satisfy the real aspiration of the country. It neither helped in solving a constitutional deadlock nor in any way assisted in bettering the inter-communal relations. On the contrary, it gave another phillip to the unsatisfied, and ever increasing Muslim appetite of more and more representation on communal lines.

The Simon Commission was followed by the Round Table Conferences in London. The first conference took place in the autumn of 1930. The representatives of the various shades of the Indian Public opinion were summoned to it in order to share the process of a constitution building for India. The Congress that was busy with the Civil disobedience movement abstained from the first session. Later on, after the conclusion of the Gandhi-Irwin Pact, Mahatama Gandhi attended the second sitting of the conference as the sole spokesman of Congress. He was completely disillusioned by the formidable opposition that he faced, in a triple alliance between the British, the Indian Princes and the Muslims. The forces of Nationalism, struck in vain, against the forces of conservatism, reaction and communalism that ultimately triumphed over the former. As a consequence the British Prime Minister Mr Ramasay Macdonald added another constitutional link in the long chain of communal representation in India. This decision is commonly known as Communal Award of 1932.[52] It was based on the Lucknow Pact and its new feature included firstly the reservation of seats for women which were specifically to be divided between varying communities. Secondly it recognized the Depressed classes as a community separate from the Hindus and as such, was granted its own electorates. The Government contemplated that these special Depressed classes constituencies would be a necessity, atleast, for another two decades. In a supplementary to the Award the Muslim Community was given a representation of 33.33 per cent in the Federal Centre.

It is apparent that the primary aim of the award was to weaken Hindus and make Muslims politically powerful. By recognizing religious communities, economic group and class interests it did a great damage to the Indian political situation. Dr Sen rightly observes: "It thus made territorial, national or non-communal patriotism difficult; it discouraged non-communal grouping in politics; it encouraged communalism in politics and the development of political parties on communal and class divisions. It washed away the concept of common citizenship".[53]

Gandhiji seriously objected to the creation of special depressed class constituencies which led to the putting away of depressed classes from the general body of Hindus. He wrote to Mr Ramsay Macdonald that he would undertake a 'fast unto death' as a protest against this political segregation. The fact was undertaken on the 30th September but very soon an agreement known as the Poona Pact was accepted as an amendment to the communal Award. The Pact replaced the separate depressed class electorates by Joint Electorate and reservation of seats, and thus arrested a total disintegration of the Hindu fold.

The Government of India Act of 1935 gave another

constitutional impetus to the sinister communal politics that British had so successfully built so far. It provided for the establishment of a fully responsible government in all the provinces. The representation in the Legislatures was arranged in accordance with the 'Communal Award' as modified at the Federal Centre and for purposes of representation, the Act retained the principle of communal representation on the same lines as in the Provinces.

The Muslims agreed to the provisions of the Act, due to the following reasons:

1. The continuance of separate electorate and 'weightage';
2. The provision of 'Safeguards', for minorities;
3. The assumption of the formation of composite or coalition character of Government, in the Provinces as well as the Centre;
4. The neutralizing influence of the representatives of the Indian States.

The Congress, however, rejected the Pact outright. Its policies were not governed by the dictates of communal gains. They were inspired by the larger interests of a Nation that sought an ultimate liberation from the foreign yoke. The Congress felt that amidst an array of checks and restrictions, provided through numerous 'reservations' and 'safeguards', the Act was nothing short of a deliberate mockery of self-government. Jawaharlal Nehru described the Act as a 'new charter of slavery'. Yet despite this opposition, the Congress contested the elections 'not to co-operate in any way with the Act but to combat it and seek the end of it".[54]

The Federal provision of the Act of 1935 could not be put into action. The provincial part of the same was carried into effect and its working exercised a profound influence on the history of the future relations in India for it was with that the separatist elements of the Muslims took a serious turn. In the British India as a whole the Hindus, including the Scheduled Castes formed sixty-five per cent as against the Muslims who formed twenty-seven per cent of the total population. The Congress with the support both of the majority as well as to some extent of the minority community, scored a thumping victory at the polls and out of eleven British provinces it obtained a clear majority in seven and therefore formed one party Ministries. In the remaining four provinces of Bengal, Assam, Sind and Punjab, none of the parties which contested the elections could obtain a clear-cut majority. Obviously in these provinces, a kind of inter-communal coalition Government became inevitable.

The Indian National Congress summarily belied Mr Jinnah's hopes of forming Congress-League Coalition in those provinces where the former had secured an absolute majority in the Legislatures. Much controversy has been raised regarding the propriety of the above decision of the Congress high command. It is said that the Congress by not conceding the demand for coalition ministries accentuated the communal question to an incurable extent. One cannot definitely predict what shape events would have taken if the Congress had acted otherwise. But if history can furnish any logic, then it was apparent that the past few years of Congress-League relations had clearly revealed that the policy of Muslim appeasement, that the Congress had hitherto followed was nothing short of a policy of National suicide.

The Congress by conceding the principle of communal representation, had already committed a blunder in 1916. It could not therefore afford to repeat the same mistake. Moreover, judging from the purely constitutional point of view, Congress was right in its stand; for the working of the Dyarchy in 1919 had amply shown the futility of forming Inter-communal coalitions.

The truth is that even if the Congress had agreed to the wishes of the Muslim League, still there were no chances of any amicable settlement of the Indian political dilemmas. There has never been, and there could not be a happy alliance of the forces of Nationalism with those of communalism.

To sum up, the second phase of the adoption of the principle of communal representation thus precipitated one of the major constitutional crisis of the modern Indian History. It not only poisoned the Hindu-Muslim relations, but after the advent of Congress to power, it paved the way for a future partition of the country.

Obviously with each measure the British instead of restricting the communal representation continued to widen its scope and nature. Such a policy enhanced stimulus to Communalism. It impeded the evolution of healthy inter-communal relations in two ways.

Firstly, it encouraged Hindu-Muslim rivalry by making them fight with which other for every seat and office in the public institutions. The following extract from an official report sent by the Punjab Local Government to the Government of India gives a vivid illustration of the same: It said:

> "The evils of communalism have perhaps been more apparent in the field of Local self government than in any other sphere. Before the introduction of the reforms, the representation of the Muslim Community on local bodies was nothing like that to which it was entitled on purely democratic principles, and it may be conceded that it would have been a task of great difficulty for the first Minister for local self government, a Muslim, to resist the claims of his co-religionists to a greater share of representation at such bodies. Nor is it possible on the point of principle to take objection to the measures which he initiated in order to achieve his object. These measures included the lowering of the franchise and of qualifications for membership, and the distribution of seats where communal electorates existed, on the basis of the mean between the population and the voting strength of the different communities. It cannot, however, be denied by any class of student of the history of the last few years that one result of this policy has been to increase communal feeling. The principles underlying the Minister's policy have naturally been very unpopular with the Hindu community, not only in themselves, but also as embodying a position which Punjab Hindus could not accept in wider spheres without serious consequences to their place in politics. On the other hand the ministers have on the whole been firm in resisting the considerable pressure brought to bear on them to extend the system of communal electorates to places where it was not previously in force, though in several such places the reconstitution of election".[55]

Secondly, it made each individual bitterly communal and fanatic in his outlook. In the day to day life, the politically enlightened people made an appeal to narrow communal allegiance of their co-religionists. C.S. Iyer rightly observes:

> "If the electorate is not communal as it is today, the appeal to fanaticism will have no chance. If the communalist flourishes, it is because he has a separate electorate, according to which only Muslims can vote for a Muslim candidate while non-Muslim vote for the other candidate, who may be a Hindu, a Christian or a Parsee."[56]

The institution of communal representation cut at the very roots of the evolution of a common citizenship in India. The consciousness of being a citizen with like privileges and obligation is what goes to make a strong and stable nation. In the prevailing context of things, it was not so. It was not the concept of an Indian citizen but the feelings of being a distinct and separate citizen that passed to the politically conscious people. The split growth of citizenship became prominent because the state did not recognize an Indian as a citizen, but it recognized a Muslim citizen and a Hindu citizen. It is thus apparent that the very foundation of a unified consciousness of a common ideal of corporate existence which the development of democratic principle envisages was destroyed in its infancy.

Curiously enough, the British adopted this principle in spite of the fact that they knew it to be a harmful principle. Lord Morley in a communication had long ago foreseen the future when in the following words he warned Lord Minto.

> "Please remember in granting separate electorates, we are sowing dragon's teeth and the harvest will be bitter".

Certainly the harvest that came in the form of the partition of this country was much more than bitter.

The Political aspect of Communalism entered its last phase after the Congress Ministries resigned from the Provincial Governments in 1939.

This event was celebrated on Friday, 22 December, 1930, by the Muslim League as a "day of deliverance". Henceforth the principle of communal representation was replaced by the principle of `self determination', which came to be interpreted in different ways.

The Congress insisted that the 'only adequate instrument for solving communal and other difficulties' lay in drawing the future constitution of the country, which should be determined by Indians themselves. As such, unconditional and complete independence of India was considered by the Congress as the only effective way of exercising the right of self determination.[57]

On the contrary, to the Muslims the exercise of the above right consisted in the establishment of a Muslim State. Mr Jinnah interpreting the same said:

> "We claim the right of self-determination as a nation and not as a territorial unit and we are entitled to exercise our inherent right as a Muslim Nation, which is our birthright, whereas you are labouring under the wrong idea that self determination means only that of a territorial unit. Ours is a case of division and carrying out two independent states by way of settlement between two major nations, Hindus and Muslims, and not of any existing union which is *non-est* in India. The right of self-determination that we claim postulates that we are a nation and as such it would be the self determination of the Muslims and they alone are entitled to exercise that right".[58]

In the true Muslim League tradition, of making its own interpretation of all principles of politics a minority community had, by virtue of the Lahore resolution of March, 1940 became a Nation and the exercise of the right of self determination included everything which achieved for that nation an independent state of Pakistan.

The British response to the Indian aspiration was as usual coloured by a conservative and an extremely reactionary attitude. Lord Linlithgow, the Viceroy of India, expressed the intentions of the Government in the historic declaration of 1940. This declaration commonly known as the August Offer expressed the Government's concern that full weight should be given to the views of minorities in any constitutional revision. The Government sympathized with the desire of framing a new constitution which should be primarily the responsibility of Indians themselves. Yet, it was made clear that the British "could not contemplate transfer of their present responsibilities for the peace and welfare of India to any system of government whose authority is directly denied by large and powerful elements in Indian National Life".[59]. British made no constructive effort to ameliorate the Hindu-Muslim relations in the country which had been gradually deteriorating after the accession of Congress to power. On the contrary, they continued to magnify the differences and made them permanent by making constitutional awards based on communal principle.

From the above, it will be clear that as usual the British tacitly gave recognition to the newly developed communal trends with Muslim League Politics. In other words, the constitutional recognition of the Nationalist demands was to remain subject to the communal veto of the Muslims.

The British stand became much more clear in the years that passed by. In the year 1942, the British War Cabinet in order to "rally the moral support of the major political groups, particularly the Congress behind the soldiers, sailors and airmen defending the frontiers and coasts",[60] as also to avert an "armed clash with Indian Nationalism"[61] sent Sir Stafford Cripps to discover the `ways and means' through which the Indians could rightly exercise the right of self determination.

The Cripps proposals in their long term plan made a definite advance on the 'August Offer'. It envisaged:

(i) to give India complete freedom and self government as soon as the war was over,

(ii) the new Indian Union was given the choice to accept Dominion Status within or without the commonwealth,

(iii) A constitution for India was to be framed by the Indians themselves. The British Government pledged itself to accept its conclusions subject (as before) to the fulfillment of British obligation,

(iv) To meet the Muslim demand, it was suggested that any Indian proginee which wished to contract out of the proposed Union might do so and form a separate Union of equal status,

(v) In its short term plan the Cripps proposals made it clear that 'during the critical period which now faces India and until a new constitution can be framed, the Interim Government, except the Control and direction of the Defence, be constituted with the effective participation of the leaders of the principal sections of the Indian people".[62]

The Cripps Plan was rejected both by the Congress and the League. The League was disappointed that a clear-cut assurance of Pakistan was not made. The Congress leaders claimed an immediate grant of complete independence. They were not prepared to go for it through instalments. They had seen enough of it in the past. Mahatma Gandhi rightly described it as "a post-dated cheque on a bank that is obviously failing".

The failure to arrive at any amicable communal settlement both at the political and social fronts led to an unprecedented 'rising crescendo of riots', which was likely to precipitate almost in a civil war between Hindus and the Muslims. In an atmosphere of mutual distrust and hatred, all efforts to create a State of peace and order failed miserably. In any social maladjustment, it is usually difficult to point out to one single constituent as the main factor of all troubles, yet amongst the Indian conditions that prevailed during the seven years that preceded the partition of India, it is not difficult to observe that communalism saw its worst phase due to the frustrated and frantic outlook of Muslim League and its leaders. They were bent on destroying the unity of the country be it at the point of 'sword'. In the true medieval tradition of the Muslims, a cry of 'Islam in danger' was raised and time and again it was declared that:

> "The attainment of the goal of a complete sovereign Pakistan was the unalterable objective of the Muslims in India, for the achievement of which they will, if necessary employ every means in their power, and consider no sacrifice or suffering too great".

Clearly enough, the principle of self determination in India was ultimately reduced to the following formula. To the Congress it was the challenge to British, to 'Quit India', to Muslims it was a request to first 'Partition' and then 'Quit India'. This was a political right for the exercise of which the Congress was prepared to suffer the violence of the Imperialist rulers and the League was prepared to shed the last drop of Indian blood to achieve Pakistan. The deadlock and distrust between the two Communities aggravated rapidly.

It was against such a background that Lord Wavell who had succeeded Lord Linlithgow as Viceroy in October 1943, made his sincere efforts to bring about a compromise between the rival protagonists of unity and partition. He suggested a plan that was developed on the tacit support of the Desai-Liaquat Pact of January 1945, where Congress and League had agreed to their participation in the Executive Council of the Viceroy. The essence of the Wavell plan lay in the replacement of this existing council by one representative of Indian political opinion; they were in effect a more detailed re-statement of the short term proposals of the Cripps offer. The plan proposed to 'represent the main communities and to include equal proportions of caste Hindus and Muslims'.

Once again it was the communal principle that was adopted here and as such it led to irreconcilable controversy. From the Congress standpoint, the use of the terms 'Caste Hindus and Muslims' was a misrepresentation of the terms. (Congress and Muslim League in the Desai Liaquat formula). The Congress seriously objected to it to accept such terms as firstly to take a retrograde step from politics to communalism. Secondly it led to an acceptance of the view that Congress was a purely Hindu organization. Thirdly, even though Congress had accepted the principle of Hindu-Muslim parity, it was not prepared to abdicate its claim to the leadership of the Indian Independence movement, and to betray the irrationalism of the policy of Muslim League and its leader Jinnah knew no bounds. Professor Lumby rightly observes that Jinnah was judging every concession from its relation to the 'grand objective' of negating 'Hindu domination' and achieving 'Pakistan'. He writes:

> "As soon as the League had won acceptance of the principles of Hindu-Muslim parity, it had put up its price. Jinnah was now complaining that the Muslims would command only one third of the votes in the Council, which must mean that he wanted parity not only with the Hindus but with the Hindus plus the minorities. And so the League would make a crescendo of demands which would act as a perpetual stumping block to the progress of the country towards independence until at least revolution or civil war came to break the deadlock".

It is true, indeed that the policy of Muslim League, not only engulfed the whole country in an atmosphere of mistrust, neurosis, and threats, of 'inter-racial and inter-communal strife', but it intensified the state of communal tension by torpedoing every attempt of solving the political deadlock.

The emergence of such an uncomfortable situation alarmed a Britain worn out by war. It was now keen to settle up the question of self-determination for Indians at the earliest for it had grave misgivings and fears of any future volcanic eruption of the native discontent which might prove disastrous for its Empire. It also wanted to tame the demon of communal massacre which had been let loose a long time back by its indifferent policies.

A quick decision was prompted by the accession to power of a labour government in Britain in the late summer of 1945. It took the 'unprecedented and boldly imaginative step' of sending three of its foremost Ministers to break the Indian political deadlock. The Members of the Mission were to be Lord Pethick Lawrence, the Secretary of State for India, Sir Stafford Cripps, the President of the Board of Trade and Mr A.V. Alexander, First Lord of the Admiralty. Primarily, they were supposed to help the Viceroy, Lord Navell in outlining a programme of forming a constitution making body, and in the task of constituting an interim executive council supported by the major Indian parties. The Mission arrived in India in March 1946 and began its negotiation with the major political parties and representatives of various other interests and communities.

The Cabinet Mission envisaged in its plan the establishment of an Indian Union, arranged in three tiers of authorities.

(1) At the top, the Central Government was to control defence, foreign affairs and communications, and to consist of an executive and a legislature drawn from British India and (after negotiation) the Indian states.

Any question raising a major communal issue in the Legislature would require for its decision a majority of the representatives present and voting, of each of the two major communities, as well as of a majority of all members present and voting.

(2) At the bottom, the provinces, enjoying a wide measure of self government, were to constitute another tier. The residuary powers were to be vested in the provinces.

(3) Between the above two tiers, a provision was made for a

possible midway tier. If any of the provinces so chose, they could form themselves into provincial groups with their own executives and legislatures. Each group was to so determine the subjects, outside those reserved for the Central Government while it wished to control in commerce.

(4) The Cabinet mission proposed also that the constitution-making process should start with the calling of a constituent assembly representing all parties. Its members were to be filled by the recently elected Provincial Assemblies on a communal basis.

(5) While the constitution making would be going on, it was suggested that an Interim Government, with all portfolios, even of the war member, assigned to Indians, was to run the administration of the country. It is apparent that the Cabinet Mission Plan was in the nature of a compromise formula between the communal and the national interpretation of the right of 'self determination'. It gave to the Congress a united India and to the League a reality of Pakistan was assured. But all schemes failed due to the rage of communal grouping in an atmosphere of disturbed communal relations.

The Muslims League did not agree to the work of constitution making. On the contrary, its policy of 'hate and civil strife' led to communal massacre in the country. The League now intended to precipitate the realization of its Pakistan dream through coercion and through creation of trouble in various places by launching a mass civil disobedience movement. On August 16, 1946, the League observed its 'Direct Action Day'. It was marked by hooliganism and looting in Calcutta resulting in large-scale deaths and injuries. The total toll of 'communal carnage in Calcutta was 15,000 dead and wounded. The way things went wrong can be estimated from the following description. It says:

> "Even small boys and girls were killed by mobs. In one place, a three year old child is stated to have been killed and nailed to the door. Fiendish mobs raiding residence as are said to have thrown down children from second and third floor balconies in some places. Mobs armed with axes, daggers, *lathies* and other weapons raided houses and shops, baltered the doors, looted, butchered or maimed the residents on whom they lay hands, threw

petrol and kerosene on the building, set fire to it and went on their way to carry out similar fiendish work elsewhere".[63]

The above description can give an idea of the communal war that had spread throughout the length and breadth of India. The riots of Naokhali and Punjab were the worst of all the bloody massacre that overtook the country and these riots continued even after the partition of the country.

A word may be added here about the conditions that prevailed in the country during the last year of British rule in India. Judging from purely sociological point of view, these riots were a reflection of the disturbed mind of the people. No blame can be put either on Hindus or on Muslims. It was a general degeneration that had been made to set in by the frustrated leaders of the Muslim League in India. To the politically enlightened Muslim if self determination consisted in political separation, it logically followed that riots were an instrument of rousing the necessary political consciousness among the Muslims, without which Pakistan would not have become a possibility.

The Muslim political consciousness was thus a consciousness of a religiously fanatic, crowd, which was no longer its ownself, an automation that was being guided by the law of sword. It was not the consciousness of one's own stand and relationship that was working in the minds of men. It was first an impulsive changeable and irritable group mind that was working in the forefront. The conscious personality, when one would think as an Indian had vanished. Hindus and Muslims were possessed by "the spontaneity, the violence, the ferocity and also the enthusiasm and heroism of primitive beings.[64]

Here one can aptly ask whether all the Hindus or the Muslims were so inherently bad as to lend their ears to the mischief mongers. Secondly, what was the British Government doing to set right such a State of affairs? Did this authority that had ruled this land for more than a century, owe no responsibility towards such a tragic situation?

Finally, what was the most practical solution of restoring communal peace and harmony?

The answer to the first question is obvious. There were people like Gandhi who wanted above everything else a reconciliation between Hindus and Muslims. He accepted the challenge of the Hindu and Muslim masses who were vying for each other's throats in Calcutta and Noakhali in Bengal and in Bihar. He braved the risk of visiting the disturbed areas without fearing the madness that had overtaken the people of whom 80 per cent professed the Muslim faith. On 8 December, 1946, he wrote from Noakhali:

> "My present mission is the most difficult and complicated one of my life. I am prepared for any eventuality. `Do or Die' has to be put to the test here. 'Do' here means Hindus and Muslims should have to live together in peace and amity. Otherwise, I should die in the attempt".[65]

The truth is that psychologically people constituted a very disturbed mind. The fact that they had been transferred into a group put them in possession of collective mind which makes them feel, think and act in a manner quite different from that in which each individual among them would feel think and act were he in a state of isolation".[66]

This psychological grouping amongst Hindus and Muslims was constituted out of the elements of fear, uncertainty, prejudice, and bitter communal and racial hate. As such, it was not the isolated appeals that could have brought the change. What was needed was the disintegration of the collective mind, the narrowly communal and the narrowly animated collective mind.

Apropos the second question, there is not much that needs elaboration. To the Imperialist mind any destruction of the native life had been a pet game for, it usually goes to strenghten the foundations of the Empire. As regards the current situation, although many of the British administrators did want to quieten down things, they could not do so as it was the Frankenstein Monster of communal frenzy, that they themselves had so tentatively reared, who was in action. It could not stop before it could devour its on creature. The British had thus to pay its price by quitting the land. It was a land that they took to civilize and left it more barbaric than ever.

We leave it to the historians of a future date to write how British shared the White man's burden in India.

Finally coming to the third question, it is obvious that in the existing conditions the only obvious solution was partition, for

Jinnah had made it amply clear during his stay in London when the Indian leaders went there in November, 1946, that he expected India to be divided into a Hindu state and a Muslim state, and added that he shared Mr Churchill's apprehension, "regarding the possibility of civil war and riots in India".[67]

This statement was read as a warning: Pakistan or civil war? and it also thus provided the only solution.

To sum up, it is clear that it was communalism that once again was the determining factor in the political question in the country. The Indian National Congress was compelled by the ever increasing and ever deepening chain of communal disturbance involving mass murder, arson and loot accompanied by unthinkable atrocities and horrors, to favour the vivisection of India. In spite of various difficulties, the working committee of the Indian National Congress once again reiterated its adherence to the Cabinet Mission Plan and made a desperate appeal to all sections to cooperate in the event of transfer of power to Indian hands. In a resolution passed in March, 1947, it observed:

> "In this hour when final decisions have to be taken, and the future of India has to be shaped by Indian minds and hands, the Working Committee earnestly calls upon all parties and groups, and all Indians generally, to discard violent and coercive methods, and cooperate peacefully and democratically in the making of the constitution. The time for decision has come and no one can stop it or stand by and remain unaffected. The end of an era is at hand and a new age will soon begin. Let this dawn of the new age be ushered in bravely, leaving hates and discards in the dead past.
>
> In view of the new developments which are leading to a swift transfer of power in India, it has become incumbent on the people of India to prepare themselves jointly and cooperatively for this change, so that this may be effected peacefully and to the advantage of all. The Working committee, therefore, invites the All India Muslim League to nominate representatives to meet representatives of the Congress in order to consider the situation that has arisen and to devise means to meet it."[68]

It was a call in the wilderness and did not evince the least response from the Muslim League. It abstained from cooperating with the Congress in any political matter whatsoever.

Meanwhile, Lord Mountbatten arrived as the new Viceroy of India. He started his chain of meetings with the Indian leaders by making an appeal for the acceptance of the Cabinet Mission Plan which could to some extent keep a united India.

After a hazardous process of negotiations and consultations both in India and England, the Mountbatten plan was announced on June 3rd, 1947.

The plan in a word represented 'the greatest common measure of the Congress, League and Sikh standpoint', for the division of the Punjab and Bengal in each of which there were small Muslim majorities into Hindu and Muslim states, the effective decision for this being taken by each Legislative Assembly voting if necessary by separate communities. A Boundary Commission was to be constituted to demarcate the exact frontiers in these two provinces, partly on the basis of ascertaining the contiguous majority areas of Muslims and non-Muslims and partly taking into account other factors such as communications, resources and the Punjab irrigation system. The Legislative Assembly was also required to express its opinion on it whether it wished to join Pakistan.

In the overwhelming Muslim N.W. Frontier Provinces, where by a curious parallel the strong pro-congress 'Red-Shirts' organization led by Abdul Ghaffar Khan had held office since 1937, a referendum was provided to allow the people to state which political group they wanted to align themselves with. Similarly the Muslim majority district of Sylhat in South Assam was asked whether it chose to join East Bengal in forming the second new Muslim State.[69]

Without any major hitch on either side, the plan was swiftly carried through. Out of the former provinces of the British India, two independent dominions of Pakistan and India came into existence, each free and equal and of no less status than the United Kingdom and each with its own Constituent Assembly.

Reviewing the whole situation, Pandit Jawahar Lal Nehru in a broadcast to the nation made on 3 June, 1947, declared the painful acceptance of the partition of India. He said:

> "It is with no joy in my heart that I command these proposals to you, though I have no doubt in my mind that it is the right course. For generations we have dreamt and struggled for a free, independent and united India. The proposal to allow certain parts to secede if they so will is painful for any of us to contemplate. Nevertheless I am convinced that our present decision is the right one even from the larger view point. The United India that we have laboured for, was not one of compulsion and of coercion but a free and willing association of a free people. It may be that in this way we shall reach that United India sooner than otherwise and then we shall have a stronger and more secure foundation".[70]

It was against such a background of communal degradation and human helplessness that the right of self determination was exercised at the altar of communalism in India. The harvest of the seeds of "exploitation and counterpoise" which British rulers had sown so sedulously, atleast culminated in their own exit. But they left the country divided. The last constitutional measure of the British Parliament awarded the Government of India Act of 1947 which created two Dominions. One was a secular state of India and other one was a theocratic State of Pakistan. It was indeed a tragic and yet a major triumph of communalism that was ever recorded by history. With this victory of the communal principle over the National aspirations, the political phase of communalism came to an end in India.

NOTES AND REFERENCES

1. *The Problem of Minorities* by K.B.Krishna. In the Proclamation by Queen Victoria addressed to Princes, Chiefs, and people of India, it was clearly stated that, 'whereas for diverse weighty reasons, we have resolved by and with the advice and consent of the Lords Spiritual and temporal and commons in Parliament assembled to take upon ourselves the Govt. of the territories in India heretofore administered in trust for us by the Hon: East India Company... It is our father — will that so far as may be, our subjects, of whatever race or creed be freely and impartially admitted to offices in our services, the duties of which they may be qualified by their education ability and integrity duty to discharge...'.

2. *Rise of Christian Power in India.* Major, B.D. Basu. Calcutta, 1931, Chapter. XCVK.
3. *Speeches and Documents on Indian Policy,* by A.B. Keith: *World's Classics,* Oxford, 1922. ii. pp. 73-74. In 1833 it was enacted that "no native of the said territories nor any natural born subject of His Majesty resident therein shall by reason only of his religion, place of birth, descent, colour or any of them be disabled from holding any place of office or employment under the said company and the court of Directors explained its import as follows"
'The court conceive this section to mean that there shall be no governing case in British India; that whatever other tests of qualification may be adopted, distinction of race or religion shall not be there, that no subject shall be excluded from the post usually conferred on uncovenanted servants in India or from the covenanted service itself, provided he be otherwise eligible' (*The History of the Congress* Vol. I, p. 6. B.P. Sitaramayya. (1946 Edn.)
It is interesting to note that "already by 1861 the British Parliamentary system had proved capable of translation to British soil overseas. In obedience to the British colonies in North America, Australia and New Zealand which had long possessed representative Government in the narrow sense (i.e. popularly elected legislatures controlling legislation but not administration) had acquired responsible government.
4. *Indian Constitutional Documents.* Vol. I Com. Edn. by P. Mukherjee. 1600-1818, Indian Edn. 1918. Thacker & Spink and Co. Calcutta, pp. 211-22.
5. *India - A Re-Statement* by Sir Reginald Coupland, 1945, p. 81.
6. Report on the Indian Constitutional Reforms (Montford Joint Report, p. 35).
7. Memoranda submitted to the Indian Statutory Commission by the Government of India, 1930, Vol. I, pp. 127-28.
8. *Ibid.,* p. 128.
9. Proceedings of the Bengal Legislative Council, May 3, 1918, p. 58.
10. *Ibid.,* p. 58.
11. See Parliamentary Proceedings, 1892.
12. Memoranda, *op. cit.,* p. 128.
13. *Ibid.,* p. 128-29.
14. Sen., *op. cit.,* p. 56.
15. Lord Morley's speeches on the Indian Council's Bill 1909, delivered in the House of Lords, March 4, 1909.
16. Quoted by Krishna, p. 90.
17. The Memoranda, *op. cit.,* p. 134.
18. Lumby, *op. cit.,* pp. 14-15.

19. Hector Bolitho, *op. cit.*, p. 65.
20. Government of India Records, Legislative Department 1917.
21. See Montford Report.
22. Sen, *op. cit.*, pp. 62-63.
23. Hansard, XCVII (1917) 1695.
24. Coupland, *op. cit.*, p. 111.
25. Indian Constitutional documents (1600-1918) Vol.1, compiled and edited by P. Mukherji, Calcutta, 1918, pp. 475-76.
26. See Montford Report.
27. See Proceedings, Imperial Legislative Council, September, 1918.
28. The Government of India Fifth Reforms Despatch, No. 4, dated 23rd April, 1919.
29. Memorandum, *op. cit.*, p. 148.
30. The following table gives particulars of the extent of representation and the weightage which the Muslim community received under the Act of 1919

States	*Percentage of Muslim voters to the Total Voters in General Constituencies.*	*Percentage of Muslim Elected Members to Total No. of Elected Indian Members*
Punjab	43.7	48.5
UP	14.1	30.0
Bengal	45.1	40.5
Bihar and Orissa	10.9	25.0
C.P.	8.4	13.0
Madras	4.7	14.0
Bombay	17.7	35.0
Assam	30.1	35.5
Legislative Assembly	16.5	34.4

31. The Government of India Resolution, May 1882.
32. Memoranda, *op. cit.*, p. 158.
33. *Ibid.*, p. 161.
34. The Report of the Royal Commission upon Decentralization 1907, paras 7, 8 and 9.
35. *Ibid.*, para 50) Memorandum, p. 158-59.
36. See *Ibid.*, Memoranda, p. 159.
37. Government of India Resolution, dated 16th May, 1918.
38. *Young India*, 26th Dec., 1924.
39. Proceedings of the All India Muslim League, 1926.
40. The Reforms Enquiry Committee 1924, para 69.
41. Memoranda, p. 167.
42. See the All India Congress Committee Resolution adopted at Bombay Session, May 1927: Madras Session, Dec. 1927.

43. See the All India Muslim League Resolution, adopted at Calcutta Lahore Session 1927.
44. See the All India Liberal Federation Resolution, adopted at Bombay Session, December 1927.
45. See the Proceedings of the All India Hindu Mahasabha Resolution, adopted at Delhi Session, February 1928.
46. See Nehru Report, 1928.
47. An attempt was made by Mr Jinnah to bring about a reconciliation between the two groups in the Muslim League and the Muslim All Parties Conference. Mr Jinnah after consulting leading men prepared a draft resolution on the basis of which a settlement could be made. It was in this draft resolution that he formulated his Fourteen Points as necessary for safeguarding the rights and interests of Musalmans. These Fourteen Points may be summarized:
    - (i) The form of the future constitution should be Federal, with the residuary powers vested in the Provinces.
    - (ii) A uniform measure of autonomy for Provinces.
    - (iii) All Legislatures and other elected bodies should be constituted on the definite principle of adequate and effective representation of minorities in every Province without reducing the majority in any Province to a minority or even equality.
    - (iv) In the Central Legislature, Muslim Representation shall not be less than one-third.
    - (v) Representation of communal groups to be by separate electorates provided that it shall be open to any community at any time to abandon its separate electorate in favour of joint electorate.
    - (vi) Any territorial redistribution not in any way to affect the Muslim majority in the Punjab, Bengal and the N.W.F. Provinces.
    - (vii) Full liberty of belief worship, and observance propaganda, association and education shall be guaranteed to all communities.
    - (viii) No Bill or Resolution or any part thereof shall be passed in any Legislature or any other elected body if three-fourths of the members of any community in that body opposed it as being injurious to the interests of that community.
    - (ix) Sind to be separated from the Bombay Presidency.
    - (x) Reforms to be introduced in the Frontier Province and Baluchistan as in other Provinces.
    - (xi) Adequate share for Musalmans to be provided in the constitution in all services, subject to requirements of efficiency.

(xii) Adequate safeguards for the protection and promotion of Muslim culture, education, language, religion, personal laws, and charitable institutions and for their due share in the grant-in-aid.

(xiii) No Cabinet either Central or Provincial to be formed without at least one-third of the ministers being Muslim.

(xiv) No change of the constitution by the Central Legislature except with the concurrence of (Sic).

48. The Indian Statutory Commission Report, Vol. II.
49. *Ibid.*
50. *Ibid.*, Vol. II, p. 41.
51. Coupland, *op. cit.*, p. 133, (See Simon Report, Vol. II, p. 17).
52. Parliamentary Paper (Command 4147) of 1932.
53. Sen, *op. cit.*, 103.
54. Pt. Jawahar Lal's Statement, 10th July, 1937.
55. Letter No. 5845, dated the 3rd October, 1927.
56. Iyer, *op. cit.*, p. 308.
57. Proceedings of the Indian National Congress, October, 1939.
58. The Speeches of Jinnah.
59. *The Making of the Indian Constitution (1939-1947)* by Anil Chandra Banerjee M.A. Ph.D., Vol. 1, Pub. by A. Mukherjee and Co. Calcutta, 1948, pp. 24-25.
60. See *India* by Cotto Philips.
61. See *The Transfer of Power to India* by Lumby.
62. See *The Making of The Indian Constitution (1939-47)*, compiled by Dr. Banerjee.
63. See *The Indian Review*, September, 1946, p. 491.
64. *Psychologic Des Foules* by Le Bon's (*The Crowd: A Study of the Popular Mind*. Fisher Unwin (12th impression, 1920), p. 36.
65. Fischer, *op. cit.*, p. 165.
66. *Group Psychology and the Analysis of the Ego* by Sigmund Freud, MD. LL.D. The Hogasth Press and the Institute of Psycho-Analysis, London, Fifth Impression (Authorised translation by James Starchey) 49. (Quotes Lee Bon, *op. cit.*, p. 29).
67. Fischer, *op. cit.*, p. 107.
68. Resolution of the Congress Working Committee, March 6-8, 1947.
69. See *Mission with Mountbatten* by Allan Compbell Johnson (Robert Hale).
70. Benerji, *op. cit.*, p. 353.

The Summing-up

Having examined the different aspects of the growth and development of communalism in its political phase, we are now in a position to attempt a summing up of our observations.

Firstly, the most important element in the life of the Indian society during this phase was the establishment of the British as the supreme political power. It is proved conclusively and significantly by the way they governed India, and, the result to which their domination led, that the force that holds political power in a society also holds the key to the harmonious and healthy development of the relations between the various sections of that society.

The pith of the Communal problem in India did not so much lie either in the fact of indigenous differences, or in the fact of British ascendancy. On the contrary, the crux of the problem lay in the way in which it was dealt by the State. It is self evident that any sociological problem can assume a menacing gravity if it is not tackled properly.

A state, in its simplest definition, is a politically organized society. It acts through the instrumentality of its government which is the active repository of the political power of the 'organized society', for which it acts. The alien Government of India, as is apparent did not derive its power from the people it ruled. The power was usurped at the point of bullets and bayonets and therefore, it was exercised in a manner that suited the British interests as against the interest of the Indians.

Communalism, would not have assumed such a ghastly form, if the people at the helm of affairs had acted in the interests of the nation. The British are responsible in as much as they governed the country in such a manner that instead of eradicating Communalism, they did all that they possibly could to aggravate the evil. The political power of the British did not become an instrument for easing the indigenous tensions, so as to develop the society into a healthy nation. On the contrary, their power was in itself a dividing force. As such it pursued a policy that inevitably culminated in the national split.

Dr Prasad rightly observed:

> "As a matter of fact, governments reflect the existing differences and seek to correlate their policy to them, with a view either to bridge them or to rely on them. Or, they `muddle through' without bestowing much thought on the claims of social integration. In domestic, imperial and foreign affairs, Britain has prided herself on a policy of drift".

Referring to the British policy in India, he further added:

> "In the course of piecemeal adjustment to various factors and exigencies of the Indian situation during the last eighty years, the British Government did strike on policies and actions calculated to sustain and accentuate the differences between the Communities, - the omission to eradicate illiteracy and poverty, differential treatment, separate electorates, extraordinary delays in political settlements and, lastly, the inversion of the true order of things by declaring all political advance contingent on prior agreement".

As such, Dr Prasad concluded that the cure for Communalism, lay in replacing the existing political system by another system which might pursue a policy consistent with the interest of the Indians. He said:

> "All this serves to re-inforce the contention that the Communal problem is part of the wider political problem, that of replacing the present system by one more, alive to a consistent policy of social concord and of infusing the exercise of power with the moral purpose".[1]

This aspect of Communalism was deliberately ignored by the British. In the true Imperialist tradition they could not think of a political set-up in which they might be replaced.

They could think only of one thing viz. that in ruling India, they were simply sharing the white man's burden, on the face of this earth. Added to it was their self-created fear or a clever ruse that if the British left India, the natives would be reduced to a state of utter chaos and anarchy, where every Mohammedan and every Hindu would perish in a ceaseless fight with each other. Charles Roe, who was the Judge of the Chief Court of Punjab, while expressing his opinion on a peculiar measure in connection with Government's due policy in meeting native opposition, in his memorandum dated the 25th November, 1893, opposed application of the English methods to Indian conditions.

He said:

> "I think the true way of meeting this opposition is to state plainly that the circumstances of England and India are so entirely different, that general principles highly beneficial in the one way may be most injurious in the other....
>
> "In India, the facts are wholly different. The `people' consist, not of men of the same or kindred race and of much the same general way of thinking, but of numerous wholly different races, with utterly antagonistic creeds and feelings. It is only the `Pax-Brittanica' that keeps these races from flying at each other's throats.
>
> "The Government on the other hand is, and always has been, a power deriving its authority in no way from the people', but from an entirely independent source. It is essential to its very existence, it is indeed the basis of its moral claim to exist at all that it should be, fully capable of effectually controlling any or all classes of the `People',
>
> "A change of government means a change from order to anarchy"*[2].

This has been, in fact, the stock attitude of all the colonial powers in the World, and the English were no exception to it. The Imperialist apologists make much capital out of the Religious differences that certainly dominated the Indian social life.

The fact of religion, would have been a good excuse, if the Communal problem had been peculiar to India alone. Curiously enough, it happened to be a concomitant of British Imperialism. Like India, British Empire had many other parallels to its credit. As K.B. Krishna wrote:

> "Communalism is the product of the Imperialist capitalist

> feudal structure. It is the compound structure of traders in politics with Imperialism".

In Palestine between Arabs and Jews, in Ceylon between Sinhalese and Tamils, in Kenya between the English and the native settlers, the Communal question was identical in its essentials, if not in degree as between the Hindus and the Muslims in India. As Krishna wrote:

> "Imperialism utilizes and intensifies class-struggles between the Arabs and the Jews as in India between the Hindus and the Moslems".[3]

Comparing the Indian problem with its counterpart in Ceylon, He adds:

> "In both places, the origins are to be sought in the growth of the professional and the commercial classes and their desire for a share in the administration of the country and in the need of the Government to counterpoise one class against another. In both places, it was asserted by their respective Governments that they were not fit for responsible government. In both cases, the original idea of representation of interests was changed to representation of communities, not in the historical sense, but in the religious sense. In both cases while the responsible Government was denied, the natural course left was to concede small administrative changes coupled with counterpoise; Moslems against Hindus; Tamils against Sinhalese".

Krishna continues with this analogy and with special reference to communal representation he writes:

> "In both cases when once the principle of communal representation was recognized, it was spread to other communities. Partly was it due to the differentiation of classes, partly due to the British policy of counterpoise. In India it spread to Sikh, Anglo-Indian, Christian and untouchables and in Ceylon to Malays.
>
> "In both cases as the communities were given more representation they clamoured for more. Above all the ostensible objects for which communal representation was sought by the professional classes were not secured.

> Communal Representation disintegrated and demoralized the Society into cockpit of creeds and castes. It coloured their outlook on life with Communalism. It hindered the growth of party feelings. It encouraged religious parochialism. It accentuated rather than diminished racial differences".[4]

Rajni Palme Dutt also agrees with the above views and he writes:

> "Communal strife is thus a special product of British rule and in particular of the latest period of British rule or of the declining Imperialist ascendancy".[5]

Be it as it may, there can not be two opinions to the view that the British aggravated Communalism. Their responsibility lies in the diplomatic manoeuvre of diverting the energies of the Indian struggle of emancipation from the national to the communal plane. It is here indeed that we also have an explanation to Mahatma Gandhi's declaration at the Second Session of the Round Table conference that the quarrel between Hindu and Mohammedan is "coeral with the British advent and that it will dissolve when the people of India are free"

Turning to the role played by the Muslims in the growth and development of Communalism in India, one cannot absolve them of the charge that, as a community, they formed a "split-personality". The fault does not lie with individuals or with leaders; it lies deep in the culture or inheritance of Islam. Their religion, their mode of life, their sense of values, their objects of loyalty, and, above all, their norms of prosperity, demanded a considerable self-abnegation on their part to make an adjustment with the changing conditions of the modern world.

It is apparent that the Indian Muslims failed to condition themselves to the changed environments. The challenge to accept a new order of life as thrown by the impact of Western civilization, could not be met by the followers of Islam. In a world of competing Communities when the frustrated Muslims discovered their backwardness in a world of competing communities it was too late to make a recovery on lines that instead of being Communal they could be National. To them it was their community alone that constituted a Nation, and, it was only this Muslim Nation that needed social uplift, economic security and political liberty in order to make enable the Indian followers of Islam to come up once again as an equal to Hindus who had stolen a march over them. It is also clear that a separatist tendency suited Muslim interest much more than the Nationalist way; particularly, when such an attitude was approved by the British rulers of the land. Given the ingredients of split personality, a split theology and a split nationality; and a land where the instrumentality of the State was pressed into the service of the Imperialist policy of "exploitation and counterpoise", it was in the logic of the historic evolution that Communalism should triumph, over the forces of national emancipation.

The third important element that aggravated the Communal problem came from the Hindu community itself. None can blame the Hindus for their numerical majority and material ascendency over the Muslims but there is much to be said in regard to their parochialism in the social field. The Hindus have most of the time treated the Muslims as untouchables.

There is enough element of truth in the otherwise exaggerated remarks of M.A. Ansari that "you may be a pucca nationalist and four square Gandhite, yet you will be treated as an untouchable as soon as you announce to a Hindu that you are a Muslim". Whatever reasons the Hindus might have to justify their conduct, the Muslims could not but feel aggrieved at this attitude.

The truth is that "discrimination" of any kind is a vicious source of tension, while "social discrimination", is the worst form it can take. The practice of social discrimination to which even the Muslims were not immune, constituted the base on which communal hatred and antagonism got into the blood of Hindus and Muslims of India. Communalism in India could not have attained that intensity and degree to which it reached if the Hindu social order had not suffered from too much of rigidity or from the curse of untouchability.

The concept that India constituted two Nations was baseless and unwarranted by the facts of History. It was a myth and a "camouflage to cover up humiliation in the social sphere and inequality in the economic sphere".[6]

The solution of the Communal problem as envisaged by the

scheme of partition was a solution both of 'irrational resolutions' and 'national despair'.

Pakistan possibly could not ameliorate the inter-communal relations in India. It was born out of sheer frustration and selfishness. History stands witness that the partition has failed to settle the minority question. Pakistan could neither do this nor resister a complete victory of the principle of self-determination. Jinnah, himself admitted that the so called two nations would continue to plague India even after partition. This is clear in an interview reported by Edward Thompson. "Two Nations, Mr. Jinnah: confronting each other in every Province? Every town? Every village". That is the only solution. That is a very terrible solution Mr. Jinnah".[7] "It is a terrible solution. But it is the only one".[8]

Jinnah wanted Pakistan so that Hindus should not dominate over Muslims. A free India, the Muslims believed, would be a Hindu-dominated India. This apprehension was not altogether ill founded. One hundred million Muslims would always be a minority among three hundred million non-Muslims (Hindus, Sikhs, Parsis, Christians and others). The Pakistan that he envisaged was sure to give Muslims all the political power and jobs and control over all industry and trade. Clearly enough "Pakistan was thus the answer to the rich Muslim prayers and middle-class Muslim's dreams. A religious state offered them social safety and political and economic monopoly".[9]

It becomes vividly clear that the chief factors that motivated communalism were primarily economic and the psychological; the Socio-religious factors being of secondary importance. In the day-to-day living of the various communities, these factors brought in tension, which lent a communal colour even to the political questions of the Indian Nation. The separatist tendencies were well exploited by the vested interests, only to create a vast gulf between a people who had been living together for centuries.

In its political phase, communalism continued to be a creed of social-tension, mainly because of the conditions created by the social rigidity of the Hindus, the religious fanaticism of the Muslims and the diabolic diplomacy of the British. It is apparent that to disappear it needed a triple effacement.

NOTES AND REFERENCES

1. Beni Prasad, *op. cit.*, p. 163.
2. Home Dept. B. Pub. Jan. 1894. Nos. 309/414.
3. See *Communal Representation* by Dr. K.B. Krishna.
4. *Ibid.*
5. *India to-day and tomorrow* by R. Palme Dutt. People's Publishing House Ltd., Delhi, 1955, p. 225.
6. *Pakistan (the Problem of India)* by Dr. Shaukat Ullah Ansari: Minerva Book Shop. Anarkali, Lahore, 1944, p. 28.
7. See the example of Ulster. The Partition did not solve the minority problem, since while the Protestant minority of 6 per cent in Eire may acquiesce in the new regime, the same cannot be said of the Catholic minority of 33 per cent in Northern Ireland *(The Future of India* by R. Coupland, 1943, p. 15.
8. See, *Ibid.*, p. 72. (Quoted from *Enlist India for Freedom*, 1941, p. 52).
9. Louis Fischer, *op. cit.*, p. 152.

Part III

The Epilogue

The Epilogue

The investigation of the problem in hand undertaken in this study leads to three obvious conclusions.

Firstly, that communalism is the consequence of a disturbance in a very complex equilibrium and that ordinarily, it denotes social tension as engendered by the rivalry between various communities.

Secondly, that three distinct factors have been the prime movers of communalism in social, religious, and political phases.

Finally, that in its political phase during the British Raj communalism signified a creed which predominately governed the relations between the Hindus and the Muslims.

Taking up the first point for further elucidation, we find that every society in this world is a subtle and complex equilibrium which, often, gets disturbed. It is indeed impossible to find a society whose equilibrium does not get disturbed. In fact, it is through this successive change of equilibrium into a disturbed state and back to a state of poise, that the world moves on. Conflict and cooperation do follow each other. In other words, it is through the eventual synthesis of thesis and anti-thesis that history is created.

In a given society, a community is the moving force behind the series of changes that continue to emerge in a spiral like motion. Such a change, however, does not come without being accompanied by tension. We know that community is like an organism; that it is a dynamic concept, that it is capable of growth and is absolute in nature, and that above all, being expansible it is proselytizing in its attitude. Naturally, therefore, when a community (be it Hindu, Muslim or Christian) exhibits its full nature while participating in the life of a society, it is likely to disturb the equilibrium since different communities shall be acting and reaching at a varying pace and sometimes in conflicting directions they are likely to precipitate tension.

The variability of communal motivation and communal progress, forms the basis of communal ideology, known as colonialism, which in simpler terms is nothing but an attribute of a "Community in Action".

Here we can raise two pertinent questions. Firstly, is the growth of communalism unavoidable? Secondly, if it is not unavoidable what are the possible ways of mitigating its evils?

The answer to the first question is quite simple. We can say without hesitation that it is not possible to avoid communalism. The reasons for it are obvious. Firstly, communalism has two aspects. In its broader aspect it is culture. If a Hindu thinks in terms of its own communities good, if he works for the welfare of the members of his community, he is not a worshipper of communalism as an evil, on the contrary he is just acting in the most natural way, for he is what his community has made him.

The trouble arises when the same person acts in a way that may prove detrimental to the members of the other communities. It is here that communalism shows the other edge. It becomes an evil. The promotion of culture ceases, when a community tries to coerce other groups. It gives birth to communal antagonism. The rivalry once germinated, develops faster towards the breaking point. The process of irritation, retaliation and counter retaliation as a consequence of disturbance in the complex equilibrium precipitates social tension.

Human nature being as it is, it is not possible to eradicate communalism altogether but it can be controlled in a way to lessen the social tension that it brings. To quote Quincy Wright:

> "Tension may be regarded in its broadest sense as the condition arising from inconsistencies among initiatives in the structure of a society. The resolution of these inconsistencies results in decisions which regulate the utilization of the society's energy. It may be, that the amount of tension in any society varies as the product of the degree of rigidity of its structure and the amount of its energy, thus suggesting an analogy to an electrical system in which tension or electromotive force varies as the product of resistance and current strength"[1].

He further adds:

> "Such an analogy has only the roughest application,. It may suggest, however, that a scientific examination of social tension should avoid the assumption of common parlance that social tension is an evil which ought to be eradicated. Tension is not the germ of war though it may bear element in the causation of war. As high electrical tension is dangerous to human life and may become so great as to destroy the structure in which it functions, so high social tension may lead to violence or war and even destroy the structure of society. Yet without a minimum of tension, an electrical system will not operate at all. So also societies will not function, much less progress, unless there is some tension within them. It is tension among inconsistent initiatives that make possible choices, direction and achievement of goals. Tensions contribute to the causation of war, but they also contribute to the causation of progress"[2].

It brings us to the second question that we raised earlier as to when it is certain that communalism is not only unavoidable, but to some extent 'contributes to the causation of progress', the only thing to be seen is those possible steps that can lessen the evils that go along with communalism in its lower aspect. In other words, we face the problem of diminishing social-tension as engendered by the action and interaction of various communities in the spirit of rivalry and competition.

The answer to this question can be easily given if we can understand the implications of the, second part of our conclusion, that the economic, psychological and Socio-religious factors are the prime movers of communalism. It is on these three planes of human existence that we can truly discover means by which the evil side of communalism may be mitigated, and we may have a social existence with less tension amongst the communities.

The Economic factor as we have already examined is the most fundamental factor of human life everywhere. Engeles rightly remarked:

> "The economic structure of society always forms the real basis from which, in the last analysis, is to be explained

> the whole superstructure of legal and political institutions, as well as the religious, philosophical and other conceptions of each historical period"[3].

This may rightly appear to be an exaggerated view, yet it is an exaggeration of a great truth. Life is indeed, nothing but an economic riddle. Ultimately, for each one of us, whether we are Hindu, Muslim, Parsi, Sikh, Christian or Anglo-Indian, living is but a ceaseless struggle directed in search of the means of existence. The first problem that stares every man in the face is how shall I live without food, cloth and shelter? The first love of man is his self preservation, it is neither community nor culture. Since group life makes this quest easier, he begins, to owe allegiance to the group that supports him. Communalism therefore is the creed that he worships from the day he receives economic protection. But does ones own community necessarily alone give one all protection? Do all other communities in a given society snatch that security? This is a dilemma which an average individual fails to rightly understand. It is this failure of right understanding that gives birth to tension. It is this individual grievance that in no time assumes a communal colour. If one Hindu has been put to an economic ruin then it invariably leads to the psychology of communal affront meted out to the entire Hindu community. But is it always a right way of judging things? What about the thread of loyalty? Even in this complex and fragile equilibrium of economic relationship between different continuities, what part does the thread of economic loyalty play? A Muslim peasant is as devoted to the Hindu Zamindar as a Hindu possibly can be. A Hindu soldier may be as devoted to the Muslim ruler as a Muslim may sometimes fail to be. In a chequered pattern of employers and employee, perhaps the thread of loyalty does cut across the communal barriers. It is this thread of loyalty that can be strengthened further.

Limitations

But this can be possible only under certain limitations and with calculated attempts. The first limitation is that of the ownership of the means of production? Is it a communal ownership and if so does it cater for the needs of the members of one community alone? Does the land belong to a Hindu Zamindar or does it belong to the peasant who tills it? The land or the factory in itself is neither Brahmanic, nor untouchable, nor Islamite?

The second limitation lies in the fact that even if the means of production be non-communal in their ownership, they are invariably in the hands of those who exploit the non-possessors, irrespective of their caste, creed and community.

If we review the economic history of mankind, we can easily see that in all ages and in every society, the means of production and consequently the wealth of the nation have usually been the monopoly of a few. It is indeed a strange irony of fate that although men are born free and equal, yet they live under conditions which are less free and more unequal. There cannot indeed be a different Muslim inequality, a different Hindu inequality. Muslim slavery is as painful as Hindu slavery. It is this fact of inequality that should be given primary importance, instead of emphasizing on denominational distinctions.

Whereas it is impossible to attain perfect and absolute equality for everyone, it is not difficult either to minimize inequality or to create a body politic, wherein greater social justice may be administered to its members. We should realize that poverty is an equal curse to every human being to whatever group he may belong. We should also realize that no community is in itself bad or good. The basic cause of disturbance in the Indian communities, or any other rival groups elsewhere, lies in their inability to afford a basic minimum of daily existence. Walter Lippman summing it up comments:

> "If the state fails to do that (i.e. to protect the standard of life of its people), its independence is threatened, as we can see in the case of Austria; its national unity is imperilled, as we can see almost everywhere in the exacerbation of separatist tendencies (witness the movement for Pakistan in India)....."[4].

Communalism in India was thus a terrible consequence of economic conflict. It was an economic question, a question created by the growth of a petty bourgeoisie middle-class, that intensified the split in the Indian national movement.

Sinha aptly summarizes:

> "Want when unconscious, will lead to complicated devices

> of communalism. Want when conscious would lead to a volcanic upheaval of society...... Allied to this want is the uncertainty of income..... The search for certainty causes the organization to preserve group of violent sectional politics... Want and insecurity are therefore, the major obstacles to liquidation, of separatism and group hatred...... Radical cure of communalism demands abolition of want, uncertainty and unjustified in equality".[5]

All this can be achieved by the liquidation of the various instruments of exploitation. Indeed such a tendency towards liquidation of these oppressive instruments is already in evidence in modern times. People have now much more faith than ever before in the distribution of National wealth from a fewer hands into as great a number as possible. This can be done through the state. As Laski says "the instruments of property' - that is to say, land and capital used in production - must be administered by the State"[6]. It is just what Stuart Chase accurately describes as "overhead planning and control of economic activity".[7]

The aim is that of introducing an economic system that may incorporate the idea of collective organization of the community in the interests of the entire mass of the people, a system that will be brought about through common ownership and collective control of the means of production, distribution and exchange.

Thus, it is only by envisaging a socialistic pattern of society that economic inequality and consequent inter-communal rivalry in the country can be minimized, poverty eradicated and healthier communal relations re-established. Equality of opportunity in every office, administrative, political as also in all economic pursuits can be the best and surer safeguard against communalism. In short, socialism is the most ideal cure for communalism on the economic plane".

In our quest to discover ways and means to eradicate communalism, we may now turn to the psychological aspect of the problem. Here we can examine communalism in its dual aspects—as promoter of culture and of social tension.

Communalism so long as it amounts to just love of one's own community, serves the noble cause of culture. It is then nothing but "a group phenomenon with a life of its own". It then gives an individual his highest possession; in fact, the very form of his being, the behaviour patterns, the language, the techniques, the values and the beliefs. Thus, it is said that the tendency of individuals to be aggressive or docile, to be loyal to a particular group or to be independent, to be cooperative or competitive is a phenomenon of culture. The same is true of the tendency of the group to be belligerent, or peaceful, to be totalitarian or liberal, to be conciliatory or controversial.

A culture as such, is extremely difficult to change: it is the product of an unalterable history. It is an integrated complex, no part of which can be changed without modifying the whole. A Hindu is bound to live as a Hindu and a Muslim shall continue to be a Muslim, each with his own characteristics, that will be transmitted as a whole by each generation of parents to the children from their very birth. Therefore, if we find a particular community aggressive in its outlook, or fanatical in its ideas, any change whatsoever seems to require an early separation of the children from parents and a subjection to a new culture inculcated by institutions maintained by the elite of that culture.

But is it possible to bring about a radical change in the nature of way of living and culture of a people on a mass scale? Further, even if it be possible, is it indeed human to throttle a precious possession of civilization. A coexistence of people also implies a coexistence of their way of life. In fact, each culture is a unique contribution. As Dr Indra Sen writes:

> "A culture, the ensemble of the life of a people, its practical adjustment of life, its crafts, fine arts, literature, philosophy, morals and religion, its social structure and politics, seem to constitute an organic growth intimately connected with the character and the temperament of the people and its geographical situation and historical antecedents. It is in its motive and forms as unique as the individual human personality of the people. And therefore each culture is a unique value and contribution to the general human culture, the totality of fundamental living wealth of men".[8]

Thus, when we take it for granted that the cultural values as developed by a community are a unique contribution, that they are meant to be preserved and not to be destroyed, it is essential to see that all those evils, that lead tension in the complex equilibrium of a society are rooted out. The question that poses itself is from where do these evil tendencies come?

Apparently, the transformation of communalism as culture to communalism as social tension may seem to be a conflict of diverse material interests and gains. It may also give us an impression of transformation from one's love for one's community, into more intense and exclusive love along with a recently developed sense of hostility against another community for one reason or the other.

However, we are of the opinion that the seeds of disturbance, of hostility and of antagonism are sown in the minds of men from their birth. As man grows, the disruptive attitudes, the dogmatic beliefs and unchangeable stereotypes also grow with him as he begets them as an indistinguishable part of his communal heritage. It would be premature to present a definite analysis here but we might recapture the points already stressed.

Firstly, we can look to the concept of ambivalence. Such a state begins with a child and it continues as he grows into a man. Therefore ambivalent situations lead to individual tensions and influence communal tension and hostility on a national scale. Every ambivalent situation is unpleasant and is commonly relieved by displacing the hate and the concomitant aggressive tendency upon someone else. For example, Jinnah was sometimes considered to be an 'Ambassador of Hindu Muslim unity'. But with the emergence of Mahatma Gandhi as the chief exponent of the Indian National Congress, he was overshadowed. There emerged in the mind of Jinnah, a simultaneous operation of two irreconcileable wishes; one leading towards a submission to the National interest and the other leading towards a submission to the communal love. This ambivalent situation led to the displacement of Jinnah's hatred against the Hindus as a out-group, till India as a whole was involved. As a writer remarks, "... In order that internal conflict may be reduced and internal cooperation augmented, the process of displacing hatreds upon the out-group continues until the world as a whole is involved. A bipolar world emerges in which the tension in each human mind and in each lesser human group is relieved by displacement of the target of aggressive disposition upon that group which is an outgroup to all".[9]

Referring to the possible solution for such a psychological cause of communalism, Professor Quincy Wright observes:

> "The solution of the problem of excessive social tension might be sought in methods of early child training so as to reduce the initial ambivalence displacement of aggressive tendencies upon common enemies of humanity such as pestilence, poverty and war itself. Institutions might be modified so that instead of encouraging the process of displacement, they will encourage solution of ambivalence through decision within the individual mind or within smaller groups".[10]

Secondly, we must look to the important role that frustration plays in our individual and social life. In such a case, it is not the conflict of opposing attitudes within the individual mind that matters. The basic conflict is that between the goals and achievements.

We have already examined at length as to how a failure to achieve success in one's coveted goal, brings frustration that leads to both adaptive and maladaptive consequences. The coming of blockages is indeed the greatest shock in the life of an individual, a group or even a nation. Every blockage, brings with it tension and rivalry. In a society of competing communities any such contingency, is bound to create an acute state of communal rivalry and social tension. We have seen how in various phases of communalism, different sections of the masses, continued to face irremovable blockages. The Hindu caste, the Muslim religion and the British rule, have been the most offensive and humiliating blockages in the life of the people of India. These impregnable barriers continued to be a source of serious frustration. Communalism would not have been there as a creed of communal hostility and antagonism, if the Hindu social system had been less rigid, Muslim religion less intolerant and British Imperialism less devastating in its nature.

We have also seen the entire trend of the relations amongst the Hindus and the Muslims under the British. There relations were tremendously governed by the frustration suffered by each community. Imperial policy did not allow a normal development of inter-communal relations. The native attempt to liquidate alien rule was brutally frustrated by the English, who cleverly turned the aggressive reaction of the different communities against each other.

The communalism of the Hindus and the Muslims was, therefore, more a manifestation of the maladaptive consequence of the frustration suffered by each, due to the conflict between the goal of an independent and free statehood and the British attempts to frustrate their efforts.

Obviously, if we desired to eradicate communalism as a creed of communal antagonism and social tension, we can do so only if we also remove the blockages that bring frustration to the members of a community in its free march towards progress.

Secondly, in order to lessen tension and bitterness, it is also essential that the maladaptive consequences, viz. the tendency to aggress, should be replaced by a greater reliance on adaptive consequences of both the individual and group frustrations. It can be done only if the masses properly understand the relation between the ends that they count and the means that they adopt to realize them. Professor Quincy Wright suggests:

> "This source of tensions, it is suggested, may be ameliorated by better education concerning the effective relation of means and ends, and by education directive attention to ends capable of achievement with the means at hand. Such education may reduce frustration, and may cultivate habits of rational adaptation of means to ends and of considering the relative value of different ends whether in economics, in politics in culture or in social relations".[11]

What holds good for the individual, should hold good for the community as well. Although we can educate an individual, it appears somewhat difficult to educate an entire community. Will a community be able to go for adaptive consequences of frustrations? Can a group be made so rational-minded as to be able to choose the right means for right ends. In all likelihood it is a difficult task, but it is possible to have the desired effect if a community gets a leadership, which is rational minded and which may guide the community into the right direction - a direction which will steer clear of all communal hostility and social tension.

Such a leadership can of-course grow only if the members of the community are rightly trained and educated for a healthy communal and social living.

A rational minded leadership and a right kind of education, however, are not enough to face alone the challenge of communalism; for it will continue to breed tension and disharmony as long as different communities or groups go on entertaining and cherishing certain false beliefs.

We refer here to the role that is played by stereotypes and false identifications and personifications on the psychological plane; which are prone to be a menace that primarily, leads to a perpetuation of communalism. Prof. Quincy Wright observes:

> "The primitive mind tends to explain natural phenomenon as the acts of persons and tries to combat than by attracting or placating the natural or supernatural person deemed responsible. Civilized man tends to generalize about racial, social, economic or other groups on the basis of insufficient instances, and to attribute to all persons in the group undesirable characteristics identified with the group. This process of stereotyping, identification, and attribution tends to develop group antagonisms".[12]
>
> Here again, the true solution lies in cleansing the minds of men. The communal stereotypes can be erased, only by an educational process, 'providing more adequate information and demonstrating the inaccuracy of the popular stereotypes', that people of one community continue to harbour against those of other communities, for instance, Hindus think that Muslims are usually unfair and fanatic and Muslims have a stereotype, that all Hindus are timid and Kafir. Stereotypes grow out of group prejudices. They are learned in the same way as the table manners: by association with people who have that kind of table manner".[13]

It is widely believed that the accumulation of prejudices a person acquires from his culture through his family as also most of the stereotypes are the result of ignorance and lack of intercommunication. Robins says:

> "Most individuals live within a fairly narrow range of social environments. Each environment bears down on

> the individual with its own special standards of attitudes and behaviour".[14]

The only way to liquidate these stereotypes is to reduce the social distances so that a free communication may lead to a better understanding of each others ways of life. Minorities may not harbour ill-will against the majority and the majority community may also try to be intimate with the minorities.

Finally, there are some who attribute communal tension to the influence of the mechanism of projection. For instance, a Muslim may project his aggressive dispositions or dominance drives upon another person (say a Hindu) with whom he happens to be in controversy. This makes the Muslim sure of the aggressive intentions of the Hindu and induces him to take defensive measures to protect himself from the assumed aggression of the other. The party will act the same way. "Individual projection reflects itself in the opinions of conflicting groups". It leads to some sort of preparation which may be both offensive and defensive in character. The armament race proceeds and tension rises. Hindu-Muslim relations in India have many a time broken through overt conflict due to such a process of individual projections.

Only a discriminate and tolerant leadership can help in reducing the tension in this plane. Quincy Wright says:

> "Better mechanism and better adjustment between the mores and the counter-mores in society might ameliorate this source of tension".[15]

The various psychological factors examined above can act alone, or in certain situations, they may all be present together. The above analysis, however, clearly reveals that tension basically begins in the minds of men. As Professor Wright remarks:

> "They suggest how major political, social and economic tensions may be traced from the tensions in the individual mind, whether to conflicts of individual human attitudes with one another, to conflicts of goals and techniques, to conflicts of beliefs and realities, to conflicts of standards and drives. They also suggest methods by which the `deference of peace' may be constructed in the minds of men".[16]

Obviously, if we desire to eradicate communalism as an evil, to lessen social tension, and to better the relations between the various communities, it is the proper training of the minds of the men that we have to look-after.

This can be done through a proper system of education which may help in fostering a sense of mutual understanding, as also appreciation of each other's way of living.

If education really, means 'the development of the whole man', it is essential that this development should be a process by means of which an individual may learn to coexist and to try to have an open mind free from all prejudices, ill will and hostility. No individual or community can continue to aspire for an endless accumulation of power at the cost of another individual or community. We have to live and let live. It can be done only through a sound system of education, which may teach people to live through a process of adjustment and not through intolerance and aggression. In short if we have to learn to be loyal to the community, we have also to learn to put brakes on the craze to seek greater communal power. Such a communal tendency can be controlled through education. As Johan Dewy remarks:

> "Education is the process of remarking experience through giving it a more socialized value through increased individual experience, by giving the individual better control over his own powers".[17]

The individual should, therefore, be properly educated to understand the nature of social living, to tolerate its varied cultures and to appreciate the different patterns they present. He should learn that his lesser loyalty to the community has to yield before the greater loyalty to the nation. As Bertrand Russel remarks:

> "If a man's life is to be satisfactory, whether from his own point of view or from that of the world at large, it requires two kinds of harmony: an internal harmony of intelligence, emotion and will, and an external harmony with the wills of others".[18]

In both these matters, it is a sound education that is needed most. What is desired is not the growth just of a good Hindu or a good Muslim, but of a good citizen, whether he is Hindu or Muslim. This can be achieved by imparting education, at an early age, as the objective of bringing up a good citizen is related intimately to attitudes and loyalties. Bertrand Russel rightly remarks:

> "This collective failure to use the intelligence that men possess for purposes of self-preservation is due, in the main, to the insane and destructive impulses which lurk in the unconscious of those who have been unwisely handled in infancy, childhood and adolescence".

Referring to a gradual deterioration of a regard for human values he further adds:

> "The source of all this does not lie in the external world, nor does it lie in the purely cognitive part of our nature, since we know more then men ever knew before. It lies in our passions; it lies in our emotional habits; it lies in the sentiments instilled in youth, and in the phobias created in infancy. The cure for our problem is to make men sane, and to make men sane they must be educated sanely".[19]

People are not by nature good citizens. Art must make them so if a stable just and prosperous social order free from the evils of communalism is to develop. It can be done through a sound education. It is through it alone that we can bring about better Hindu-Muslim relations. The great Victorian reformer John Ruskin said:

> "You do not educate a man by telling him what he knows, not, but by making him what he was not".[20]

It is when we come to the moral factor that we face the most difficult situation, primarily because the concept of morality, in certain socio-religious practices of various communities is too deep seated and firm. The devotion with which these practices are pursued, the religious fervour with which they are passed on from generation to generation, cannot be easily obliterated from the minds of men. We have already examined in detail how the observance of certain practices is not given up even when these practices become outmoded and cease to fulfil any vital necessity of the community simply because it adds to the communal strength and power. Therefore, from the point of view of a community, their effacement is both undesirable and difficult. In fact, it is as impossible as the disappearance of the sense of religion itself.

Curiously enough, this dogmatic and aggressive character of the communal customs and traditions, having different appeal for different communities, being moral and religious to some, but not to others breeds communalism and social disharmony. The pseudo-concept of morality has thus been a powerful sustainer of communal tension since it is a relative concept and possesses different meanings for different people. Once the 'difference' is there, tension automatically follows in its train.

Similarly, religion too has been the most important, the most positive and perhaps the most effective promoter of communalism as a creed of social tension.

It may appear paradoxical that in the name of religion, most irreligious and immoral acts have been done in the world.

Communities have fought not only for the preservation and propagation of their faith but have fought and lived in the worst state of communal hostility and antagonism because of religious differences. Their quarrels have not been confined to the mere upholding of one's creed as the most righteous, and one's gods and goddesses as the most beatific deities of the universe. They have expressed their feelings in sanguinary feuds, like those between the Roman Catholics and the Protestants in Europe and the daily recurring communal riots between the Hindus and the Muslims in India.

Communalism has thus not only been a measure of economic and psychological state of inter-communal rivalry and tension, but has also been an unfortunate commentary on the havoc that different customs and creeds, temperaments and traditions and rites and religions of various communities have wrought in their life.

It is needless to reiterate that those practices, which combine in themselves both a moral trait and a religious sanction, if misinterpreted and wrongly practised are likely to be a source of constant conflict and communal tension.

The truth is that, fault lies not in morality, but in the immoral application of morality. What is good for a Hindu must also be good for a Muslim and a Christian and any other human being. There cannot be a Hindu morality and a Muslim morality as there cannot be air or water which is either Muslim or Hindu. Any such distinction is superficial and arbitrary. In India such denominational and sectarian distinctions were invidiously maintained as amongst the Hindus and the Muslims, the Brahmins and the non-Brahmins, the high caste and the Shudra. As such, they perpetuated communalism. In a set-up where we desire to remove communalism, these distinctions shall have to go.

It will not be unwise to re-emphasize the part untouchability has played in disrupting communal relations. This socio-religious practice had created an impregnable barrier between one community and another, repelling all forces of mutual adjustment and understanding[21] between one Hindu and another as also between a Hindu and a Muslim. In the words of Mahatma Gandhi:

> "To remove untouchability is a penance that caste Hindus owe to Hinduism and to themselves. The purification required is not of untouchables but of the so-called superior castes. There is no vice that is special to the untouchables not even dirt and insanitation. It is our arrogance which blinds us, superior Hindus, to our own blemishes and which magnifies those of our downtrodden brethren whom we have suppressed and whom we keep under suppression.
>
> "Religions like nations are being weighed in the balance. God's grace and revelation are the monopoly of no race or nation. They descend equally upon all who wait upon God. That religion and that nation will be blotted out if the face of the earth which pins its faith to injustice, untruth or violence. God is light, not darkness. God is love, not hate. God is truth not untruth. God alone is great. We, his creatures are but dust. Let us be humble and recognize the place of the loveliest of His creatures".[22]

Thus, if communalism is to go, this curse that, "clouds our vision, limits our experience, hardens our heart, narrows our sphere of responsibility and prevents our ideals of justice, love and sincerity from being perfect",[23] should also go in as a prerequisite.

Similarly, the fault lies not with religion but with its ritual. Religion has always been and should ever be a matter of individual conscience for it is a 'dynamic' force and it does not originate from social taboos.[24]

Therefore, if we intend to eradicate the communal spirit that antagonizes people on a religious plane, we shall have first to eradicate those rituals which do not go well with the spirit of the faith and time. No religion ever teaches actions that may be hostile to ones neighbour or that may not confirm to the needs of the society. A solution to communalism demands such a dynamic adaptability of those tenets of ones religion that manifest themselves through conflicting concepts of morality, as practised through communal customs and rites.

The idea of mutual understanding and adaptability as a solution of communal trouble has been emphasized repeatedly. Regarding the communal trouble between the Hindus and Mohammedans, an eminent leader echoes the voice of millions when he declared:

> "So far as the Hindus and the Mohammedans are concerned, there should be an emphatic recognition of each other's rights, and each should be prepared to undergo some kind of sacrifice in favour of the other. Let me give an instance to make my meaning clear. Every devout Mussalman objects to any music in front of a mosque, and every devout and orthodox Hindu objects to cows being slaughtered. May not the Hindus and Mussalmans of India enter into a solemn compact so that there may not be any music before any mosque and that no cow may be slaughtered"[25].

It is an irony of fate that once the inter-communal relations get disturbed, it becomes difficult to tackle the problem by making appeals on the rational place. The emotional disturbance can be tackled only by diverting the emotional energy from the wrong to the right channels. It is the independence of mind that is needed; and an outlook, which leads not to fanaticism, but inspires a natural spark of catholicism. The power that is unleashed by emotional derangement whether it is excited by the innocent symbols of different communities or it is incited consciously, can be tamed as we have already said through liberal education, if not through 'compacts' or constitutional checks and balances. Bertrand Russel expressed this idea:

> "This is the task of a liberal education; to give a sense of the value of things other than domination to help to create wise citizens of a free community and through the

> combination of citizenship with liberty in individual creativeness to enable men to give to human life that splendour which some few have shown that it can achieve".[26]

To sum up, when it is an accomplished fact that no community can give up its socio-religious practices, the solution to the communal problem can be sought not in their effacement but in their proper evaluation. We can pose a pertinent question here - a question which at the same time is a touchstone for all possible claims of communal morality and righteousness? Does observance of certain conflicting customs and socio-religious practices, go to promote the national interests? Does the communal value attached to them also embrace certain national values?

If they do, they may indeed be preserved and pursued, so long as they do not lose their national import. If they do not, they may be forsaken in the larger interests of the nation.

Clearly enough; if we desire to eliminate the parochial and narrow aspect of communalism, we shall have to make national interests the norm of all communal valuations. It shall have to be done irrespective of their being entertained either by Hindus or Muslims, by a majority community, or a minority community or by any other community whatsoever.

Dr M.A. Ansari, discussing a solution to the Hindu-Muslim problem, supports the thesis advocated above. He says:

> "While attempting to solve the Hindu-Muslim question we should not however, mistake the sysmptom for the disease. The political and religious differences which are straining the relations between the two communities are but outward manifestations of a deeper conflict, not peculiar to India or unknown to history. It is essentially a problem of two different cultures, each with its own outlook on life, coming in close contact with one another".

He adds:

> "The best remedy lies in a recognition of the right of each culture to exist, in a development of a spirit of tolerance and respect and in the encouragement and cultivation of cultural affinity by the establishment of national institutions where young people of both the communities

> will come into touch with each other and get opportunities to study and understand the ideals underlying the civilisations of both... It is time this dangerous isolation and colossal ignorance were ended".[27]

Clearly, one of the possible solutions of communalism lies in forsaking its narrow aspect that usually leads to social tension. The need is firstly, of acquiring a greater knowledge of each others sentiments and an appreciation and tolerance of each other's culture, which symbolizes the higher aspect of communalism, secondly, an attempt to foster a spirit of sympathy for each other's communal ideals, and, lastly, the making of a proper evaluation and bringing of a dynamic adjustment of communal values, as tested on the touchstone of national interests.

It is only in a democratic and a secular state that the development of such a tolerant outlook in the people belonging to different caste, creed and community can become a possibility. However, it is not only a secular concept of the State and Government alone that would bring the desired effect. The key to real success lies in the hands of the people and their outlook on ideal citizenship. As Bishop (now Cardinal) V. Gracias remarks:

> "By a secular state, we understand a civil society or nation in which no single religion is given a privileged position by the Law of the land, and a Government which does not officially practice a particular religion, or favour any one religion at the expense of the other. But it may be observed that in this concept of a `secular state' it is the government that is specially concerned. But since the men who form the Government and its officials are of-course, free like other citizens to have their own religion and practise it, one can easily see that it will be a delicate and difficult task for them to maintain complete `secularism' in their official acts and contacts. While a secularization policy excludes religions favouritism, legislators and administrators are naturally inclined to favour their own personal religion, or even unconsciously act under its influence".[28]

Not much can be said for such a contingency. After all, the change of human nature is more a matter of personal understanding and individual habit rather than of sermons. However, the best recourse, as suggested above lies in a proper system of education. But that training can bring fruits only in a climate of democracy and secularism.

A word may be added about that aspect of communalism when religion and politics get mixed, and form a most explosive compound in day to day social living. We have seen as to how and with what unfortunate consequences such alliance was made by certain groups in India. Speaking on this aspect of communalism, which should not be tolerated in any social set-up, Jawahar Lal Nehru, a great exponent of the secular concept of State, says:

> "There might have been in the past various reasons which came in the way of such policy being given effect to, although I think that even in the past those of us who accepted any measure of communalism erred and acted unwisely, and we have suffered greatly for our unwisdom. However, in the past, conditions were different; but when a country is functioning independently there is no alternative except to follow this. The only alternative is civil conflict. We have seen as a matter of fact, how far communalism in politics has led us; all of us remember the grave dangers through which we have passed and the terrible consequences we have seen. In any event, now there is no other alternative; and we must have it clearly in our minds and in the mind of the country that the alliance of religion and politics in the shape communalism is a most dangerous alliance, and it yields the most abnormal kind of illegitimate breed".[29]

It can also be clearly seen that such an approach is not exclusively an instrument of solving the minority question. Any approach on such dangerous lines can be equally harmful to the majority community. In the words of Nehru:

> "But the combination of politics and religion in the narrowest sense of the word, resulting in communal politics - there can be no doubt - is a most dangerous combination harmful to the country as a whole, it is harmful to the majority, but probably it is most harmful to any minority that seeks to have some advantage from it. I think even the past history of India will show that. But in any event a minority in an

> independent state which seeks to isolate and separate itself does some injury to the cause of the country, and most of all it injures its own interests, because inevitably it puts a barrier between itself and the others, a barrier not on the religious plane but on the political plane, sometimes even to some extent on the economic plane; and it can never really exercise the influence which it legitimately ought to aspire to exercise, if it functions in that way".

To sum up, it is apparent that on the moral plane, communalism flourishes because of the barriers that are created in society; whether the barriers are of socio-religious scruples or of group isolation on religious grounds. A society, if it is has to exist can not afford attempts of social or political exclusivism on religious grounds. A real organism, as a society is, can grow well only of its parts in the form of various communities lead a life of mutual interdependence and understanding, in a true democratic and tolerant spirit.

Secularism is perhaps the only cure for communalism on the moral plane.

Any scientific enquiry which concerns itself with suggesting cures for communalism would be incomplete, if it failed to answer the pertinent question; 'whether the ways and means suggested here can prove to be of some real good'?

It is not possible to give any categorical answer to the question posed above. Firstly, if certainty be the claim of these cures; the facts of history are there to belie our judgment. Even when mankind has on the whole definitely progressed towards a positive improvement in material conditions, in mental understanding and moral codes, the tension between the castes, creeds and communities has not lessened to any appreciable extent. That is not all; for in India, communalism as a creed of social tension, has always had the support of the most prosperous, the most educated and even of those who claimed to be the most morally enlightened. Secondly, if we concede the inefficacy of the remedies suggested, we will be equally guilty of self contradiction and of raising a superstructure of questionable stability.

The truth however, lies in the fact, that even when history scoffs, it does so, not so much on the propriety of human effort, as on the incorrigibility of human nature. Moreover, an absolute evil can not have an absolute cure either. Thus, when we assert that Communalism in one form or the other, is bound to persist, as long as there are different communities, we are not sounding a note of despair, but just attempting to describe a historical truth.

Social-tension can end only with the end of society itself. But just as the malignant aspects of a disease can be mitigated by applying proper remedy, social-tension also can be reduced to an extent, where, in spite of its presence in the body-politic of the society, it can not prove pernicious to the system. In the field of Socio-therapy when an attempt is made to cure sociological ailments, the treatment has to be prolonged over a sufficiently long period. It is needless to mention that it shall need a change and re-adjustment in its application, from one age, one condition and one society to the other.

On the basis of the investigations in the socio-political history of communalism made in the preceding pages, we do emphatically hold that it is only on the lines delineated here that we can eradicate communalism in India.

A glance on the contemporary scene reveals that free India is trying its utmost to tackle this problem on its different levels. In the year 1948, Shri Ananthasayanam Ayyangar, member of the Constituent Assembly moved the following resolution which was passed by the House with a minor amendment. The resolution is possibly the best answer to the challenge of the forces of communal disruption. It says:

> "Where it is essential for the proper functioning of democracy and the growth of national unity and solidarity that communalism should be eliminated from Indian life, this Assembly is of opinion that no communal organization which by its Constitution or by the exercise of discretionary power vested in any of its officers or organs, admits to or excludes from its membership persons on grounds of religion, race and caste, or any of them should be permitted to engage in any activities other than those essential for the bonafide religious and cultural, (social and education) needs of the community, and that all steps legislative and administrative, necessary to prevent such activities should be taken".[30]

Speaking on this resolution, Jawaharlal Nehru said:

> "The point so far as the Government is concerned is that we should function as closely as possible in accordance with the spirit of the Resolution. Further, the purpose of this Resolution, I take it, is also to give a lead to the country in this matter, so that the country may realize as clearly as possible that the only right way for us to act is to do away with Communalism in its political aspect in every shape and form".

Turning to the social and economic aspect of the communal problem with reference to a democratic concept of State, he further said:

> "There is another aspect of this matter which must be remembered. We talk about democracy and unity and all that and I hope we shall rapidly have more and more democracy and more and more unity in this country. A democracy is not purely a political affair. The Nineteenth Century conception of democracy, that is, each person having a vote, was a good enough conception in those days, but it was incomplete and people think in terms of a larger and deeper democracy to-day. ...Now it is patent in India to-day that there are huge differences between certain groups, classes and individuals. There is a big hiatus between those at the top and those at the bottom. If we are to have democracy, it becomes necessary and essential for us not merely to bridge that gap but to lessen it very greatly: in fact, to bring them closer together as far as the necessities of life are concerned, leaving out for the moment luxuries and the rest, though ultimately there seems to me, to be no particular reason why any particular group or class should be favoured even in regards to the luxuries of life... Now, because there are such great differences in India, it becomes incumbent upon us, not only for humanitarian reasons but from the standpoint of the fulfillment of democracy to raise up those people who are low down in the social and economic scale and to bring them every possible opportunity.... Therefore we have to think always in terms of raising the level of all

> these who have been denied opportunities in the past. I do not personally think myself that the best way to do that is on the political plane by the reservation of seats and the rest. I think the best way and the more basic and fundamental way, is to advance them rapidly in the economic and educational spheres and then they will stand on their own feet".[31]

Nehru also deplores the system of bestowing favours on one group or community in the form of separate electorates, certain reservation of seats or making adhoc appointments from one community or the other as the British had done. Such a system not only annihilates a normal growth of healthy communal relations but also whets communal appetite by giving a false notion on strength. In this connection he said:

> "There is a great danger whether you deal with an individual group or community, of giving certain props to that community which give it a false sense of strength which does not belong to it. The props are external to it, and when they are removed suddenly make the community weak. A nation ultimately ought to stand on its own feet. So long as it relies on external props, it is not strong. It is weak. So these external props, as I might call them - that is reservation of seats and the rest - may possibly be helpful occasionally in the case of the backward groups, but they produce a false sense of political relations, a false sense of strength and ultimately, therefore they are not so nearly as important as real educational, cultural and economic advance, which gives them inner strength to face any difficulty or any oponent":[32]

Emphasizing the non-theocratic character of the Indian State, Nehru has declared:

> "Our State is not a communal state, but a democratic state in which every citizen has equal rights. The Government is determined to protect those rights".[33]

All these policy statements bear out how the ways and means proposed above are being given a practical shape. The fact that the Sovereign Democratic Republic of India is striving on these very lines to eradicate communalism, lends concrete support to the suggestions of this thesis. On the economic plane it has adopted Socialism as its creed. In the educational field, it has planned a system that go a long way in dispelling the darkness in the minds of men. It has abolished untouchability and its practice in any form is forbidden. Last but not least, free India has embraced the idea of secularism.

It is a beginning on the right lines. Its merit is not to be judged by our times but by posterity. One can hope that with the passage of time communalism as a creed of social tension is bound to disappear in a land which has pledged to secure to all its citizens:

> "Justice, social, economic and political;
> Liberty of thought, expression, belief, faith and worship;
> Equality of status and of opportunity and to promote among them all;
> Fraternity assuring the dignity of the individual and the unity of the Nation;".[34]

NOTES AND REFERENCES

1. *Problems of Stability and Progress in International Relations,* by Quincy Wright: University of California Press, 1954, p. 160.
2. *Ibid.,* p. 160.
3. *Herr Engen Dirhring's Revolution in Science,* p. 32 (Quoted from *The Good Society*. by Walter Lippmann: Boston, Little Brown and Company, 1950, p. 68.
4. Quoted by Sinha in *Guide to Communal Problem in India,* p. 218.
5. *Ibid.,* pp. 218-19.
6. *The State in Theory and Peace* by Harrld J. Laski, p. 222.
7. *The Economy of Abudance,* by Stuart Chase, p. 310.
8. *Future Culture of the World* by Dr. Indra Sen, *Hindustan Times,* Sunday of December 9, 1956, p. 1.
9. *The Psychiatric Aspect of War and Peace* by Franz Alexandar, *American Journal of Sociology,* XLVI, Jan. 1941, p. 526.
   Also see: *Personal Aggressiveness and War* by E.F.M. Durbin and J. Bomby, New York: Columbia University Press, 1939.
10. Quincy Wright., *op. cit.,* p. 165.
11. Quincy Wright., *op. cit.,* p. 165.
12. Quincy Wright., *op. cit.,* pp. 165-66.
    Walter Lippman: *Public Opinion,* New York: Harcourt Brace & Co., 1922, p. 79.
    Quincy Wright, *A Study of War,* p. 1288 ff.

13. "The Reduction of Inter-group Tensions". A Survey Research on Problem of Ethnic, Racial and Religious group Relations. Williams Robin M. Jr. (Bull 57) N.Y. Social Science Research Council, 1947, p. 90.
14. *Ibid.*, p. 91.
15. Quincy Wright., *op. cit.*, p. 166.
16. *Ibid.*, p. 166.
17. *The Pivotal Problems of Education* by William F. Cunningham. The MacMillan Company. N.Y., p. 18.
18. *Education and the Social Order* by Bertrand Russel, London, George Allen and Unwin Ltd., 3rd Ed. 1947, p. 244.
19. *Ibid.*, pp. 246-47.
20. Quoted in *The Education of Good Men* by M.L. Jacks; Victor Gollancz Ltd. 1955, p. 7.
21. In a series of interview that the author of this dissertation conducted amongst the Muslims of the rural and urban areas, he was repeatedly given the discriminating factor as an important cause, that has kept Muslims in a state of permanent hostility towards the Hindus. What is true with Hindus and Muslims, is exactly true on a larger scale amongst the Hindus themselves in the South.
22. *Ibid.*, p. 742 (Mahatma Gandhi: Thirty Ninth Congress - Batgauna-1924).
23. *Ibid.*, p. 807 (Mr S. Srinivasa Iyengar, Forty First Congress. Gauhati, 1926).
24. *Symbolism - A Psychological Study* by Dr. Padma Agarwal, Manovigyan Prakashan, Banaras, 1955, p. 224.
25. Congress Presidential Address: Second Series, Natesan & Co. Pub. Madras, 1934, C.R. Das in his address to Thirty Sixth Congress, Ahmedabad 1921, pp. 78-79.
26. *Power - A Social Analysis* by Bertrand Russel, p. 319.
27. *Ibid.*, pp. 829-30 (Dr. M.A. Ansari: Forty Second Congress, Madras 1927).
28. Quoted in *Group Prejudices in India - A Symposium* by C.N. Vakil and Sir Mani Lal B. Nanawati.
29. *Independence and After* (A collection of speeches of Jawaharlal Nehru) Sept. 1946 to May 1949. Pub. Division., Govt. of India, p. 47.
30. See Proceedings of the Constituent Assembly, April 3, 1948. Words 'Social and Educational' were added as an amendment.
31. Speeches of Nehru, *op. cit.*, p. 49.
32. Speeches of Nehru, *op. cit.*, pp. 49-51 (A speech delivered at the Constituent Assembly (Legislative), New Delhi, April 3, 1948.
33. *Ibid.*, p. 45.
34. "Preamble to the Constitution of India", p. 1.

Bibliography

(A list of the important documents consulted in the course of the preparation of this study is appended herewith. Some other documents, which might throw more revealing light on the problem, could not be consulted as they were not made available. Either they were described as destroyed or as "Not transferred to the National Archives". Their number has not been given below.

The Records of this Department available at the National Archives of India ranged from the years 1861 to 1935. The past - 'thirty-five records have not been transferred so far to the Archives and are still lying with the Ministry of Law.

The Government of India were at an earlier stage, kind enough to permit me consultation of the confidential as well as the non-confidential records of the Legislative Department upto the year 1947. It is a matter of regret, however, that this facility was withdrawn at a later stage. Even some ninety pages of material that had been extracted from the pre-thirty five records remained lying with the Ministry of Home Affairs and it was not been considered advisable to release the same for use.

Since all the documents were not made available, it has not been possible to incorporate much of this highly valuable information lest it should give an incomplete picture).

Table: 1 (A)

DOCUMENTS PERTAINING TO THE LEGISLATIVE DEPARTMENT OF THE GOVERNMENT OF INDIA

Year	*Subject*	*Date*	*Number*
1874	Religious sites	A. November	5 to 7
1874	Religious sites	A. December	148
1875	Religious sites	A. March	50
1875	Hindu-Muslim Riots	B. January	3
1880	Religious Societies Act of 1880	A. January	18 to 79
1889		A. September	1-19

(Continued till Page 384)

Year	*Subject*	*Date*	*Number*
1889	Religious Societies Act of 1880	A. April	1-7
1895	Additional Members of Council	B. October	109-111
1898	Additional Member	B. August	30
	-do-	-do-	5 to 7
1899	Additional Member	B. November	37
1900	Additional Member	B. January	6-9
	-do-	B. August	7-9
	-do-	B. September	44-45
	-do-	B. October	43-44
1901	Principles for Hindu Muslim Holidays	B. October	7
1902	Sikh Temple	B. September	100 & 103
1908	Bandematram Paper	B. July	145
		B. March	158-163
1910	Jewish Community Rep.	B. January	146-149
1913	M.A. Jinnah	B. February	149
		B. September	51
		B. July	78-79
1914	Slaughter of Animal Bill. C.P.	A. November	4 to 7
1914	Ed. policy of Govt. of India.	A. January	24 to 33
1914	M.Ed.	A. July	1
1916	Md. Community of the Punjab	A. October	199 to 202
		A October	199-202
1916	Indian Ch. Community	B. April	44
1916	Indian Commercial Asstt.	A. October	203
1917	Ah. Md. Raffiuddin	A. January	18 to 25
1917		B. March	4 to 6
1917	Md. Education	B. March	72-74
1917	M.M. in Fr. Deptt.	A. March	16-19
	M.M. in Fr. Deptt.	B. March	177 to 179.
	Communal Rep. Md.	B. March	16 to 18
	Constitutional Reforms Sastri	B. October	409-411
	Ed.	B. October	376-378.
	Md. Ali. Shaukat Ali	B. November	107-109.
1918	Rep. Anglo	B. Jan.	103
	Md. Ed. Cess.	B. May	15
	Burial of Mohammedans	B. December	167-168.
		B. Dec.	207-208.
	His Excellency's speech	January	11.
	Constitutional Reforms	B. October	62-64
	-do-	B. December	47-49
	-do-	B. December	7-9
	-do-	B. December	222
	-do-	B. December	223

Year	*Subject*	*Date*	*Number*
1918	Resolution	A. November	1-3
	Riots	B. December	139-141
1919	M. League	B. August	17
	Memorial Anglo-Indian Empire League	B. July	4-5
	Resolution	B. October	50 to 81
	Punjab Disturbances	A. October	176-178
	M. Ed.	B. November	451-453
	Punjab Disturbances	B. September	34-35
		B. September	27-28
		B. October	22-24
		B. October	124-126
		B. November	519-520
		B. November	174-176
		B. November	521-523
	Punjab	B. November	37-39
	Satyarath Prakash	October	7
1920	Ajmal Khan correspondence	B. May	278-280
	Anglo Indian	B. March	81-84
	Congress	B. June	117-119
	Const. Reforms	B. July	203-205
	Disturbances	B. November	16-18
		B. November	161-103
		B. November	425-427
	Disorder Enquiry Committee Report	B. October	162-164
	Electorate	B. May	204-206
	European Representation.	B. April	275-277
		B. April	124-126
1920	Hunter Commission Report	B. April	245-247
		B. April	127-129
	Imp. Leg. Council	A. May	1-19
	I.N.C.	B. July	221-224
	Jallianvallah Bagh	B. November	19-21
		B. November	148-150
	Md. Ali. (Aligarh)	B. September	83
		B. February	6.
	Assam Moslems Rep.	B. April	181-183
	M.Ed.	A. May	185-188
	Md. Sudras	B. June	325-327
	Pol Developments	B. June	65-68
	Racial Discrimination	Deposit July	2
	Cow Slaughter	B. November	567-569

Year	*Subject*	*Date*	*Number*
1922	Nomination of Abbots	Deposit. Nov.	8
	Release of Gandhi	A. & C. Sept.	4
	Akali Movement	A.& C. Jan.	260-329
	All India Services	A& C.B. Oct.	390-542
		A & C. April	199-225
	Bareilly Disturbances	A&C Feb.	6
	Electoral Rules	A & C. August	219-236
	Disturbances	Genl. B. Oct.	4-10
		A&C, March. B	247-295
	Pol. Condition in India	A & C. March Deposit.	4
	Repressive Policy	Gen. B. August	18
	Riots	B. A&C. May	66-67, 129
1923	Ahir, Kshatriya M. Sabha	B. & A.C. Sept.	269
	Viceroy's Royal Prerogative as to cancel or transfer sum or property for religious purposes.	Genl. April D.	10
		A& C.B. Sept.	375-395
	I.N.C.		
	1.C.D.M.	A&C (L.A.) B.June	470-515
	Md. Education	B. May	446-464
	Greed Minorities	Genl. B. July	130
	M.R. Endowment	Genl. April.	21
	J.S. Committee	Genl. Deposit. Nov.	35
	Mosques & Temples.	A&C. (L.A.) March. B.	1-29
			299 Report
	Md. Institutions.	A&C. (C. of S) May. B.	446-464
	Guru Ka Bagh	A & C. (L.A.) B. March	483-485
1924	European Nominations	A.C./24	53-XI
	Anglo Indians	May	Genl. 18
	Anglo Indians	May	53-XI/24 A.C.
	Bedi G. Singh nomination	April	A&C. 4 Deposit
	Depressed Classes.	B. April	A&C/130-132
	Representation		(C. of S) F. No. 16 VII/24.A.C. 5-XI/24. A.C. 53-XIII/24. A.C.
	Gidney's nomination	B. April.	A. & C. 77-119
	Indian Christians		53-X/24. A.C.

Year	*Subject*	*Date*	*Number*
	Jain Community		53-XV/24. A.C.
	Riot. (Mohammadens) C.S.		20-XVI/24 A.C.
1925	Communal rep. in All India Services.	F. No. 70/25 E.	
		F. No. 260/25 General.	
		F. No. 24-I/25 - A.C. (C. of S.)	
	Communal Holiday	F. No. 423/25. Genl.	
	Holidays		
	Sikhs	F. No. 359/25. Genl.	
	Arya Samajists	F. No. 359-II/25. Genl.	
	Jats	F. No. 359-III/25. Genl.	
	Sikhs	F. No. 359-4/25. Genl.	
1926	Jain Community	F. No. 53-II/26. A.C.	
			128-I/25. A.C.
	Minority community		96/26-G.
			155/26-E.
	Muslim Minority in Greece		158/26-G.
	Procession		16-IX/26. A.C. (L.A.
			-do- C. of S.
1927	All India Services		111/27-G
	Minorities		225/27-G
1928	Hindu-Muslim Disputes.		10/28-P.
	Communal compositions		38/28-E.
	Depressed classes.		3-I/28-A
	Muslim Rep.		7-1/28-C. & G.
	Swarajists		203-I/28-C. & G.
1929	The Problems of Md. Pilgrims.		3/21 P.
	Communal Compositions	Est. F.No. 178/29	
	History of Services.	Est. F. No. 3/29	
		F. No. 223/29	
	League Minorities	F. No. 140-1/29 C&G	
	Nadar Community	F. No. 204-II/.29-C & G	
	Nominations.	F. No. 204-I/29. C&G	
		F. No. 1 XXVII/29 C&G 37	
1930	Communal composition		113/30-E
	Com.		L.C.O.F. 12/30-E
	Services.		
	Muslims.		F. 202-I/30-C. &G
	Moti Lal Resigns		F. 101-IV/30 C&G
	Nomination of		101-IX/30 C&G
			101-XLII/30 C&G
			112-II/30 C&G
			112-XIII/30 C&G
			112 XII/30 C&G

Year	Subject	Date	Number
1931	Anglo Indians		150/30.E
	Clerical Staff.		148/31 E.
	Comm. Comp.		148/31 E.
	Com. Disturbances		146/x 31-E
			9/31 E.
	Idul Fitr.		189/31 C&G
	Muslims		79/31-E.
	Muslims		104/31 C&G
			474/31 C&G
1931	Nominations		247/31 C&G
			144-III/31 C&G
	Pol. Disturbances.		146/31-E
1932	Anwar-ul-Azam. Mr. Mohd.		12-VI/32-E
	Returns		1/32/E
			83/32-E
			2-11/32-E
	Communal Composition		151/32-E 41/32-E
	Communal Unions		304/32 C&G
	Ch. of Commerce.		368/32 C&G
	Sikhs		12-III/32-E
			12-IV/32-E
1933	Anglo Indians		157/33-E
	Communal Comp.		26-11/33-E
			172/33-E
			7/33-E
	Communal Unions		246/33 C&G
	Madras Act.		127/33 P.
	Muslims		75-VIII/33-E
			75/IV /33-E
			26/V/33-E
			26-III/33-E
	Nominations.		106-VI/33-C&G.
			106-XI/33/C&G
			104/33 C&G
1934	Comm. Rep.		144/34-E
	Sikhs		22-I/34-E.
			67/34-E.
1935	Annual Returns (Services)		F. 389/35-E
			F. 10-II/35-E
			16/35-E
			15/35-E
	Comm. Rep.		70/35-E.
			70-II/35-E
	Communities		104/34-E
	Nominations		IV-35 C&G
			V/35 C&G

Documents pertaining to the Home Department of the Government of India.

The records of the Home Department contained the most relevant subject-matter on the study. Unfortunately not much use of the same could be made because the Government of India did not allow me to consult their post-1901 records. The following pages contain the number of those important documents of the above Department, information supplied by which has been incorporated in this study.

Table: 1 (B)

PUBLIC DEPARTMENT RECORDS (1748-1800)

Year	*Subject*	*Vol. No.*	*Date.*	*Nos..*
1748-1800.	Brahmins	2 (18, 36, 42)		
	Brahmins	3 (21, 22, 50)		
		8. (256....)		
	Revolution At Delhi	2. (12)		
		3. (62)		
		4.		
	The Hindus	3. (24.)		
		5. (72)		
		8.		
	Riots in Calcutta	9 (581)		
		10. (42,44)		
	At Murshidabad	12 (311, 418-19, 592)		
	At Calcutta	14. (138)		
		9. (581, Pub: Dept)		
	Public Department Reference .. F, G, H, I, K, L, M, N,			
	O.C.		13th May. 1779	(Fort William)
	O.C.	10(42)	10th April, 1780.	No. 1,2,3,4,5
	O.C.	(44)	10th April, 1781.	No. 20.
	O.C.	14 (188)	24th June 1773.	No. 15(B) PP 1581-88
	O.C.	8(256)	25th August, 1772.	No. 1, 2. 348.
	O.C.	3(21-22)	Pub: Progs. 1755.	Pages 429, 430, 431, 432. No. 635-636
		15.(154)		

(Continued till Page 397)

Subject	*Year & Date*	*No:*
Records pertaining to Wahabi Movement: 1858-1864		
Pub:	30th April 1858.	106
Pub:	17th September 1858.	31
Pub:	22nd October, 1858.	11-12
Edn:	24th September, 1858.	1-5
Pub:	4th May 1860	7-10
Pub:	31st May 1860	23-27
Pub:	15th September 1860	56(B)
Pub:	1st August 1864	3-6(A)
Pub:	7th September, 1864	25-26'(B)
Pub:	7th November 1864	8-9(A)
Pub:	10th February 1860	31-35
Pub:	14th September, 1860	51-(B)
Judl:	12th November 1864	55-(B)
Judl:	13th May 1859	13
Judl:	20th May 1859	13
Ednl:	24th September 1858	1-5
Ednl:	10th June 1859	1-4
Ednl:	30th December 1859	1-2
Ednl.	16th February 1861	1-3-(A)
Correspondence Regarding Wahabi Movement, 1865-1870		
Judl:	7th June 1865	9-10-(A)
Judl:	12th February 1870	28-29(A)
Judl:	19th February 1870	18-20(A)
Judl:	30th July 1870	28-29(A)
Judl:	17th September 1870	44-46(B)
Judl:	27th September 1870	51-69(A)
Judl:	19th November 1870	1-3/(A)
Judl:	10th December 1870	39-(A)
Judl:	17th December 1870	26-27(B)
Judl:	31st December 1870	48-49(B)
Judl:	2nd April 1870	24-27(A)
Judl:	10th April 1870	56-58-(B)
Judl:	10th September 1870	59-60(B)
Judl:	May 1866	26-28(A)
Judl:	8th January 1870	8-15(A)
Judl:	25th October 1865	55-57(A)
Judl:	27th September 1865	70-74(A)
Judl:	27th March 1869	30-33(A)
Judl:	24th April 1869	15-19
Judl:	19th June 1869	60-62

Subject	*Year & Date*	*No:*
Judl:	21st August 1869	39-41(A)
Pub:	January 1886	296-97(B)
Judl:	9th October 1869	10-11(B)
Police:	30th October 1869	12-13-(B)
Judl:	1st January 1870	21-(A)
B.I. Association:	18th September 1869	Pub: 6-(B)
Ednl:	21st May 1870	38-40(A)
Judl:	30th July 1870	55-59(A)
Muslim Riots: Between Police in Bengal	7th March 1868	Pub: 42-44(B)
	13th August 1870	Pol: 49-52(A)
Syed Ahmed	9th July 1870	28(A)
Political Agitation	3rd September 1870	Pub: 124-125(B)
Religious Agitation.	24th March. 1865	Pub: 136-138(A)
Religious Agitation.	3rd September, 1870	24-25 (B)
Religious Agitation.	10th December, 1870	65-69 (B)
Religious Agitation.	31st January, 1865	99-101(A)
	4th April 1868	Pub: 23-(B)
	1871 as below:—	
Caste: Question of recognizing of Prisoners in jail	8th July, 1871 (P. 1305-6).	Judl. 36-37
Resolution on the encouragement of Muslim Education	19th August, (P. 741-1906)	Ednl: 2-8
Muslim Holidays	1st April, (P.2219-84)	Publ: 89-91
Muslim Holidays	23rd September, (P.5159-70)	72-79
Muslim Holidays	4th November, (P. 5393)	117-18
Mohurruam: Riots in Bareilly	5th August, (P.4359-87)	Publ: 145-47
Papers on the subject	23rd December, (P 6825-63)	Publ: 135-39
Tribes & Castes. Revd: M.A. Sherrings Work	30th September,	64-65(B)
	1872 as below:—	
Aligarh Police	March 1872	48-49(B)
Aligarh Police	March (P.645)	Publ: 290-292
Grant in aid for extending Muhammaden Education in Mysore	November	Ednl: 44-(B)
Castes by M.A. Sherrings	August 1872	Publ: 554-5(B)

Subject	*Date & Year*	*No:*
Holidays	January	Edn: 6-8(B)
Md. Proceedings	September	Jud: 120&131(B)
Mohammedans in British India-A Lecture by Karant Ali	September	Jud: 120& 131(B)
Mohammedan Education in N.W.F.P.	August.... (389-396)	Edn: 38-45
Plunder of villages	May (1541-42)	Pub: 307-08
Riots		
Wahabi Reports	November (3247-3248)	Jud: 124-132.
	1873 as below:—	
Caste & Customs	July 1873	Pub: 247 & 248(B)
Caste & Customs	August (P. 2053-2055)	Pub: 431-433
India on the Eve of		
the British conquest	January	Pub: 371
the British conquest	June	Pub: 481-83
the British conquest	July	Pub: 230
M.A.O. College & Schools	June (P. 459-469)	Edn: 69-73
Muslim Education	June (P. 471-509)	Edn: 74-111
M.A.O.	October (P. 703-704)	Edn: 15-17
Moplah Outrage	December	Pol: 83-85(B)
	1874 as below:—	
Hindu-Muslim Holidays	December 1874	Pub: 5 & 6(B)
Muslim Education in Bengal	January 4.	Edn: 1&2
Muslim Education in Bombay	March 30.	Edn: Part B
Muslim Religion (Lucknow)	July	Edn: Part B
Muslim Religion (Lucknow)	August	Edn: 48-50-(B)
Riots between Mohammedans & Parsis in Bombay	February	Pol: 68-71 (B)
"	April (P.115-143)	Pol: 30-41
	May	Jud: 40
Parsee Riot Memorial	June (P. 197-202)	Police: 9-11
Parsee Riot Memorial	August (P. 273-276)	Police: 30-37 & 39-39(B)

Subject	*Date & Year*	*No:*
Moplah Outrage	January (11-13)	Police: 8-10
Religious and Educational Trusts	April	Publ: 154-159(B)
Paper of Mohammedan & Parsees Riots	June (P.197-202)	Pol: 9-11
"	August (P.273-276)	Pol: 34-37
Wahabi Sect. Correspondence	May	Jud: 6 (Part B)
Religious Movement in Rampur	May	Pub: 334-335(B)
	1875 as below:—	
Despatch regarding the state of law for the suppression of Riots	April 1875 (197)	Pol: 48
Hindi as court Language in Bihar	November (355-362)	Edn: 11-13
Pamphlet	January	Pol: 21-23(B)
	1876 as below:—	
Outbreak	October (1351-1360)	Jud: 123-127
	1877 as below:—	
Mosque	September 1877	Pub: 36-37(B)
Riot	December	Pol: 9(B)
Temple	August (481)	Pub: 91
	1878 as below:—	
Roman Catholic Community	August 1878	Ec: 7 & 8 (B)
Grants Rules of Govt: For schools	June	Edn: 3 & 4 (B)
Temples	June	Jud: 132 (B)
	1879 as below:—	
Aligarh M.A.O.	March 1879 (145-149)	Edn: 31-33
Disturbance in the Rampur County	April	Pol: 43-49(B)
Riot Tax	January (1-103)	Pol: 44-46
Rioting Hazaribagh Europeans	November	Jud: 206-208(B)
	1880 as below:—	
Caste	September 1880	40. (B)
Muslim Institution in South (Hindu)	August	Jud: 125 (B)

Subject	*Date & Year*	*No:*
	1881 as below:—	
Caste, Census	March 1881	4 & 5 (B)
Riots at Banaras	July	69 & 70 (B)
Outbreak at Rampur	March (121-150)	Pol: 35-41
Hindu-Muslim Disturbances	November	Pub: 47-51 (A)
	1882 as below:—	
Caste & Occupation	September (163-165)	Census: 5-6
Hindu & Muslim Schools	June	Edn: 37-38 (B)
	June	Edn: 43-44
Muhammadans: Music before the Mosque	July	Jud: 350-351 (B)
Religious procession	July	Jud: 1-2 (B)
Music and Procession	May	Jud: 45-54 (A)
	1883 as below:—	
Brahma Samaj Community	July 1883 (1867-68)	Pub: 253-254.
Caste Census	March	1 (B)
Hindu Association Bangalore	April	Pub: 204-205 (B)
Mohammadan College at Calcutta	September (P. 523-538)	Edn: 12-20
	February (P.183-185)	Edn: 144-47
Madarsah for Muslim	May	91-92(B)
S.S. Reports	June	Jud: 404-05 (B)
	1884 as below:—	
Hindi	May 1884 (P 731-40)	Pub: 82-90
Moharrum	May	Pol: 16-22(B)
Mohammadans of Salem	April	Jud: 95(B)
Religious Thought	May	Pub: 163-65 (B)
	1885 as below:—	
Ameer Ali Introduction of a Bill	October 1885 (P. 1549-61)	Jud: 174-85
Education of Muslims in Punjabi	November (P. 883-884)	Edn: 23-24
	December (P. 983-985)	Edn: 34-35
Muslim Education Reformed paper by Dustgir	October	Edn: 23-25 (B)

Subject	*Date & Year*	*No:*
Hindu-Muslim Victim buried in one pit	January	Jud: 157-58(B)
Correspondence relating to the general impact of Madras Presidency	February (P. 187-205)	Pub: 212-14.
Mohammadan inhabitants of Cuttack	September	Jud: 56-57 (B)
Moplah disturbances in Malabar.	July & May	Pol: 101-10 (B)
Mohammadan Nobleman.	September 1885 (1409-13)	Jud: 229-30
Mohammadan Observer	December	Pub: 183(B)
Riots at Broach	December	Pub: 160-61(B)
Refusal to allot money to temples	February	Arch: 38-41(B)
	1886 as below:—	
Education of Muslim Printing of Paper.	January	Edn: 31-32(B)
Hindu-Muslim Riots.	October (851)	Pub: 110-112
Kith compendium of Castes & Tribes	February	Books & Pub: 31(B)
Moharrum (Delhi)	Nil	
Mohammaden Buildings	December (273-75)	Archaeology 16-17
Mohammaden Schools in Bengal	October (721-27)	Edn: 82-85
Mohammaden Scholarships	August (495-96)	Edn: 57-58
Riot at Broach	January (17-35)	Pol: 44-49
	1887 as below:—	
College Mehonda at Madura	December'87 (695-96)	Pol: 97-101
Mohammaden Education	September. (463-67)	Edn: 28-31
Hindu-Muslim Literati Titles	February	Pub: 201-02 (B)
Hindu-Muslim Riots during Dasarah at Etawah	January (15-50)	Pol: 55-59

Subject	*Date & Year*	*No:*
Hindu-Muslim. Report on religious feelings N.W.P. & Oudh.	August 1887 (1941-43)	Pub: 205-06.
Hindu-Muslim Riots at Delhi, Ambala, Hoshiarpur and Ludhiana.	April (131-190)	Pol: 84-91.
Riot at Alaper in the Badaun District	August (289-90)	Pol: 63-67
	1888 as below:—	
Mohammaden community Claim for State patronage	October 1888 (1117-29)	Edn: 1-11
	1889 as below:—	
Report on Third Md; Educational Congress,	March 1889	Book & Pub: 214-215 (Part B)
Hindu Festivals during Moharrum	March	Pub: 413-17
Mohammaden Claim for State Patronage	February (P.747-87)	Edn: 47-52
	1890 as below:—	
Rioting at Binodpur	August 1890 (1623-27)	Pub: 145-50
Native Muslim Association	February (153-294)	Edn: 34-61
Caste:	August 1890. (1465-66)	Pol:: 75-76
Bakr-Id: Disturbances at Darbhanga	October	Pub: 434-36
	1891 as below:—	
Amrit Patrika & Tribune. (Rohtak)	February (213)	Pub: 352-54
I.N.C. Bengal Govt. Orders	January (1-2)	Pub: 1-4
Memorial by Hindus of Agra	February (81-107)	Pub: 61-91
Play in England on Mohammed	March (359)	Pub: 91-95 & 201-202(B)
Mohammaden Riots	August (1151-1156)	Pub: 74-78
At Malikgunj with Murder	July	Jud: 362-63 (B)

Subject	*Date & Year*	*No:*
Near the lines of 25th Madras Infantry	October (2089-96)	Jud: 179-191
In Shain Bazaar	November (2349)	Jud: 180-81
Committed at Jamkhabad Infantry	March	171-172 (B)
In Banaras: Petition of release	June	64-65 (B)
Official Report (Banaras)	June	28-30 (B)
Riot at Calcutta	June (783-794)	Pub: 62-67
Riot at Calcutta	August (1151-1156)	Pub: 74-78
Rioting Shan Bazar.	October (2031)	Jud: 63-64
	1892 as below:—	
Riot in the Akyab Jail	May 1892	Jails: 36-41 (B)
	1893 as below:—	
Cow-Protection Movt. Gazipur	December 1893 (2427-31)	Pub: 155-57
Movt. of Troops	August	Pub: 127-28 (B)
Movt. of Troops	August	Pub: 196. (B)
Despatch to Hindu-Muslim Correspondence regarding riots	December (2489-2575)	210-13
	October	Pub: 23-33 (B)
Mohammadens	September (1431-47)	Pub: 1-3
Riots	September	Pol: 9-10
Appointment of people firing of black cartridges	November (1507-09)	Pol: 146-147
"	December (1535-41)	Pol: 67-70
Azargarh Movt. of troops	July	Pub: 58-59(B)
N.W.P. & Oudh	July	166-169(B)
In Rajor on Iid.	July. (1171-1202)	Pub: 186-207
H.M. Bombay Correspondence	October (1621-24)	Pub: 34-36
Bombay-Azangar Report	November (2137-2232)	Pub: 167-189
Riot at Saran	Nil	
Bombay Azangarh report	November 1893 (P. 2233)	Pub: 190-91.
Report to S. of. S. H-Muslim Riot or causes.	December (2489-2575)	Pub: 210-213

Subject	Date & Year	No:
	1894 as below:—	
H.M. Riots.	March (P. 395-409)	Pub: 258-65
Cow Slaughter	May (P. 713-739)	Pub: 195-212
Hindu Community Petitions	June (P. 783-796)	Pub: 134-143
H.M. Riots	February (P. 237-247)	Pub: 246-252
Riots. Supply to SS.	March	Pub: 258 -265 &
Riots Supply to SS.	September	Pub: 345-364
H of B.	July. (P. 995-996)	Pub: 1-2
Kine-killing	November. (1801-1810)	Pub: 196-223
Despatch from & to S.S. on K.K	August (1177-1178)	Pub: 111-114
Question on Cartridges	February	Pol: 64-65(B)
Question on Cartridges	August (967-1000)	Pol: 226-247
Question on Cartridges	August (248-257)	248-257(B)
27th Punjab Infantry	November. (1467-1479)	Pol: 176-186
Police special alliance in Bombay	December (1501-1502)	33-35
B.-H. Muslims Report	January.	Pub: 155-56(B)
Kine-Killing	January	Pub: 309-414 (B)
Riot at Isakhil	June (957-989)	Pub: 344-349
Riots in Assam	April (471-505)	Pub: 110-131
Riots in Assam	April (577-581)	Pub: 208-217
Riots in Assam	February	Pub: 181(B)
	June (937-953)	Pub: 337-340
Riots in Assam	May (755-756)	Pub: 258-261
Riots in Assam	June (831)	Pub: 214-215
Riots in Assam	July	Pub: 30-33 (B)
Riots in Assam	July (1041-1044)	Pub: 159-165
Riots in Bombay	May	Pub: 260 (B)
	June	Pub: 132-133 (B)
	August	Pub: 214-220(B)
Riots in India:		
Ball Cartridges;	January (37-38)	Pol: 76-80
	1895 as below:—	
Reports	April 1895	161-64(B)
	May	109-10(B)
Hindus Riot at Poona	February (39-116)	142-55(B)
Religious Endowment.	February	223-24(B)

Subject	Date & Year	No:
H & Muslims	March (319-21)	275-78
Parliamentary Questions and Reports	March	145-52(B)
	April	22-23(B)
	May	264-65(B)
Vernacular Pamphlets.	June 1895	88. (B)
Md. Mosque at Madras	June	Eccl: 26-31 (B)
Memorial of M. of Lucknow.	July	73-77 (B)
Moharrum	January (49-131)	Pub: 123-46.
Riot: At Kalungunda. Madras.	February	Pub: 180-83.
Despatch of troops to Porbunder to quell	February	337 (B)
Temples	May (625-627)	Pub: 239-42
	1896 as below:—	
Kine Sacrifice.	April 1896 (365-73)	Pub: 214-24
Riots in Bengal	November (1051-53)	Pol: 24-25
Bapatla	December (1145)	Pol: 59
Kalugunda Riot.	January	Pub: 376-78 (B)
Orders, Dhalia Riot.	February. (215-231)	Pub: 247-50
At Nagpur	December (1923-34)	Pub: 214-25
	1897 as below: —	
Grain Riots. Kottur Bellary District.	January (29-30)	Pol: 40-46
In Kistna District.	April (285-87)	Pol: 72-74
Kine Slaughter (memorial) Rangoon Muslims.	March. (211-12)	Pol: 223-25
Riots of Mappilas in East Ernod, Malabar.	March (73-220)	Pol: 31-64
Report of a Riot in Nagpur district	May 1897	Pub: 26(B)
Central Provinces.	June (685-86)	Pub: 171
Troops at Calcutta	July	Pub: 36-47(B)
Koyas	August	Pub: 76-78(B)
Local Govt's Report;	August (1313-14)	Pub: 376
Calcutta 30th 187	October (1683-87)	Pub: 124-57
Rawalpindi	October	(destroyed)
Disturbances at Fort Mandalay	December	Publ: 178-79(B)

Subject	Date & Year	No:
	1896 as below:—	
Deputation of Anglo Indians to S.S.	October 1898	Pub: 170-73(B)
At Mandalay on 14th October 1897	January	Pol: 157-62
Calcutta Riots.	January (7-9)	Pub: 55-57
	August	Pub: 134-38(B)
Patrolling of Ry; Lines.	January	Pub: 166 (B)
Caused by Bhutias at Jalpaiguri	April	Pub: 11
Jalpaiguri	May	Pub: 221-(B)
Parliamentary Questions and answers	June	Pub: 101-02(B)
Multan Muhammad	July	Pub: 117(B)
Rishra Bakr-Iid Rishra Riot	July	Pub: 80-81(B)
Kine Killing Rangoon.	November 1898	Pub: 281 (B)
Bombay Riots.	March	Pub: 242-58(B)
	July	Pub: 284-88 (B)
Despatch of Troops to Salem	November	2(B)
Despatch of Troops to Salem	September	68-(B)
H.M. Riots		
Parliamentary Questions	-do-	303-304 (B)
	-do- (4057, 4059)	&305-308(B)
Riot Plague	March	Pub: 56-57 (B)
	April	44-45(B)
	May	Pub: 131-132(B)
	November	Pub: 1-(B)
Riot: Rising	January	Pub: 223-229(B)
	February	Pub: 6 (B)
	1899 as below:—	
British & Rajputs	July 1899	Books. 919-29(B)
Caste Disabilities Act	February (207-208)	Judl: 53-56
Khaddar	May.	319-21(B)
Plague Riot in Nagpur,	April	661-69(B)
Riots	October	Pub: 213-217 (B)
	November	136-38 (B)
Dera Gazikhan	October (2365-86)	212
Cochin-Velur	April	230 (B)

Subject	*Date & Year*	*No:*
Palarpur	November	(Not available)
Radhanpur	June	244-45(B)
Riots Plague	August 1899	Sanitary 1(B)
	January (271-79)	Sanitary 297-303.
	May	Sanitary 319-21(B)
	April	Sanitary 661-69(B)
Alleged forces akin tea-gardens	April	Sanitary 661-69(B)
Troops for aid	December	Pub: 70-73(B)
Mawa Kottai	December	Pub: 110-(B)
	December	Pub: 45 (B)
	December	Pub: 111-12(B)
	1900 as below:—	
Hindus and Muslims	January	Pol: 78-79(B)
Muharrum	May	Pub: 145 (B)
Mussalmans not exempted	May 1900 (481-83)	Pol: 70-71 (B)
Riots At Moniwa	September (991-1023)	Pol: 60-62
Tinnevelly District	February	Pol: 77-79 (B)
Tanjacheri, Malabar,	December	Pub: 261 (B)
Vizagapatam	November	Pub: 265-68(B)
Dhulia (H&M)	-Do-	Pub: 47-53(B)
Gowripur	August	Pub: 102 (B)
Vizagapatnam	July	Pub: 235-38(B)
Firing in Cawnpore.	August	destroyed
Cawnpore Riot.	July	Pub: 4
Munda, Assam	August (1877-1941)	Pub: 326-53
Riots in Assam Tea.	April 1900	Pub: 147 (B)
Riots in Assam Tea.	July	Pub: 205-206(B)
Plague: Riots	August (2541-49)	195-199
	March	37-(B)
	May	196-(B)
Tinnevelly	November (1233-43)	Pol: 86-87
	March (289)	Jud: 141-142
	May (461-65)	Pol: 61-62
Trials of Durwans' Mill	January	245-47(B)
	January	268-70 (B)
	1901 as below:—	
Mohammadan University Book.	November 1901	Edn: 4

Table: 1 (C)
CONSULTATION FROM CALCUTTA REVIEW

Subject	*Vol. No.*	*Page No.*
Amalgamation of I&R Army	XXXVI	144-157
		144-145
Anglo Indians	VIII	548-568
Aurangzebe	XII	297, 322
Bengal	III	165, 171
Bengal. P. Settlement	I	189, 192
Land System of Oudh	XLII	309-383
Brigg's Work	XXIII	1
Dawn of Muhammodan	VI	112
Buddhism	IV	241-281
		253
Relation of Buddhism to the Religions of the time.	XCVIII	83-124
		117
Rise principle and tendency	XIX	256-297
Caste	XV	36-74
Caste	XXXI	150-169
Christianity. Method of Conversion of Jesuits	XV	403-405
Early Pro. Indifference		416-417
Mutiny	XXIX	377-438
East India Charter	XVII	422-451
Education	XL	138-158-161
Minto on M&M Edu.	III	255, 371
Encouragement to Md. Exclusiveness, in Education	XXXVII	205
Causes of Md. Disbelief	XIV	445
Idolatry in India	XVII	114-177
Islam	XXIV, XXV	265-287, 197-226
Madras Native Army	XXXIII	127-157.
Missionary	XLIII, XVIII, XXIV	243-272
Moghal Empire	XCV	175-187
Muhammadans	IV	418-475
	XLVI	349-390
	XII	385-88

(Continued on next page)

(Table 1(C) Continued)

Subject	*Vol. No.*	*Page No.*
	XXIII	1-37
Oudh	XLVI	435-484
Punjab & Mohammedans	XXXIII	286-305
Ram Mohan Roy	IV	355-393
	XLIV	219-233
Lunindar	VI	305-353
Caste	I	136-139
	XXX	8
	XXX	430
	XIV	485-487, 418,
	XXIX	291, 303.
	XXXIII	
	XXXIII	
	XXXV	
Mutiny	XXIX	389, 392
	XXX	101-105, 424, 423.
	XXXVIII	159-161, 103-105, 10-13.
	XLII	423
	XIV	535-39.
	XXXVI	
	XXXI	449
	XXXII	110-112
Abdul Wahab	NOC	879
Wahaboe	NOC	73-104.

TABLE: 1 (D)
The Official and Non-Official reports

1. Report of the Bombay Riot Enquiry Committee (1925)
2. Report of the Burma Riot Enquiry Committee (1938)
3. Report of the Cawnpore Riot Enquiry Committee (1931)
4. Report of the Disorder Enquiry Committee (1920)
5. Report of the Franchise Committee (1931)
6. Report of the Peshawar Disturbances
7. Report of the Raja of Pirpur Enquiry Committee
8. Report of the Sedition Committee (1918)
9. Report of the Indian Statutory Commission, (Simon Commission, 1930)

(E) Secondary Sources

Abdul Latif Syed	(1) South Indian Musalman and Education
	(2) Mohammedan Education in Bengal
Abul Fazal Allam	Ayeen Akbery
Abdul Wal	Ethnographical Notes on Mohammedans of Bengal
Abdullah	The Foundations of Muslim Rule in India
Adhikari, S.P.	Before and After Independence. A Study of Racial and Communal Attitudes in India
Adler Alfred	Understanding Human Nature
Aga Khan, M.M.	(a) Lord Mintos Viceroyalty
	(b) The Memoirs of Agha Khan
Agha Khan	India in Transition
Aghor Chander Chattopadya	The Original Abode of the Indo-Aryan Races
Agrawal Dr Padma	Symbolism - A Psychological Study
Ahmed Jamiluddin	(1) The Indian Constitutional Tangle
	(2) Muslim India and its Goal
Ahmed Sir Sultan	A Treaty Between India and United Kingdom
Ahmad Khan Sir Shafat	(1) Muslims in New India
	(2) The Indian Federation
Aiyers, P.S.S.	Indian Constitutional Problem
Alexander Horace	India since Cripps
Ali C. Rahmat	(1) The Millat and the Mission
	(2) The Millat of Islam and Menace of Indianization
	(3) What does Pakistan's National Movement Stand For
Adinaryana, S.P.	Before and after Independence. A Study of Racial and Communal Attitudes in India. p. 108, Br. J. of Psy. Vol. XLIV, 1953
Allaport, G.W.	Prejudice - A Problem in Psychological and Social Causation (1950)
	All India Parties Conference Report 1928

Ambedkar, B.R. (Dr.) (1) Untouchability
(2) Ranade, Gandhi and Jinnah
(3) Thoughts on Pakistan
(4) Castes in India
(5) Annihilation of Castes
(6) Inaugural Address at the Depressed Classes Conference
(7) Pakistan or Partition of India
(8) What Congress and Gandhi have done to Untouchables

Ameer Ali Syed — India and the New Parliament

Amein — Wisdom of Prophet

Amery, L.S. — India and Freedom

Anderson — British Administration in India

Andrews — India and Simon Report

Andrew, C.F. (1) Indian Independence
(2) India and Britain - A Moral Challenge

Ansari, Dr. Shaukutallaha — Pakistan - the Problem of India

Archir, J.C. — The Sikhs - A Study in Comparative Religion

Ashok Mehta, and Achyut Patwardhan — The Communal Triangle in India

Ashraf, K.M. (1) Life and Conditions of People of Hindustan
(2) Pakistan

Atlekar, M.D. — Caste System and its Relation to Total Life

Atula — Hindus and Musalmans of India

Awabzada, N. — Indian India

Ayyar, R.S.V. — After the Reforms - Communal Vs. Democratic Psychology

Asariah, V.S. — Caste Movement in South India

Bahadur, A.C., Mukerjee — Communal Tension (in Indian Review)

Bakar Ali. — Hindu Muslim Problem

Baljon — Reform and Religious Ideas of Sir Syyed Ahmed Khan

Banerji, A.B.	Indian Tangle
Banerjee, A.C.	Indian Constitution, Documents Vol. I and IV
Bapat	Nationalism Vs. Communalism
Barker, E.	Ideas and Ideals of the British Empire
Barton	India's Fateful Hours
Barua	Reflections on Pakistan-cum-Pakistan.
Barkatullah Mohammad	The Khilafat
Bashir-ud-din	(1) Non Co-operation and Islam. (2) Some suggestions for the solution of the Indian Problems
Basu, Major B.D.	Rise of Christian Power in India
Beauchamp Joan	British Imperialism in India
Beylic, H.	Other Sheep
Beni Prasad	(1) Few Suggestions on the Problem of Indian Constitution (2) State in Ancient India (3) Hindu-Muslim Question (4) Communal Settlement
Bernier	Travels in Mughal Empire
Besant Annie	(1) How India Wrought her Freedom? (2) India—a Nation
Bevan Edwyn	Thoughts on Indian Discontent
Bhai Parmanand	The Hindu National Movement
Bhatti, V.K.	Khalistan
Bhattacharya, J.N.	Hindu Castes and Sects
Bahadur Lal	The Muslim League - Its History, Activities and Growth
Bhandakar	Lectures on the Ancient History of India (650-325 AD)
Bhoopat Kar	Facts about India
Bienenfeld, F.H.	German and the Jews
Birla, C.D.	In the Shadow of the Mahatma
Birley, R.	Czechoslovakia
Bizley Sir Herbert	The People of India
Bolithough Hector	Jinnah's Biography
Boughet, A.C.	Hinduism

Bower	An Essay on Hindu Caste
Brailsford, H.N.	(1) Hindus and Muslims in his subject (2) Rebel India
Brinton, Crane	Anatony of Revolution
Brockway, A.F.	Non Co-operation in other lands
Brown Milton	Sahibs
Buchanan, D.H.	The Development of Capitalist Enterprize in India
Burkly	Quran
Butler Sir Harcourt	India Insistent
Byron, Robert	Essay on India
B.B.C.	India and the Four Freedoms
Calcutta Review	Spink & Co. (All Volumes)
Campbell, G.	(1) British India in its relation to the decline of Hindooism and the Progress of Christianity (2) Mission with Mount Batten (3) India as it may be: an outline of proposed Govt. and Policy
Cameron	An address to Parliament on the part of G. Britain to India in respect of the Education of the Natives and the Official employment
Casey, R.G.	An Australian in India
Chadwick, H.M.	Nationalities of Europe and the Growth of National Ideology
Chakravarti, Atulanand	(1) Hindu and Musalmans (2) Call it Politics
Chakravarti, Raj	Reconciliation Why and How - a plea for immediate action
Chakravarti, Rajagopalachari	Ambedkar refuted
Chirol Valrutine	Indian Unrest
Chopra, P.N.	Some Aspects of Society and Culture during Mughal Age (1526-1707)
Choudary, Afzal Haq.	Pakistan and Untouchability
Choudary, H.C.	Congress in Power
Choudary, Binayendra Mohan	Muslim Politics in India

Christian Literature Society — Problem of Race and Religion
Churye — Castes and Race in India
Cobbana, A. — National Self Determination
Cockpain, C.B. — Indian Federation - The Muslim Impasse
Cocktho, M.E.A. — Question: Whither India
Commager, H.S. — Majority Rule and Minority Right
Congress Presidential Addresses
Comnell, A.K. — Discontent or Danger in India
Coupland, R. — (1) India A Restatement
(2) Indian Politics (38-42)
(3) The Future of India
(4) Indian Problem. (1833-35)
Cowel, F.R. — History, Civilization and Culture. The Historical and Social Philosophy of Sorokin
Cox, E.C. — A Short History of Bombay Presidency
Craddlocks, S.R. — Dilemma in India
Cross, M.E. — People's Right to Know
Cumming John — (Ed.) Political India
Currane (J.A. Jr.) — Militant Hinduism in Indian Politics. A Study in RSS
Curzon (Marquis) — British Govt. in India
Dalal, Sir Ardeshr — An Alternative to Pakistan
Dalal, M.N. — Whither Minorities
Dar, Bashir Ahmed — Why Pakistan?
Das, C.R. — India for Indians
Dadda, D. — Landlordism in India (1931)
Davis Kingsly — Population of India and Pakistan
Deb. — Blood and Fears
Desai, A.R. — Social Background of Indian Nationalism
Diwakar, R.R. — (1) Satyagraha - its technique
(2) Satyagraha - its annihilation
Dubios (Abbe. J.A.) — Description of the character and manners, and customs of the people of India of their institutions - religious and civic
Dunbar, Aurther — India in Crisis
Durlabb, S. — (1) Famous letters and ultimatum to the British Government

(2) Complete Records of Unity Tasks
(3) Famous Trials of Gandhi, Nehru and Azad

Durrani, F.K. Khan — Meaning of Pakistan
Dutt, Uncle — The Rediscovery of India
Dutt — Origin and Growth of Caste in India
Dutt, R.P. — (1) Indian Problem and its Solution
(2) Problem of Indian Nationality
(3) New Chapter in Divide and Rule
(4) India Today (1940)
(5) The Crisis of Britain and the British Empire (Lawrence and Wishart Ltd., London, 1953)

Dutt — Effects of Foreign Rule
Dutt, T.K. — Grave Digger's in India
Eaton (Jearette) — Fighter without a sword
Edilu — Inside India
Ellan, J.P. — Swaraj - The Problem of India
Ellenborough (Lord) — Correspondence with Duke of Willington
Emerson, G. — Voiceless India, N.Y. (1930)
Encyclopaedia of Social Sciences
Encyclopaedia of Brittanica
Encyclopaedia of Ethics and Religion
Farquhar, Dr. J.N. — 'Modern Religious Movement in India' (1915)
Fisher, L. — (1) Mahatma Gandhi
(2) Indo-British Tangle, *Tribune* Lahore, November, 2, 1942

Franchise Committee Report, Calcutta (1919)
Friedmann, W. — The Crisis of the National State
Fuller, J.F.C. — India in Revolt (1931)
Ganapat Rai — Edn. Pakistan X-Rayed. Lahore Publishing and Station Qry. 1946
Gandhi — (1) Famous Letters
(2) Young India (1927-35)
(3) Correspondence with Government
(4) Satyagraha
(5) To the Students

	(6) Hindu Muslim
	(7) To Protoganists of Pakistan
	(8) Non-Violence in Peace and War
	(9) Delhi Diary (Prayer Speeches) Sept. 47 to Jan. 1948
	(10) Communal Disorders
	(11) Hindu Dharma
	(12) Untouchability
	(13) India of my Dreams
	(14) Ethical Religion
	(15) Indian Nationalism
Ganga Ram, Rai Bahadur	A Great Indian Problem and a Suggested Policy
Garret, G.T.	Enlist India for Freedom
Ghurye	Castes and Classes in India
Goodall Norman	Can India Unite (1943)
Gour Hari Singh	Communalism and Nationalism. (Indian Review Madras) 29 Time 1928, pp. 383-85
Govind Sahai	San-42-Ka Videsh
Gokhale	Speeches of G.K. Gokhale
Graham, G.F.I.	The Life and Work of Sir Syed Ahmed, 1909
Greanes, E.	Hinduism and National Movement (Hind Review V. 22, 1910. pp. 538-46)
Grigg, E.	(1) British Foreign Policy
	(2) League of Nations and the Protection of Minorities of Race Language and Religion
Grisworld	Insight into Modern Thought
Gulshan Rai	Caste System of Hindu and Absorption of Foreign Elements among them (Hind Review V. 67, pp. 6-130, 1935)
Gunther, S.	Revolution in India
Gupta	Indian Nationalism
Gur Dutt	Cultural State in Bharat Varsha
Gwyr, J.T.	Indian Politics - A Survey
Hamza, El.	Pakistan - A Nation (Sir Md. Ashraf). Lahore

Haq, Ch. Afzal	Pakistan and Untouchability
Haq, Sir Azizul	The Man behind the Plough
Hansard	Parliamentary Proceedings
Harold, J. Laski	India at the Cross-Roads. (Yale Rev. V. 21. pp. 486-502, 1932)
Hasan Ali, Mrs. Meer	Observations on the Musalmans of India. (W. Crooke, 442, 1832-1932)
Hawsin, H.M.	Race and Colour Prejudices. Rev. 31. V. pp. 351.71. 1911
Hawell, E.B.	Indian Architecture
Hawley, Amos H.	Human Ecology - A Theory of Community Structure
Haughton, Bernard	Struggle for Power in India
Hertz Fredrick	Nationality in History
Heyd Uriel	Foundation of Turkish Nationalism
Hillman Aurther	Community Organisation
Hindustan Review	Is Caste System Essential to India? Vol. 29, pp. 1-10, 1914
Hobhouse, T.	Elements of Social Justice
Holderness, T.W.	Peoples and Problems of India
Holy Land, J.S.	Indian Crisis - The Background
Hull William, I	India's Political Crisis. Baltimore: John Hopkins Press, 1930
Hunter, Sir W.W.	(1) Progress of India under the Crown (Soc. Arts. V. 41. pp. 329-458-9_.
	(2) A Brief History of Indian People
	(3) The Indian Musalmans
Husain, Mirwa Akhtar	Taarikhe Muslim (Hindi)
Husain, S. Shafat	Solution of Communal Problems. (In Indian Rev. (Mad) 28. 732-734. Nov. 1947)
Hutton, J.H.	Caste in India
Ibbeston	Pubjab Castes
Imam, Sir Ali.	Nationalist Muslims - Conference at Lucknow, 1931
India Empire Solution	Pub. No. 3-6, 9-11, 1930-31
India Under Lord Moreley	Quarterly Review No. 426. No. 426. pp. 203-24, 1911

Indian Annual Register Vol. II, p. 403. M.A. Jinnah

Indian Quarterly Register 1924-1929

Indra Prakash The History of Hindu-Mahasabha

Ingham, K. Reformers in India

I.R.T. Conference Proceedings 1931-33. Federal Structure Committees and Minority. 3 Vol. 7th Sept. 1931- Dec. 1931

Indian Statutory Congress Report

Iqbal Mohd. Presidential Address (1930)

Ishwari Prasad (1) A Short History of Muslim Rule in India (1939)
(2) The History of India

Jaffar, S.M. (1) Cultural Aspects of Muslim Rule in India
(2) Education in Muslim India

Jagdish Saran Sharma A. Descriptive bibliography of J. Nehru S. Chand & Co. Delhi. Fountain No. 14, '55

Jagirdar, P.J. India's Major Problems

Jawahar Lal Nehru (Also 'See Jinnah) Recent Essays and Writings on the Future of Indian Communalism, Labour etc. Allahabad Kitabistan, 1937. 153. pp.
Autobiography

Jeejebhoy, J.R.B. Non-Co-operation, its pros and cons

Jessie, Bernard P. The American Community Behaviour

Jinnah, M.A. Some recent speeches and writings. (Ed. By Jamaluddin Ahmed)

Jinnah-Nehru Correspondence

Johnston, James Can Hindu rule India? London. P. S. King and Sons Ltd. 1935. XV. 144 pp.

Joseph, B. Nationality, Its Nature and Problems

Joshi, P.C. They must meet Again (Bombay, Peoples Publishing House, 1944. 44 pp.)

Kabir Humayun (1) Muslim Politics, 1905-42
(2) Indian Muslims. (Jan. 56. Indo-Asian Culture)

Kailash Chandra The Tragedy of Jinnah

Kali, P.D. — UNESCO Report on Communal Tensions (H&M)

Kamal Uddin Khawaja — House-Divided: Eng. India and Islam. (The Islamic Review, 1922)

Karaka Dosabhai Framji — (1) History of the Pariahs including their manners, customs, religion and Present Position
(2) I have shed Tears
(3) Betrayal in India

Karandikar, S.L. — Pakistan-Ke-Sankat

Karl Marx — The Future Results of British Rule in India (N.Y. Daily *Tribune*. Aug. 1853)

Karim Razaul — Pakistan Examined

Karne and Majumdar — Racial Problem in Asia

Kaundinya — Federation or Partition

Kaye, Sir John and Mallesson, Col. G.B. — History of Indian Mutiny. (6 Vols.)

Ker Shote — Effect of British Rule

Keshav Prasad — Hindustan-Aur-Pakistan-Ka Ithihasic Vishleshan

Ketkar Sridhar, V. — History of Caste in India. (Vol. II Ithaca. N. Y. and London (1909-1911)

Khan, Abdul Majid — The Communalism in India - its Origin and Growth

Khadduri Majid — War and Peace in the Law of Islam

Khama Mehr Chand — Pakistan a Hindu View. New York. Institute of Pacific Relations. 1942. 32

Khan Sir Sikandar Hayat — Outlines of a Scheme of Indian Federation

Khosla, G.D. — Stern Reckoning

Kifayatullah Mufti — Jamiat-e-Ulema-e-Hind

Klineberg. — Tensions Affecting International Understanding

Kohn, Hans — India and Nationalism

Kour, Lalit Mohan — Effects of British Rule in India, 1873

Kote Wal, J.F. — (1) The India Charter
(2) Whither Bharat (or)
(3) The Mission from the Moon-land

Krishna, K.B. Dr. — The Problem of Minorities in India

Kulkarni, V.B. — Is Pakistan Necessary? (Hind Kitabs) Bombay, 1944

Kreech and Cratchfield — Theory and Practice of Social Philosophy.

Kriplani, J.B. — (1) I.N.C.
(2) Gandhi - The Statesman
(3) Nehru-Jinnah Correspondence

Lajpat Rai — The Arya Samaj

Lajpat Rai — 'Unhappy India. (Banna Pub. Co. Cal. 1928)

Lal Bahadur — The Muslim League

Lane-Pool Stanelay — Medieval India under Mohammadan Rule

Latif, Dr. Syed Abdul — (1) The Muslim Problem in India
(2) The Cultural Future of India
(3) A Federation of Cultural Zones for India
British under its Races and its History

Levin and Others — Authority and Frustration

Lovett Sir Vernay — History of the Indian Nationalist Movement. John Murray - 1921. London

Lumby, F.W.R. — The Transfer of Power in India

Macdonald, J.R. — Awakening of India, 311. pp. 1910

MacIver and Charles, M. — Society - Introductory Analysis

Mac Munn Maj. Gen. Sir G.F. — Hindu-Muslim Enemity. National Review V. 88. p. 103. Sept. 1926

Macartney, C.A. — National States and National Minorities

Madhokar Srivastava — Hindustan on the Cross-Roads

Madni — Open Letter to Muslim League

Malik, B.K. — Individual and the Group - An Indian Study in Conflicts

Manu Subedar — Communalism in India (In Indian Review (Mad) 33. 696-698. Oct. 1932

Man Shardt Clifford — The Hindu-Muslim Problem in India, 1936

Margret — Cultural Patterns and Technical Change, UNESCO (Tensions and Technology Series) Margaret

Mason	Essay on Racial Tension
Masavi	Caste and Structure of Society
Maulana Habibur Rahman	Jamiat-E-Ulema-E-Hind
Maulana Syed (Urdu)	Musalman-Ka-Roshan-Mustak-Beel
Mayter, O.C.G.	Conversation of Outcastes (As Rev. V. 26 pp. 603-11, 1930)
Maz, A.C.	The Congress a National Movement
Mazumdar, Amvika Charan	Career of the Congress (Ind. Rev. Vol. 15 pp. 977-88, 1914)
Mazumdar, D.R.	Race and Culture of India
Mehr Ali	Trip to Pakistan
Mehrally Yusuf Jaffar	Trip to Pakistan (Padma Pub: Bombay, 1944)
Mehta Ashok and Nair Kusum	The Simla Triangle (Kitab p. 263, 1942 and Bibliography)
Mehta	The Simla Triangle
Meinrich	(Psychology'. Supressed People. 148. pp. '37. (A Study of Untouchables)
Memorial of Parsees	On Bombay Riots to Salisbury
Meston Lord	Reservation of seats for non-Brahmins (Indian Rev. (Mad). 21. 198, 200, 1920)
Meston Lord	Nationhood for India
Miller, H.A.	Races, Nations and Classes
Minto, Lady	India, Minto and Morley
Minto	A Collections of Speeches
Mirza Bakar Ali	The Hindu-Muslim Problem
Mirza Akhtar Husain	Tareekh-e-Muslim League
Mitra	Annual Register (All Vols.)
Mitra, H.N.	Punjab Unrest Before and After
Moconachie, J.R.	Desirability of a definite recognition of the religious elements in government education in India (East India Association, Vol. 32, No. 21, pp. 1-31, 1900)
Mitra, S.M.	Moslem-Hindu Entente-Cordiale (V. 28, pp. 12-28, 1909)
Mitra, S.M.	Analysis of Indian Unrest
Modi, Sir Homi and Dr. John Mathai	A Memorandum on the Economic and Financial Aspects of Pakistan

Author	Title
Mohammed Noman (1942)	Muslim India
Mohammed Mirza (urdu)	Musalman-i-Hind-kit-hayata-sayasi
Mohammad Ali, Maulana	Presidential Address. I.N.C. (Coconada) or (Kakinada)
Mohammad Ahmed Mirza	Non-Cooperation and Islam. Lahore: 1921 115. pp.
Mohammad Ahmed	'Khalifatul Masih II'. Some Suggestions for the solution of Indian Problem (456.pp. Quadian. 1930)
Mohindra Singh	Depressed Classes
Mohammad Yusuf	India's Muslims and Reforms. (Asian Rev. V. 29. pp. 638-43, 1933)
Moon, Edward Pendal	The Communal Question. In his (Faber & Faber Ltd. 1944. New York.) Strangers in India' London
Moon, Edward Penderal	Strangers in India
Moraes, F.R.	Promotion of Inter-Communal Goodwill-Harmony in India
Moreland, W.	"From Akbar to Aurangzeb"
Morely, Viscount	Recollections
Muhammad Ashraf Kunwar	Life and Conditions of the People of Hindustan. 1200-1550 AD mainly based on Islamic sources, 1935, pp. 103-359
Mukherjee, P.	Indian Constitutional Documents
Mukherjee, S.	Communalism in Muslim Politics and Troubles over in India (1947)
Mukherjee, R. Kamal	Economist Looks at Pakistan
Mukherjee, Radhakumud	An anthropological and Sociological study (Padma Pb. Bom. 1943. iv. PP. 100)
Mukherjee, S.	Communalism in Muslim Poliltics and Trouble over India (Calcutta Oriental Agency - 1947 vii. 171. pp.
Mukherjee, Prof. Hiren	Indian Struggles for Freedom (Bom. Kitab Sec; Edn. 1948)

Munshi, K.M. — (1) Akhand Hindustan
(2) The Indian Deadlock
(3) Zonal Division of India

Murphy, Gardner — In the minds of men: Study of Human behaviour and social tension in India

Muslim Politician — Muslim demand for Pakistan. (New York Institute of Pacific Relations. 1942. 32. pp)

Mussalman — An Explanation of the Lahore Resolution of the A.I. M. League: Bombay, 1942

M.R.T. (Edn.) — India's problem of her future Constitution

Nanavati Sir Manilal, B. and Vakil C.N. — Group prejudices in India. A symposium, Vora & Co. Pub. Hd. 1951

Narayan, J.P. — Towards Struggle

Narendranath Raja — (1) The Hindu Minority (As Rev. V. 28. pp. 92-102: 1932)
(2) Memorandum on the Rights chained by Hindu Minorities in N.W. India

Narendra Krishna Sinha — Communalism - A study in comparison (Indian Rev. (Mad) 30. 5-6 Jan. 1929)

Nasif Ahmad — Basis for Pakistan

Nayale, B.N. — Indian Liberalism (A Study Padma Pub. Bom.)

Nationalism in Conflict in India. — Bombay Home Study Circle 43.310. pp

Nazir Yuar Jang — The Pakistan Issue

Nehru — (1) Speeches
(2) Autobiography
(3) Unity of India

Neville, R. — Houses Divided (In life: Chicago. 23.19-20)

New York Times — Nehru Flings a Challenge. pp. 10-11-19. 1942)

Nicholas Beverley — Verdict on India

Noman — Muslim India

O'Malley — Modern India and West

Oldhan, W.B. — Race and Colour Prejudices in India. (A.S. Review. V. 32, pp. 62-71, 1911)

Pant, D.	The Commercial Policy of the Moguls
Pannikar Kayalam Madhava	(1) Psychology of the Hindu-Muslim Riots (Contemporary Rev. Vol. 131, pp. 230. Feb. 1927)
	(2) Communal Representation. (In India Review (Mad) 21, 301-303. May, 1920
Parkin Raleigh	'Indian To-day'
Patel	On Indian Problem
Payare Lal	(1) Gandhian Technique in the Modern World
	(2) Mahatma Gandhi - The Last Phase
Peirzeda Syed Sharfuddin	Ed. Leader's Correspondence with Mr Jinnah
Peshawar Disturbances Enquiry Committee	
Philiph, C.H.	India
Pole	India in Transition
Pollen, J.	"Divide and Rule". India's Destruction. (As. Rev. V. 5, pp. 137-146, 1914)
Prabhu, P.N.	Hindu Social Organisation
Prabhu Rao	Mind of Mahatma Gandhi
Pranjpye R.P. (1931)	The Crux of Indian Problem
Prem Nath, M.A.	Our Fault. Lahore, Pub. 1944
Parliamentary Proceedings	(1) House of Commons
	(2) Indian Constituent Assembly
Punjabi	(1) Separation
	(2) The Confederacy of India (1939)
	(3) Separation - A reply to its critics
Radha K. Mukherji	Indian Communal Problem
Rahamat Ali	(1) What does Pakistan's National Movement stand for?
	(2) Contribution a I'Etude-du-conflict-Hindu (French)
	(3) Mussalman
Rajput, A.B.	Punjab Crisis and Cure
Raj Chakravarti	Reconciliation, why and how and plea for Immediate action. Bombay Hind Kitabs. 1945

Raj Kumar	Indian Political Parties
Raja of Pirpur Enquiry Committee Report	1937-38
Rajendra Prasad	(1) The League Demand (Cal: New Age Pub. 1945, pp. 24)
	(2) Pakistan (1940)
	(3) India Divided
Rama Jigyasu and Munshi and Rana Deva	The Arya Samaj and its detractors, a vindication, 294-290, pp., 1910
Ramanuja Chari, K.	Condition of Lower Castes. (Chintaman's Indian Social Reform, pp. 312-34, 1901)
Ramsay Macdonald	The Awakening of India
Ranga Iyer, C.S.	India in Crucible
Rao Rajeshwara P.	A Survey of Indian Constitutionalism
Raven, C.E.	Is War Obsolete (Religion Vs. Citizenship)
Rawlinson, H.G.	India - A Short Cultural History

Report of the Bombay Riot Enquiry Committee (1925)

Report of the Enquiry Committee, N.W.F.P.

Report of the Franchise Committee, 1931

Report of the Kanpur Riot Enquiry Committee, 1931

Report of the Sedition Committee, 1918

Reynold, H.G.	The Anglo-Indian Manifesto
Reynold, R.	White Sahibs in India
Rizaul Karim	(1) Muslims and the Congress (Cal. 1941)
	(2) Pakistan Examined
Ride, P.S.P.	Indian Unrest. The Psychological Factory (Emp. Rev. V. 56, pp. 140-45, 1932)
Roback, A.A.	The Present Day Psychology
Robert Byron	Essay on India
Ronoldshay Karl of	Heart of Aryavarta. A Study of Psychology of the Indian Unrest. London Constable and Co., 1925
Routledge, James	English rule and Native opinion in India from notes taken. 1870-1878. London Tribune and Co. 1878
Round Table	Reforms of Hindus and Muslims. No. 69 pp. 80-89. 1927

Roy, M.N. — (1) India in transition
(2) Historical role of Islam (1938)
(3) A Constitution for India
(4) The problem of freedom

Roy, S.C. — Caste, Race and Religion

Roy Smith — Nationalism and Reforms in India

Rudra, A.B. — Lectures on the Problem of India's Constitution. Patna University, 1943

Rrushbrook, L.F. — 'India in' 1924-25' (Series)

Russell, Bertrand — (1) Power - A New Social Analysis
(2) Educational and the Social Order

Russell, J.M. — Is India a Nation? (Quarterly Rev. Vol. 230, pp. 422, 432, 1918)

Roy Chowdry, A.K. — Pakistan - A Psychological Analysis J. Abnorm (Soc) Psychol. XLII

Sanjana — Caste and Outcaste

Santon, H.V.M. — The Untouchables of India and their enumeration (As Rev. Vol. 16, pp. 171-84, 1920)

Santhanam, K. — Ambedkar's attack

Sanyal, B. — Facts of Indian Politics

Sapru Committee — Constitutional proposals

Saran, Dr. P. — Studies in Medieval Indian History

Sivadhikari — (Bahadur Rai Rajkumar) Unrest in Bengal and Mr Morley's Reform. 48. XXXII. pp. (Ed. 1910)

Satya Prakash — Hindu Rastravad

Savithri Devi — A Warning to the Hindus. (Cal. Bijoy Krishnan Hindu Mission, 1939, XXV. 154. pp.)

Schiff — Present Condition of India — A Study in Social relationship

Senart, M. — Caste in India (1930)

Sen, A.K. — Islamic State

Sen, Dr. Sachin — Birth of Pakistan

Sen, Dhirendranath — The Problem of Minorities, Cal. Univ. 1940

Sen, D.C. — History of Bengal Language and Literature

Setalwad Chaman Lal H. — Recollections and Reflections

Shafat Ahmad Khan — What are the Rights of the Moslem Minorities in India

Shah, K.T. — Why Pakistan, Why not?

Shamsul Hasan — Nehru on A.I.M. League, 1938, pp. 58

Shariff — Islam in India

Sharma, Sri Ram — (1) Bibliography of Mughal India (1526-1707)
(2) Crescent in India: A Study in Medieval History
(3) Making of Modern India (From AD 1526 to the present day)
(4) Mughal Empire in India. Religious Policy of the Mughal Emperors

Shiva Rao, B. — Problem of India

Relvankar, K.S. — Problem of India

Shuster, G. Sir — Indian Democracy

Simon Commission Report.

Sinha, A.N. — To Phillip Sober - A Guide to the Communal Problem in India

Sinha, Narendra Krishna — (1) Hindu Moslem Unity (Ind. Rev. Vol. 31, pp. 153-56, 1930)
(2) Communalism - A Study in comparison. (In Ind: Rev. (Mad) 30, 5-6 Jan. '26

Sinha, Sachidananda — Caste Conference and Natural Progress (Hind. Rev. V. 52, No. 300, pp. 53-67. 1921)

Sircar Sir, Jadu Nath — History of Aurangzeb (5 Vols.)

Sirdar Iqbal Ali Shah — Pakistan - A Plan for India

Sitaramaya, P. — History of Indian National Congress Vol. I and II

Sivaswamy Aiyar Sir, P.S. — India To-day (74 pp. Mad. 1922)

Smith, R.A. — Why India fights India (In Saturday Evening Post Philadelphia, 220; 24-25, Dec. 6th 1947)

Smith, Vincent — The Oxford History of India from the Earliest Time and the End of 1911

Smith, W.C.	The Muslim League: Modern Islam in India
Soper, E.D.	Racism - A World Issue
Strachey, S. John	Coming struggle for Power. India its administration and
Suleri Zind-Din-Ahmed	My leader being an estimate of Mr Jinnah' work for his Indian Muslims. Ind. Ed. Lahore. Lion Press 1945. 11. 195 pp)
Sunder Lal	Hindu Muslim Aykta
Surdar Alikhan Syed	Unrest in India considered and discussed
Syed Ahmad Khan	Review on Dr. Hunter's Indian Mussalmans
Symond, R.	Making of Pakistan. (So-called superiority of the Brahmins). Modern Rev. V. 14, pp. 611-17, 1913)
Tagore, Rabindranath	Nationalism (London: McMillan & Co., 1950)
Tara Chand, Dr.	Influence of Islam on Indian Culture
Tara Singh	Why we must avoid Civil War
Temple, R.C.	Travels of Peter Mundoy in Europe and Asia
Thadain, R.V.	Historical State Trial of the Ali Brothers and Puri Brothers, Karachi, 1921)
Thompson, E. and Gareet, G.T.	The Rise and Fulfilment of Br. Rule in India
Thompson, E.	Enlist India for Freedom
Titus, P.M.	Communalism - A Sociological Analysis, (*The Indian Journal of Social Works*, Bombay, March, 1942)
Tritton, A.S.	The Caliphs and their Non-Muslims subjects
Tufail Ahmad Monghori	Mussalman-ka-Roshan Mustak-beel
Tyabji	Why Mussalmans should oppose Pakistan?
Universal Races Congress	Paper on Inter-racial Problems
Vogt. V. Ogden	Cult and Culture (1951 Macmillan Co. N.Y.)

Vairanapillai, M.S.	Nationalities in Indian Politics
Vokil, C.N. and Nanavati, Sir, Manilal, B.	Group Prejudices in India - A Symposium (1951)
Wadia, A.S.N.	Reflections on the Problem of India. 174 pp. 1913)
Wafford Clare and Harris	India Afire
Wallock, Wilfred	Indian Awakening
Wilson, S.G.	(1) Modern Movement among Moslems (2) Some Indian Problems
Winslow, Elwin Verrier	Dawn of Indian Freedom
Wint, Guy	Indian Democracy
Woolacotta, J.F.	India on Trial
Wright, Prof. Quincy	Problem of Stability and Progress in International Relations
Yar Jand Nawab Bahadur Wazir	(ed) Pakistan Issue. (Correspondence between the leaders.
Yunus, M.	Industrial Pakistan (Muslim University Union. Pub. No. 3. Aligarh 1945)
Zacharia, H.C.P.	Renascent India

Index